P9-DUQ-454

Magic In The Air

Marc Paulsen and Piper Cub J-3 N7074H, 1963

Magic In The Air

My flying stories from a time when anyone could own an airplane

Marc E. Paulsen

Magic In The Air

Inquiries:

visibilityunlimitedpress.com
info@visibilityunlimitedpress.com

503-330-1226
or
Visibility Unlimited Press, 7332 S.E. Thiessen Road
Milwaukie, Oregon 97267

First edition, 2012

ISBN 978-0-9774737-3-1
Printed in Hong Kong

Cover photo:

Marc Paulsen with his Piper Cub, 1946 Model J-3, 85hp

About the author

Marc Paulsen was born of Danish parentage in Willow River, Minnesota, in 1933. He chuckles when noting the doctor's charge for his birth (in the doctor's home) was five dollars! In 1942, his family moved to Portland, Oregon, where Marc's father worked helping build a new aluminum plant which would furnish material for World War Two airplanes.

Marc was adventurous, leaving home on a number of exciting excursions while still in his early teens. Considered independent and somewhat rebellious (which he readily admits), early teenage escapades included hitchhiking through many states, riding steam freight trains with hobos and working at a surprising number of unique and diverse jobs. At age fourteen, he spent a month all alone "feeding cattle" in high ranch country which required driving a team of draft horses. With only one year of formal high school, his father finally "laid down the law" and said, "Either go to work full-time…or go to school!" Marc chose work.

Achieving journeyman status as a bricklayer at age twenty-one, Marc became a foreman at twenty-two, was drafted into the U.S. Army at twenty-three and shipped to Germany on a troopship. In the service, he was taught to type, learned Army administration, was assigned work as a mechanic's "helper," ran a carpenter shop, and finished his tour as a Specialist 4th Class project manager with two Sergeants First Class, two thirteen-man squads, a pair of two and a half ton trucks and a Jeep, driver and interpreter...all *reporting directly to him.*

On return, he worked at many occupations which included brickmason, masonry contractor, general contractor, national trade show manager, metal salvager, interior design and furnishings store owner, sawmill project manager and airplane sales…and quite a few others in between.

Avocations have included fishing and hunting, auto racing, motorcycle racing (he has a Class-A Main-Event motocross trophy), antiques, rare book collecting, owning antique autos, writing, world traveling and flying.

Marc's infatuation with airplane flight began in 1943 when, as a ten-year-old, he looked up to the skies and gazed in amazement as great formations of Boeing B-17 "Flying Fortresses" soared overhead on their way from manufacture in Seattle to the sunny climes of California and the U.S. Southwest. They were flying to new airfields built expressly for training "advanced" pilots who would ultimately fly them into WWII combat.

When Marc's older cousin returned from Army Air Corps duty after the big war, he purchased a flight for Marc in the renowned Piper "J3" Cub. The moment he became old enough (and earned a modest amount of money) he began flight lessons. Although a full 12 years elapsed from his first flight lesson until the day he received his pilot's license, his interest in airplanes never flagged. Marc proceeded to own 10 different airplanes and enjoy an exciting involvement with aviation that lasted over twenty years, all at a time when small used airplanes were surprisingly inexpensive.

Other books by Marc Paulsen:

Dominican Republic Guidebook
1989 - in advance of 500th anniversary (1492-1992)
of Columbus' discovery of the New World

Audacious Escapades
In The Fabulous
Columbia River Gorge

The Amazing Story
Of The Fabulous
Medjool Date

Short Stories
for
Quick Readers

Foreword

"As good as it gets!"

In an interview, a respected personality of national renown was inspirational indeed! The person, who had been highly successful in a number of disciplines and human relations, summed up: "If, throughout life, you do things that thrill and excite you, lift your spirit and consume you and you're honest and try your best to do it all well, then…that's 'as good as it gets!'"

Life is a journey of discovery and adventure, a lifetime quest for fortune, happiness, contentment and fulfillment. It may be true that "no man is an island" but, in the final analysis, only you can determine what is most important to *you*…what it is that pleases you or touches you to your very core. Family, friends and associations aside, your life journey is a private tour for you alone to make "as good as it gets!"

A scholarly group studying "finding happiness" published its conclusion…that a fulfilling journey of adventure, occupation, inquiry and quest for knowledge is much more satisfying than the achievement of riches and fame. They discovered that many people who had gained riches and fame wished they had done more that was beneficial for others as well as being adventuresome and challenging to themselves.

Life seldom has been dull and many times thrilling and mesmerizing. I'd have achieved a much higher degree of financial success if I had stuck with one or only a couple of occupational disciplines. But, would dedication to one path have been enough? *Not a chance!* I don't have great monetary wealth…but I surely have had many wild and crazy enjoyable experiences. Upon reviewing my failures (I've had a number), even they have been a source of personal value.

May *you* seize ***your*** day and make *your* life as adventure-filled and interesting as possible to *your* very last gasp of breath.

The short stories in this book are all true and intended to inspire. With only one life to live, may you succeed in doing well intriguing things that capture your imagination and then *your life* will be…"***as good as it gets!***"

Acknowledgement

I am grateful to Jeff Oerding, longtime pilot and airplane owner ("Airplane, Single & Multi-Engine Land and Instrument" rated) who selflessly contributed his editing knowledge and aviation expertise to assist me in assuring that as much of this book as possible is accurate. It was Jeff who aided in areas of specific airplane flight terminology and aerodynamic details. His painstaking time-consuming efforts are more appreciated than he will ever know. Thank you, Jeff...for your exceptional and significant contribution!

My editor/sister Diane Paulsen-Heberling deserves substantial credit for her untiring efforts reviewing numerous drafts and providing much appreciated journalistic expertise. It was she who did a large share (many, many hours) of the text-edit "heavy-lifting" for this project. Thank you, Diane!

A warm thanks to Vahan Dinihanian, Lorraine Troh Gabel, Jerry Jacques, Norm DesJardins, Jack Barnes, Trevor Norris and other aviator friends whose continuing encouragement helped keep me on track to complete this work. Their enthusiasm, contributions and helpful suggestions for the project made the book better and the long hours of effort seem much shorter.

Contents

Contents

Storiettes

Epilogue

Back From Oblivion...

Introduction

A time when "everyman" could afford to own an airplane

"May I speak with Mr. Piper?"

I scarcely could believe I was doing this…actually attempting to talk directly with one of the most revered names in the history of world aviation. But, those are the kinds of things that happen when eager young people with adventure on their minds enroll themselves in programs of "self-improvement."

In class, the instructor of the "Human Relations and Salesmanship" course suggested that people in high places frequently welcome the opportunity to talk with young folks and pass along their hard-won wisdom to those attempting to work their way up the ladders of success. My first attempt ended in utter failure when I contacted a successful local company. The company had as its "logo" what appeared to be a man's given name and, when the telephone receptionist was asked to connect me with the big man, I was gently informed (to my shock) that no such person existed. The company had simply chosen a good solid American name to use…and it worked! They did, in fact, become a major success but, for my search, I elected to pass on this company and find another with which to connect for my class assignment. My thoughts next turned to a manufacturer whose products were being sold all over the world.

The year was 1961. I was twenty-eight. Although beginning airplane flying lessons at seventeen (then starting three more times and not finishing for one reason or another), my thoughts remained connected to the idea of flight. I'd already flown many times in the aircraft considered throughout the world to be a legendary icon of flight training, the "Piper Cub!"

The renowned and celebrated Piper Cub airplane almost single-handedly established and solidified private aviation in the United States. From its introduction in the 1930s through the middle of the Twentieth Century and beyond, "Cubs" were used to train tens of thousands of aspiring pilots. By 1961, more than ***30*** variations of the basic Cub airframe had been marketed. During those years, there had been times when a perfectly flyable Cub could be purchased "used" for as little as $300. Amazing! Man had dreamed for thousands of years of joining the birds in their conquest of the heavens…and now ordinary people could sprout wings and soar with eagles for not much more than the comparable price of a fancy new refrigerator. At my first important job, in a portable sawmill when I was 16, one of the company employees bought a used Cub for $500...less than *two months* of his pay.

"Hello?" A formal-sounding voice answered on the other end.

"Hello, Mr. Piper. My name is Marc Paulsen and I am an admirer of you and your outstanding airplanes."

"Well…I'm happy to hear that. Is there something I can help you with?"

A world-famous man, he sounded genuinely willing to talk! I continued, being totally open.

"Uhhhh…Mr. Piper, I'm taking a class on improving myself by learning all I can about business. Our instructor said highly-successful people like you are usually willing to give some pointers to people on their way up."

"My, you flatter me with talk like that. All I've done is do the best I can to make the best possible airplanes."

A real conversation had begun! He hadn't cut me off, a result I had contemplated when considering how busy most top executives can be.

"I've read all about you and your airplanes and have already flown in a number of them while taking flying lessons…most in Piper Cubs. I've learned much about your working history and the story of your airplanes. I'm not trying to flatter you because I know how much you've done to advance aviation."

"That's fine. What can I do for you today?"

"I like your planes and I plan to become a pilot. It is well known how successful you have been and I was hoping to get some business advice. I hope this is not too intrusive on your time."

"Oh no. At my advanced age, I'm not so important to the company that I can't take some time out for conversation. I'll be happy to help you if I can."

Astoundingly, we talked for over a half hour. The man was as gracious as could be. Maybe I reached him at an opportune moment...but it seemed to me, from his attitude, that he was probably the same in most of his dealings with people. Can you believe that I made this call from a phone booth? He stayed patiently on the phone and bided his time even when I occasionally found it necessary to insert more coins into the pay slot!

My urge to call in this unusual way had been triggered during work while on a job in a small town a hundred miles from home...our class instructor had said we should not delay but take action when we summoned the courage. The only reason the call ended was my lack of coins to feed into the payphone. I believe Mr. Piper might have talked another hour. He seemed to be in no hurry to end the conversation and was impressed with my deep interest in planes and flight. Along with offering some wisdom and sound advice, he urged me to get my pilot's license and then a plane. Later, I would do just that, but in reverse order. The very next year I bought a Piper Cub...and then earned my license.

As a matter of astonishing coincidence, to take a few minutes off while writing this introduction, I turned on the television for a quick "break." On the Discovery Channel at that precise moment, the screen depicted the famed "Tuskegee Airmen" in training during early WWII. Not twenty seconds elapsed when five yellow Piper Cubs in a row appeared...and the narrator explained how the young men were being trained in these airplanes which Mr. Piper had made a veritable icon of flight history. *Imagine that!*

Ryan PT-22 (primary trainer) 1941- 43, 1,568 built

When I was 13 years old, a favorite activity was biking to a nearby airport that sported a whole flock of both of these war surplus ships illustrated... all offered for sale at the grand price of $500 each, as is. For a wishful young boy, viewing rows and rows of these beauties was captivating indeed. Many of them were in excellent condition...and, with average worker yearly incomes about $3,000 at the time, they were considered affordable for numerous young people aspiring to become aviators.

Cessna AT-17 Bobcat, 1939-1943
WWII multi-use twin-engine - 5,400 built

Made with a substantial amount of wood, it was referred to disparagingly (or maybe jokingly) as the "*Bamboo Bomber!*"

When *Anyone* Could Own A Plane

Hard to believe, but there really *was* a time when anyone who skillfully managed earnings could buy an airplane! This phenomenon in the world of aviation was fairly short...about 15 years between the end of World War Two and the end of the 1950s!

During the four years of the big war, America produced a staggering number of airplanes ranging from the Piper Cub to the behemoth Howard Hughes HK-1, nicknamed the "Spruce Goose." The HK-1 wasn't finished during the war but it was conceived to be used as a military troop and cargo carrier while guns still blazed. The speed with which our country's industry cranked out complicated warplanes was absolutely astounding!

Most light aircraft producers shifted to war production. Working as subcontractors, they produced aircraft designed by other companies and built military versions of their civilian designs. The industry produced flight-trainer planes for crews learning to fly larger transports and bombers. They also produced olive-drab versions of light-planes for transporting officers and other important wartime personnel. The wartime Grasshopper Fleet used versatile maneuverable planes like the Piper Cub J-3 and other small ships for front-line service in liaison work, observation, artillery spotting and evacuation of wounded.

The statistics are remarkable! From 1939-1945, aviation manufacturing became the largest single industry in the world. In the United States, it rose from 41st place to first. In 1939, fewer than 6,000 planes a year were produced. Production doubled in 1940 and doubled again in 1941 and 1942. In the first half of 1941, it produced 7,433 aircraft, more than had been produced in all of 1940. From January 1, 1940, until V-J Day on August 14, 1945, more than 300,000 military aircraft were produced for the U.S. military and its allies--with almost 275,000 after Pearl Harbor! In the peak production month of March, 1944, more than 9,000 aircraft came off the assembly lines. By the spring of 1944, more aircraft were being built than could be used so production began to be curtailed.

When the war ended, there was no immediate need for most of those wonderful flying machines. The large majority of them became surplus and, of that majority, many were offered for sale to the public at "fire-sale" prices.

On my bike route, there was a complete Curtiss P-40 "Warhawk" fighter plane parked next to the mailbox of a man who had a war surplus aviation parts business down his country lane. Each time I rode by, I'd pull up to that plane and gawk in amazement while dreaming what it would be like to fly such a beautiful and storied ship. This was the ship the famed Flying Tigers flew in China. That it now was valued so little as to be used for a simple advertising sign boggled me. The same plane in the same condition fifty years later would bring around a million dollars as a rare antique.

The massive number of war-surplus ships in good operating condition offered for sale inexpensively held down prices of "pre-war" civilian used planes. The feast of available planes provided a virtual feeding frenzy for people adept at carefully controlling their finances. If one was good at saving and handling one's money, a Joe Q. Average could be a proud airplane owner.

By the 1960s, small plane manufacturers had begun to fill the gap of diminishing surplus planes with new plane offerings. New technology made possible fancier planes with more exotic radio and navigation equipment, more horsepower and more seating space. More technical equipment made possible by rapid advances in the high-tech semiconductor industry made possible light plane "instrument" flight into the same airspace as the large airliners. Businesses with substantial financial capabilities took advantage of the improvements and expanded their use of private airplanes.

Those were among factors that began to force prices up. Boom-times of the 1960s found many people and companies making a lot more money so airplane manufacturers made even more expensive bigger and faster ships...ultimately building even much more expensive private jet aircraft.

Concurrently, opportunist lawyers representing family members of pilots lost to accidents saw the chance to make big money by suing manufacturers for "suspected" deficiencies in small airplanes which possibly might have caused crashes. "Suspected," because whenever a small plane crashes, it generates very emotional responses from close family and they can be very quick to blame the aircraft. While such blame occasionally may be a fact, by far the greatest number of air crashes are a result of pilot error. Nonetheless, when a private plane crashes taking a few lives with it, there is usually someone ready to sue whether or not the airplane was at fault. After a few giant settlements granted by overly-sympathetic juries, that situation began to bleed manufacturers of funds and, in fact, caused a number of them to go out of business. The remaining companies found it necessary to buy exceedingly high-priced product liability insurance to protect themselves thereby forcing airplane prices even higher. There has been no letup of this situation. Insurance continues to be a very high cost element of both plane manufacturing and an airplane's purchase price.

Airplanes are different from other vehicles. In any given group of 1000 people, it is possible to teach a large number of them to operate a boat or car, run a machine tool, cook a meal or knit a sweater. Flying a plane is a "horse of another color!" In the unforgiving environment of the open sky, planes will stay there only if operated with exacting meticulous attention to detail. Mental attitudes, physical condition, native intelligence, mechanical abilities, quick *correct* decision-making capability and close attention to the task at hand are all mandatory attributes necessary to launch an airplane into the air and return it safely to terra-firma. That is why only about one in a few hundred people are airplane pilots. To join this exclusive community and stay in one piece is what sets pilots apart from groundlings. They operate closer to St. Peter and the angels than the best of evangelical preachers but are not given quite as many second chances!

Summarizing...if, for whatever reason, it is necessary to locate a pilot in a crowd of a thousand people, just wait for a plane to fly over and usually the first person to look up to the sky will be your person. *Once a person of the air...* ***always a person of the air!***

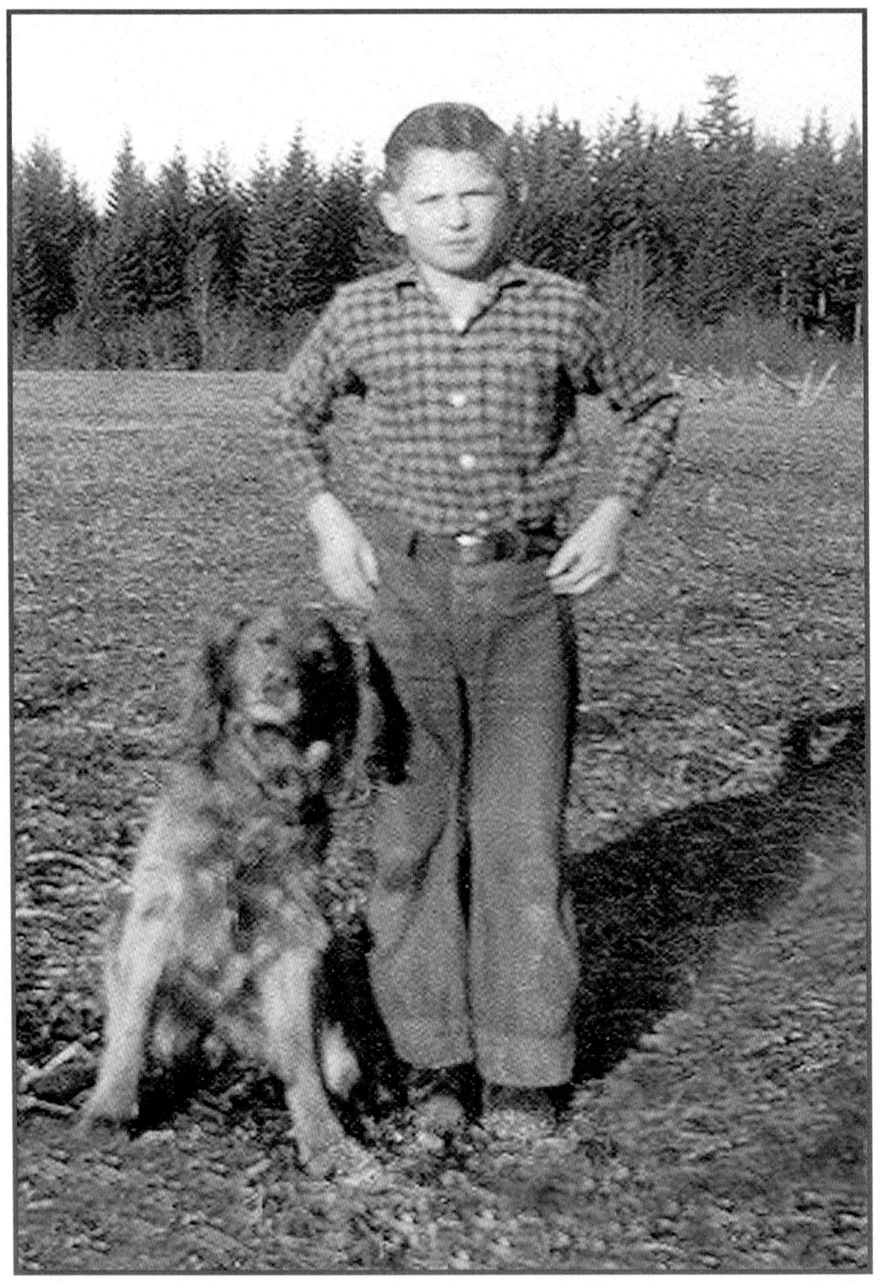

The Author At Age 10 with "Duke"

Ecstasy Discovered

Nineteen-forty-three in Portland, Oregon, was a noteworthy year for this ten-year-old. That was the year I learned words like duration, rationing, oleo margarine, priority, furlough and the gravity of the word "missing"....as in "*missing in action.*" It was also the year the soon-to-be famous Thunderbolt fighter plane was introduced, the year Henry J. Kaiser built a Liberty ship in only fourteen days (in the Portland, Oregon area) and also the year that, as a ten-year-old, I actually touched my first real airplane.

The word "duration" had tremendous meaning and much significance for many civilians during World War II. If you operated a business the government considered superfluous to the war effort, there was a very good chance Uncle Sam would redirect you (with a *mandatory* directive) toward assisting in the production of war goods. Not much historical information is available about the high number of small businesses that switched from making peacetime goods to manufacturing wartime necessities. Far out in our countryside, a fellow who owned a small custom machine shop converted his little operation to making parts for military tanks. It was always surprising seeing his workers loading cargo with military markings on trucks bound for strategic factories elsewhere. On my way to school each day was another unique operation which had been a manufacturer of Honduras wood veneer used on fine furniture. When the war began, it changed to making balsawood-based life-rafts for the many "Liberty" cargo ships turned out in the wartime shipyards in Portland and Vancouver, Washington. We boys loved the place! The factory workers allowed us to pick up scraps of balsa wood that we could use to build model airplanes.

The government "grounded" all private aviation for the "duration" of WWII except that commandeered or otherwise utilized for national service, such as the Civil Air Patrol, military liaison, etc. And how many people remember the national 35-mile-an-hour speed limit for all private vehicles? When not going to school, my chores included milking our cow, tending our pig and chickens or cleaning the neighbor's massive chicken coop for very meager pay (all jobs that I sincerely hated). In 1943, I purchased a bicycle from Sears Roebuck Co. with money I earned from picking strawberries the entire summer of 1942, another job I thoroughly detested! It's hard to imagine these many years later that the bicycle cost $32.95...which would be the equivalent in modern dollars somewhere around ten to twenty-five times more if values were "indexed."

To expand my horizons, I might be found climbing the deeply rutted, wartime-abandoned motorcycle climb hill a few blocks from our home. For other relatively harmless fun, I occasionally would hike or bike around the neighborhood simply to explore. It was on such an exploring junket with an adventurous friend that the fateful decision was made to do "it."

"It" was somehow to get inside a fantastically-shaped and apparently deserted building situated next to a grove of fir trees alongside a giant open field. The structure was located in S.E. Portland at the corner of 181st and Division Streets. We had biked past it many times and always wondered what in the world could be inside such a strange and unusual building, one that nobody seemed to care about and appeared deserted. In all the world, there can't be many buildings that appear to be round but are actually six-sided with no corners. Why had we never seen the slightest bit of activity in or around the building? It was indeed bizarre!

Youthful curiosity demanded we see the inside of this strange structure no matter what drastic measures might be necessary. It took the two of us to get the job done and doing it put me on a many-year track that ultimately would result in many exciting adventures..

A pleasant sunny day revealed my mischievous friend and me darting between trees and sneaking around the building searching for a weak spot in its security defenses. Five sides were fitted with very high and wide doors. One door was inadequately fastened and, together, we were able to pry it open just far enough to squeeze through. Inside, as our eyes adjusted to the near darkness, we beheld a sight that froze us in quiet amazement.

Scanning the dim scene, we made out the shapes of many huge objects much like giant fat beanstalks leaning against the walls and resting in vertical positions. There was scarcely enough room to walk because the building was so full of whatever this was.

On close inspection, we discovered the shapes were disassembled parts of small airplanes standing on their noses, with their wings placed alongside. We recognized what they were because there was hardly a kid alive who didn't either make model airplanes or wished he knew how so we knew a fair amount about planes. But, certainly, we had never seen anything like this!

Imagine! All these wonderful flying machines stacked tightly together in so many pieces! Even with our limited knowledge, we understood that these pretty little ships of the sky were laid away for the "duration." Years afterward, I would own and fly one of the very same models we viewed here with childhood awe. Building model airplanes, plus this sight of a couple dozen small planes all stuffed tightly together were among the seeds that germinated into my passionate determination to one day become a pilot.

As the war progressed, many more opportunities to see airplanes up close intensified my excitement with aviation. My dad and I occasionally would drive by a new emergency airstrip a few miles from our home, built to save trainees and advanced fighter pilots in case of serious emergencies in the air. It also became convenient for fighter-pilot instruction and practice. It was wildly exciting for airplane model-building boys to watch real Lockheed P-38 Lightnings, P-40 Warhawks and P-39 Bell Airacobra fighter planes roar in and out with their monstrous whining engines and bristling multi-machine gun mounts.

At that airstrip, I especially remember seeing a massive stack of "Jeep-cans," which were gasoline cans used throughout the war and sized to fit a special holder in the rear of Jeep utility-vehicles. They were filled with aviation fuel and stacked four or five high for a few hundred feet alongside the runway. The veritable mountain of cans numbered in thousands. It seems amazing that aviation fuel might be handled in such a manner, but war obviously produces a lot of unusual situations.

All during the war, it was exhilarating to hear the drone of engines in the sky, look up, then see hundreds of giant ships flying in formation as they ferried from one strategic area to another to execute their duties in connection with the great conflict.

The venerated WWII Lockheed P-38 Lightning - 10,037 built

As an 11-year-old, it was exciting to observe these glorious ships close-up at a nearby training strip used by fighter pilots.

Fairchild P-19 (primary trainer) - 6,397 built

This trainer buzzed overhead constantly in our area.

A couple more years went by and the great *second* "War to End All Wars" was over. I was thrilled when a cousin returned home from his service in the Army Air Corps, came by to visit and, upon learning of my interest in flight, offhandedly asked if I would like a ride in a real airplane.

Would I? Was there any question? Without delay we headed for the nearest airfield and, surprise, it was the very same one with the strange roundish building...which was now back in service as an operational aircraft hangar. Just a short time after the war ended, I had visited it a few times to view the activity. Airplanes were being reassembled and refurbished in a shop on the premises. I smelled the unique aroma of curing airplane "dope" the mechanics used to seal and tighten new fabric as they applied it to patch or recover the small planes. It was the very same smell that we airplane modelers had about us as we covered miniatures with paper-tightening "doping" liquid. It was a grand smell. I loved it!

We learned the hangar and airstrip had been created by Hank Troh, a noteworthy and highly respected early Oregon pilot and, during the war, a flight instructor to many Air Corps cadets at the Tex Rankin Flight Academy in Tulare, California. He had operated the airport on 181st and Rockwood Road from 1934 through 1941 when it was closed for the war's duration. After the war, it had other operators. Hank and a business acquaintance, Harold Wagner, then purchased one hundred acres of land on which to build a larger flight operation a couple of miles nearer the city of Portland.

Two dollars and fifty cents for a twenty-plus minute flight seemed an outrageous price for my cousin to pay for me to take a short airplane ride. Heck, I could buy a BB gun for that kind of money. However, since my much-older cousin was paying, I figured I should take him up on this chance of a lifetime. The moment the airplane engine started, I knew I had to become a pilot. It was just plain ***magic!***

This, my first flight, was in a Piper Cub model "J-3," possibly one of the very same we had earlier sneaked into the round building to view. When we departed Mother Earth and levitated, I decided then that the day must come when I would be the one in control. What I could not foresee then were the wild airplane escapades that the future held in store for me. Some of those would present many sobering realities about the importance of proper planning and the careful analyzing of risks (***before*** a flight).

That first flight was an amazing adventure into the realm of fluffy white clouds, birds and maybe...angels. People on the ground looked like tiny ants. What a fabulous sensation to view the broad expanse of miles and miles of one's own surroundings all at one time. I was permanently hooked!

Later, at age seventeen, enough money had been saved to begin flying lessons and I was lucky to get connected with one of the finest long-time pilots in our area. It turned out to be the ***very same Hank Troh,*** on whose earlier airport with the strange building I'd had my first ride. Now, he had built a much larger airport called Troh's Skyport...and had a new 150hp Piper "Super Cub" that was mostly used for training.

Hank had the enviable personal history of being one of the Pacific Northwest's illustrious, capable and well-known early pilots. It is very probable that the reason I am alive today is because of the native flight knowledge, diligent perseverance and unmitigated gall (when beneficial) of this man, my first flight instructor.

Like many in aviation after the war, Troh resumed his flight business figuring that a very large segment of the nation's future would be in the air. Practically every magazine shortly after the war had articles on how the world was in the new age of aviation for the masses. The success of our military planes overseas in the war had convinced the public that soon almost everybody would be able to fly! I recall artists' conceptions in magazines illustrating assorted hobbyists, "geezers" and "auntie Mauds" flying their own little "puddle-jumpers" around much as they might drive to the grocery store. Early after-the-war writers misjudged that every "Tom, Dick and Harry" would soon be flying over to visit their neighbors! Within five years or so, the majority of the new airstrips were out of business after the operators learned that only people with just the right mental and mechanical characteristics can become pilots.

When I took my first flight lesson, the new "air-age" idea had begun to wear off. People quickly realized that when something goes wrong in a plane, one doesn't just pull over to the side of the road and live happily ever after. Couple that with the statement a friend pilot liked to repeat when I was learning to fly: "An airplane is a great way to travel, *if your destination is another airport*." By the time I began my lessons, flying was getting narrowed down to only the seriously committed.

In my situation, because I also was a hunting and fishing aficionado, my resources were spread thin and, as a result, I ultimately began learning to fly three completely different times. Yep, that's right…three!

It would be fun to look back through those first amateur logbooks which each got lost before I got around to beginning again. I'd fly a few hours…not enough for "solo" flight...and then run out of money. A couple of years would go by and then I'd get some money ahead and get the urge

Marc, age seventeen...year of 1st flight lesson.
Motorcycle is 1947 BSA 30.50 c.i. twin.

again. Up I'd go with another fresh logbook only to run out of cash again... mainly because of also spending a bundle for hunting and fishing trips.

Among more memorable early flying experiences were some of my instruction flights. Hank Troh had a fabulous method of teaching student pilots to remember important aircraft procedures. For me, his most unforgettable one involved "carburetor heat." In airplanes that have carburetors (not all airplanes have them, but most small planes do), the carburetor is prone to a possible dangerous buildup of ice in certain weather conditions when the throttle is closed. Such an ice buildup can stop the engine and, if it stops at low altitude in a landing pattern, it can mean big trouble.

Sikorsky H-34 helicopter - 2,108 built

While serving in the U.S. Army in Germany, 1957, Marc (left) and friend Ron Pearce are set for a flight from Nellingen (near Stuttgart) down the Rhine River in this Army chopper.

As we would enter the landing pattern, Hank would wait…almost with glee...for me to close the throttle. Flying his Piper Super Cub, I would be in the front seat and, if I forgot to pull the carburetor heat on at what he considered just the right moment, he would lean forward and "whap" me smartly dead-center on the back of the head with a fifty cent piece…HARD! When not expecting it, such a hit is one heck of a shock. They don't make instructors like Hank anymore. Guaranteed, his students remembered the importance of carburetor heat and it is doubtful that any of them ever lost an aircraft for lack of it! From his early days of flight he had learned that the key to consistent success in the air is assured by careful preparation and intense training!

At some point during a flight, Hank might reach over to his left, pull back his lever of the dual-unit throttle setup, hold it closed against my efforts to open mine...and yell out as the plane began to drop, "Where are you going to land it?" And…he expected the right answer every time! Once, when I picked the wrong field, he let me fly almost into an irretrievable situation...before he took over the controls and masterfully set things right (only five feet from the ground...yep...FIVE FEET)! This guy really knew how to get one's attention! We then headed back up and gained altitude, he pointed out my mistakes and made me do it all over again…immediately. He didn't put up with any nonsense and he especially didn't appreciate cowards or daydreamers. If you lacked the potential ability to be successful and also the stomach for his brand of teaching, that was fine with him. You simply could learn somewhere else. But, if you stuck with him, you learned some great basics which became a natural part of your technique for the rest of your days. I'm sure some of his pushy instruction served me well a number of times since those nervous days of trying to please him and his demanding style.

The years passed and soon I was twenty-nine years old and still had no pilot's license. I yet had the desire, but the usual number of life experiences had interfered and, it just hadn't happened. That is, until one very momentous day! That was the day a fellow I'd met decided to offer his small plane for sale.

Werner Reimers was a young highly-skilled aircraft mechanic who had his own airplane. I met him at a nine-hundred-foot private airstrip where Werner based his Piper J-3 Cub. The strip had been created by Virgil Buroker, one of Oregon's pioneer pilots and was located on Portland "outskirts" near the intersection of 162nd and Halsey Street, right in the middle of private homes and apartments. It was a sort of "leftover" from earlier times when the surrounding properties mostly had been farms. A friend of mine kept a Piper 150hp "Super Cub" there and occasionally would ask me to fly with him to "***cut holes in the sky***" (one of his favorite things to say). Werner was there on a day when my friend and I visited the airstrip to go flying and told me his Cub was for sale. After discussing the airplane and hearing him quote $1,250 as his total asking price, we struck a deal.

I didn't have that much money but he was amazingly flexible on the terms and said, "Well, if you don't have the cash, how about giving me $500 down and paying the rest off at $50 a month. I could hardly believe that, as briefly as he had known me (a period of about two months), he would trust me to pay him on that basis. But, that is exactly what he did. I wrote a check to him for $500 and we simply shook hands on the deal. No paperwork. Just a "gentlemen's agreement!" I was almost in shock after the simple handshake...and then he said, "***It's your plane!***"

In retrospect, that wasn't necessarily *the* most surprising part of the deal. No…it was what he said next. As we shook hands, he said matter-of-factly, "Of course, the sixty-five horsepower engine in the plane is very high-time (well-worn) and so, whenever you are ready, I will major-overhaul (complete engine rebuild) the engine for you...A*T NO ADDITIONAL COST!*" At the time, I thought it was a good deal. I just didn't realize then how good! And, like a true gentleman, he kept his word.

A few months later, when I learned a little more about airplanes, I bought a wrecked J-3 Cub like mine that had an 85hp engine (*more power*) needing a complete overhaul…one that was built on the same basic engine case as the 65hp in mine. I swapped engines with the new plane and Werner agreed to rebuild the 85hp on the same basis. To my great delight, he delivered it back to me as a beautifully painted, brand spanking new chrome-cylinder "*major*" overhaul that included a shielded wiring harness and a number of other new extras not expected. I was dumbfounded and overjoyed. I very soon wrote a check for the balance so this little jewel that was now like brand new throughout would, for sure, be my very own.

From that day forward, each flight I took in the Piper Cub was sheer enchantment. As I became proficient, I could do loops from cruising speed and take off in a little over one-hundred-fifty-feet. It got to the point where I had to force myself to pay attention to my contracting business because I found myself thrilling to the chase in the little ship almost every day.

Such were my introductions to the fascinating world of airplane flight which easily rate in the top of my lifetime accomplishments. In essence, the first exciting experience of discovering the world of real airplanes at age 10 was the seed that germinated into a lifetime of pursuing widely-varied adventures and escapades...many producing exhilarating thrills and a few chills!

My first plane...*true love!*

The legendary Piper Cub - 19,888 built

The first Cubs had relatively small engines. The author installed an 85 horsepower engine which gave it greatly improved performance and superb flight characteristics.

Received from Marc
Paulsen $500.00 as ~~part~~
down payment ~~on~~ for
$1250.00 ~~for~~ on Piper J-3
N7074H (Werner Reimers)

This is how business used to be done. Not much more than a scrap of paper and a gentlemenly handshake!

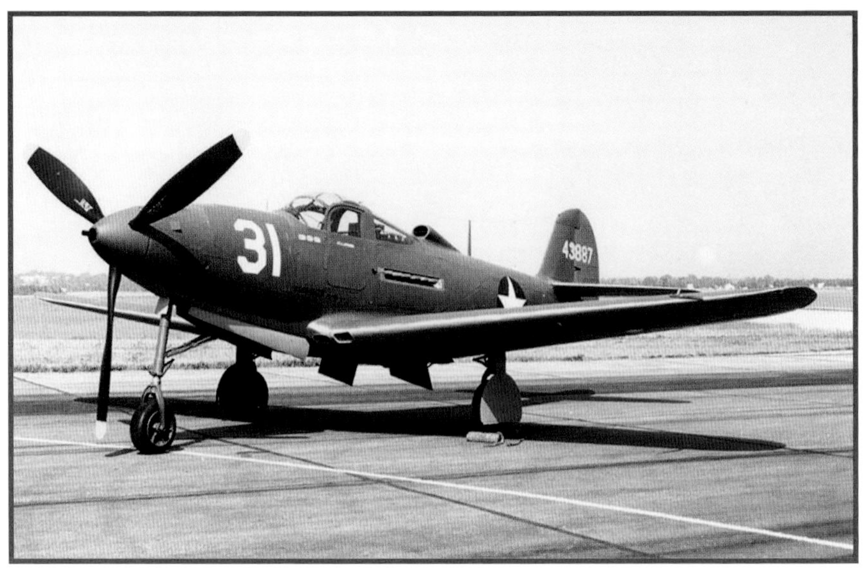

Bell P-39 Airacobra - 9,584 built

This was one of the fighter planes I watched fly on training flights near our home in 1942.

CUSTOMER'S COPY

Troh's Air Taxi

Troh's Skyport

PIPER SALES & SERVICE

The Oldest Flight School In Portland Vicinity

1949 S. E. 156th Ave. & S. E. Division St.

PORTLAND 16, OREGON

ALpine 3-5864

N.C. 7074H Date Nov 5 1962

M Marc Paulsen

Address

Sold By	Cash	C.O.D.	Charge	On Acct.	Mdse. Ret.	Pd. Out	CREDIT CARD
	✓						

5.3	Gals. Gasoline 80/87	1.91
	Oil	
	Hours Minutes	

GASOLINE PRICES DO NOT INCLUDE STATE TAX.

09859

BARCO INC. - OAKLAND 53712

Rec'd By

Imagine stopping for airplane fuel in the 21st Century and expecting a fuel attendant to deal with you for this kind of money!

Hank Troh didn't mind back in 1962. Hank was one of Oregon's premier commercial and flight instruction pilots and a very accommodating "fixed-base" operator. He would do anything in his power to advance aviation.

Hank gave me my very first flight instruction in 1951...until I ran out of money (which wasn't very long...I was just seventeen) and so had to postpone getting my pilot's license. Later, when I resumed flight lessons, it first was with Hank's operation in a shiny Piper 150hp "Super Cub," a very classy plane in which to learn what relatively few master... successful flight operation of a "heavier-than-air" flying machine.

Maybe Means No

Who (or whatever) out there in the great-beyond designed "homo sapiens" surely had this one pegged for travail. I hadn't had such a rude adjustment to my life since being drafted into the Army. Who came up with the idea that would wipe out two whole months of my blood, sweat, and tears...*in one swat.* Was it just a lapse of brainpower on someone's part or was destiny actually out to destroy me and my good works? From either direction, my project was compromised.

Sailplane? You fellows have a *real* sailplane? I couldn't believe it! This was too good to be true. I had just purchased a Piper Cub from an aircraft mechanic who kept it at a private airstrip near Portland, Oregon. As he was introducing me to the strip's owner one day, he asked the owner if he'd been in the sailplane lately.

I piped up and asked, "Who owns a sailplane?" The strip owner, "Dave," allowed that he and nine other men were members of a sailplane club that owned a WWII "surplus" sailplane.

I just *had* to hear about it and asked every possible question. I'd owned my Cub for only a few months and was enchanted with flying. Anything that took to the air got my attention. Dave looked me over and said, "Well, if you'd like, come to our next meeting. We could actually use a couple more members."

I couldn't accept fast enough! While in the Army in Germany, I'd seen gliders soaring in the Bavarian Alps and flying them seemed awfully romantic to me. It was fascinating to look up and watch as they soared in big graceful circles like giant white swans...true *poetry in motion!*

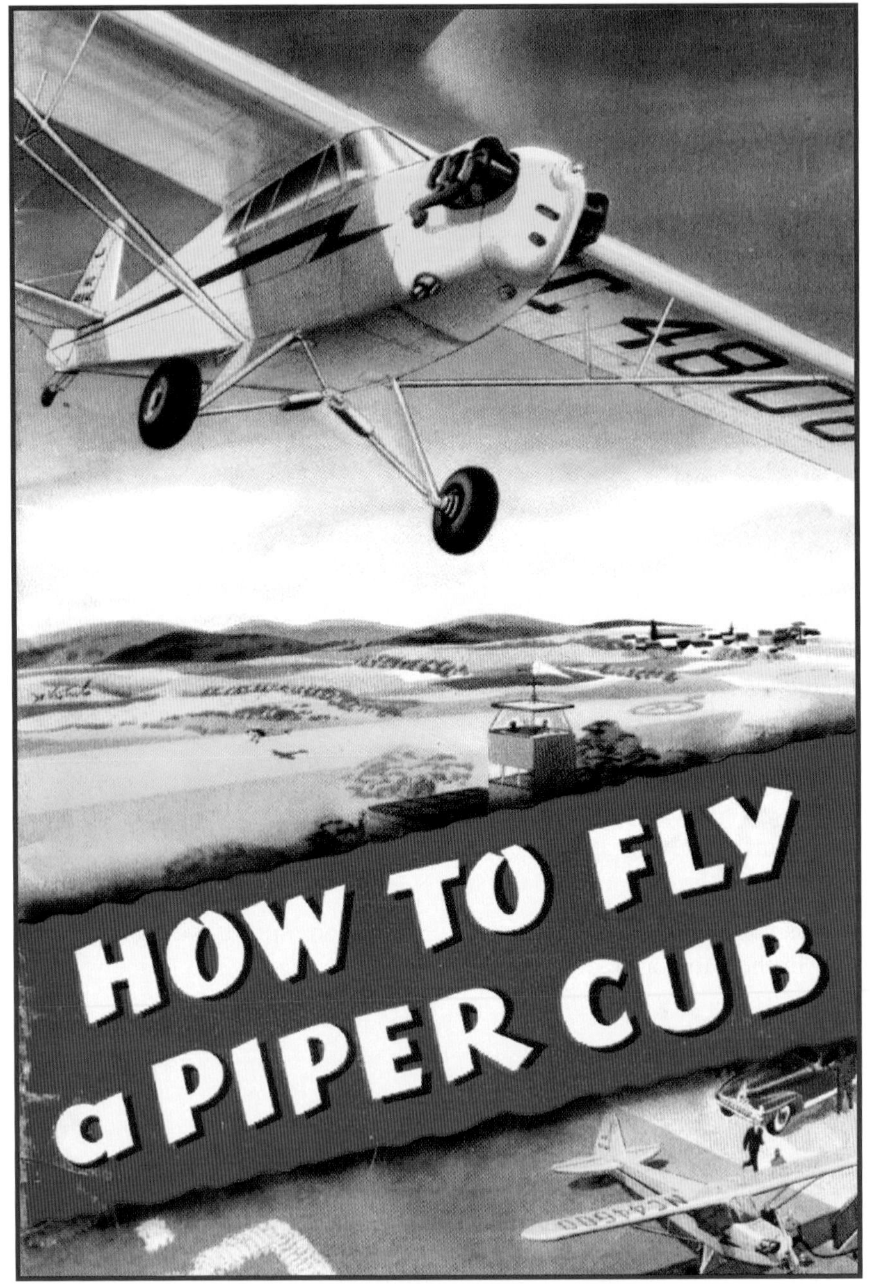

A Piper promotion - 1945

The first sailplane club meeting I attended was a bizarre affair. The members were all fairly "laid-back" guys, including a letter-carrier, a fire-fighter and a couple of state government employees. Only two out of the ten were self-employed, a far cry from the profile of most airplane owner groups. By far, the biggest share of airplane owners I'd known were either self-employed or at least modestly aggressive...*a different breed of cat!* It was quite obvious that there were no "Type-A" personalities here. And…what was the agenda? They talked about voting to *disband the club* and *sell the sailplane!*

What in heck was this? I had come to the meeting because I was excited about the possibility of joining their group. How *could they* disband? I'd been told that I almost assuredly could be a member…and *for only a hundred bucks.* I wondered about that. How could they let a member be a "one-tenth-owner" for only a hundred dollars? But, that was the situation.

The story seemed to be that they needed more members...hopefully one who owned a plane capable of towing their sailplane.

Aha! Now it came out. They really needed a member with a *tow-plane.* They had been hiring tow-planes at substantial cost and, when they didn't feel like spending as much, they towed the sailplane behind cars on the runway, an inferior substitute. Such tows would allow them to fly only around the landing pattern and settle back down. Their dream was to get a plane owner into the club, one with an appropriate type of plane, and then lean on that person to tow their sailplane. It all became clear.

I was introduced as a new member even as they were considering disbanding their club…*strange indeed!*

Then, other business was discussed and it came out that the club had been offered a free booth at the forthcoming *Boat, Trailer and Sport Show,* a massive yearly event for the world of outdoor sporting activities to be held in the Memorial Coliseum in Portland, Oregon. The space was offered free because the club was chartered as "Non-profit."

Boy, I'll say they were *non-profit!* Their treasurer's report indicated that they were lucky to be operating at all. I enthusiastically piped up and suggested that a free booth should be a great venue for gaining new members. One key member looked over at me and said, "If you think it is such a great idea, I move we make you the chairman of the event." *And like that*, not only had I become a new member, I was now an event "chairman." Wow, what shooting off your mouth can do! *Get you in big trouble, that's what!*

One of the members had almost finished a home-built sailplane that he said we could use for exhibition. He suggested we stand the fuselage

3240 N. W. 29TH. AVE. PORTLAND 10, OREGON
CAPITOL 3-7101

PD 4077 11-60

PLUMBING, HEATING and INDUSTRIAL SUPPLIES • FIRE PROTECTION SYSTEMS

PIPER J-3 N7004H WITH
YELLOW WINGS INCLUDING SPAR, GAS TANK, ENGINE MOUNT, ~~TIP~~ #1859 CLIP-TIP PROP, SPARE RUDDER, GENERATOR, TURN & BANK AND 2" VETURI. —

SOLD FOR #635.00 AND ROUND TIP METAL PROP AND — ~~CLIP~~ MY COST ON CLIP TIP REPAIR.

Oct. 24, 1962

R.W. Edling

recd. $300.00 cash.

Receipt for a damaged Piper J-3 Cub

I bought this wreck, which included an 85hp engine, so I could swap engines with my 65hp Cub. The seller used the nearest piece of paper for this "Bill of Sale." After the swap, I resold the remainder of this ship along with my "run-out" 65hp engine for only a bit less.

up, out, and directed away from the booth. They all thought that might be really dramatic. I wasn't sure but thought…*maybe...*

These guys got me to do their entire show for them…a slick move. I reviewed their charter and they truly were considered a charitable organization. How the heck they got that designation is a mystery, but they had it, so I planned to put the "charitable" part to good use.

I visited the Memorial Coliseum to view the space we were to be given. It was prime space dead-center in the big ring right in the middle of the most important items that were to be exhibited: *large yachts.* A brilliant thought crossed my mind. What if we could hang our sailplane…*the whole thing*...from the ceiling of the Coliseum. Wouldn't *that* be dramatic? I'm not sure what it was in me that snapped but a little later my brain told me it would be even better if we were to hang the sailplane ***plus*** a ***real airplane*** from the ceiling. So…I moved ahead in that direction!

About this time, I was flying my Piper Cub for sport almost every day. One day I flew to Hillsboro Airport just west of Portland. "Hillsboro Aviation" was the Piper dealer. While there, in a discussion with one of their key pilots, I told him about planning to hang a sailplane in the Coliseum. One thing led to another and soon we were talking to his airplane sales manager. The upshot? They agreed to provide a two-place Piper "Colt" airplane if I could figure out how to get it hung from the ceiling. Hurray! If I could pull it off, this would be a *very big deal.*

Back to the Coliseum I went to meet with the owner and manager of the big show. The boat show was owned and put on by a man of about sixty. This very busy man gave me only a few minutes of his time. He said, "The space you will occupy is right in the middle of my best-paying customers, the *large yachts*. You will have to be in ***first!***

Yachts then need to come in...so you must do whatever you do and *get out quickly* so they can get in. You say you plan to hang two airplanes from the ceiling? I'll give you ***twenty minutes*** to get them in, up, and get out! You run over that time and you'll have to get all your stuff the hell out and you'll be out of the show…***pronto and permanently! Do you understand?"***

"Yes, I believe I do."

"Can you do it?"

"Yes, I believe I can."

"**No,**" he responded, "***You don't understand!*** I don't want to hear what you ***believe*** you can do. I mean, do you ***agree*** to do it? ***In twenty minutes?"***

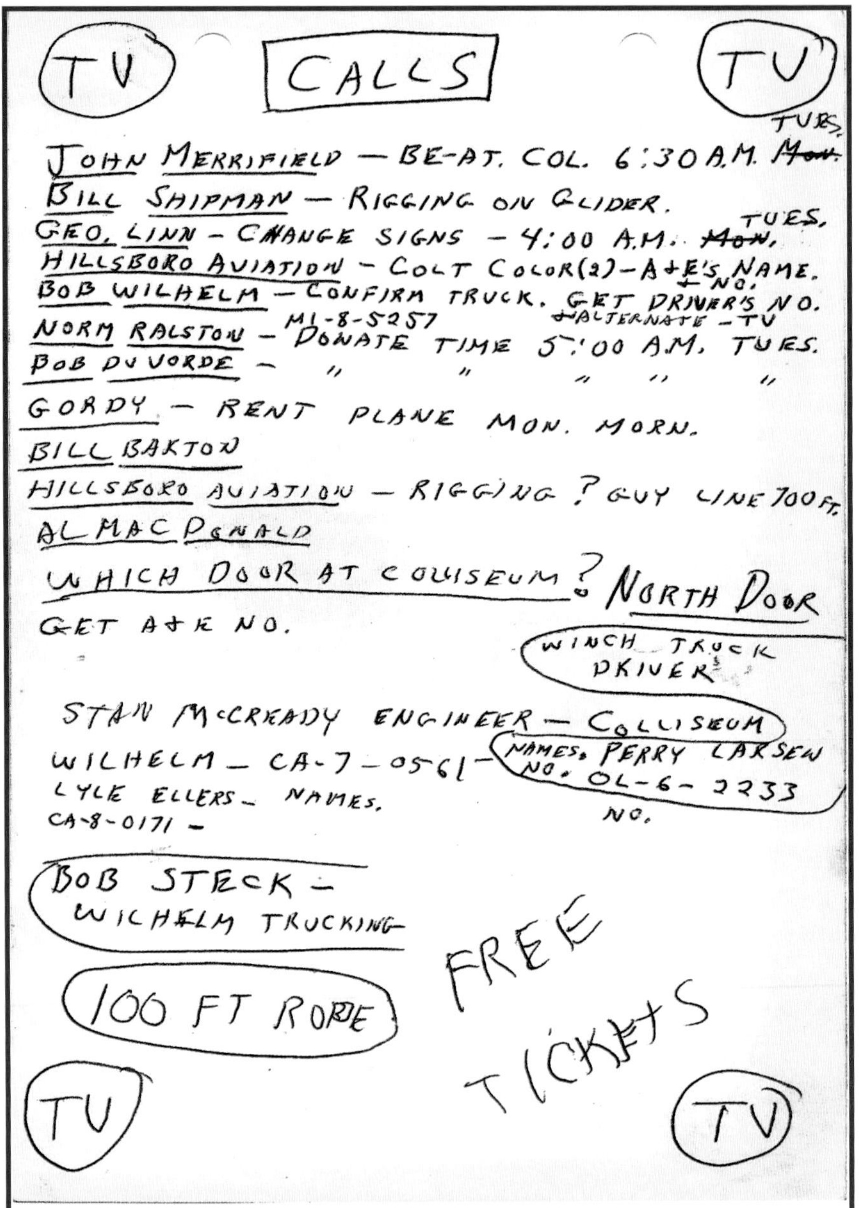

TV CALLS TV

JOHN MERRIFIELD — BE-AT. COL. 6:30 A.M. ~~MON.~~ TUES.
BILL SHIPMAN — RIGGING ON GLIDER.
GEO. LINN — CHANGE SIGNS — 4:00 A.M. ~~MON.~~ TUES.
HILLSBORO AVIATION — COLT COLOR(2) — A+E'S NAME. + NO.
BOB WILHELM — CONFIRM TRUCK. GET DRIVER'S NO. + ALTERNATE — TV
NORM RALSTON — MI-8-5257 DONATE TIME 5:00 A.M. TUES.
BOB DU VORDE — " " " " "
GORDY — RENT PLANE MON. MORN.
BILL BAKTON
HILLSBORO AVIATION — RIGGING? GUY LINE 700 FT.
AL MAC DONALD
WHICH DOOR AT COLISEUM? NORTH DOOR
GET A+E NO.
WINCH TRUCK DRIVERS
STAN McCREADY ENGINEER — COLLISEUM
WILHELM — CA-7-0561 — NAMES. PERRY LARSEN NO. OL-6-2233
LYLE ELLERS — NAMES. NO.
CA-8-0171 —
BOB STECK — WILHELM TRUCKING
100 FT ROPE
FREE TICKETS
TV TV

One of my original notes listing people and tasks involved with hanging airplanes from the ceiling of the Memorial Coliseum.

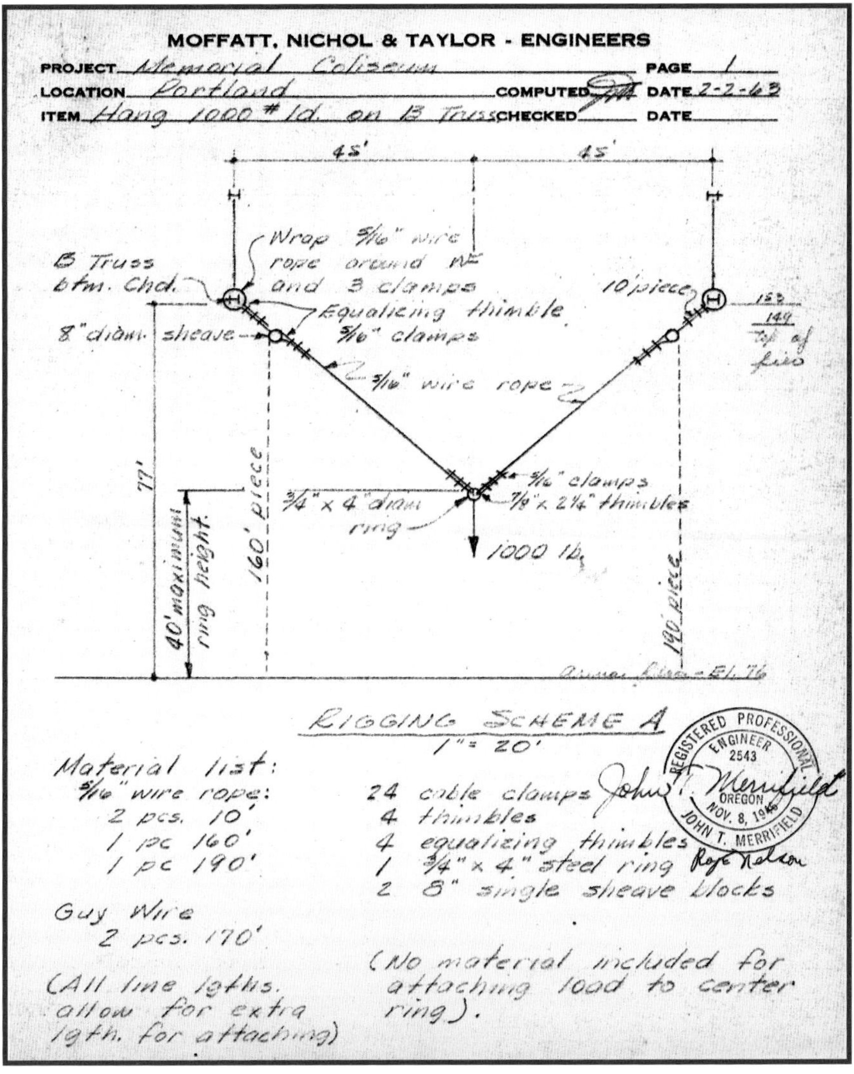

Original drawing detailing rigging of cables and fittings

Graciously prepared for our project at no charge by John T. Merrifield, Engineer. It details exactly what, how and where cables and fittings were to be attached to the Coliseum ceiling/roof to properly distribute the loads. John had a long and distinguished career as a civil engineer in Portland, Oregon, with the firm of Moffatt, Nichol & Taylor. While with that company, he designed a number of prominent structures in Portland, which included the Memorial Coliseum, the Morrison Bridge, the Hilton Hotel and Good Samaritan Hospital.

I thought about it for a few moments. This man was dead-serious about the twenty-minute figure.

"Yes, I will do it."

"Good. ***That's what I need to hear!"***

Twenty-minutes was an extremely short time for a program like this. I asked him, "How in the world do you get people to agree to things like this?"

"Son, when you ask someone to do something, there are three answers you can get: **NO**, **MAYBE**, and **YES**. Just remember, ***MAYBE means NO!*** When you get the answer you need (if it's a yes), then you get telephone numbers of everybody involved so you can call them even out of bed for action, if necessary. In this business, there is ***zero room*** for mistakes. Mistakes cost us a fortune. I expect you to perform or we'll jerk your stuff out and pile it in the street in a heap. It's that simple."

(Years later, I would become a national "Trade Show" manager myself and this lesson from a "good ol' boy" served me well.)

My first move was to visit the city manager in charge of Coliseum operation and maintenance. The man in charge quickly told me not to bother him unless I could get the man who designed the Coliseum to draw plans for the cable rigging necessary for such a project. He was concerned about the roof crashing down! Hmmmm….this was going to be a little tougher than I'd thought—no satisfaction from that man and I would have to please him before anyone else.

So…on to the local offices of the big architectural firm that designed the building. Fortunately, the Coliseum was only two years old so all of the work was still fresh in everyone's mind. I still had to contact the right man, the lead designer.

By a happy quirk of fate, I did, and, fortunately, he was the one man who could do the job. He was friendly and open to the possibility. And then, by golly, he said yes, he would get a drawing out for me at no charge since we were a "charitable" organization. So far, so good! He must have decided it was so unusual and interesting that he would be generous with his time and help us out.

Then, back to the Coliseum manager! He had said if he got the plan and it clearly stated that it was O.K. to hang the planes, then I could go ahead.

With this O.K., it was back to Hillsboro Aviation to talk again to the airplane sales manager. This time we went to the airplane mechanics and talked it over. They said it would take three mechanics to take the plane apart, put it on a trailer and haul it, and five men to put the ship together on the floor of the Coliseum...who could then hang it up in the twenty minute time frame. They sounded optimistic and thought for sure it would be a fun challenge.

It was agreed all around they would do it and thought for sure, that, with five men, they could meet the time schedule...if each person involved did his job properly. My job would be to oversee it *all.*

The architect produced drawings in a short time and, with plans in hand that specified the exact type of cable rigging required, I went to visit the largest industrial hardware company in the city.

They also wished to help. Again, I leaned heavily on the charitable organization element. They “charitably” furnished all the necessary cable and fittings for the job and delivered them to me on time at no charge. Was I ecstatic? *I'll say!*

I visited a trucking company that did the heaviest hauling in the area, figuring they'd have a truck set up with winches for rigging. They did and the owner was very gracious! After he heard that the big hardware company had agreed to help, he said, “Sure, it sounds like an interesting project and I'll send a winch-truck with a driver.”

My cup runneth over! Things were progressing amazingly well. That “charitable” designation seemed to produce an almost magical, positive result! With all the complicated, interrelated activities taking place, I'd found it necessary to halt all work in my modest contracting business and, was now spending full time on this profitless pursuit. But, it got so fascinating that *I had to do it!*

The last stop was the riggers' union hall. I begged and pleaded with the riggers' business agent..and he finally agreed to ask a rigger and rigger's helper to assist us and do the “high” work. The Coliseum ceiling was about one hundred feet high, a very dangerous height for amateurs. Again, those magic words, “charitable organization,” levered the project to success. I thought, “Dang, maybe I should figure out how to get control of a ‘charitable' organization of my own.”

It took me over two months full-time, seven days a week, getting this gambit all together. But, *it did come together.*

The day of the airplane lift came. What the old boy who ran the Boat Show operation had told me about getting everybody's personal phone numbers proved important. It helped make sure everyone involved was prepared to be there ***on time!*** What I'd been told about ***NO, YES***, and ***MAYBE*** was really true. I didn't mess around with any ***“maybes”*** on this job!

The airplane mechanics worked like clockwork. They had pre-assembled lightweight fitted-cable hanging-harnesses in their shop and were all set up and ready to roll the moment they arrived with the real plane (in pieces).

The rigging truck was parked and waiting just outside the big exhibit entrance door and the riggers showed up early.

We got the planes inside, assembled and hanging from the ceiling in ***eighteen minutes***…fabulous teamwork all the way around. Miraculous! After deeply praising and thanking the workers, I went home to get some much-needed rest. The show was to begin the next day and I wanted to be there at the opening bell to witness the viewers' astonishment at this gigantic production. Just imagine…not one, but ***two airplanes*** hanging from the ceiling of ***the biggest open-spaced building in the state.***

Jumpy all the next day in anticipation of the evening, I looked forward to standing around and listening to attendees as they gazed skyward in amazement at this unusual accomplishment.

The day of the great show opening, I arrived at the Coliseum in time to be sure that most of the other club members were in our booth. It was exciting walking through a long entry tunnel leading toward lights of the massive arena…anticipating looking up at those beautiful airplanes in the Coliseum sky!

Eagerly peering up, all I could see *was a mass of color and white.*

I rubbed my eyes. I looked again.

In my gaze was a ***colossal mass*** of giant white and multi-colored objects! What in the world was I seeing???

What I was seeing…was the ***gaudiest and most massive conglomeration of immense Japanese paper fish decorations imaginable!*** Dang! The whole place was filled with them. Dang again! The guys running the show had them put up during the night (after I had left) and hadn't had the decency to inform me ahead of time…***way ahead*** …like when I first talked to the old hotshot showman. Why hadn't ***HE*** told me I would be in direct competition with a mass of behemoth frivolous paper fish?

To see and concentrate on the planes was a stretch! That's how big and overwhelming the fish display was. Many of the giant beautiful paper fish were ***as big as a plane fuselage*** and camouflaged my airplanes.

I could not believe it! ***Two months*** of some of the most difficult negotiating, begging, pleading and hustling *had come to this*. And, it had cost me two months of my year's income as well. If you think I'm exaggerating the size of those blasted fish, study the news photo from the local paper illustrating the entire inside of the arena with all the big yachts plus every-

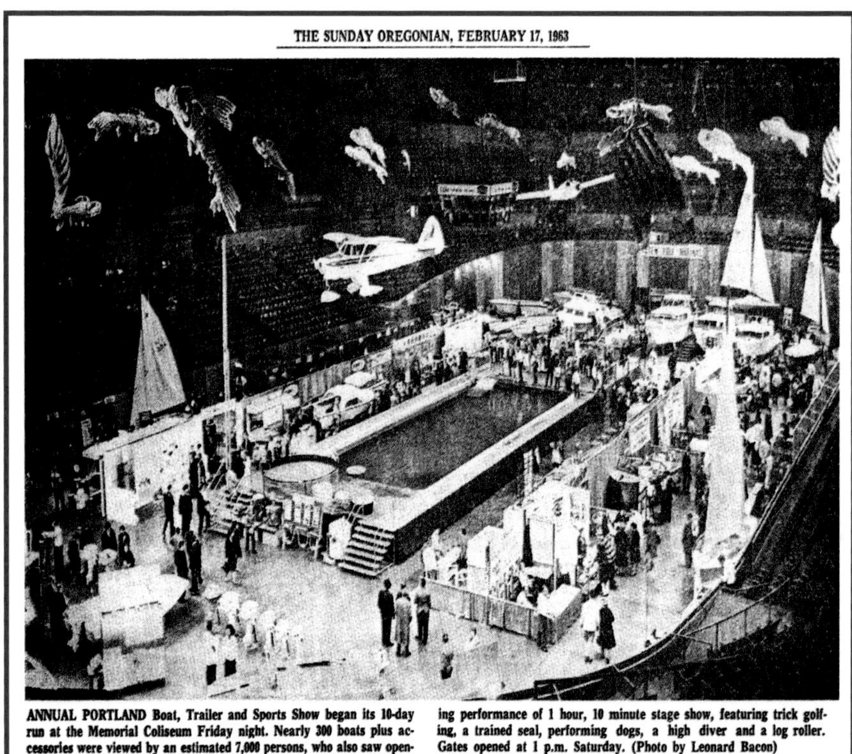

THE SUNDAY OREGONIAN, FEBRUARY 17, 1963

ANNUAL PORTLAND Boat, Trailer and Sports Show began its 10-day run at the Memorial Coliseum Friday night. Nearly 300 boats plus accessories were viewed by an estimated 7,000 persons, who also saw opening performance of 1 hour, 10 minute stage show, featuring trick golfing, a trained seal, performing dogs, a high diver and a log roller. Gates opened at 1 p.m. Saturday. (Photo by Leonard Bacon)

This was the local newspaper's photo of my and my several crews' production. Notice the giant paper fish...so monumental in size that they almost negated our entire effort!

thing that was hooked to the ceiling. If you ***really squint***, you can make out the sailplane hanging among those infernal paper fish. I swear I never want to see another paper fish in my lifetime!

And *then*, this whole story got even crazier! The show went well for the club. We signed up half a dozen new sailplane club members, including a nice gentlemanly "Flying Farmer" who had a Piper Super Cub, the ideal sailplane tow-plane. The club now was really ready to move forward!

Right after this big event I went back to my full-time contracting to make up for some of the money not earned from two months of working without pay. I had a couple of months of out-of-town work lined up a hundred miles from home and didn't make it back to a club meeting for three months, figuring that I'd "paid my dues" so everything would be O.K. whenever I did show up.

Checking with one of the members by phone, he gave me the date and time of the next meeting. He sounded a bit odd on the phone, as though something strange was going on.

The meeting was held in an airplane hangar of one of the members who had a private airstrip. Walking through the hangar door, I was amazed to see all of them working on the construction of a brand new Schweitzer two-place trainer sailplane "kit." And…*nobody* looked up as I walked in. Not a soul said a word.

I walked over to Dave, who had invited me into the club. He didn't look up as I asked him what was going on. He sheepishly mumbled that the board had held a meeting in my absence and decided that I was a little too much for them! They had decided to return the money I'd paid in... thereby canceling my membership. His only comment of justification was, "***This is kind of a family club***." The implication was that because I was single and not "tuned in" to their type of "easy-going" operation, I was somehow not their kind of "family." They surely had *that* right!

Nonetheless, I was beyond speechless. If I hadn't done all the work at the Coliseum setting up an outstanding display, they most likely would have disbanded the club. They had all told me earlier that they hadn't planned even to take advantage of the free booth. They did so only because I got involved and put the airplanes up. The Super Cub owner they got as a new member joined only because I knew him and had invited him to the show!

Now they had new members, new life, a new sailplane, a going operation and a fancy tow-plane…and they basically threw me out of the club *for promoting too forcefully.* I just shook my head in disbelief…*and left.*

Did I learn any kind of a lesson from all this? Well...from my perspective, flying sailplanes is mostly a "solo" sport. Most "advanced" sailplane pilots fly alone. When I joined, I did it more as a lark and for "camaraderie" to mix with people involved in the world of flight. I didn't plan to become a permanent sailplane "aficionado." I think these guys realized that and decided that I wouldn't fit in. And, you know what, *they were right!*

Oh, by the way, about fifteen years later I read one of the most shocking articles I ever read in a newspaper. Dave, the guy who gave me the word I was "out" of the club…***was arrested for hauling marijuana in an airplane and sentenced to a couple of years in prison!***

Laister-Kaufman TG-4A - 150 built

A two-place glider similar to the one owned by the sailplane club

Statement of Financial Condition - Oct 25, 1962

Willamette Valley Soaring Club, Inc.

L-K Glider sold Oct 24, 1962 - $1200.00 (with trailer)

Outstanding membership shares $1050.00 (11 members)

Dues and flight charges unpaid $37.50

Cash on hand less memberships $85.41 (net worth)

Property - Parachutes, barograph, tow ropes and cables, etc.

Mark your flight charges are $2.00

WHS

William H. Shipman, Treas.

My bill for dual flight-instruction time in the flying club's two-place Laister-Kaufman WWII "surplus" training sailplane. Members with instructor "ratings" gave member-students free "dual." A membership cost $100.

DATE 19 59	FLIGHT FROM	FLIGHT TO	AIRCRAFT MAKE AND MODEL	CERTIFICATE NUMBER	ENGINE	H. P.	CLASSIFICATION ASEL				DURATION OF FLIGHT
3-1-59	Troutdale	Local	Aeronca 7AC	N3657E	Cont.	65	:30				30
3-6	TROH'S	"	PA 18	7069P	Lyc	150	:30				30
3-7	"	"	PA 18	3894P	"	"	30				30
3-8	"	"	"	7069B	"	"	30				30
3-8	"	"	"	7069B	"	"	35				35
3-11	"	"	"	7069B	"	"	30				30
3-29	"	"	PA18	7069B	"	"	30				30
5-10	"	"	PA 18	7069B	"	"	30				30
2/7/60	Troutdale	"	Cessna 140	9601A	cont	90	30				30
2-12-60	TROUTDALE	"	CESSNA 140	2061N	CONT.	85	1 00				1 00
3-4-62	TROUTDALE	LOCAL	CESSNA 140	N9620A	CONT	90	1:05				1 05
THE RECORD ON THIS PAGE IS CERTIFIED TRUE AND CORRECT:							6:40				6:40
PILOT________	ATTESTED BY________						CARRY TOTALS FORWARD TO TOP OF NEXT PAGE				

INSTRUMENT	INSTRUCTION	DAY	NIGHT	DUAL	SOLO	REMARKS INSTRUCTOR SHOULD ENTER IN THIS COLUMN THE NATURE OF EACH MANEUVER IN WHICH INSTRUCTION IS GIVEN, AND THE TIME SPENT THEREON, AND SHALL ATTEST EACH SUCH ENTRY WITH HIS INITIALS, PILOT CERTIFICATE NUMBER, AND PERTINENT RATING.
		30		30		Introduction Flight [signature] 31461-CFI
		30		30		turns Coord, climbs H Troh 31762
		30		30		Stalls climbs glides G J Widmayer 626160
		30		30		T.O. & L H Troh 31762
		35		35		T O + Landgs D course G J Widmayer 626160
		30		30		circuits + Bumps H Troh 31762
		30		30		T O + landings G J Widmayer 626160
		30		30		T O + landings G J Widmayer 626160
		30		30		ORIENTATION [signature] CFI 552845
		1 00		1 00		TURNS - STALLS - SLOW FLT. - T.O. + LNDGS
		1 05		1 05		ORIENTATION FLT. [signature] CFI-A-1482921
		6:40		6:40		ENTER IN THIS COLUMN DETAILS OF ANY SERIOUS DAMAGE TO AIRCRAFT. IF MORE SPACE THAN THAT PROVIDED ABOVE IS NEEDED FOR ANY DETAILS OF FLIGHT INSTRUCTION OR AIRCRAFT DAMAGE, USE PAGES PROVIDED IN BACK OF BOOK.
CARRY TOTALS FORWARD TO TOP OF NEXT PAGE						

Entries in my third flight logbook. I ran out of money in my first attempts at learning to fly because I also spent heavily on fishing and hunting during the same time periods. Check the sixth entry down in the Remarks section. "***Circuits & Bumps***" was a favorite "tongue-in-cheek" entry by Oregon's legendary commercial pilot/instructor, **Hank Troh**. It referred to practice "***takeoffs and landings***."

The Northwest's Most Outstanding Gov't. Approved Training School

SKYWAYS
FLIGHT SERVICES

INSTRUCTION — CHARTER — RENTAL — SERVICE — SALES

PORTLAND - TROUTDALE AIRPORT
TROUTDALE, OREGON
PHONE: MOhawk 5-2141

Customer's Aircraft N____ Date 3-9 1962

M Paulsen

Address

SOLD BY	CASH	CR. CARD	CHARGE	ON ACCT.	CR. MEMO	OUR AIRCRAFT N9620A
	X					

QUANTITY	DESCRIPTION	RATE	AMOUNT	TOTAL
1:00	FLIGHT INSTRUCTION			7 00
1:00	AIRCRAFT RENTAL		9 00	
	USE CHARGE		1 00	10 00

FLIGHT PURPOSE: TNG X | RENT | INST | NITE | XC | VET | ROTC | OTHER | S.A.

QUANTITY	DESCRIPTION	RATE
	LINK INSTR. (BASIC) (ADVANCED)	
	GROUND SCHOOL INSTRUCTION	
	BOOKS & SUPPLIES	
	PILOT SERVICE TRIP NO.	
	CHARTER TRIP NO.	
	GALS. OCT. GASOLINE	
	QTS. SAE OIL	

TOTAL INVOICE pd 17 00

ALL claims and returned goods MUST be accompanied by this bill

This receipt shows the hourly charge for a Cessna 140 two-place trainer and the instructor. Typical skilled craftsman pay at the time ranged from $3 to $6 per hour.

Cessna 140 - 7,664 built

A great trainer! I spent quite a few hours in one at $10 per hour (solo).

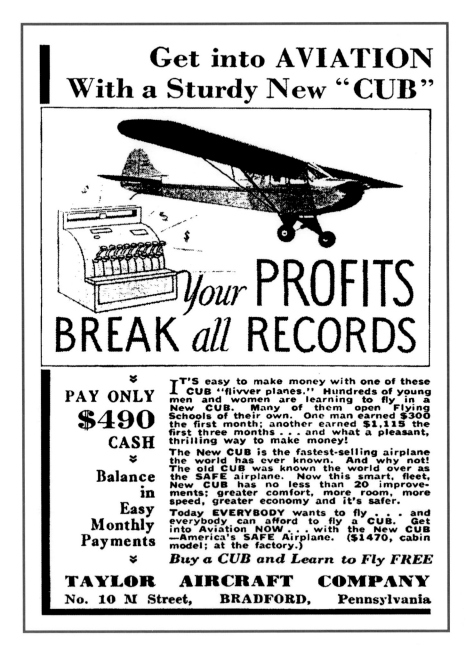

Get into AVIATION With a Sturdy New "CUB"

Your PROFITS
BREAK all RECORDS

PAY ONLY
$490
CASH

Balance in Easy Monthly Payments

IT'S easy to make money with one of these CUB "flivver planes." Hundreds of young men and women are learning to fly in a New CUB. Many of them open Flying Schools of their own. One man earned $300 the first month; another earned $1,115 the first three months . . . and what a pleasant, thrilling way to make money!

The New CUB is the fastest-selling airplane the world has ever known. And why not! The old CUB was known the world over as the SAFE airplane. Now this smart, fleet, New CUB has no less than 20 improvements; greater comfort, more room, more speed, greater economy and it's safer.

Today EVERYBODY wants to fly . . . and everybody can afford to fly a CUB. Get into Aviation NOW . . . with the New CUB —America's SAFE Airplane. ($1470, cabin model; at the factory.)

Buy a CUB and Learn to Fly FREE

TAYLOR AIRCRAFT COMPANY

No. 10 M Street, BRADFORD, Pennsylvania

1936 ad - The famed Piper Cub...began life as the *Taylor Cub.*

Terror Comes In Twos

Listening to the good-old-boy hangar talk, it was crystal clear to me that Charles Lindbergh flew across the Atlantic Ocean through gloom of night and pea-soup weather *without* all the extra instruments that my flight instructors said were absolutely necessary now for survival in the air. These grizzled old flyers indicated that any pilot worth his wings can fly through just about anything…be it black of night or solid-cloud weather...with only a "needle-and-ball," an "airspeed-indicator" and an "altimeter" for guidance. "Needle-and-Ball" was the slang term for what (was) formally called a "turn and bank" indicator...(now called a "turn-coordinator"), a primary instrument that shows that your airplane is in a skid, slip or turn. That is, if you have learned how to read it! This early level-flight indicator was crucial for blind flying at night and in bad weather conditions with limited or zero visibility…long before more sophisticated instruments made their way upon the scene.

After hearing these stories enough, it was settled in my mind that, if I were to become a really proficient, true-blue, hotshot *Aviator Extraordinaire*, I would have to learn to fly blind on the "needle and ball."

At this time, I was a very high-time student pilot having accumulated *well over* one hundred hours in the air. It was time for me to check out the mysteries of the clouds! I hadn't got around to getting my pilot's license at this point in my flying career because that would have required slowing down long enough to attend boring ground school classes and, besides, I owned my own plane so could fly it at will.

A number of stories the veteran pilots told involved hapless neophyte pilots popping out from bottoms of clouds minus plane wings after they accidentally got into a solid overcast, became disoriented, then over-stressed the airframe to the point of in-flight breakup—a very spooky thought!

This could never happen to me! I would simply learn fast and well and then exercise cool, calm and calculated intelligent control when faced with that inherent danger lurking in those beautiful giant mountains of fluff.

Listening intently, I'd heard old hands point out that the unfortunate souls who lost their plane's wings (and their lives) had missed great opportunities to save themselves by simply putting their ships into a spin and spiraling safely down out of the clouds to clear sky. In scenarios like this, it is assumed that pilots should know beforehand if there is sufficient distance between the cloud bottoms and Mother Earth. According to aerial pundits, all one had to do after clearing the cloud bottoms was execute a normal spin recovery maneuver, pull out into level flight and live to fly happily ever after. It all sounded elementary.

The day came when I had both a free afternoon and a newly-installed "turn and bank" indicator. I had just picked up my 85hp Piper J-3 Cub from a wizard aircraft mechanic who had done a fantastic job of building a classy looking new instrument panel for me. The panel consumed every square inch of the tiny available space directly in my path of vision. I scanned this exotic construction, which looked to me much like a junior-grade Boeing 707 display (all seven instruments)! And, dead center of all this equipment, was that grand new "needle and ball"…just begging for an opportunity to meet a cloud. Earlier, while flying in my friend's Super Cub, I'd had the opportunity to spend quite a bit of practice time *in clear weather* learning to control an aircraft with help from the "needle and ball."

This bright summer day had spawned some colossal pure white billowing clouds. Formed as monumental building blocks in the sky, they were isolated in distinct separate units with a lot of airspace and clear sky above, below and around them.

Here, then, was the perfect situation for this novice pilot to gain sharp new expertise in a simple, inexpensive way. I didn't have to pay an instrument instructor some vast sum of money to demonstrate something I could teach myself in my own plane. I reminded myself that *no one taught the Wright brothers!* It was thus settled in my mind.

Takeoff for this adventure was from Troutdale airport, a few miles up the Columbia River from Portland, Oregon. Notwithstanding my limited experience, I'd thought out this whole process very carefully, had planned for every possible detail I could imagine and was positive I hadn't overlooked a thing.

First, I'd practiced spins at great length to cover the possibility of my losing complete control inside a cloud and having to use the "good-old-boy-method" to recover control of the plane, the one I'd heard while sitting around the proverbial cracker barrel "hangar-flying" with other pilots. When a non-pilot, I'd been amazed that a mere human could actually recover from, level out, land and walk away from an apparently death-defying spin. Even the thought of spinning out of control in an airplane is enough to give willies to most earth-anchored souls. Aha! I'd learned the facts about how non-threatening a spinning aircraft really is. However, I'd never be the one to reveal the secret of much revered aerobatic pilots who make spins a vital component of their great air shows. The public shouldn't know that a controlled "tailspin," or simply "spin" in a plane is a very tame and surprisingly simple and safe maneuver.

I'd even thoroughly planned for the very remote possibility of having to bail out of the plane in an emergency. The WWII surplus seat-pack parachute I had decided to wear for the occasion had been recently re-packed and inspected by a licensed parachute-loft manager at a nearby airbase. I already had jumped three times successfully albeit gaining some seriously-bruised muscles due to my two-hundred-pound frame paired with a relatively small war-surplus chute canopy. My jump-log refers to the "chute" used as a Military "T-10" type (which was *relatively* small). At any rate, I felt I could muster the courage for "jumping" if it was really necessary. In truth, the very thought of stepping into space and leaving my precious little plane behind to auger into the earth was more than my flying psyche wished to contemplate. But, if forced, I felt that I could do it.

On this summer day there were at least two thousand feet between the cloud bases and ground level and the clouds were positioned just southwest of the village of Estacada twenty or so miles from my point of departure. The location was well out of the way of commercial air lanes and most private plane traffic. Certainly, no airliners would be anywhere near this area. There is a lot of sky for private planes when one considers how very few of them there are in relation to the size of the great canopy of blue above.

Lastly, I had scanned the airman's "sectional" chart of the area closely...concluding that the ominous-appearing fan-shaped "Military Climb Corridor" indicated on the chart (used by high-powered Air National Guard jet fighters) was plenty far away from my planned

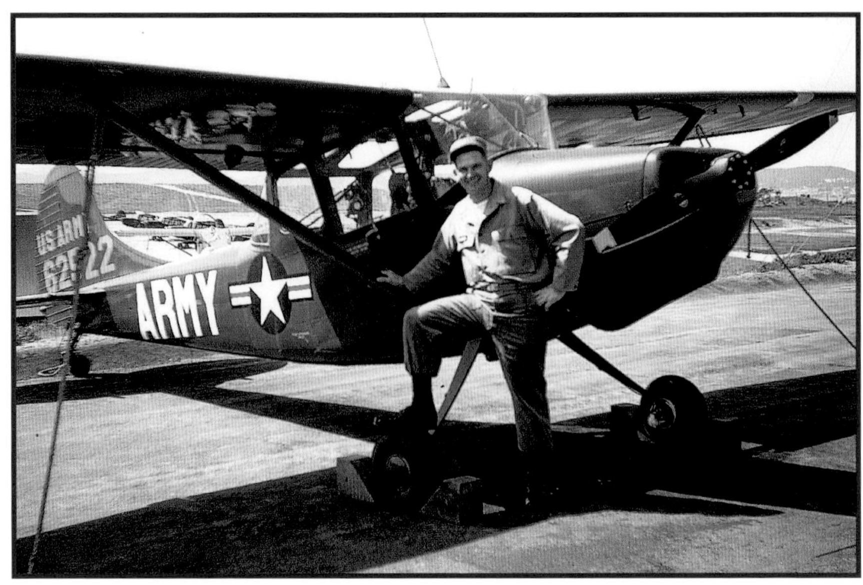

Cessna L-19/O-1 Bird Dog - 3,431 built

The Author dreaming about future flight while serving with the U.S. Army in Fort Ord, California, 1957.

Marc checking out a Hiller OH-23 Raven - 1,773 built

activity. That was clear because the "corridor" was indicated in a very obvious and precise location on the chart so this eliminated my fear of any direct involvement with those planes. Confident that no planning stone was left unturned, I looked forward to an extraordinary experience. No question about it. By late afternoon, I hoped I'd qualify as a real *instrument pilot! (Just kidding, of course!)*

I had recently purchased one of the early portable and *then expensive* VHF (Very High Frequency) aircraft radios. It was from the venerated radio equipment firm, Hallicrafters, a model TRV-128A and its use made possible transmitting and receiving radio calls from tower-controlled airports. It worked reasonably well (most of the time) but had major drawbacks, one being a very short-lived ***12-pound battery pack*** that cost a small fortune! It also had a severely-limited range and only one radio frequency which necessitated calling ground control on the tower frequency. With only one frequency, getting ground control instructions from the tower controller always proved to be a great time waster while waiting for other better-equipped planes to be moved ahead of me. After a fashion, it did the job. As long as they would go along with my limited radio situation, I'd resist spending more money.

Ground control cleared me to taxi, so I held the brakes and increased power to the engine (the combination of which maintained the tail in a raised attitude)...then moved out onto the taxiway.

Upon arrival at the end of the "active" runway, the tower cleared me for takeoff and, after a hundred and forty foot roll, the plane rose into the sky. Immediately pulling the stick back, a very steep dramatic climb was initiated. A day would come when I would regret repeating this steep climb maneuver…but that's another story.

About a third of the way along the runway, I called the control tower, requested and was given permission to make a right-turn departure to the south. The air traffic thinned out quickly upon leaving the busy Troutdale airport and the sky became all mine. I winged my way along gaining altitude...all the while contemplating the secret, thrilling activity I was about to undertake.

After about fifteen minutes, I approached the area and began searching for an appropriate cloud for my clandestine purposes. Fortunately, there were a number of giant, mile-square blocks of clouds far enough apart to let me choose my very own cloud system.

The cloud bases proved to be about 2500 feet above ground, an almost perfect altitude for spin recovery, if such a drastic measure became imperative. Earnestly, I hoped it wouldn't be necessary to test this granddaddy of all great questionable hangar-flying folk tales: the theory of spinning out of a cloud!

Arriving at 3500 feet of altitude and at about the vertical center of a nearby giant cloud block, I circled outside of it for a while, practicing holding my headings and altitude while looking straight ahead at only the instruments. This, to get that true feeling of absolute blind control that I knew all big-plane pilots surely must experience as they slip gently down the glide slope (a radio-frequency-produced invisible highway in the sky) in the klag (solid clouds). The process seemed to work well and, after *at least a half-hour of practice*, it seemed I was ready to go for the real test: true "*instrument-only*" flight!

Moving out about a quarter mile from the big cloud block, I set up a straight-and-level flight approach to it. The game plan was to fly straight into the cloud for maybe twenty seconds until I was in pure white and solid blind flight, execute a 180-degree turn using the needle and ball in a timed turn to assist me in exactly reversing my direction…then fly straight back out of the cloud for twenty seconds. If everything went according to plan, the plane would pop back out of the cloud just about when the second hand on my panel clock indicated that one minute had elapsed. In my junior birdman way of thinking, this type of practice, if controlled adequately, should help me learn the rudiments of instrument flight. If Lindbergh made it all across the Atlantic in the middle of the night with only the same basic dials and gauges, couldn't I teach myself instrument flight without difficulty in a relatively modern airplane? So, in I went!

The first flight progressed perfectly throughout. I couldn't believe how easy this was and that it didn't present the least difficulty. Again and again and again I flew back into the clouds to get the hang of it. I'd fly in straight for twenty seconds, ascend for twenty seconds, hold the new altitude and fly straight for twenty seconds, then execute a timed 180-degree turn and backtrack out simply reversing the process. It all went without a hitch, so...how about trying something a bit more difficult? Fly in for a while, execute a 360 and a 180-degree turn in the cloud and fly back out into bright sunshine...and do every combination of climb, turn, descent and level flight I could think of. It was all working with textbook perfection and I now could understand clearly how pilots were able to wing their way across the Atlantic with only a few instruments and the turn and bank indicator, a.k.a. "needle and ball."

It was surprising what short shrift had been given the "needle and ball" by the air and ground instructors I'd had. This truly was flying at its ultimate.

Although the cloud interiors concealed the outside world, the day was so bright and sunny that the big cotton candy-like cloud interiors were fairly light and bright inside and, although opaque, flying inside was quite pleasant. It felt much like living inside a safe all-white cocoon, and I experienced a giddy, warm, glowing feeling of security and serenity as I continued this wondrous activity for an hour or so.

Tiring of the repetition, I decided to take one last plunge in before heading back to the airport…so flew straight in for about thirty seconds, completed a climb, then a period of level flight and had just started a second climb still on my way in…*when it happened!* My exquisitely laid plans *exploded with a flash!*

It happened with a jolt comparable to a howitzer shell fired at a plate glass window from four feet away! We're talking *major danger, major fear*...giving the word *incredible* whole new meaning!

While inside the cloud…and for just *the* ***slightest fraction of a moment***, my gaze had wandered out into the bright white nothingness to the right side of the plane when, ***at that precise moment***, a giant dark, forbidding, ominous shape ***shot past*** exactly level with me and no more than fifty feet away.

The shape had come almost directly at me ***like a lightning bolt****…and was* ***gone behind me in an instant!*** The action happened so fast that my brain did not clearly register the event for a moment. In another instant, a sharp jolt of rapidly moving air hit me like a brick. It was a ***big jet fighter's*** tremendous "*slipstream!*" My little plane jerked wildly for a moment, pitched up, then sideways…tipped on edge and hovered there for an instant, then settled back down. I fought like mad to keep my senses and concentrate on the "needle and ball" to return the Cub back into level flight. The hurtling object had been pushing as much air as a gigantic truck…but *about ten times faster* and *a lot more.*

I sat frozen...motionless as if suspended in a space-time-continuum. My brain strained to shift my thinking processes forward. ***My God!*** This had to have been an illusion. My planning had been to perfection, I thought, and hadn't left even the slightest bit of room for strange or unusual occurrences.

In a state of utter shock I flew on. Split seconds elapsed.

They seemed like minutes!

This had to be a dream.

And then, with the impact of what seemed a hundred lightning bolts at once, my foggy mind registered the detailed reality of what I'd seen. ***I almost had been vaporized by a head-on collision with a F-94 jet-fighter plane.***

I obviously had overlooked one detail…namely, that the local Air National Guard F-94 all-weather-interceptor squadron did, in fact, leave the area through the military "climb corridor," the location of which I had checked very carefully…*but I hadn't yet learned* they were free to **return** ***from almost any direction***…including ***where I was right now!***

I sat absolutely petrified…frozen in place, totally unnerved and staring vacantly ahead into the white space where the apparition had appeared and then disappeared with what seemed the speed of light.

As my brain recalled the sight and redrew the picture I had just witnessed, I realized the near miss had been so close that I actually had seen the faces of both the pilot and the radar operator. Now, as I slowly began to think clearly again, the complete scene materialized in my mind and I shuddered. The jet had missed me by the aerial equivalent of a split-hair and, as that realization came solidly home to me, my next thought was ***even more horrifying.*** Jet fighter planes ***always traveled in pairs!*** Where was the second one? *Was he following???*

Weakly, I summoned all the courage I could muster. This was absolutely no time to lose mental control and do something even more foolish, which might cause the wings of my plane to fail during a violent maneuver. But, ***what*** should I do?

Now, I asked myself a shotgun series of unnerving questions:

Turn right or left? Ascend or descend? Put the ship in an instant spin and plunge toward the ground? What? What? ***What*** should I do?

Had the ship that whipped past me been the first fighter or the second? If it was the first, how far behind was the second fighter? And…would it be ***high? Low? Where in the world would it be???***

Panic made a wild grab at my senses and began to squeeze me like a vise. I fought panic off desperately to retain a semblance of calm…I had to do something now...and had to do it instantly! *But what?*

I began a left turn for no special reason. ..although a direction away from what I had just witnessed.

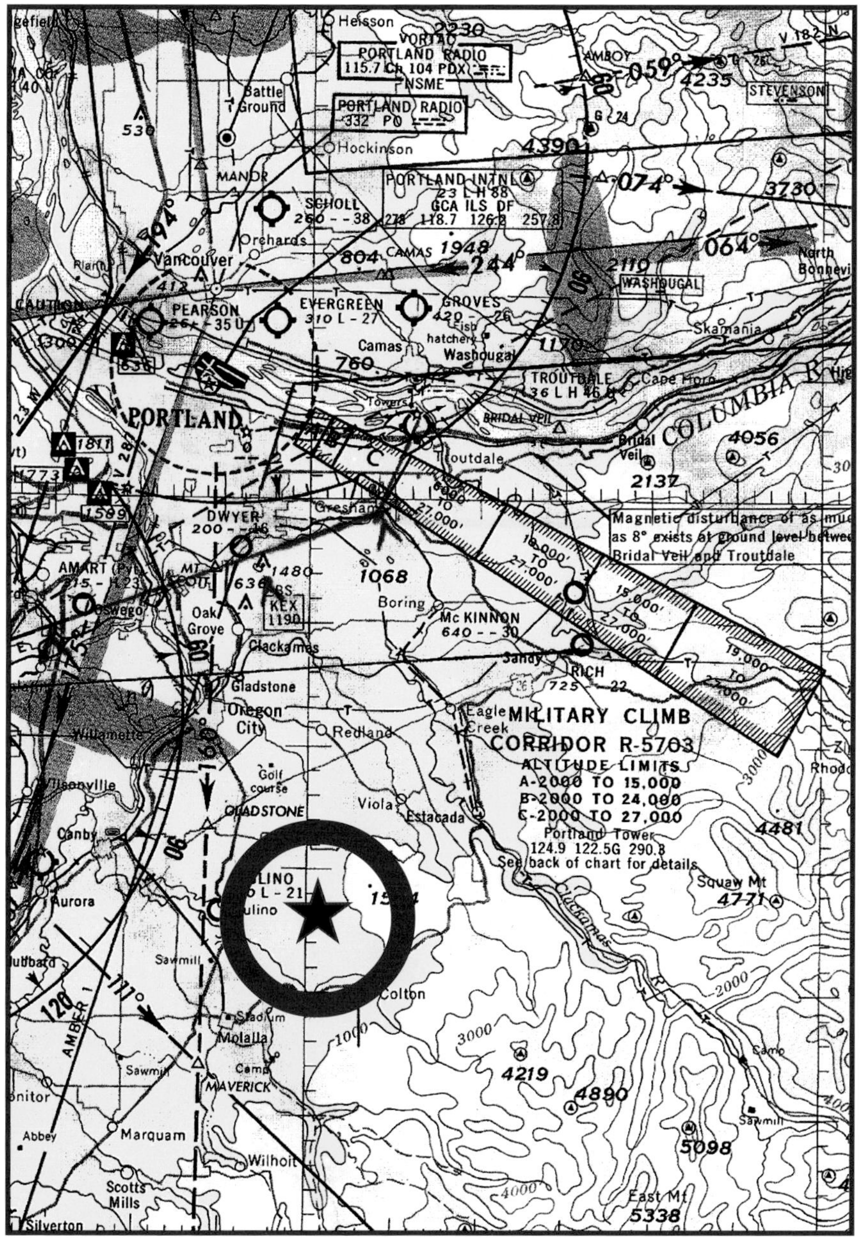

Aeronautical chart indicating location of my F-94 encounter.

I prayed. I held the turn. I thought…I didn't think...I shivered…I shook…I quaked and...*nothing more happened.*

Then, an almost comical thought struck me and I laughed aloud in my fright. Had the pilot and radar operator seen me? If they had, were they now looking at each other with as much disbelief as I was experiencing?

It seemed I could almost hear the conversation:

Pilot to Radar Operator: "Mike! Did you see that? Holy mackerel, Mike! That was a, a, a, a, a, a ***Piper Cub!*** *Did you see that?* Huh?…Mike! My God, Naaaahhhhhh.....I don't believe it! I've got to be dreaming. Son of a gun! *It couldn't be!* ***A PIPER CUB...IN THE MIDDLE OF A CLOUD???"***

A hopeful notion flashed into my thinking. I reasoned that when the fighter zipped past me, he appeared to be returning to his base and was therefore, probably descending with his compatriot following, if, indeed, another fighter was behind him. So...if I climbed at the same time as trying desperately to turn back and fly out of the clouds, I might avoid the second plane by flying over him. I instantly pulled up into a slow climb.

My little jewel of a Cub droned on.

I thought wildly, "Will I get speared by the second plane?"

I nervously waited for the terrible moment at which life as I had known it on this planet might suddenly cease to exist…*in a puff of smoke!* If the worst happened, it would all be over in a microsecond and I probably wouldn't feel a thing, so I waited for eternity to present itself and maybe... the hand of St. Peter reaching out for me from gloryland.

Still Nothing.

More Nothing.

Nothing but pure white!

Fighting to control my still shaking body, I pulled back on the stick and gained more altitude, then straightened out level and on a compass heading that would take me out of this infernal cloud. I promised God I'd take care never to do anything this stupid again. That's interesting…I'm not even very religious…funny how *that* works. All this had taken place in only a few moments.

I waited...waited...and continued holding the plane steady.

Nothing! No follow-up event!

Just smooth level flight.

Then, like the dawning of a spectacular new day, I was back in brilliant sunshine…enchanting, ambrosial, delightful, glorious sunshine…and ***I was still alive!***

The "all-weather" Lockeed F-94 Starfire fighter plane - 855 built
...my nemesis in the klag!

Years later, I still recall this event with absolute crystal-clarity in the theater of my mind. The picture of the scene forces its way back into my semi-conscious thinking and, like Scrooge from Christmas past, I am compelled to envision it again as if I were there yet. I still see microscopic details of that massive fighter-plane thundering past a mere few feet away. And there in the giant airplane are the two statue-like airmen sitting at attention…bolt upright in their cockpits concentrating on their instruments and staring straight ahead. And then I wonder:

Did they *see me?* And, if so, do they sometimes think these same thoughts?

Day lodge
Christmas Valley, Oregon

This was the second beautiful building built to entice property buyers with what was promoted to be a retirement paradise in the Oregon High Desert which can be rather chilly much of the year. As a masonry contractor, I built the stone chimney and the fireplace within.

A Douglas DC-3 airplane played a major role in pushing forward the developer's dreams of big riches in this project covering many square miles of "outback" desert sand. The plane was used to fly prospective buyers here from big cities.

This project was the site of one of my spooky airplane incidents...one which illustrated beyond any shadow of doubt the possible deadly consequences which might be expected when pilots overlook what they perceive to be minor details.

The Christmas Valley Caper

Picture this: You are middle-aged. You live in Los Angeles. You live in a typical California ranch-style house. You've worked hard all your adult life at the same repetitive job. You have a modest savings account plus a modest retirement program. You can remember how beautiful the Los Angeles area *used to be* when glorious *orange groves* were where now there are monotonous, boring subdivisions *wall to wall*. The traffic has become so bad that the freeways seem to be one big parking lot inhibiting your path to and from your work and driving you crazy.

Then one bright day you pick up the Sunday paper and *there is your salvation!* A company with a proven history of success in retirement community development advertises what sounds like an inexpensive retirement Utopia. What has this to do with aviation and flying? Plenty! What follows is a story of aggressive promotion and distortions of reality, with airplanes helping provide the key to riches for the developers.

The time? The early 1960s. The setting? The beginning of one of the longest economic booms the U.S. has ever known. The players? The person described above and a company that had recently put together the right combination of location and timing and made a lot of money developing a retirement community. Of course, as is the American way, they wanted to do it again and again…and make even more money. *A lot more.* And, *make it easier this time.*

Whether by accident, or by specific design, the company discovered *Christmas Valley, Oregon.*

Now, you must agree, that name has a happy and pleasant ring to it. The fact that the area consisted of a lot of hot sand and sagebrush in the summer and shivering cold sand and snow-covered sagebrush in the winter somehow just didn't come through very clearly when the promoters' voices crooned that wonderful word, "*Christmas!*"

What must the decibel level have been of the horse-laughs of those creative people who named the area in the first place? Nonetheless, the development company made an amazing discovery when they visited *Christmas Valley.* They found that land could be bought for prices starting at four dollars per acre.

At any rate, these city characters sneaked into the valley with a very small bag of cash and in short order ended up the proud owners of *twenty-six-thousand acres* of it. Unfortunately, the acreage they bought was not in one big solid unit but rather in oddball-sized chunks that zigged and zagged and checker-boarded and only occasionally joined one another. It was a lot of land but a chopped-up maze. Many buyers of lots never did pinpoint the actual location of their prizes even though they searched for days with the developers' map in hand. But, boy, did the developers make it look great on a giant artistic wall map! And, the first thing the developers did was *brilliant.* They built a mile-long gravel *airstrip* in the middle of the vastness.

Then they platted the property out in lots on a large (no, *gargantuan*) sheet of paper and drew in roads to the lots on the big wall display.

Next, they built a beautiful rustic lodge with a restaurant and large meeting room adjacent to the airstrip. They devised some fantastic large easel-mounted "artist's-conceptions" along with colorful brochures and sharp-looking architectural models all illustrating how this fabulous undertaking was *going to look* "finished" and set them up as a grand display in the shiny new lodge.

Finally, they rounded up quick-talking salesmen-types and fitted them out with classy upscale gabardine western dress outfits, elaborate Texas-style cowboy boots and the biggest cowboy hats they could find (Stetson's best, of course). These were smooth-talking dudes!

Lastly, they bought a war veteran twin engine C-47 (known as the venerable DC-3 in civilian transport service) and spent a ton of money fixing it up to make it look new and spiffy. They then advertised free champagne flights to the newest retirement destination: the legendary central Oregon plateau where famed explorers John Charles Fremont and Kit Carson fought their ways through during the pioneer western expansion. The new trusting-soul residents had to fight not only isolation boredom, hot blowing sand or chilling cold, but also a 75-mile drive to the nearest supermarket!

SOLD TO MARC E PAULSEN JR

SHELL AVIATION CREDIT CARD INVOICE

CITY & STATE Portland Oregon

AIRCRAFT LICENSE NO. 7094H

CARD NO. 387 151 251 2

439427

THIS COPY CANNOT BE USED FOR TAX REFUND PURPOSES.

GIBSON AIR SRV
BEND ORE 1260 DATE 10 1 62

The charges shown are hereby transferred to SHELL OIL COMPANY

SHELL PRODUCTS	QUAN.	PRICE INC. TAX	TAXES STATE	TAXES FED.	AMOUNT	
Shell ____ Aviation Fuel	76	40	7	4	3	84
AeroShell Oil Grade ____						
SALES OR LOCAL TAXES						
	TOTAL			$	3	84

The amounts shown include all taxes which the vendor or any prior vendor must pay or is obligated to collect.

CUSTOMER'S COPY

RECEIVED BY X

With the economy growing briskly (that period of the 1960s was nicknamed the "soaring sixties" by economists) and people like the afore-mentioned wishing they somehow could escape the god-awful congestion of a city gone mad, it didn't take much effort to fill the flashy refurbished flying-machine with folks dreaming of living in a promised utopia in dusty desert double-wides.

Back and forth zipped the DC-3, a.k.a. "Gooney Bird" (so nicknamed by WWII military fliers) with its cargo of heaven-on-earth hopefuls.

I happened upon this scene just after the project had gained enough momentum to warrant a salesman descending on me (when all I'd done was drop in to try their restaurant while traveling through).

One super-smooth pseudo-cowboy-cum-sales-agent tried to convince me to buy one of their more exclusive "commercial" lots for only about ten thousand dollars. We're talking about a lot of hot sand here…one could look to the horizon in any direction and see nothing but heat waves. The only "development" that existed at that time was the handsome lodge/restaurant with layouts on paper indicating where property (according to rosy projections) was going to be "developed" to the size of a "city." I chuckled and kept my hands glued in my pockets.

Fast forward a couple of years:

Shortly after acquiring my Piper J-3 Cub, I flew through this same

Christmas Valley and landed at the airport for lunch at the restaurant. No "lot" salesman tried to separate me from my hard-earned greenbacks, so I chalked it up to an interesting stop and went on my way.

A little later a contractor friend of mine called me and said he had a subcontract job for me at Christmas Valley. Knowing the area and the questionable "development" well, I was standoffish about it, but he convinced me that although the project looked a bit "shaky," he had done work there and been well paid for it…*promptly*. And, he said he knew the project manager well, which made me feel a bit more comfortable about the idea of working there.

Accepting the job, I became better acquainted with the project and also a few of the people working in the lodge restaurant. Others met were some people building a new artificial lake nearby. However, I still thought the project was *highly questionable.*

A couple of months after finishing my job there, I decided to fly in for lunch. Arriving about ten o'clock on a sunny morning, I landed on the gravel strip and taxied to the gas pumps.

Aha, a momentary flash of pure inspiration struck me!. Why park at the airstrip when I could taxi onto the road and then a couple more blocks right up to the restaurant and surprise the locals. Except for the random days when the DC-3 landed, there was seldom any air traffic. In perspective, the nearest highway was twenty-five miles away and the road to it was all gravel. So, to the restaurant I taxied, wheeled the plane right into the parking lot in front of the entrance, locked one brake (most planes have individual brakes) and pivoted around, ending up between two pickups and pointed directly at the front door.

The prop hadn't stopped turning before a dozen dazzled people rushed out to see this noisy interloper. Swinging out of the cockpit, I hit the ground lightly and strolled toward the entrance. After enjoying a western rib steak capped off with dessert, I headed back out to my shiny airplane feeling seven feet tall!

The airplane had no electrical system, so it was necessary to start the engine by standing alongside the plane just behind the propeller, reaching forward and grasping it...then giving it a gentle twist downward (called "propping"). It usually started on the first pull because its dual "magneto" piston-firing system was in excellent condition.

Reaching into the ship, I switched the ignition on, leaned forward and prop-started the engine to life...then swung back up into the saddle of my aerial mount and settled down to exit the parking lot.

Whipping the airplane around, I accelerated it out onto the road in front of the restaurant and into a full-powered bush-pilot left turn toward the end of the airstrip. With the throttle full forward, the plane blasted up the road for two hundred feet plus, went airborne, gained seventy-five feet of altitude, banked hard to the right and proceeded a short distance to line up with the end of the runway. I then yanked the throttle back and, as the plane began to descend like a rock, moved the control stick sharply to the left to head directly at the runway for a straight-in approach, pushed on the right rudder with my foot to straighten out from the sharp turn... annnnnd?....*the plane didn't straighten out!* In fact, the stick and rudder didn't seem to move much at all. Horrors! The controls were frozen with the plane still in the sharp left turn!

The plane continued down steeply toward the runway end in a very scary nose-down attitude with the rudder seemingly locked in "hard left" position. Having relatively minimal flying experience in general, and in a state of severe panic, I yanked the stick back toward its center-neutral position, but it moved very little. The earthward descent continued in a sickening out-of-control left-hand bank.

The earth came up to meet me at the left side of the gravel runway's end with an inhospitable whang...crunch...bump...swoosh...and a giant cloud of dust!

As I felt around to see if I was still alive, I realized I was jammed against the front seat, the airplane having finally stopped…standing unceremoniously on its nose where the beautiful brand new shiny metal propeller had been a split second before, and, with the tail pointed almost straight up twenty feet in the air. If that wasn't enough, the plane ended up directly in front of the only hangar on the field and in full view of the main road along side it.

I scanned the inside of the ship searching to find the cause of this catastrophe. In the flick of an eyelash, I spotted the reason I was jammed against the front seat: I had no seatbelt on!

Where was it? In extreme haste to get airborne before the viewers went back inside the restaurant, I'd popped into the air without benefit of the seatbelt, a simple but critical oversight. This particular seatbelt was military surplus which I'd elected to use because, not only did it hold well, it looked ultra-professional, having a width of about three inches and many gizmos and buckles. These same gizmos and buckles did me in! The belt had flopped over and down onto the left rudder pedal and become entangled with the control wires leading back to the tail control surfaces. When I tried to apply right rudder to straighten out the ship, the belt firmly held the pedals from moving.

I wasn't out of the plane ten seconds before the first witnesses came rushing up to view this amazing event. Although it was quickly over, there still lingered the cloud of dust and the ship remained standing on its nose with its tail high in the air.

If that wasn't humiliating enough (especially after making the takeoff such a dramatic effort), within minutes at least twenty more people from all points converged on this scene of destruction! Darn!!! I was mortified! Uhhh…wait. What's way beyond simple mortification? Well…whatever it is, that's how I felt. Dang! My ego was cut down to the size of a bean!

Appearing as if by magic, where in the heck had these people come from? In later crashes (yup, there were more), I noted that almost all nearby people rush to such a scene, inadvertently shaming into quaking masses of jelly hapless birdmen like me who perform really stupid maneuvers.

After it was ascertained by all present that I was not grotesquely mangled (some appeared to be disappointed by that), they began to ask embarrassing questions.

"What happened?" one titillated bystander asked.

"Did your engine quit?" queried another.

"Did something in the airplane break?" asked a third.

The only good news was that apparently there were no pilots present among the crowd of gore and excitement seekers. The best I could do was fib and mumble meekly, "I think a control wire must have broken inside the fuselage."

That statement turned out to be a perfect response, as nobody could see inside the fuselage, and it seemed to make perfect sense to those unacquainted with the intricacies of flight. At least, it slowed the pointed questions and made me feel a bit better. But, *not much!*

Checking damage, the propeller was bent in a major way and the carburetor broken off. Other than those items and a few paint scratches on the bottom of the engine cowling, it looked as though I could get the parts and, most probably, simply repair the damage myself. There wasn't much that could be done for my wounded pride. Regardless of how neatly I had explained away my crash, the fact was that I had crashed right in front of God and everybody in Christmas Valley.

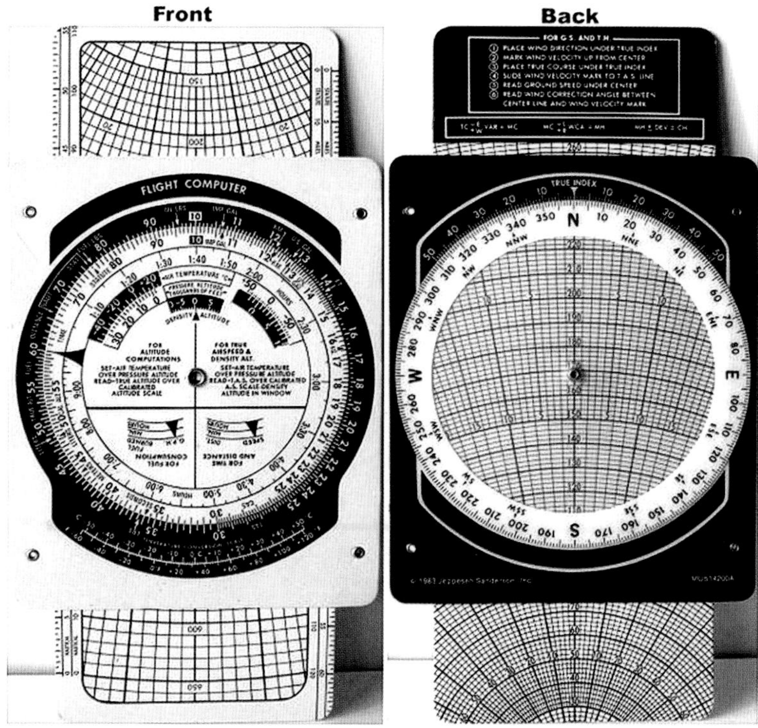

"E6B" pilot's flight computer from the 1960s

As a student pilot, I had to learn to operate this infernal mechanism. It was one of the numerous requirements to gain a pilot's license and not easy to master. Because my earliest flying experiences were in my own airplane (a ship which flew so slowly that most of the data learned from operating this gizmo did not apply), learning how to use it was mostly an irritant (my opinion). Later, when I flew more advanced planes, improved radio navigation gear made the use of it largely unnecessary so it is now mostly an interesting antique.

A local resident gave me a ride the twenty or so miles to the nearest place a bus for home could be boarded. The bus driver viewed my six foot long damaged propeller in wonder as he made room for it in the baggage stowage-compartment in the lower part of his machine.

I returned a few days later in my pickup truck with a friend who then drove the pickup home. I made sure that we arrived at the airstrip on the least busy day of the week so we wouldn't have to answer any more embarrassing questions from curious by-standers.

After replacing the repaired parts on the plane, I flew directly home. It would be a long time before I could show up here again without running into more knowledgeable interrogators who might expose my ineptitude for all to know.

Note: Christmas Valley today is a thriving little community. It was discovered over the years that water could be pumped from wells in quantities large enough to support giant hay-growing operations. Although it has a population of contented citizens, it is far less than the utopian metropolis-of-the-future pictured by developers of years past.

1967 Cessna 150 - 23,949 built

I bought this one from a bank in 1970 (a bank repossession) for only $1,750. For airplane cost comparisons, good average employee pay that year was around $12,000. This plane had a "run-out" engine (needing overhaul) but two very good radios and was otherwise in excellent condition...and...it was only three years old! This model of airplane is still used for student pilot instruction...and it has gone up in value considerably. Picture this! The same plane now 44 years old and well maintained is worth a lot more money and will look exactly as it did those many years ago.

Aerobatics
And The Wayward Radio

Unbelievable! One hour of searching from the air and not a sign of them. It was hunting season in Eastern Oregon's high desert and I couldn't find my friends who had given me a detailed description of precisely where they would be. They had told me what vehicle they'd be driving, its color, how many would be in the hunting party and what they were hunting for: *Antelope!*

Not finding my friends was baffling! Supposedly, almost any place or anyone can be found using an airplane…especially out in open flat country. But *not this time!*

Earlier in the week, the group and I decided I would fly my Piper J-3/85hp (freshly reconditioned after a fairly outlandish mishap) to meet them on the desert and fly them around, one by one, so they could each get the lay of the land. If we happened to see some antelope in the process, so much the better.

Although it may have been illegal at that time to harass wild animals, it was okay to spot them, depending on a few variables such as how far you were from them and whether spotting was or was not your basic intent. There was a time when chasing animals with an airplane was not only legal, it was considered good sport by aristocrats when only they could afford airplanes. (Some of the greatest flying stories ever involve the first woman bush pilot in Africa chasing down big game for safaris.) At any rate, using the plane sounded like a good sporting time for all of us, and we looked forward to it with great anticipation.

I arrived just east of Burns, Oregon, population about 3,000, around two o'clock in the afternoon and spent an hour-plus looking for my friends over a massive area about six or seven miles by ten miles square…something like *40,000 acres!*

A few cars and a number of pickups were visible, but not their white Chevy four-wheel drive pickup truck. This was going to be difficult! The sagebrush was averaging about six to ten feet high with open spots here and there (great cover and habitat for antelope) and, from a long distance at low altitude, a pickup easily could be hidden from view. At high altitude, one could see *down* into the brush quite well but not make out individual makes or models of vehicles. After climbing high enough, I did see a few white and light-colored vehicles, but, when dropping low, none of them belonged to my friends. It took a tremendous amount of time and fuel climbing back to altitude because ground level was 5,000 feet above sea level and airplane performance diminishes as the air becomes much thinner at higher levels.

Tiring of searching, an inspiration overcame me. It might be fun to practice some aerobatics!

Having the latest gear is important to me and I'd just purchased one of the very first small portable VHF (Very High Frequency) radios ("receiver" only) measuring 5x7x2 inches. From reading an ad in a flying magazine, I had been lured into buying it at an exorbitantly high price. When it finally arrived after a looong wait, I was chagrined at how small and "rinky-dink" it was for the whopping price, for me about 2 days' pay! In the ad it was pictured importantly and craftily re-proportioned to appear about six times bigger than it actually was.

When I observed its shabby quality, I couldn't believe the sellers had the gall to ask the price they did. But, it did work, after a fashion, and it would tune in other VHF aircraft radio talk (if all conditions were just right). At any rate, the radio was my constant companion and now it was occupying a place of honor sitting neatly on top of a plastic gas can which was carefully strapped down on the "tandem" seat in front of me. The can was fastened. *The radio was not!*

A Piper J-3 Cub is flown from the rear seat when solo (pilot only) because, when only one person is in the plane, flying from the rear seat balances the plane properly. The radio was thus in a convenient location for the odd occasion when I might pick it up, plug my earphones into it and listen for that glorious sound of other fellow birdmen conversing with one another. This was usually done in vain out in sparsely populated areas due to the radio's relatively short range.

At this time, I was attracted to anything and everything to do with flying. Among flight paraphernalia, I had some frivolous items, some not. I was wearing a bright red jumpsuit (O.K…on the side of questionable) but these were my Eddie Rickenbacker (or maybe) Red Baron days!

Here I was at 3000 feet above ground with both doors open, 90 degrees outside and, if the doors were closed, about the same temperature inside. A Piper Cub's two horizontal half-high doors are long enough to span both tandem seats (on the right side only). The doors together make up an area about three feet high and are split in the middle so that the bottom door folds out and down and the top door swings out and up. This opens up much of the side of the airplane to the outside world and presents a fabulous view.

I had worked up a fairly flashy aerobatic program that usually consisted of going from level flight into a series of ever-steepening wingovers, smoothing out to level flight and up into a cruising-speed loop…then doing about five more loops in a row, followed with flight straight up to a vertical stall which developed into what is called a "hammerhead." After dropping out of the hammerhead, I'd usually pull up from the bottom straight up to another complete dead-stop stall, drop out of that into a spin, then recover from the spin, pull up and jerk into a snap roll.

Occasionally, when feeling a little extra "nervy," I would attempt a "slow-roll"...during which gasoline would dribble from the fuel tank in front all over the windshield. At this time, my slow rolls were imperfect to the point of sometimes falling out of them into a downward spiral. The theory of aerobatic flight is that, if one has enough altitude, no matter how badly a maneuver is done, the airplane simply will end up headed down...from which an easy recovery is possible. I skipped the slow rolls this day.

My wingover/vertical reversements turned out well and, by the time I got tired of doing them, I was almost going beyond vertical on the high side in the turns. By that time, every hunter on the ground within twenty miles (and my friends) could spot me, so they would know that I was searching for them.

It was loop time, which I had down pat. In practice I'd done forty or fifty cruising-speed loops consecutively, and hit my slipstream at the bottom of each one. Almost any pilot with a Cub can do that so I moved into a series of loops. Hey, what the heck, now I'll just go into an absolutely mind-boggling, straight-up "hammerhead" stall and hold the plane until hanging motionless...then let it drop into a "tailslide" falling straight back down. (Not too far, however, because old-timers had told me rushing air could bend my rudder if the plane dropped back down too fast.) Then I'll go into a perfect drop off to the left away from the open door and into a screaming straight down dive. That was the plan!

Sooooo...out of the last loop I dropped down into level flight, smoothly pulled back on the stick and up, up, up, up, straight up...upppp...upppp... slower...slower...slower...and STOPPED DEAD while pointed straight up!

At this precise point, the ship began its fall straight down backwards and I imagined that, if I had a smoke system like those impressive airshow pilots all use, the hunters and my friends below would then see me falling backwards straight down through a pall of white smoke...disappearing in it momentarily. The plane continued down and then, at the correct moment, I gave it a little power, kicked in left rudder, dropped off to the left and felt the thrill of the plane in a free fall as it pivoted on its center axis toward a vertical descent.

At the same moment, I realized that the precious brand-new, one-week-old expensive VHF radio in the front seat...had *risen up in a state of rocketship weightlessness* right at the start of the plane's free fall to the left. The radio acted as if it had come to life and could control its own movements. As the dropping plane fell to the left, the radio, in the slowest of motion, began to move ever so gently up and toward the open door…just like a levitated astronaut floats freely in an earth-orbiting vehicle.

Now, basic physics forces were at work here! The radio lay on the gas can loosely and would stay there as long as all of the maneuvers I was doing were what we call in pilot's lingo, "coordinated"…that is to say, as long as the aerobatic movements of the plane through the air were ones that maintained a force of gravity of 1G or more downward. Only the super-pro aerobatic pilots do a lot of "negative-gravity" maneuvers. I admit, I typically did mostly coordinated maneuvers mainly because the other kind are scarier than hell and a plane like a Cub might simply come apart from overstress.

By the time I grasped what was happening to my prized VHF radio, the airplane was already in a preordained and unchangeable plunge down side-ways toward the center of the earth and the radio was heading inexorably up and toward the open door. When it passed through the door, I stretched

72 683 1029 4

ORIGINAL INVOICE

SOLD TO: MARC E PAULSEN JR / 617 SE 102ND / PORTLAND OREGON 9 63

TERMS: PAYABLE WITHOUT DISCOUNT UPON RECEIPT OF MONTHLY STATEMENT OF PURCHASES.

SOLD BY: AERO AIR INC / HILLSBORO ORE / 72 183 02202

PURCHASER'S SIGNATURE X Marc Paulsen

DATE 10 13 62

THANK YOU

MERCHANDISE OR SERVICE	QUAN.	STATE TAX	FED. TAX	TOTAL PRICE	AMOUNT	
TEXACO AVIATION GASOLINE - GRADE 100	8.0	.01		44	3	52
TEXACO AIRCRAFT ENGINE OIL - GRADE						
AV 847196		TOTAL CHARGE $			3	52

PRICES AND AMOUNT INCLUDES ALL APPLICABLE FEDERAL, STATE AND LOCAL TAXES AS SHOWN.

AIRCRAFT LICENSE NO. 7024H

TAX EXEMPTION CERTIFICATE NO.

CERTIFICATE OF INTENTION (TO BE SIGNED BY DEALERS IN STATES REQUIRED) THE UNDERSIGNED HEREBY CERTIFIES THAT THE PURCHASER OF THE MOTOR FUEL INVOICED HEREON AT THE TIME OF PURCHASE EXPRESSLY DECLARED IT AS HIS INTENTION TO USE SUCH MOTOR FUEL FOR A NON-TAXABLE PURPOSE AND TO FILE CLAIM FOR A REFUND OF THE TAX THEREON.

SIGNED: Tom DEALER

FORM S-199D (AVIATION) 12-59

forward with all my might and made a mad grab for it, realizing too late that my seat belt prohibited me from reaching very far…and then watched aghast as the radio continued its journey slowly out through the door and up the bottom of the wing as the plane continued its drop down and away.

It was a situation that seemed to play in astonishingly slow motion, with my attention diverted totally to the radio and its progress up the wing as it slowly rotated...appearing weightless. In desperation, I did what a pilot would never do in a hammerhead stall aerobatic maneuver. While still falling on the plane's left side, I hammered the right rudder pedal all the way to the floor hoping that somehow I could miraculously hold the plane in a sideways fall that would allow the radio to fall back down the wing and right back into the airplane. Hopeless, for sure!

But, guess what? After the radio got up the wing about halfway, in the briefest of moments the plane and the radio fell at the same speed and the radio stayed right where it was. Then I was jolted back to reality as basic aerodynamics took over and the plane went totally out of control, shifted into a spin and spun down and away...and out of sight went my radio!

Immediately, I pushed the stick forward increasing my airspeed and then pressed the right rudder, stopping rotation of the spin...then pulled back on the stick and recovered to level flight. Desperately, I looked into the air around, up, down and all about...trying to spot the errant falling radio. I wasn't sure exactly what I'd do if I saw it, but felt compelled to try to spot it. Sure enough, there was the radio about two or three hundred feet below me, slowly rotating as it gained earthward speed with a vengeance. Instantly putting the little Cub into a very tight downward spiral, I tried to…maybe catch it?...Huh? What the heck, you ask, was I going to do if I did catch up with it? Nope…I didn't catch up with the radio!

However, I'll tell you that on the way down, while in a temporarily warped state of mind over the impending doom of my prized radio, I was thinking crazily that I might get ahead and somehow turn the airplane on its side and then...the radio could fall back into the cockpit. Now, that is how *wild* my thought processes were working because of this potential loss. "Potential" in this tiny moment of time…because the radio hadn't yet hit Mother Earth. My thinking was, of course, a "pipe-dream," perhaps temporary insanity! There was no way anything but radio "doom" was going to transpire.

Surprisingly, I *was* able to follow the radio with my eyes all the way down while making extremely tight, high "G-force" turns to keep it in sight. I wasn't thinking about the G-forces…only the approaching loss.

Realities in life are driven home to we humanoids in a myriad of quaint variations. Some have seen a connecting rod crash through the block of an engine. That's final! Some have had their favorite coffee cup crash to the ground into pieces after forgetfully leaving it on the top of the car and speeding away. That's a final! Others have watched in horror as a poorly-fastened outboard motor jumped off their boat and disappeared in a whirlpool of vanishing dollars…another final event! There is a multitude of ways in which people have been separated from valuable goods through their own stupidity and the fickle forces of fate. And, by golly, this was a brand new one! And let me tell you, this one was final! Now I know where the TV and movie folks got the idea for all those boring slow-motion scenes they think are great for emphasizing drama. This scene developed into that very type of thing as the radio dropped a couple of thousand feet. All the time, it was rotating as I circled it...and finally calculated there was no way I was going to do anything but watch my radio, paid for with hard-earned dollars... crash and smash! For quite a while the radio was still alive and well in midair...until it reached the ground! Then, a new awareness struck that the engine was still running and the plane flying slowly in suspended flight to nowhere...while I had been engrossed in the contemplation of my impending loss.

I circled for a while, working my way lower to make a pass directly over the radio's crash site just above ground level. Of course, the possibility of there being much left was nil but, amazingly, it landed in a very small flat clearing in very high sagebrush...and that, my friends, led to another crazy adventure which produced the next story.

"Radial" engines often produce big smoke at start-up.

A beautifully restored Boeing "Stearman."

Grumman F8F Bearcat - 1,265 built

Flying my little Cub cross-country, I stopped at a high desert airport to fuel up. Upon taxiing up to the fuel truck, an amazing sight appeared. A magnificent Bearcat like this (with one of the biggest radial engines ever put in a fighter plane) was nearby, fastened by the tail to a giant steel ring on the apron with the biggest hunk of rope I'd ever seen, maybe three inches in diameter. This was still a time when these monstrous surplus WWII machines were available for purchase by ordinary citizens at prices which many could afford. The main ownership difficulty a purchaser might have, would be paying for the prodigious quantities of fuel required to make such an airplane run. In this case, the proud and very nervous owner was in the pilot's seat at the controls. As I jumped out of my ship, the Bearcat came to life with a thundering roar that could be heard for miles around. As the plane tugged at the big rope, stretching it out straight as a string, the pilot slowly increased the throttle until apparently, he ran out of nerve. I wondered at the time what kind of damage that monumental propeller would do if the big rope parted and someone was in the way. Needless to say, everybody in sight gave this big baby plenty of room...and all were ready to run like the wind if that giant rope failed.

The World's Shortest Airstrip?

Looking down from a couple hundred feet of altitude on the remains of my recently-purchased expensive VHF (very high frequency) portable radio ("receiver" only) which had just popped out of my plane while I was performing aerobatics, I could see the radio laying far below on the high-desert floor, and felt an intense pang of stupidity over my self-induced loss. Highly disturbed, I decided to check out the possibilities of landing to see if, supernaturally, my wonderful piece of equipment might still have some "radio-life" and salvage value. The radio miraculously could have landed on a soft, tall sagebush and spiraled down gently enough to still operate...*or something*.

I could see the radio, which was cream color and in plain sight. It had landed at the edge of a small round clearing set in the middle of about a square mile of intensely thick ten-foot-high brush. Comparing the size of the radio against the overall size of the clearing, I could see that the open area was too small in which to land an airplane. Or, so it seemed at first.

Numerous tire-track dirt roads crisscrossed this desert. The closest visible set of tracks that I could see was quite a distance from the clearing, on the edge of which the radio rested. If I could land on those tracks, then there would be a few-hundred-yard fight through *some of the most unyielding brush ever*...to retrieve my radio!

A high landing speed would result due to the ground level of 5,000 feet above sea level which has very thin air. Additionally, the temperature was around 90 degrees. The plane eased onto the ground very neatly but the fast rollout felt like running over a field of rocks!

After getting out of the plane and struggling through the thick brush toward the clearing, I quickly became lost. Reassessing this whole situation, the smart thing to do, it seemed, was to get back in the air in the plane and look over the entire area. It took a fair amount of time stumbling through more brush to find my way to the road...and finally back to the plane.

Hopping back into the ship, I took off and was able to see the clearing almost immediately. I'd missed the radio by only a hundred feet or so when on the ground. And to think I'd spent a couple of wasted hours stumbling around in a de facto jungle looking for it! Then a brilliant thought. Why not see if I could land in the tiny clearing? That would mean no more walking, no more getting lost while fighting scratchy underbrush...and no wasting of more time. Repeat, this was a small clearing for such a high altitude, thin-air, hot-day takeoff. And, not just small…more like minuscule! And…with ground level at five thousand feet above good old sea level, how would I gauge my performance to make sure I could fly back out? Of course, I knew I could fly in…anyone could do that…even a fool like me.

The situation required a meticulous calculation:

Circling the pocket-sized clearing, I looked carefully down and then over to the nearby road on which I had landed the first time...to mindfully compare distances. Choosing landmarks of a tree and a bush alongside the track which were about the same distance apart as the clearing was wide, I landed again on the road. I then made as short a takeoff as possible...and upon breaking ground within the two landmarks, determined it should be feasible to land and takeoff in the clearing (if everything went exactly right)!

Well, it was time to get set to make the landing. I circled three or four times building up intestinal fortitude and made some low, slow passes surveying the site. Taking some exceedingly deep breaths, I wondered if I really should go ahead with this questionable idea…and finally thought, "What the heck!"...and set up an approach for landing.

Landing an airplane perfectly takes a lot of practice. Generally speaking, if one throttles the engine down, gets close enough to the ground and keeps the tail down and the ship straight, the airplane glides down and lands safely. Landing wasn't a problem here. (*Taking off* is what would be treacherous!)

At elevations this high above the sea, the air is so thin that most airplanes would rather land than fly...the airplane moves through the thin air much faster as it touches down.

The plane dropped into the clearing like a rock, met the ground and braked to a halt. Here I was...locked into what had to be the world's shortest airstrip and surrounded by brush up to ten feet high!

Now I could recover my fallen VHF radio. Fascinating how the human mind works…or maybe doesn't! I'd gone to this major effort, actually risking damaging or crashing the plane and, who knows, maybe even losing my life, just to recover this item that had experienced what must have been a *forty-G stop*. Now, I was pacing around the clearing perimeter searching for the radio's remains, with the forlorn hope that there actually might be some value left.

Find it I did! I'd heard that an item like this radio reaches terminal velocity of around one-hundred-eighty miles per hour in a straight-down fall in thin air. Maybe more! Interestingly, the radio's case was fractured into only about thirty pieces. A look inside this expensive purchase revealed that the quality of construction shockingly resembled an item I'd once got in the mail *free* after sending so many box tops. (I had risked my plane for this?) It was grossly-overpriced junk! It was so poorly made, it was surprising that it had worked *at all.* Next, back to face reality!

Zounds! What was I doing here...landing in a space this small? Boy, this "airfield" really *was* teeny!

Had my calculations been correct? Could I take off? Could I get the plane back into the air? *Did I have a choice?*

From inside the almost perfectly-circular clearing, the surrounding sage and brush rendered ***nothing*** else visible. Tiny plants for about one hundred feet ahead tapered up to a full height of about ten feet. The loam-sand surface was hard. That was good. But the distance for a takeoff roll looked frightfully short. That was bad. I'd planned for the take-off thoroughly. That was good. But my knees were shaking. That was bad.

Ripping out as much low sage behind the plane as possible with bare hands, I made a very short track out into the brush. Carefully picking up the tail of the plane, I physically dragged it through what little was cleared, released my grasp and the plane stayed level...with the dense brush holding the tail up.

Reaching forward, I propped the engine from behind, started it and climbed up and into the plane. Taking one exceedingly deep breath while simultaneously praying, sweating, panting and shaking nervously, I pushed the throttle all the way forward and held the brakes to the floor.

Releasing the brakes abruptly, the little ship moved forward *very slowly* at first. Then, as the tail cleared the brush, the plane began picking up speed and bouncing as it rolled over lumps of earth. Yes, the plane moved faster...but slow motion must have been invented for high altitude takeoffs!

The center of the clearing passed by.

Now, it was ***time to fly!*** There was nowhere to go but through the brush...or up. ***Please, Lord!***

I eased the stick back slightly. Too much would increase the drag and slow the airplane down, dooming me to fate in the brush.

Then, with that old *Piper Cub magic*, the high-performance wing created just enough lift as the airspeed increased. ***Airspeed was the answer!*** Fortunately, the Cub had it!

At that point, the plane levitated just enough and the wheels skipped over the tops of the brush…touching every plant on the way out even as we reached the ten foot high stuff...with me sweating out the possibility of the wheels catching in a high bush and flipping the plane forward onto its back. Finally, the wheels stopped bouncing along the brush and the plane climbed above and into the clear air.

Whew! Made it. *Just barely!*

Was the risk worth it?

Well, upon looking over the retrieved radio more closely, it would make a great keepsake by which to remember this chancy experience. I thought about having it bronzed like a pair of baby shoes. I kind of wish I had. In the next life I'm going to do things like that. I promised myself not to buy any more mail order items sight-unseen without first thoroughly checking product reviews!

And…what did I learn about short-field takeoffs from that foolish experiment? To not cut it so close in the future! That is what I told myself after I had calmed down, stopped shaking, and let the fact sink in that my airplane was not damaged and the results could very easily have been drastically different...*Amen!*

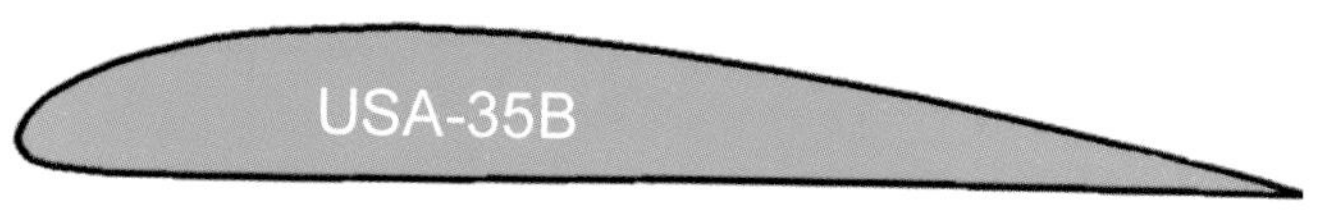

High-lift wing cross-section

About "high-lift" wings:

Old pilots tell that when William T. Piper got involved with the Piper Cub back in the nineteen-thirties (then it was the "Taylor" Cub), one of the things he liked most about the airplane was the USA-35B airfoil shape of the wing, often called the "Clark-Y" by many pilots (including me) because the two are almost identical and Clark-Y is easier to say. The "USA" is for "U.S. Army." The lifting power of this wing design is legendary. That "airfoil" design is what made possible the original thirty-seven horsepower Piper Cub's successful flight with two people. Charles Lindbergh's "Spirit of St. Louis" had a similar "Clark-Y" wing. Piper airplane models from the J-3 to its iconic twin-engine "Aztec" used this same high-lift wing "airfoil." Alaska bush pilots worship this wing design and its derivatives which make possible carrying great numbers of people and thousands and thousands of tons of freight, equipment and merchandise in the illustrious one-hundred-fifty horsepower "Super Cub" on both large "tundra" tires and as a seaplane on floats. If a Cub won't lift itself and its load out with a short takeoff run, then one better get a jet helicopter to do the job.

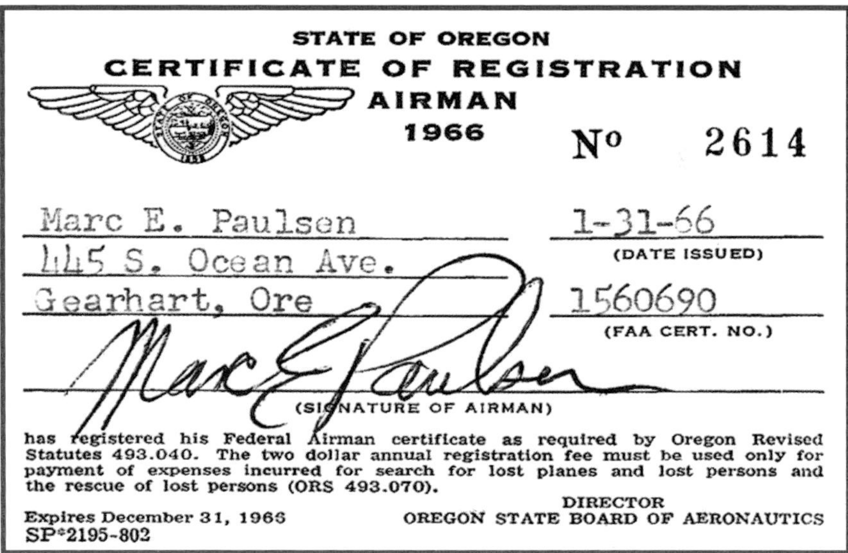

STATE OF OREGON
CERTIFICATE OF REGISTRATION
AIRMAN
1966
No 2614

Marc E. Paulsen — 1-31-66 (DATE ISSUED)
445 S. Ocean Ave.
Gearhart, Ore — 1560690 (FAA CERT. NO.)

Marc E Paulsen
(SIGNATURE OF AIRMAN)

has registered his Federal Airman certificate as required by Oregon Revised Statutes 493.040. The two dollar annual registration fee must be used only for payment of expenses incurred for search for lost planes and lost persons and the rescue of lost persons (ORS 493.070).

DIRECTOR
OREGON STATE BOARD OF AERONAUTICS

Expires December 31, 1966
SP*2195-802

Aerial Shenanigans

Our local Cessna dealer/distributor elected to put on a massive "fly-in" sales extravaganza. This took place about a year after my purchase of a Piper J-3 "Cub." During my first year of plane ownership, I flew it constantly, gaining a good feel for the ship and its flight characteristics, and installed a more powerful 85 horsepower engine which, when occupied by the pilot only, made it an outstanding performer. My plane was based at a tiny 900-foot-long private field on which another high-performer was also located. That plane was a late model Piper *150hp* "Super Cub."

Johnny Roberts, Hood River, Oregon, with his "custom" version of a Super Cub

During winter, when cloudy weather was "below minimums" for flying activity, the Super Cub owner and I sometimes contested whose plane could get off the ground quickest. We even went so far as applying an old bush pilot gambit we had heard about…placing a fence post across the runway to help our planes bounce into the air after a very short takeoff run. We both got fairly proficient at short-field takeoffs.

Upon hearing about the Cessna dealer's fly-in, we decided to try our skill in flight contests included in the program. The first test was a "short take-off and landing" contest. It was open to any type of aircraft and based on a "handicap" arrangement that took into account radically different airplane sizes and horsepowers. With a wind blowing at eighteen mph, my little ship with its big engine handily outperformed everything, including my friend's Super Cub. My landing to a full stop (with low power, control stick back and brakes locked) measured no more than eighteen paces or, *about fifty feet!* The next test was a "spot-landing" affair in which participants were instructed to climb to a thousand feet above the airport, shut off their power, execute a 360 degree circuit and land as close as possible to a preset point in the center of the runway. A new flyers' organization provided a large "perpetual" trophy which was to be awarded annually and engraved with the name of each year's winner. By another stroke of good fortune, I won that event as well. The new organization disbanded the next year and...***I still have that trophy!***

The "Perpetual" trophy
...that wasn't!

This is the "Perpetual" trophy I won at the Oregon Pilots' Association's Troutdale Chapter "Spot Landing" contest at Troutdale, Oregon, in 1963. The trophy was to be awarded annually to each year's winner from that year forward...and the winner was to be given possession of the trophy for that year. That "OPA" chapter disbanded the next year... leaving the "one-name" trophy *"Perpetually" with me!*

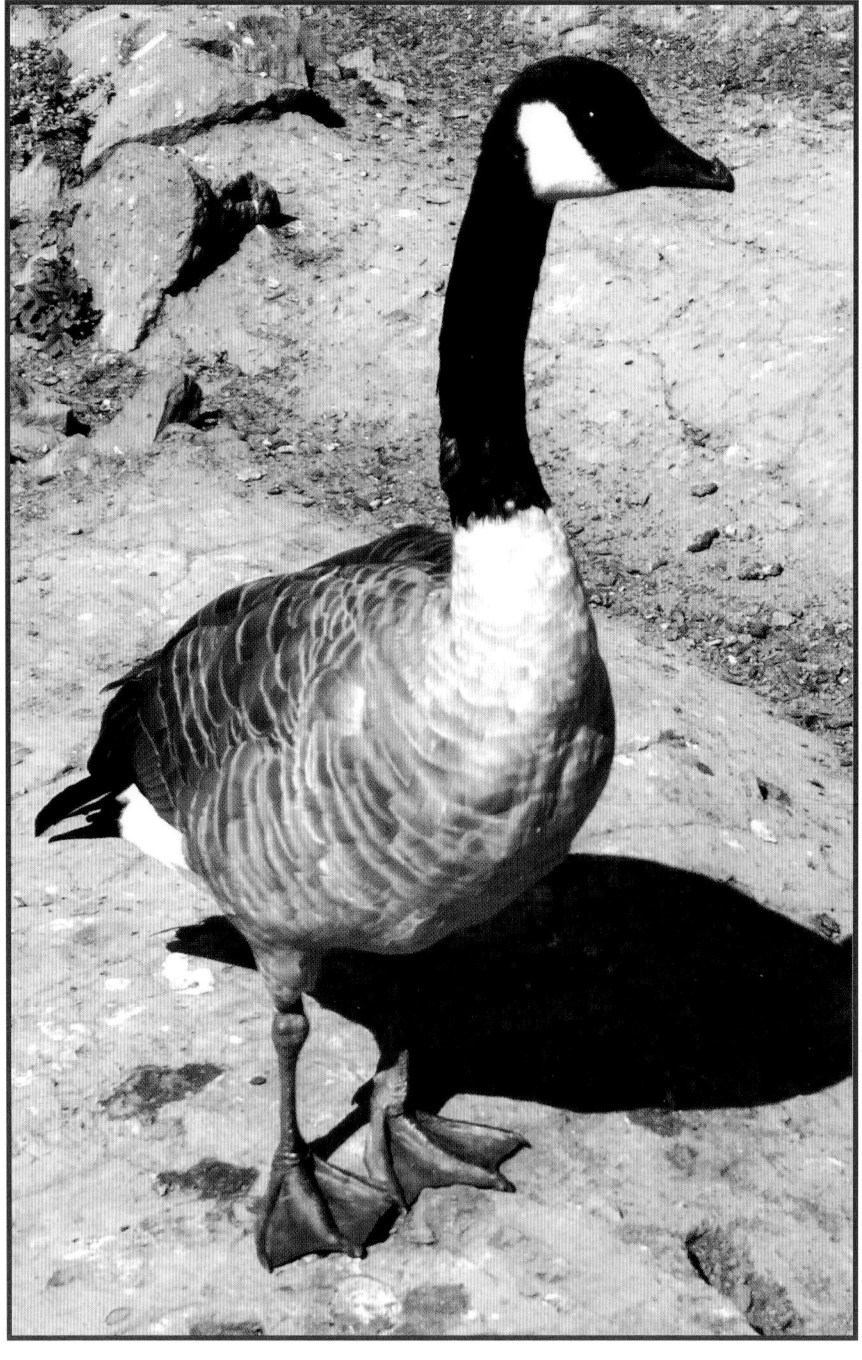

Honk If You're A Honker

Putting a wild goose on the family's dinner table at Christmas was always one of my heart's desires, especially since we are Danish and historic Danish tradition is serving goose at Christmas time. My Dad was a avid hunter and exposed me to the outdoor world from earliest childhood. Dad's hunting experiences taught me how difficult it can be to bring home the dinner in the form of a goose. He seldom came home with these wily creatures in his game bag, but not for lack of trying. Most geese in northern Oregon gather to feed on private grain fields on hills above the Columbia River, but...if you don't have the right connections with ranchers, you are hard-pressed to do much productive goose shooting. Thus, my Dad would have to try his luck at public shooting grounds…usually with mediocre results.

There was a time when Dad's work would be set aside in a flash for the opportunity to go shot-gunning for game birds. Of the different game birds available, the Canadian Goose, affectionately known as the "Honker," was one of the most difficult to shoot. However, one time in my life I managed to bag a Honker. It thrilled me! It may not sound like much but, in the world of waterfowl hunters, it's a small but notable milestone.

After the goose was shot, it didn't drop but faltered, set its wings and sailed over water-filled irrigation ditches and levees for a mile or so. It took me from late afternoon into darkness to traverse all that miserable terrain to find the bird…dead in thigh-high wheat stubble in a field a mile square. This on the second and last day of the hunt.

That was my only success with goose hunting. After the hunt, I drove 300 miles home to my bachelor apartment to find in my mail a "Greetings from your Uncle Sam" mandatory invitation to join the U.S. Army. (This was the 1950s when the U.S. military "draft" was the accepted method of staffing our Army.) You can bet the exact date of that goose hunt is well remembered.

The old-timers on that trip taught me a lot about the lore of geese and, from that day to this, my respect has been high for the majestic Canada Goose. Although not too successful hunting geese, my experiences with them did qualify me to know a fair amount about them.

Before the Columbia River was dammed completely from source to mouth, big Canada Geese accumulated by the millions along the upper river shores. In later years, after learning to fly and buying a small Piper "Cub" plane, I found it interesting to cruise along the spectacular Columbia Gorge observing smaller flocks…much diminished as a result of the multiple dam construction.

On one occasion, a few hours of time away from business found me flying my little J-3/85 Piper Cub above the river. Approaching historic Vista House, unusual objects appeared in the air directly in front of me about a half mile out and below my altitude a hundred feet or so. Typically, all one sees from a slow private plane are seagulls, crows and an occasional hawk or buzzard.

Drawing closer, it became apparent that these were very big geese. No question about it…they were *Canada Geese*. They appeared to be in one large vee-formation of sixty or seventy birds. Unbelievable! I had never imagined that a small plane would come this close to geese in flight. There is no way a non-hunter can comprehend the fires of subconscious desire such a confrontation produces within the breast of a hunter-gatherer.

I aimed for the flock!

In the heat of the moment, my goose-addled brain didn't immediately register that I wasn't hunting, didn't have a gun, and was locked in an airplane at two thousand feet. If that wasn't enough, approaching below was an inhabited area probably running over with sensitive bird-watcher types...and flying near birds would be harassing wildlife, something that in modern times can cost you money, your airplane and maybe some time in jail.

To the side went my left hand…to shove the little round red-tipped-knob throttle lever forward with gusto. I decided to be a bit whacko and try fly-

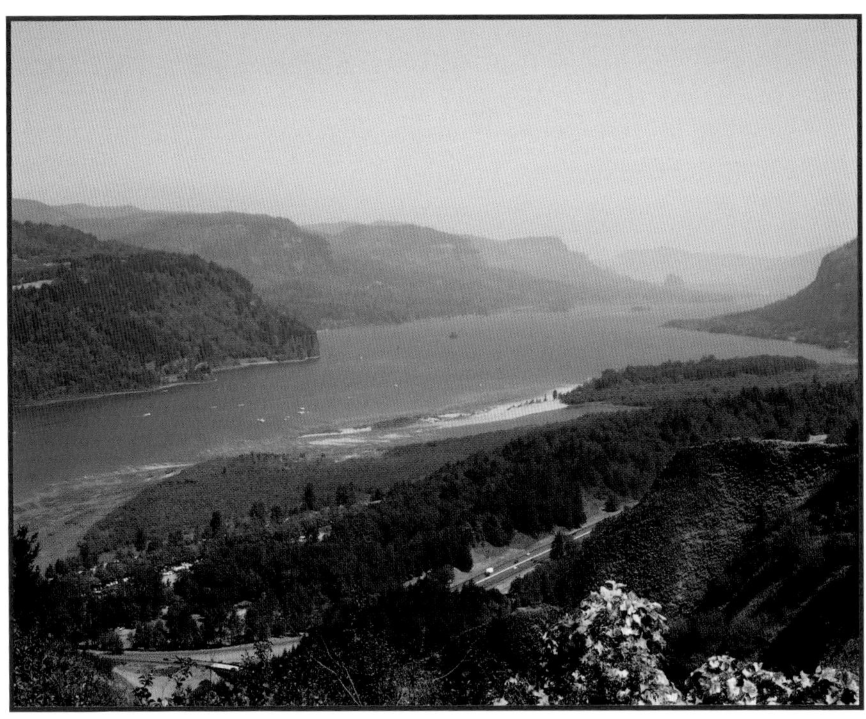

The fabulous Columbia River Gorge

ing formation with the geese. Amazing what people will do in moments of less-than-clearly-considered zeal. In a warped hot-pursuit way of thinking, these geese were fair game for major sport. Hey, we were sharing the same airspace and we all had wings so why couldn't we fly together for a while?

The plane closed in on the flock!

Have you ever thought about how birds in the sky actually operate? They always seem to be up there just flying along. But they really are feathered flying machines with a semblance of a brain and the accompanying ability to think, see, reason and react to assorted circumstances especially when it might directly affect their welfare. It was soon obvious that birds are quick-witted indeed when threatened.

The closer the plane got, the larger the geese appeared. It was surprising to realize that the plane was actually flying right up behind these big birds with relative ease. In sneaking up on ordinary birds such as crows or ravens, the tiniest hint of moving the airplane toward them would cause them to dive and disappear. These geese held their formation like a flight of Air Force cadets fearful of crashing if they moved out of position by one inch. Outstanding discipline! They held their positions…no matter what!

One thing became obvious immediately. Approaching close enough to see their distinct features, a couple of the geese were looking back over their shoulders (they have shoulders?) at this giant noisy foreign dragonfly…clearly with concern. We were rapidly coming eyeball to eyeball. Their concern seemed to be highly controlled and they appeared to be talking to each other and discussing the situation as if contemplating what actions they should take to escape this threat.

Flying close, I eased back on the throttle and transitioned to slow flight mode behind them.

They sped up...*to stay ahead.*

We evened out at the same airspeed, approximately forty miles an hour in level flight. The plane could go a bit slower but not much without falling out of the sky. Maybe the geese could have gone faster but probably not without having goose heart attacks. It seemed they had pushed their speed to the limit by their briskly flapping wings and were flying as fast as they could.

We stayed even.

The group, holding formation, must have taken an order from whichever was the bird squadron leader because, as soon as they decided they couldn't outrun the plane, they initiated an evasive maneuver to dive and turn away. Their move was in absolute unison and perfectly coordinated. These fellows were masters of the sky and they didn't waste a lot of fuel doing nutty things like airplane pilots do. They continued to hold formation as if they were all glued together and made every move count. Impressive! Could we somehow domesticate this group? In their spare time, we might get them to teach Blue Angel flight candidates precision flying.

The plane dived and turned with them.

They pulled up and executed a climbing turn.

The plane followed.

They abruptly dived.

Down went the plane!

They set their wings for a glide.

The plane stayed right on their tails.

The entire proceeding was bizarre! Imagine, flying formation with a flock of geese! A fascinating part was that the geese seemed almost human as, one by one, they turned their heads back and coolly looked me over. It was as if they were carefully gauging my airspeed and, with that information, considering their next evasive maneuver. No serious panic here...only group resolve to maintain an unwavering discipline. Here were magnificent birds worthy of much respect.

Now...if you are an Audubon-type person, please know that no birds were injured in this aerial flirtation, and all of them most likely lived happily ever after. And, hey, instead I could have been out in a hunting blind somewhere...sneakily waiting for these same birds to come down to be blasted with my shotgun!

You might think the story would end here. But *it didn't.*

As my interest in the activity began to wane, one goose appeared to be tiring. He broke formation, set his wings and began a long descending glide down and away from his flying buddies.

It just didn't seem right to let that "lone ranger" go without following him down, and it surprised me how easily the Cub maneuvered to stay right with him.

The goose moved right.

The plane moved right.

He pulled up.

The plane pulled up.

It was eerie.

This bird "goose-plane" was made of bones, flesh and feathers and yet it was flying just like a real airplane. It was as if the two of us were now flying wing man formation and he was going like a bullet! We were doing around sixty or more on the way down. He gave up trying to beat his wings to hold or increase altitude. He just continued gliding down. It looked like he was about out of wing-flapping energy...and a simple matter of time until he had to do something rash.

While mulling this over, a jolt of unpleasant awareness struck me that, not only had we descended to a low altitude, we now were rapidly approaching the center of the suburban village of Gresham after covering around ten miles or so. Engrossed in my aerial nature studies, I'd failed to pay adequate attention to my position. Now my situation became precarious. It was possible some real bird watchers might accidentally glance up at the sky and see us flying together. It might appear to some as if a giant motorized hawk was bearing down on a poor defenseless bird...a bird of which children's nursery rhymes are made.

Facing the possibility of someone reading my plane number and calling the bird police, I climbed to a higher altitude and departed the area.

While pondering the potential outcome in the event someone had got my number and reported me, worry now occupied my thoughts. Cruising along, I mulled over the potential consequences of my indiscretion.

What would be my plea? Temporary insanity?

Ah, well... it had been a kick and apparently no wildlife had been injured so what the heck!

My nervousness increased during the swift return to home base...and getting down and out of the plane pronto was my earnest desire (as if that might somehow reduce my exposure to discovery, punishment and shame).

The government required giant one-foot high registration numbers in plain sight on the sides of planes. Not pretty! Why didn't I think about the number exposure up there when it counted and either forget pursuing the geese or at least try to hold the plane in a configuration that would make the numbers difficult to see?

A couple of days went by and I was a recovered man.

Hadn't heard a thing from the FAA, the FBI, the CIA or the Audubon Society. Apparently, a clean getaway had been made. Amazing the feeling of relief that produces!

A few more days went by and this incident had been assigned to history, when one local morning newspaper featured an interesting story and a big photograph.

Unbelievable!

There…as big as life and snapped not far from where my plane had left the lone bird...was a photo of a homeowner standing in his front yard feeding a giant Canadian Honker goose. The homeowner told a story about the wild goose arriving in his yard a couple of days earlier...apparently all worn out from its flight south. The goose was friendly and seemed to want nothing more than to stay in his yard, rest and eat. The man had been feeding the bird, hoping to see it gain enough stamina to continue on its way south. He just couldn't understand why it wasn't in any hurry to leave.

If you are wondering? Noooo...I didn't call the man (or anybody else for that matter) to inquire or talk about it. No sir, I was content simply to read about it in the paper like thousands of other people and be just as engrossed as they were!

By The Dark Of The Moon

I always found it somewhat hard to believe the fantastically wild flying stories occasionally bandied about in hangars, flight lounges and assorted bull sessions when pilots got together. As a secretly-thrilled novice who aspired to become one of that crowd, I listened with rapt attention. One of the fanciful stories sounded pretty far-fetched. It was the one that always came up about flying into and out of unlighted airfields in a pitch-black night with only auto headlights for guidance. Still, it was fun hearing the same story repeatedly and trying to picture being faced with taking off or landing at night using only the primitive method described.

Perhaps most of those tall tales originated from expedient and daring actions early airmail pilots were forced to take to complete their assigned missions. Most survived. Many did not. Their well-known deeds of daring and peculiar brand of devil-may-care risk-taking became the stuff of legend. Imagine how the sweat might pour off in a dark night landing with only the most minimal assistance. Obviously, this should be attempted by only a very proficient aviator...most likely an old grizzled and highly-experienced bush-pilot type or at least an exceedingly-grizzled young one.

In my line of construction work, business usually slowed down each fall. That season in 1963 gave me a great opportunity to take my Piper J-3/85 Cub on a flight-log time-building trip with no particular destination in mind. I frequently went on random adventures for the sheer joy of them. Trips without planned destinations were always exciting because of the inherent mystery. It was a bit like jousting with fate! As a teenager hitchhiking around the country, I met many interesting people in this way and had some surprising and thrilling adventures. It was always a great learning process.

For this flight, I took two bright yellow three-and-a-half gallon plastic cans of extra gas to strap down on the front seat of the plane and headed for the airport on a cold crisp October 31st afternoon. I had recently improved the operation of my cabin heater and was looking forward to a warm, pleasant and comfortable daylight and early evening of high-desert sightseeing and flying. As small as it is, a warm J-3 Cub cockpit is about as close as one can get to curling up in a cocoon.

After moving the plane out of the hangar, I loaded my gear into the abbreviated luggage compartment behind the rear seat...one that I'd recently paid an absolute fortune (all relative) to have slightly enlarged.

Taking plenty of time doing my pre-flight walk-around inspection, I remembered being taught by a great instructor who said that, although many pilots give short shrift to the aircraft inspection before a flight, some even seem embarrassed by appearing overly cautious. The fact is, however, the pilot who wants to live to fly another day can't be too careful. A pilot doesn't just pull over to the side of the road while flying...and step out to fix something that goes wrong.

The preflight check of the plane and all its equipment and systems showed no sign of problems. I had fueled up when coming in from a previous flight so there was plenty of oil and gas. Everything looked like a "go."

When all was ready, I hand-started the engine by swinging the propeller from the rear. Reaching forward with my right hand, I gripped the shiny recently-renewed metal prop (I had damaged it in a semi-wild adventure and had just got it out of the repair shop)...and gave it a downward pull. A couple of pulls and it fired up into a pleasant throaty rumble (OK, a junior-grade rumble) that sounded to me like the sweetest music this side of Carnegie Hall. I always got that feeling whenever an airplane engine started. It's in a pilot's blood. Guess it's that plane engines are so well built and usually so well cared for that one knows it is solid and reliable. Of course, it better be!

Hopping into the little flying machine with a large sweeping motion, I cinched myself down with the giant three-inch wide WWII surplus web seatbelt installed to hold me tightly in place for the simple self-taught aerobatics that I occasionally executed during this period of my advanced student-learning. Unfortunately, my amateurish attempts produced sloppy slow rolls which always made me nervous. When rolling upside down, gasoline leaked from the top-mounted gas cap and poured all over the windshield. Not such a good situation!

I taxied onto the grass to proceed with my preflight run-up and make the final checks of the airplane's flight-ready condition. Pilots use the old memory-jogging "**C.I.G.A.R.**" method of preparation for takeoff, checking "**C**ontrols, **I**nstruments, **G**as, **A**ttitude and engine **R**un-up" before takeoff. I checked the rudder, elevator and aileron controls for freedom of travel, the instruments to make sure there was adequate oil pressure, set the altimeter for correct field-altitude elevation (which changes constantly as barometric pressure changes...and must be adjusted each time upon entering the aircraft), set the proper elevator trim and glanced at the gas gauge. I then reached over to the throttle lever with my left hand, gripped it firmly and eased the engine speed up to the appropriate RPM, checked both magnetos for proper operation and pulled the carburetor heat lever to make sure it was working. Everything was "Skookum"...as the Pacific Indians and loggers used to say. That essentially means "very good" in Native Indian jargon.

Shoving the throttle forward briskly, I eased the stick forward, raised the tail off the ground and whipped around onto the runway in one big, smooth motion that decreased my takeoff roll considerably. I'd read and heard about bush pilots doing that at strips which otherwise might have been too short to fly out of successfully. It seemed like a classy way to get off the ground and, at heart, I always wanted to emulate bush-pilots!

The ship broke ground in about 250 feet, a little longer than usual because of the extra gear and gas aboard, but still a very short liftoff.

Heading east and lining up the plane with Mt. Hood, my plan was to pass south of the mountain over the small historic village of Government Camp, located at about 3,000 feet of elevation. On beyond, I cruised smoothly over "Blue Box Pass," elevation 4024 feet and continued into central Oregon over the farming and ranching center of Madras. Then, it was on over low broken mountains toward the high desert village of John Day, which had a small landing strip on the outskirts. The winds turned out to be favorable... from behind, which increases a planes speed over ground by the speed the wind (or air) is moving.

Getting late in the day, pending darkness made it necessary to start thinking seriously about landing and tying down for the night. A Piper Cub can be landed practically anywhere, so I wasn't as concerned about finding a landing spot as my pilot counterparts who flew larger and more expensive blacktop-loving airplanes. However, my little Cub had no electrical system and therefore no navigation lights, no interior lights, no instrument lights and no landing lights. No lights whatsoever! Not only that, I'd never flown as pilot-in-command at night and wasn't exactly sure how it all worked, so wanted to get the plane safely on the ground before dark.

Staying above the road leading right into John Day, I figured that I couldn't miss my target airstrip which was illustrated directly alongside the road on my aviation chart. A half-hour went by and it was approaching five o'clock in the evening. The late fall sky was already beginning to darken ominously with the addition of a lingering thunderstorm cloud-cover in the area. As I began to tense up with trepidation over the accuracy (or possible inaccuracy) of my calculations, the early evening lights of my target village appeared. For a few brief moments, there still seemed to be adequate daylight and the airstrip showed up quite clearly right where it was indicated on the chart. Reducing power, the little ship dropped down toward the narrow valley floor as the strip came into sight. There was no air traffic way out here and none expected so I set up my final approach straight in and "touched down" right on the very end of the grass runway. At that moment I knew how someone like the great Jimmy Doolittle must have felt after a planned flight worked out according to plan and the resulting landing on a tiny deck or field was successful...a comforting feeling of achievement.

It was amazing the speed with which a very dark night presented itself. It seemed as if a giant hand had thrown a monstrous light switch and turned off every source of light in the sky. There was scarcely enough time to search out a tie-down spot before darkness descended.

Most airports have quite a number of "tie-down" fixtures such as small steel rings that are solidly fastened to the ground...to help keep a plane from blowing away in high winds. After finding the only readily visible tie-down set-up on the field and securing the plane, I took out what gear I'd need for the night, closed the door-window and started for town on foot. My walk proved to be only about six or eight blocks.

There were very few people around. As it was about suppertime, I ambled into the only open restaurant, plunked my gear down on the floor in a corner and sat at the counter to order dinner. I was the only customer.

Small restaurants way out in western cow towns always seem to offer giant steaks and other equally generous meals for modest prices. The people

Ubiquitous Boeing "Stearman"

Because more of these were made than any other WWII biplane trainer, they are the most widely "restored" ships of their type in existence today. "Skeets" Mehrer's hangar at Grove Field, Washington, 2001.

are generally friendly as well as helpful and thoughtful. It seemed to warm one up inside to be a short-term part of the simple activities that took place in the rural villages of America. It was my instant delight to be greeted by a pretty young waitress who bounced up happily to take my order.

Her first words were, "***Happy Halloween!***"

My answer? "You're kidding! ***It is?***"

Now, for those who pay a lot of attention to calendars and holidays, this probably is exactly what one would have expected her to say. Not me. Young and single, I could do and did pretty much as I pleased. I didn't pay much attention to dates other than paydays, the opening of fishing season and that time of year when it became warm enough to water-ski. Her answer put me in a moderate state of shock, for I completely had forgotten that this was indeed...***Halloween!***

Stunned, a wave of apprehension approaching panic began to grip me. In thinking about the Halloween stunts we kids had once played on others, I then thought about what unfortunate prank damage might possibly be done to an untended itinerant airplane. I'd just put many dollars worth of work and effort into the plane and it was like brand new with all its neat modifications. I could only imagine what a fabric-covered airplane might look like about thirty seconds after a few inventive pranksters performed their breed of fun and games on it with even the dullest pocket knives or other instruments of vandalizing excitement.

The waitress served my dinner. I tried to concentrate on eating but my thoughts kept returning to that beautiful little airplane sitting innocently in the field all alone and in plain view on the edge of town. I'd met some rancher kids in the past, the general type of whom I was certain had the potential to be inventive as heck with their pranks given the occasion and opportunities of Halloween.

As I tried to enjoy my dinner while contemplating the worst, an Oregon State Policeman came in and sat down next to me. He ordered coffee, then dinner and turned to say hello. He was in a friendly mood and we discussed this and that for a while before the conversation turned to Halloween. He was expecting the usual number of wild happenings which Halloween brings to small towns where kids don't have numerous things to keep them occupied. With every word, I became more and more anxious about my plane. I told him that I'd just flown in and explained my anxiety about the fact that somehow I had completely overlooked the Halloween prank potential. I mentioned that about all I might be able to do about it was to go back to the airplane and bed down under it (for the night) in a sleeping bag...not a happy thought with the outside temperature hovering around twenty-five degrees.

The trooper responded, "I'm surprised you didn't land at the new lighted airport up on top of the hill just south of town."

I replied in greater surprise, "It wasn't in my flight guide. My approach was so long and low down the valley that I landed way below the hill, didn't see the new airport lights and thought that the strip on the edge of town was the only airport."

"Oh, no," replied the state patrolman, "In fact, the small strip is considered closed. That's why you didn't see any other airplanes. The new airport is paved, lighted, fairly long and only about a mile by road from downtown. Everybody is using it now. It's a great airport. It's been finished for only a couple of weeks."

Well, that explained it. It wasn't yet noted in my flight guide.

We talked about the situation for quite a while. I was pleasantly surprised to find the trooper genuinely concerned about my plight. As we sat together eating and talking, a brilliant thought popped into my head. Hey – if he was as concerned as he sounded, maybe he would be willing to help!

This would be the ideal time to put the great "no-runway-light-operation" story to the test. If I could get him and someone else to park their cars on opposite ends of the strip with their lights on...as in the stories told by the old-time pilots, I could make my very first night flight...one that would allow me to get my plane up to the new airport and onto safer ground. It was quite an outrageous thought considering that I had never flown at night. But then, I'd done some pretty wild things in the past (and lived through them) and just how difficult could a little night flight be, anyway? A lot of pilots fly at night!

Fortunately, I hadn't given away the fact that I was a low-time student pilot or the policeman probably would have laughed at my suggestion. Doing my best to sound like a pro, I said, "If I could get someone to park on each end of the strip with their headlights on, I could take off, fly up to the new airport and park my plane where it would be safer from vandals."

"***You can do that?***" He sounded astonished!

Anxiously, I moved in for the kill. "Sure, we small-plane pilots fly in and out of unlighted strips and make takeoffs like that whenever the need arises. It's not that unusual." Leaning back on my stool and appearing nonchalant, I imagined bush pilots probably effected such mannerisms. He asked how, exactly, a takeoff like that worked. I described it as best I could remember from the stories I'd heard...hoping to God that the guys doing the wild-flight storytelling hadn't been totally full of bull and that it would actually work.

To my delighted and nervous surprise, the trooper took an immediate fancy to the idea. He appeared to have had a boring day and was soon thinking of someone he could call to be the "other set of headlights." He decided to call the local city policeman because they were well acquainted and it was still early enough in the evening that the policeman shouldn't yet be too busy chasing adventuresome kids.

About this time, I started to worry about how I would respond flying my plane in pitch-blackness and...how I would be able to see the airspeed indicator and instruments...and, and, and, and! Whew!

Well...it was now too late! I was past the point of no return. Although I was concerned about my ability to fly in the dark, my worry about possible damage to my plane was greater.

My new trooper-friend walked out to his patrol car and spoke with the local policeman on his police radio. As I watched him through the window and mulled over the stark reality of the situation staring me in the face...I was half-hoping he wouldn't be able to make contact...but he waved happily as he apparently got a positive response after talking with his friend.

The legendary Cessna 180 outfitted with oversize "Tundra" tires

Owned and flown by friend Trevor Norris of Sherwood, Oregon. This ship represents the 180 in a highly useful configuration...one that bush-pilots in Alaska find absolutely necessary for making rough-country landings possible on some of the most formidable landscape in nature. Because my 180 had only standard-size tires, I didn't attempt landings this aggressive. Rolling dry wheat stubblefields were the limit of landing risk for me.

This was almost too much! Now I had two policemen, a state and a local, helping me break the law. I thought, "What if they somehow figure out how wrong this is in the next few minutes, or, what if someone who is a truly experienced pilot stumbles onto us and exposes my plan?"

But now we were two police cars and one very nervous amateur student pilot driving up the hill to check out the new airport...so that I could get a bit familiar with it. In far too deep to turn back, I continued to sound as best I could like an old pilot from way back and chatted away using all the salty pilot talk I had picked up listening to good ol' boy aviators.

It was gratifying to see that the new airport was well-lighted indeed. The runway lights sparkled like so many flawless-fine diamonds in the night desert air. I reluctantly uttered my approval and we headed back, snaking our way down the winding road to the old deserted strip on the narrow valley floor. As we drove, the trooper quizzed me about how this was going to work and who would have to do what and be where. With my most authoritative air, I explained how he, the State Patrolman, should position his car with his headlights on at the end from which I'd start my takeoff run and we would have the city policeman park at the far end and point its headlights on dim directly at me to give me a target at which to aim. Just talking about it made me shudder because I knew I was trapped and was having second thoughts. Hell, I was having *third* and *fourth* thoughts!

It was dark when we pulled up to my plane. I had to borrow the State Patrolman's flashlight just to find the door-latch of the plane. I could feel my hands shaking. Fortunately, the Trooper couldn't see them. In fact, my whole body started quivering from stark-naked raw fear...and then the airplane door was open. Fumbling my way inside, I searched around trying to find my own flashlight and re-stow my gear so that it wouldn't get caught in the exposed rudder controls. I couldn't believe this was happening and my thoughts were starting to lean toward thinking up some unique excuse for backing out and forgetting the whole idea.

Then my thoughts returned to the importance of protecting my great little Cub from possible Halloween pranksters. "What the heck," I thought, "Might as well go for it!"

The city policeman had already driven to the other end of the strip and set himself up with his lights in my eyes. It was obvious that he didn't know any more about flying than the State Patrolman and was eager to be a part of an activity that seemed a lot more stimulating than chasing trick-or-treaters.

Checking the plane out briefly, I didn't spend a lot of time on the preflight as I'd been flying it not more than an hour before and the engine was still warm. Taking an extremely deep breath, I leaned over, reached in, turned on the ignition switch, stepped up to the propeller from behind while holding on to the wing struts with my left hand... then reached the propeller with my right hand and gave it a pull down. The engine roared to life instantly and I jerked sharply back knowing the propeller was an instrument of certain death spinning around unseen in the inky darkness. Climbing into the rear seat, I thought, "Man, those lights at the end of the strip are bright...hope I'm not blinded by them and can keep the plane in an absolutely straight line toward them. And what happens if I don't?" The strip was unusually narrow and well fenced. I tried not to dwell on that thought.

Leaving the tie-down rope attached to the tail to keep the plane from getting away from me when the engine started, I motioned to the Trooper to untie it as now my feet were planted firmly on the brake pedals. He untied the rope, got in his car and drove to the nearby end of the strip behind me. Jockeying his car into position, he parked with his headlights shining directly at the city policeman on the opposite end of the strip. It was an eerie feeling sitting there in the darkness, broken only by car lights off to one side and others in the distance. For the final time I thought, "I sincerely hope that all those hangar stories hadn't left out any minor details which might sneak up and convert me into some news reporter's column material for the morning paper." I couldn't see a thing other than the lights ahead. My great little ship, and indeed, my life were now at stake.

Easing the throttle forward, I felt the plane bump over the rough grass. It was so dark that the only way to be sure of my movement was to look at the two pairs of headlights and compare my movement with the stationary lights. It was surreal.

Carefully, I taxied in front of the Trooper's car and swung around abruptly in front of him pointing directly at the other headlights in the distance. This was the moment of truth.

I checked my magnetos, jiggled my controls to make sure they were free and sat there for a few moments wondering if I should abandon the effort and simply tell them I thought I heard one of my magnetos stutter. I remembered a schoolteacher in a literature class reciting from a famous writing, "Discretion is the better part of valor." I thought, "I wonder if that could mean right now?"

Ah, but youth doesn't let little details like someone else's concept of good sense destroy the magic of moments like these. The last sage cliché which passed through my somewhat addled mind as I applied full throttle was: "Good judgment comes from experience and experience comes from bad judgment." I was sure as heck going to get some experience, and fervently hoped that good judgment would come to me now.

The engine shrieked in the darkness. It sounded three times louder than it did in daylight flight. It must have been because I felt boxed in with no outside reference in the dark. Also, I now heard "night-rough" for the first time. That's pilots' term for what might sound like engine trouble. Dang...was that an engine miss I heard?

As usual, the tail rose off the ground right away. Gaining speed while holding the plane level allowed me to look straight into the city policeman's lights. In the blackness, I couldn't see anything other than those tiny lights straight ahead and the glint of the prop blades spinning madly in the reflection. It occurred to me that, in the dark without a horizon reference point in front of me, it might be possible to raise the tail so high that the prop might dig into the ground and really foul things up. Of course, wandering into a wire fence at night with a cloth airplane at high speed would also provide an interesting way to start a conversation with an airplane mechanic...or a medic!

I didn't dare use the flashlight to see the instruments because that might interfere with my concentrating on the target headlights. With my heart pounding, I mentally clicked off the seconds of time that I estimated it usually took to lift off during daylight. Fortunately, the ship stayed in a straight line as it moved forward for takeoff.

The lights on the other end drew closer. I held the plane on the ground not daring to lift off too early and die instantly because of a low airspeed stall.

Then, as if a great friendly hand reached down from the sky and gently raised up the little Cub, I suddenly realized that the plane and I were no longer on the ground! Son of a gun...we were flying! As we lifted off, the nose climbed up above the headlights of the police car in front. For a short period of time, I could see absolutely nothing!

The thrill and adrenaline rush under these new conditions was indescribable. I snapped the flashlight on and checked the airspeed. It was high enough that there was no way the plane could stall. The city lights shining up from below produced a very modest amount of "skyglow" (the glow of light one sees over cities from a distance). With peripheral vision, I could see the lights of homes and other buildings. The few lights below now provided a frame of reference to keep me from getting vertigo and the possibility of disorientation.

All I needed now was to keep the plane straight and level with full power and it should climb comfortably away from the field. Then, in a matter of only a couple of minutes, there should be enough altitude to look over to the left and see the lights of the new airport come into view on the plateau above town.

What a delight it was to look down on the lights of the town and realize that I was now a member of the fraternity of night-flying "Aviators Extraordinaire." That is, if I lived through the entire exercise! I still had to make this very first night landing successful.

Sure enough, in just a few moments I gained the necessary couple of hundred feet or so needed to see the new airport just over the edge of the canyon rim. Its runway lights glowed brightly a relatively short distance away. This must be how an airline pilot feels when he sets up for a night approach at a giant airport. "But," I wondered, "how does a night landing on macadam feel and how do you make a perfect three-point landing when you can't see the ground? Can I keep the plane straight? Will I lose control and ground loop?" (To "Ground loop" is to lose control and spin the plane around on the ground, frequently causing substantial damage.) Well...I was about to meet the ground. There was no avoiding these questions now!

Interestingly, the toughest part of the whole take-off procedure was getting up the nerve during some shaky minutes immediately prior to applying the plane's throttle. The landing went surprisingly well. There were enough runway, taxiway and other lights at this new airport to give needed reference points and the runway was long. Fairly high above sea level, it had plenty of length for heavier planes. It was oriented uphill to quite a degree so I landed uphill...because the air was dead calm. I'd read numerous stories of Alaskan bush pilots landing on water that was so glassy smooth that they couldn't be sure where the surface was and they flew right into the water with disastrous results. To solve this problem, so the story-tellers explained, the pilots would set up as long an approach as possible and let down very slowly until the airplane finally touched the water. To preclude driving my Cub into the unseen surface, I emulated the water pilots and used up much of the runway "feeling" for the pavement. Finally, the tires touched down with an odd little squeak and I was safe on terra firma...a real live night pilot!

Arriving at the tie-downs in front of the flight offices a couple of minutes before the two policemen got there, I had jumped out of the plane and was in the process of tying it down when they came wheeling up. Since there were no lights on the airplane, they couldn't see me in the air and weren't sure whether I had made it or crashed on the way. It apparently had been as much a thrill for them as it had for me because, as they came up to the plane, they babbled about the ease with which I'd pulled it off and wondered if I did this kind of thing often.

We all went back to the cafe, had another cup of coffee and I bid them goodbye as they set out to capture Halloween trick bandits while I set out to find a room at the local hotel. If only they knew!

Considering the wild things I've done in my life, this lunatic escapade has to rank near the top. I'd be willing to bet that if I had spent the rest of my life performing to this level of madness in everything, I'd be so rich and famous right now that I'd be inviting you to ride in my own Lear-Jet…or...***I'd be DEAD!***

The Cessna 207 "bush-plane" extraordinaire - 626 built

Turning to look back inside while flying this long plane gave me the impression of looking through the wrong end of a telescope!

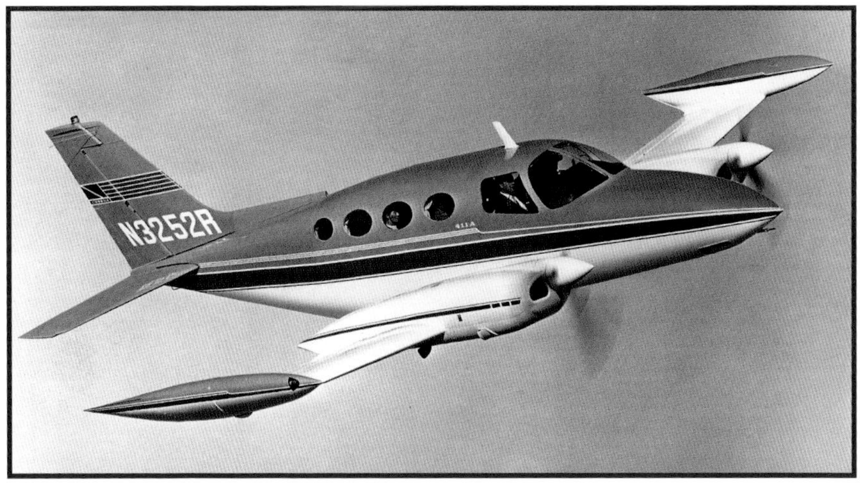

Cessna's first large twin engine business-liner, Model 411

This ship arrived on the scene in 1962...302 were made. I first saw one at Nogales airport...when flying to Mexico in my Cessna 180.

CARD NO. 947738156 S — FORM 787P 12-56

Standard

UNION 76
OIL COMPANY OF CALIFORNIA
AIRCRAFT DELIVERY TICKET

CUSTOMER Marc E Paulsen
1801 NE 162nd
Portland Ore

IF NOT UNION CARD SHOW COMPANY NAME

REC'D BY X Marc E Paulsen

DATE 9-25-62

DEALER Evergreen

7074H
AIRCRAFT LICENSE NUMBER

COMMODITY	GRADE	GALLONS	PRICE	AMOUNT	
7600 AVIATION GASOLINE	80	5-8	30	1	74
RED LINE AERO OIL	1 Qt				50
SALES OR USE TAX @ %					10
TOTAL				2	34

METER READINGS	
AFTER	
BEFORE	
DELIVERED	

PRESERVE THIS INVOICE. NO OTHER WILL BE ISSUED. THIS IS ONLY INVOICE GOOD TO SUPPORT CLAIM FOR REFUND OF TAX.

ORIGINAL INVOICE

225570
SERIAL NO.

DELIVERED BY

PRICE INCLUDES FEDERAL AND STATE MOTOR FUEL TAX (IF APPLICABLE). PAYMENT OF WHICH IS ASSUMED BY UNION OIL COMPANY OF CALIFORNIA.

Aviation fuel price back in the glory days

Compare these figures with those seen at pumps today. Now, you can't get a fuel attendant to unlimber his hose for this kind of money.

The Cessna 172 Skyhawk - 43,000+ built

This is one of my all-time favorite airplanes. I would take sales prospects up, shut off the engine and stop the prop...then quietly glide for a time...to demonstrate its outstanding stability.

Box Canyon Blues

"Downwind" is a word that pilots seldom link with takeoffs, for very good reason. It is directly related to the speed a plane requires *over the ground* to become airborne and the length of the runway being used. In the world of aviation, the word is so significant that the cartoonist who drew the long-running flying-oriented newspaper strip, "Smilin' Jack," named one of the main characters *Downwind.* Quaintly, his countenance was drawn in such a way that one never saw his full face, only a quarter-view of one side from the rear…hence his name, *Downwind!*

With airplanes, speed is relative and the word downwind plays an important part. What an airplane's speed is relative to is the force of an air-mass movement in which it flies or, as most non-pilots know it, *wind.* In its simplest form, the explanation goes like this: If the wind is blowing toward your plane at 30 mph and your plane flies at a minimum airspeed of 55 mph, then the plane will become airborne at a speed of 25 mph *over the ground* and use very little runway. Simple, hmm?

Movies depicting aircraft carriers catapult-launching fighter planes that have very high minimum airspeeds show that not only are aircraft carriers surprisingly fast, but they always steam at high speed *into the wind.* In many cases, that tactic will lower a carrier plane's required take-off speed from well over 100 mph to 50 to 80 mph or so (over the carrier deck) when combining a headwind and the fast forward speed of the carrier. Pity the poor pilot who has any type of failure on takeoff and drops over the bow into the water (and is unable to first "eject"). He will be run over by the racing carrier!

Now, one would think that the reverse of this formula must also be true. In other words, if taking off downwind with a 30 mph tailwind and flying the same plane that lifts off at a minimum airspeed of 55, then you'd simply add 30 to 55 and be off (over the ground) at 85 mph. Up to a point, that is true. However, there are some sneaker situations with various wind conditions, types and configurations of airstrips and planes that can complicate this equation very quickly and…*by square.*

For this reason, airplanes seldom take off downwind. No point in complicating life when it isn't necessary. But, sometimes…*it is necessary.* This is a story about *one of those times.*

One of the great things which can be done with a Piper Cub airplane is land on short, rough fields or fields with obstacles (locations other than "prepared" landing places) and *fly back out successfully.* The little ship has a very "high-lift" wing (developed in the 1930s) and that attribute has endeared it to generations of private pilots from week-enders to flying farmers and bush pilots. The ship's ability to land in fairly short, rough fields was what motivated my friend Del and me to load a batch of hunting gear into my J-3 Cub and head for Eastern Oregon pheasant country.

On an earlier summer flight we had discovered a good-looking hunting spot in expansive wheat fields, and now that Fall had arrived, our taste buds were primed for wild bird with all the trimmings. Using a plane and landing in wheat fields near the bird habitats would shorten our trip by an entire day compared with driving a car. What a great way to go!

As we loaded gear into the plane, I did mental calculations as to its weight. My concern was that we would be *much overloaded.* Pilots often fly with overloaded airplanes. Just ask any pilot. The trick is to know, within reason, how overloaded the plane is…and adjust your flight technique accordingly.

Shotguns, ammunition, shooting jackets, sleeping bags, cameras, food, drink, charts, etc., etc., etc. Looking Del over, I concluded he weighed in at about 175 pounds and I checked out at about 210 pounds. Flight manuals usually calculate people's weight at a standard of 170 lbs. That's great if you have a large man and a little woman or a pair of trolls as passengers, but it's not often the reality. Also related to flight manuals, airplane manufacturers seem to be a bit *optimistic* as to precisely what their planes are capable of carrying under various conditions. Most small planes which are called "four-place" will typically safely carry only three people (or fewer) under average conditions if the pilot *carefully does his "weight and balance" calculations.* Del was a "skydiver," and skydivers probably do more heavy-duty overloading of planes than any other type of flyer mainly because their gear is so heavy and they always want to load in as many skydivers as possible. So...we didn't think too much about our obvious overload. We would simply adjust for it by making longer takeoff runs.

This morning was one of those bright, clear, brisk ones which make one happy to be alive and eager to be headed for new adventure. I was going to do most of the flying so I got into the rear seat and Del propped the engine. It fired up and Del hopped into the tiny front cockpit and settled down. The front cockpit was so small that, with my long legs, it was very close to impossible for me to fly from the front. Del was perfectly happy to sit up front closest to the cabin heater outlet. I was still a student pilot and on this flight, I wanted to enter all of the flight time in *my* logbook. As Del was a "Certified Flight Instructor," he would sign my entries for important cross-country flights…plus, he liked to hunt.

Off the ground and into the air, we settled back to a long, slow climb to gain enough altitude for crossing the Cascade mountain range. We were headed for the approximate northern center of the state of Oregon, and the simplest route was over dense Douglas Fir forests and the high foothills of snow-covered peaks.

Arriving over those foothills, we finally leveled out at about 5,500 feet on our altimeter and set the throttle at cruise power. That doesn't mean much in a Cub because it cruises at only about eighty mph. The 5,500 foot reading (above seal level) put us about 2,000 feet above thick deep-green Douglas Fir timberlands below.

Del poured a cup of coffee for me from my big old-fashioned lightweight Thermos bottle. I always used old-timer inexpensive Thermoses in airplanes because, although they are lightly made and prone to easy breakage, they weigh very little and carefully controlling weight in airplanes is vitally important. The really fancy stainless steel productions are heavy... jokingly, enough to put the ship into a spin! Thus, lightweight foam cups were used for the same reason.

Drinking the liquid appreciatively, I tried to carry on a conversation with Del, raising my voice to about the roar of a young lion, but it was no use. Little airplanes have a decibel sound level that would drive a rock-and-roll drummer crazy. The J-3 is made of metal tubing covered with a very tough thin fabric, and the engine is almost in one's lap. A normal conversation can't be carried on without an intercom system. As I didn't have an electrical system, we could forget easily conversing!

A new Cessna 172 during my airplane salesman days

As an airplane salesman, I met some former WWII pilots who had fantastic tales to tell. The man standing to my right was a P51D fighter pilot who was shot down over Germany by a Messerschmidt ME-109 at an altitude above 30,000 feet. To avoid being shot out of the air in his parachute, he delayed opening it until falling to a thousand feet, then yanked the ripcord. He ended up hanging from a church steeple and was pulled down by angry townspeople who came close to tearing him apart. He was saved by a German army officer present in the crowd...and spent the next year in a prisoner of war camp until liberated by the U.S. Army.

Soon, we passed over the foothills on the east side of the mountain range and continued over an assortment of grain fields, mint fields, hay fields and cattle grazing. Then, it was on to what some of us call "scab-lands." That is land outside and beyond the cultivated ranches that is made up of rocky sharply-rolling hills with tiny creek-dotted valleys be-tween. The average elevation of this land runs from about 1,500 to 3,000 feet above sea level. It is well into the early frost zone, so the vegetation which grow best there are sagebrush and juniper trees neither of which has much value. This is the land of the celebrated range-cow and the cattle graze here on sparse grasses that do their best to exist during a fairly short growing season.

Observing the moving scene below, we saw an occasional abandoned homesteader's shack amidst the junipers…almost always near a spring and usually accompanied by a glorious row of very old, tall stately Lombardy Poplar trees. Lombardies are one of the few tree varieties which need little water (due to a very expansive root system), so almost every early high-desert homestead in the West planted them. The thought passed through my mind how much different the lives of these people were from ours. Imagine hitching your team of horses or oxen to a wagon with giant creaky wooden wheels, loading up your family and driving off into the wilderness like the wilds now passing beneath us. In most cases, there were no roads and almost no communication with the outside world...all of this to get just a hundred and sixty acres of free government homestead land that, in the final analysis, could grow only enough to support a few cows (and those beautiful trees). That's why the buildings we were observing had been abandoned.

Out of the hills and onto flatter ground, the sagebrush still held sway. Del spotted a coyote and down we went to do a little harassing. (Although scenery is moderately interesting as one flies along in a light plane, it can get very boring after a while.) Thus, upon spotting the coyote, I banked the J-3 sharply to the left and into a dive. We swooped down on the animal, missing its back by maybe six feet...and pulled up into a steep wingover to take another run at it.

Right here, you're probably thinking what bad guys we were to do such an inhumane thing. Actually, what a lot of rangeland pilots did was make the nearby ranchers happy and blow coyotes' heads off with shotguns (because the animals frequently killed their livestock and pets)...but we were content to see only how fast they could run. It's notable how differently people view things and how various acts are rationalized. At any rate, a couple more passes over the "desert dog" and we resumed our flight.

At around nine o'clock in the morning, we landed in the first pheasant field. We'd received permanent permission to hunt on this property a couple of years earlier so we didn't have to waste time visiting the rancher. We parked the plane in recently-cut stubble of a wheat field about four hundred yards from a dry creek bottom.

With our guns assembled, we hiked down to high grass along the creek. The morning went along according to plan and we visited three different fields and shot a few birds. The ground was dry enough to allow very safe plane operation and we covered a lot of real estate in short order flying from one field to the next. After we had enough birds, we munched a lunch of sandwiches and coffee and discussed which way we should return home. I visually checked our fuel supply and explained to Del that we had a little less than half a tank and, from my experience in the ship, it would last a bit less than an hour and a half. We agreed that it would not be enough to make it home so we'd have to make a stop somewhere for fuel.

Having flown over ranchlands frequently, I'd met a number of very friendly ranchers who belonged to the Flying Farmers, one of the largest flying associations in the United States at the time. This was a warmly congenial and helpful group and those I'd met would do about anything for another pilot. I told Del that I knew one member of the local chapter who lived directly south of our position, had a family airstrip and fuel and, if we flew that way, I felt sure we could stop and buy some fuel. "Way out here in the middle of nowhere, that will be our best and closest opportunity," I proclaimed to Del.

Leaving the wheat fields behind to reach my rancher acquaintance, we flew over a small range of fairly high hills ("mountains" to easterners) with tops up to 6,800 feet above sea level. Pretty high terrain for an airplane carrying a heavy load! At these altitudes, the horsepower is reduced dramatically due to thin air and a lack of adequate oxygen so it is necessary to exercise the greatest of care flying. We used a substantial amount of fuel in the climb over the hills so fuel now became an even more important issue!

Clearing the small range of hills, we were gratified to see the man's ranch directly before us and just beyond a highway paralleled by telephone wires. We had checked our charts, watched the compass carefully and arrived as expected. We spotted the airstrip, circled, observed the field's "windsock" to determine wind direction...and decided to land "upwind" due to a substantial "downwind" air mass that was blowing and, as earlier mentioned, it is always far preferable (and safer) to land *into the wind.* A negative in this situation was that "upwind" lead to a "box" canyon.

The strip wasn't really a strip at all. It was just a very long, narrow, modestly uphill two-lane driveway to the ranch house. That's the way rancher-pilots operate. They use whatever is handy as a place to land a plane and call it their "airport." These strips can be awkward for some to land on, but flying farmers who are used to operating complicated equipment in dif-

Piper J-3 Cub

A friend fellow-pilot poses with my plane after this landing we made on a small patch of ground close behind a restaurant in Oregon's high desert. The proprietor was so amazed and taken with the idea of an airplane landing on his property that he later built an airstrip on it...but charged ahead without acquiring professional advice. The resulting strip was so poorly designed that a number of "incidents" quickly occurred...and it was ultimately abandoned.

ficult settings get really handy with their own airplanes and they manage flying from these types of strips with little difficulty. But this...was one ***very challenging strip!*** It was *exceedingly narrow* consisting of only the two vehicle tire tracks running along a narrow hay field to one side and a slope of irregular rocks on the other. Did I say rocks? I meant to say "boulders." They ranged from six inches in diameter to three feet, and were positioned all along and quite close to the road, plus high enough to cause collision trouble if one might get too close. But, if a pilot exercised caution and good judgment and followed all the rules of flight, he should fly in and out with a minimum of difficulty.

We set up an approach, dropped in neatly and very gently because of the headwind that slowed our forward progress substantially. Taxiing to a shed located a hundred yards from the ranch house which appeared to serve as a hangar, we parked the plane and shut the engine down.

The wind hadn't seemed strong by the windsock's indication. We apparently underestimated it considerably. Either that or we had checked the sock at a moment of lull in the wind. We also missed noticing how much the wind was affecting the surrounding trees...which would have given us a more accurate clue to its strength had we been *just a bit more* observant.

Parking near the beat-up and weathered makeshift hangar, we now felt the plane rock back and forth harshly as we prepared to get out. Hmmm.... obviously, the wind was blowing *one heck of a lot* harder than it had seemed from the air.

Out of the plane and on our feet in whistling wind, we now noticed something else that had slipped past our hasty and inadequate observations on the way in. We were at the end of a small and high ***box canyon*** (walled off on one end!) We hadn't paid much attention to it coming in because the canyon spread out and was wide at the end from which we had approached. Now, if we followed the basic rules of flight, we must take off into the wind...***directly at the tight wall of high cliffs.***

We could see that the rancher most likely always took off headed down the road rather than uphill toward solid rock. Of course, he could pick his time and conditions according to wind situations, a luxury not available to us now for we needed to get back home to work. We walked around his hangar to the open side and got another shock. ***No airplane!***

We walked up to the ranch house and knocked on the door. No answer. He wasn't home. He must have flown his plane somewhere.

Back at the hangar shed, I told Del that, "If a pilot is in a fuel pinch, flying farmers generally don't mind if you borrow some gas from them as long as you leave some money on top of a gas barrel or a note stating that you will send them the money." Sounded O.K. to Del so I went over to check a barrel.

It was locked! A giant padlock! What a surprise! I had stopped here before and got fuel with no problem. There were no locks then. "What's the deal?" I wondered: "Has someone been stealing fuel from him?"

But, no matter. Now we had a whole new set of problems.

We immediately began a heated discussion on how to get out of the canyon and what to do about our now much more serious fuel situation... "heated discussion" because of the increasing number of critical elements involved! We agreed that the wind appeared to be in our favor for the fairly long flight to the next big airport which would have fuel. If we turned left after leaving the field, it appeared that the wind would be at our backs and would thereby improve our fuel efficiency so, in "theory," we should easily make it to that alternate fuel source with little difficulty. Luckily, the wind was blowing in the general direction of our final destination. After more discussion (because of the importance of making the *right* decision), then some bickering and finally calculating and recalculating the distances involved and the rate of our fuel "burn," we ultimately agreed that our fuel supply ***should*** be enough...and the takeoff and flight ***should*** be successful.

We then spent an inordinate amount of time arguing heatedly over *which way to take off.* We spent quite a bit of the time considering the effects the plane's gross weight and the four thousand foot elevation above sea level elevation would have. This air was ***exceedingly thin!***

Del had at least eight times more flying time than I so I finally saw fit to defer to his expertise. But in this critical situation with my airplane at risk, I truly wasn't sure. He didn't want to bash into a canyon wall so, after much more haggling, we decided to take off…***downwind.***

I climbed into the back seat of the plane. Del then grabbed the prop, spun it half a turn, the engine started and Del joined me in the ship. *We then taxied to takeoff position.*

We had decided that Del would do the flying in this very demanding situation because of his experience so he now took over the controls. It all seemed very logical. As he situated himself for takeoff, the wind velocity had seemingly increased considerably. In *the wrong direction!* Del shoved the red-knobbed throttle lever ***full-forward!***

We roared down the driveway/runway like a rocket! The tailwind must have been well over twenty miles an hour. *Probably more.*

We argued for years over exactly what happened next. Del said the plane hit a hole in the road and bounced sideways. I said he let the plane get away from him. The upshot was, that the plane started to wallow badly the instant its forward speed (created by propeller "thrust") matched the speed of the wind. The plane then started to sway wildly back and forth on the very edge of "stalling." As I remembered it, he pulled back on the stick a little to try to help the plane fly and that exacerbated an already dangerous situation. By now we were ripping along (with the push of the moving air mass) in the neighborhood of 60 mph and skipping along the strip's surface from side to side as the wings dipped furiously up and down. We were stalling (losing ability to fly because of not enough actual forward movement through the air mass) and still were almost on the ground. The plane simply wasn't flying! At this critical point, I made a mad grab for the controls to save my ship. Just as I did, we were jolted with a wild wrenching jerk at the same time that a loud sharp report echoed through the plane...and the plane shuddered violently.

I had no idea what had happened but we were still staggering crazily along the strip at full throttle with the plane clawing desperately at the air in an awkward nose-up condition. We each held our controls in death-grips and continued to blaze down the runway.

As if God himself had seen fit to take personal mercy on these two idiots, we were somehow allowed to straighten the ship out at the exact end of the field…and ***actually fly!***

Mumbling prayers to ourselves as the plane cleared the wires along the highway by inches, we both kept our eyes planted directly ahead and concentrated on holding the ship in the air and gaining altitude. As the ship finally transitioned into a normal climb, I yelled up to Del, *"What in the world happened?"*

Del yelled back, "I'm not sure, but I think that, on the rough ground, the tail wheel must have broken off and wrapped around the exposed rudder wires at the tail. That's what must have fouled up our ability to control the ship. The problem is," he shouted, "we can't see back there and, if it is broken and tangled, that could destroy our ability to handle the plane if the tailwheel flops around again and gets even more tangled!"

It seemed that Del had applied his expertise to the question and come up with a possible answer. I didn't like it much, though. If his speculation were true, the controls might lock up any time and give us a personal introduction to oblivion.

We turned the plane in the direction we had planned and flew on for a while. Our nervousness about complications calmed enough to allow us to think more clearly, so we looked out the window.

We stared down in ***disbelief*** at a landing gear strut and wheel on the right side severely smashed and bent wildly back…***directly under the plane almost out of sight.*** The plane obviously had veered far enough off the track to hit a giant rock with a wheel! That we were still in the air was way beyond a miracle.

Del was dumbfounded! We sat riveted with eyes peering through the window for minutes before we spoke again. We clearly understood the obvious. Somehow, we were going to meet the ground again...but how? Were we going to fly along meditating silently and then get mangled into pulp by a crash landing at the next stop? That we were concerned is an understatement of major proportions!

Not ten minutes later, we were jolted by another complication. The wind changed 180 degrees...*against us*. That meant we were now flying into a strong and steady *direct headwind.* What made this ominous was what the headwind-reduced mileage would do to our already scant fuel supply. We had figured that we could barely make it to the next airport with what fuel we had. Now, even this looked doubtful.

We could do one of two things. We could either try to land immediately somewhere below or continue to our planned destination and take our chances on a landing at the next airport…assuming we could even make it there.

Looking down, we quickly ruled out landing below. There was absolutely no safe place to land. The terrain was extremely rough and also crowded with various small trees and brush. And, we certainly didn't want to go back to the rocky and uneven strip we had just left.

We decided to throttle back to save fuel and continue. Unfortunately, that doesn't work too well with a slow plane in a strong headwind, as experienced pilots know. Although throttling way back greatly reduces fuel consumption, flying into a headwind reduces forward speed to a crawl. But, we had no choice. Yikes! Could anything else go wrong?

We tried to find a balance between saving fuel and still making some realistic headway. The little ship struggled but *slowly* made progress. Looking out at the damaged landing gear worried us greatly, but we couldn't stop looking. We silently kept asking ourselves: "How in the world could the airplane have taken such a tremendous hit and still be in the air?"

The next forty-five minutes seemed like eternity! If the other problems weren't enough, we yet had to fly over a mountain pass. It seemed like conditions all around us had ganged up to take away what little fuel we had.

But, our luck held out! Finally, after giving off buckets of cold sweat, we neared the Prineville, Oregon, airport we were aiming for. Fortunately, Prineville was an airport with little traffic, so at least that should be no worry. It now looked like we were going to make it! There wasn't much preparation we could think of other than to cinch up our seatbelts more tightly and quietly whisper some words of appeal to the heavens.

By chance, we were lined up perfectly for a straight-in approach to the long main blacktop runway. But, we most certainly didn't want to land on blacktop so we eased to one side to land on the sod next to the runway, figuring it would make for a less serious crash. A history of planes having to land with problems such as landing gear that wouldn't extend has proven that landing on grass can make the best of a bad situation.

Making the longest, gentlest descending approach either of us had ever made, we crossed the threshold of the runway in slow flight, eased the ship over to the grass on the left side...and began the *longest landing stall* either of us had ever done. With only one of the two main landing gear wheels operational, we were almost positive we would lose control the moment we touched the ground so we braced ourselves and waited for fate to do its worst. About a third of the way along the sod, and about a foot from the ground, the ship stopped flying, stalled and *made contact!* It hit, bounced once, twisted around and came to a dead stop almost backward but upright and...with *absolutely no further damage.* The plane rocked back and forth a little and then...*all was still.*

We looked at one another. We couldn't believe such a happy ending to this strange situation. Neither of us uttered a word. Still shaking, I crawled out from the rear and headed for the flight office. Now that we were successfully back to "terra firma," *we'd have to get the landing gear repaired!*

Author's note:

The next time you see a report of an airplane crash in the news, remember our story of how flight complications ganged up on us in our little ship (in this case, all of our own making except for the unexpected wind direction change). Other scary situations (different problems) sometimes overwhelm commercial pilots and we read the unfortunate results in the papers. What non-pilots must know is that when airplanes develop mechanical problems, or some other critical situation arises, pilots have two choices, not always their own. They must do everything in their power to land the ship…***or crash!***

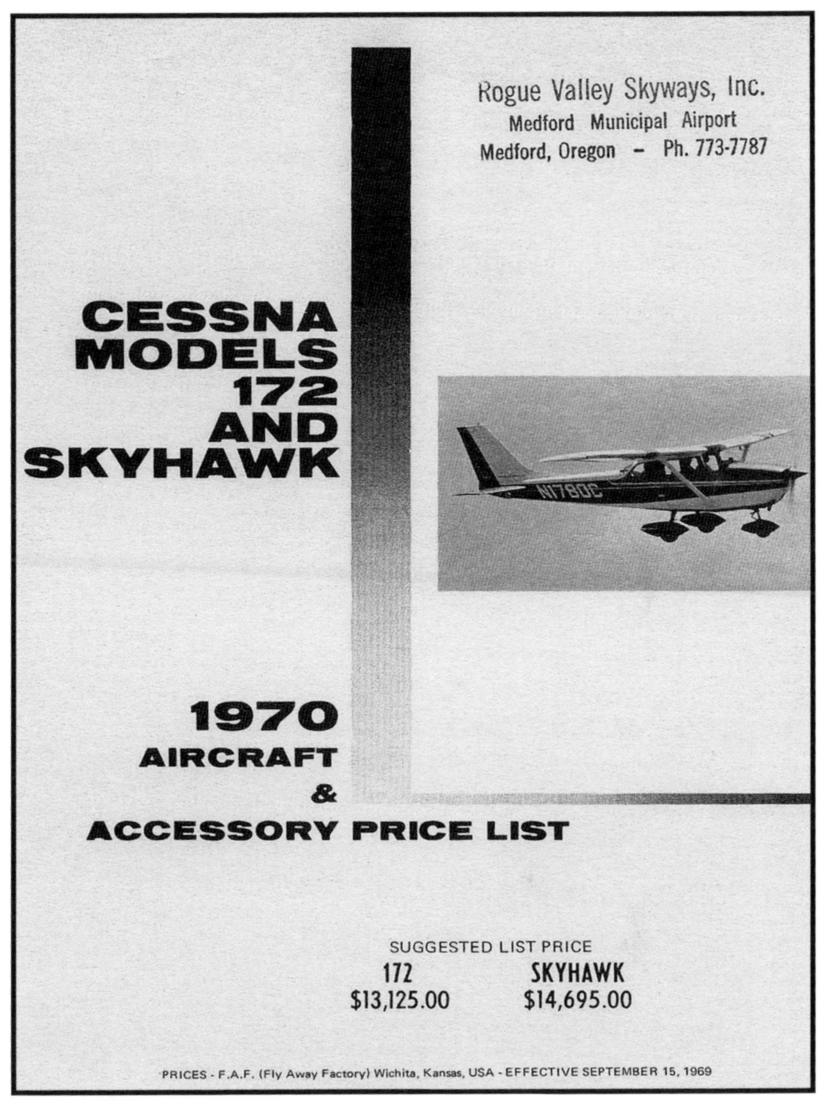

Rogue Valley Skyways, Inc.
Medford Municipal Airport
Medford, Oregon - Ph. 773-7787
CESSNA MODELS 172 AND SKYHAWK
N1780C
1970 AIRCRAFT & ACCESSORY PRICE LIST
SUGGESTED LIST PRICE
172
$13,125.00
SKYHAWK
$14,695.00
PRICES - F.A.F. (Fly Away Factory) Wichita, Kansas, USA - EFFECTIVE SEPTEMBER 15, 1969

1970 Cessna Model 172 pricelist

The "172" model was the "basic" plane...the "Skyhawk" model the same plane with additional features. This was a pricelist in use when I was selling airplanes at Rogue Valley Skyways in Medford, Oregon. The price now for the same plane (depending on "options" added) can range to as much as ***$307,000.***

My Cessna 180...a *heavy hauler!* 6193 built

Home after a very successful hunting/fishing trip. In the plane, besides two of us 210-pounders, was the Honda Trail 90 motorcycle (in 2 pieces via a "split-kit"), 2 rifles, 2 shotguns, other hunting gear, fishing gear, tent, sleeping bags, personal gear, a forked-horn mule deer, 5 pheasants, 6 ducks, 8 chukars and 2 nice strings of trout. This was my fourth airplane purchase (9 yr. old ship). Cost in 1964? $8,250 with a "low-time" engine.

Cessna 320 Skyknight, 577 built

I got to fly this slick ship on a charter from Southern Oregon to San Francisco to pick up a businessman. The man was so wealthy that he had a shiny new Cessna 206 based on our Oregon field just for ferrying guests to his private airstrip and lodge on the Rogue River, a trip also flown by our charter pilots. The 320 was in production from 1961 through 1969. The plane was essentially a stretched 310 with more powerful engines plus an extra window and six seats. Like the revered 310, it felt as solid as an airliner and was a pleasure to fly.

Night Is The Hunter

There was a time that I'd do almost anything to break free from work for a pheasant hunt. I've never been able to get over the splendor of those gloriously beautiful birds. This once-avid bird hunter thinks there isn't a prettier collection of feathers in the wild than those of the Chinese Ring-neck Pheasant.

After I got my first plane and hunting season had arrived, not a week went by when I wasn't plotting to fly to eastern Oregon in search of that fabulous winged art form….no matter that I was still a student pilot not yet signed off for cross-country flight. But then, there had to be a way around that. *There was!*

When one gets a first plane, all kinds of intelligent and important uses for it come to mind. Some of them even make sense. This one seemed to. I surmised that a bird hunt would be a great way to get some "cross-country" flight practice. Just think...I'd get to go on a hunting trip (something that always thrilled me) and this time I would receive a double thrill with the addition of the airplane flight.

I called my friend, Ray, also a pilot, and suggested to him this trip would be one heck of lot of fun, and very inexpensive as I would be picking up the tab for the transportation. I touched ever so lightly on the fact that it would also be a chance for me to get some good cross-country dual instruction entries in my logbook and allow me to save a few bucks in the process. Ray was a Certified Flight Instructor, a very convenient friend to have when learning to fly. Ray's reply? "Sure, I'd love to go bird hunting. Sounds like a great idea. When do we go and what shall I bring?"

Outstanding! In addition to his acceptance, Ray had even more good news. He had a good friend who owned a very large ridge-top ranch overlooking the famous John Day River in the Oregon high desert country, a dry-land wheat ranch that, according to Ray, would offer the possibility of some exceptional bird hunting. Not only that, Ray was sure his friend would loan us a vehicle, guide us to the best places for birds and maybe...put us up for a night or two. This was indeed a great stroke of luck.

Before daybreak on Saturday morning, we met at the extremely short private strip where I kept my new (to me) airplane. Packing item by item, we very carefully considered weight. Ray is one of these people who are slow and easy and take time to do things right. He observed, "With only sixty-five horsepower, we better make zero mistakes on our gross weight calculations. This is one heck of a short field and over east we will be operating at fairly high airfield elevations in relatively warm weather." I heartily agreed! I had already learned that weight, temperature, airfield elevation and horsepower have a lot to do with the success or failure of every flight. Numerous pilots who attempted to be first to fly across the Atlantic Ocean did not make it alive...due to too heavy a fuel load, etc. Because of this, a number crashed and burned even before getting completely off the end of runways.

I had been fully educated about some potential problematic situations by the owner of the ***extremely short airstrip*** where I kept my plane. He was adamant that pilots understood the intricacies and importance of approaching landings to his strip...***only*** by flying to the strip ***above and over*** the *seventy-foot-high electricity distribution wires on one end of his strip* and said, "Never, but ***never***, attempt to take off toward them!" He was greatly concerned that a pilot attempting such a feat would end up without enough altitude and would crash into the high-voltage wires. With only nine hundred feet of total field length and a six-foot-high fence on the opposite end, flying in and out at all was quite an achievement…but it was a great place to learn the basics of flight...and learn them *exceedingly well!*

By the time we had stowed our guns, ammunition, sleeping bags and the rest of our gear in the tiny baggage compartment, night was giving way to dawn. In the increasing light we gave the plane a thorough visual flight inspection, checking every important detail necessary for a safe flight. It all looked like we were ready to go.

With the inspection completed, I explained my plane's specific idiosyncrasies of the starting process to Ray as, at start-up it was going to be his hand on the throttle. I would spin the propeller by hand to start the engine.

As Ray was considerably smaller than I, he slipped into the front seat, no easy feat because a Piper J-3 Cub is truly a compact airplane and the seating is what one might call...absolutely *miniscule!* I remained outside for engine-starting duties, pulled the prop through half a turn...and thrilled as the engine fired on the first "contact" pull. The resultant engine roar gave me the ecstatic feeling that mechanically-oriented people experience when machines perform as they should.

If there is no "self-starter" mechanism on an airplane, "contact" is a word the prop-spinner (engine-starter) shouts out to the pilot who then turns on the ignition switch and yells back "contact." The term "contact" originated because of some unnerving accidents (blunders) in early aviation. In the birthing days of aviation, the "prop-spinner" (engine starter) would call "switch off" to the person inside the plane who would then repeat loudly "switch off" to confirm that there would be no inadvertent ignition...thereby allowing the starter to turn the prop a few times to remove oil from bottom "radial" engine cylinders or to prime or clear the carburetor. When the starting person was ready for engine ignition, he would call "switch *on,*" and, after hearing a "switch on" response from inside the plane, he'd spin the prop and the engine would start. Unfortunately, occasionally the two individuals would confuse the words "switch on" and "switch off." The result was that a number of early engine starters lost limbs or lives. The word "contact" removed that possibility of deadly confusion.

With the engine of my plane purring smoothly, in one big motion I raised my left leg up about four feet in the air and over onto the left floorboard of the airplane just in front of the rudder pedal. It helps to have legs as long as a giraffe to perform this contortion in a Piper Cub. There simply was no easy way for me to enter *this* flying machine.

For takeoff, I took over the controls...knowing this made Ray very nervous on this tiny potentially-dangerous airfield but, what the heck, if he had to, he could grab the controls out of my hands at any time (hopefully *in time*) to save our necks. After all, *he was a flight instructor!*

We taxied to the end of the airstrip that had the high wires and whipped around to line up with the strip...headed into a very light wind. A macadam street ran parallel under the wires and, to utilize every possible bit of field length, all who flew from this field began take-offs aiming down the runway with the tail resting *out in the street* six or eight feet. A wise old pilot once said, "Runway behind you is of no use"...so we were in the habit of using every last foot *of what was available*...especially with that six foot high fence just nine hundred feet directly in front of the plane on the far end. Our only more serious problem might have been getting hit by a daydreaming driver not expecting the tail of an airplane to suddenly appear in the roadway right in front of him. That hadn't happened yet at this strip, but I came uncomfortably close to being hit once.

We checked the controls to make sure they were free, scanned the oil pressure gauge, set the elevator trim and gave the engine a "run-up" to fifteen hundred RPM to check the two magnetos individually (usually about a one hundred RPM drop was expected when switched to one magneto only... which was considered O.K.). With everything looking normal, I smoothly applied power and we accelerated down the strip.

It was bizarre rolling along in an airplane past the owner's numerous endangerments: a double garage with less than ten feet of clearance from the wing, two large fuel-oil tanker trucks about six feet to the right, also his small shop on the right, then an old rubber wheeled tractor-loader and a giant pile of un-split firewood almost high enough to damage a wing tip. Next, a small aircraft hangar fifteen feet to one side and finally through a narrow path between two more high piles of split fireplace wood. All these things that were extremely close to the airplane path left an exceedingly narrow lane for anything, let alone an airplane. One mistake and a plane could hit one of these obstacles!

I'm sure that Ray was nervous cramped ahead of me into that tiny front seat, trusting his life to me. He had mentioned earlier that he didn't think of this as a bona fide airstrip, he having flown mostly from wide, long, paved runways in his flying career. But, here we were, headed directly for a six foot-high fence with very tall Douglas Fir trees just beyond. Oh, hadn't I mentioned those? To miss them, it was necessary to bank sharply right immediately after passing over the fence, because it wasn't possible to gain enough altitude to go directly over them. With a student pilot at the controls and a very heavy load of fuel, bodies, firearms and camping gear, I could envision Ray holding his hand firmly in place around the control stick between his legs. He had to be hoping to God that it wouldn't be necessary to wrench control away from me with the plane in a crazy pre-crash attitude somewhere in the middle of those giant trees ahead.

For a lot of early flyers, fields such as this were fairly typical. Having begun my serious flying here because the price was right (no high hangar rent or tie-down costs), this airfield matched early primitive conditions. Videos of hot jets landing on aircraft carriers never astound me

1961 150 horsepower Shinn, 121 built

A plane similar to this flew into our small airport at Seaside, Oregon, while I happened to be there. It so intrigued me that I made a point of meeting the pilot. He was an itinerant plane salesman and a certified flight instructor. Not wishing to pass an opportunity to fly an unusual airplane, I asked if he could "check me out" for a modest fee. He agreed and we had a great flight together...after which he signed my logbook with an entry appoving me for solo flight in this type of aircraft. My main interest was to add another unique logbook entry...and it was a pleasant surprise to find the little gem handled easily through the air, had great cockpit visibility and was a joy to fly.

as they do others. After learning to fly on this hair-raising minuscule strip through an obstacle course, it always looks to me like the carrier pilots are cheating by using catapults and arresting gear.

The ship cleared the fence and the trees by the usual narrow margin as I watched Ray poised in front...ready to grab at the controls.

Rolling out of the sharp right bank downwind, we aimed directly at the tip-top of Mt. Hood in the distance. Our plan was to fly to the north of the mountain and cross the foothills after reaching six thousand feet of altitude. From that route, we could view numerous snow-covered peaks to the south, plus look over to the vast Columbia River Gorge about twenty miles to the north.

Being a high-wing advocate, my thought was...why fly in a ship with a low wing and miss unique scenery views. Yes, there are slick aerodynamic benefits in low-winged airplanes because their structure eliminates drag-producing wing "struts"...but a slightly slower high-wing airplane offers superior views of Mother Earth. Think of the high-wing airplane salesman's pitch good-naturedly debunking the low wing ship: "*Did you ever see a low-winged bird?*"

Cruising east, the sun was rising behind famed Mt. Hood and about to appear in awe-inspiring glory! The mountain (named for an Englishman) glowed warmly with golds, pinks and oranges as the sun climbed into the crisp morning sky. How the souls of early mountain men and explorers must have been enraptured by the visual poetry of scenes like this!

As the plane droned along, we each drifted off into our private thoughts. Small airplanes make big noises in the cockpit and, without an intercom system, hearing one another is close to impossible. Because aircraft are constructed to be light, there is very little mass for absorbing the wild roar the "relatively-large" engines make. "Deafening" is a modest description of the din.

The bright scene of Mt. Hood snow now changed to the pure green of the Mt. Hood Forest, one of the most beautiful of all Douglas Fir timbered areas. We passed over a mountain trail where I'd ridden a motorcycle in earlier years as part of a large club activity.

Continuing, the terrain now shifted to dry sagebrush desert dotted with occasional wheat ranches appearing much like oases...then, across that great trout-fishing river, the Deschutes, and on through very sparsely-populated rolling hills of mixed sagebrush, wheat land and stony hillocks (not a good place for forced landings). It was necessary to pay very close attention to our "sectional chart" because there weren't many easily identifiable objects on desert hills. Getting lost in the desert is a common happening when navigating by "pilotage" (visual observation) rather than "radio navigation," an embarrassment for pilots who are theoretically supposed to know better. We crossed the John Day River and looked up and down for the ranch of Ray's friend. *It was nowhere in sight.*

Ray allowed that he had never seen the ranch from the air and had visited only by ground transportation. Landmarks, such as a ranch, can look remarkably different on land than from the air. Seasoned pilots have fits trying to mentally reconstruct from the air what they have visited on the ground. So, we engaged in a shouted verbal interchange.

Ray wanted to turn north and follow the river and I wanted to turn south. He went along with my choice most likely because of my plane ownership and I was paying for the fuel. After about ten minutes flying south, we had a second discussion. We agreed to continue for no more than two minutes…then do a 180 degree course reversal.

Finding nothing resembling what Ray *thought* the ranch should look like, we turned the plane around and headed back for the point at which we had crossed the river. Reaching that location, we continued north for a few minutes and lo and behold, there appeared a ranch that seemed to have all the markings of the one belonging to Ray's friend. There was no airstrip but Ray had remembered his friend telling him that small planes landed occasionally just across the barnyard fence to the east. We circled, checked out "the lay of the land" and, from our vantage point, landing looked possible. To get wind direction, we checked a distant dust cloud caused by a working farm tractor, set up a glide and landed the little ship just beyond a barbed wire fence about two hundred feet directly out from the ranch house.

While taxiing and turning to decide where to park, we made enough noise that we aroused people in the house and a couple of men came loping out to see who had arrived. This particular Saturday, they were not out in the fields as many were this time of year. This was good news for us because earlier, after we were airborne, Ray had informed me that he hadn't been able to make telephone contact with his rancher friend and we were taking a chance on finding someone at home.

The fellows stood watching as we shut down the engine, unlatched our belts and swung out onto terra firma. Ranchers will almost always stop whatever they are doing when airplanes are involved. Many wheat and cattle ranchers are pilots. To bridge distance, aircraft are a very logical mode of transportation for them. They usually have a lot of their own land to cover and most of them, conveniently, are quite mechanical. Many of them are members of the "Flying Farmers," an outstanding organization that offers them wonderful social contacts and involvements such as flight safety training.

By luck, the men turned out to be the rancher and his son and this day not only could they tell us where to hunt, they would be most happy to take time off to go hunting with us. Man, oh man, what good fortune! As it was still fairly early in the day, we were invited in for coffee, conversation and some late breakfast (good old Western hospitality) and to make hunting plans for the balance of the day.

The program would be to head out in their four-wheel drive pickup and first hunt the hills sloping down to the river for Chukar, the small wily game birds introduced to the U.S. from Asia a number of years ago and thriving here. Apparently, there had been a good hatch of these small desirable birds right on the ranch property.

All went well and the four of us had a great morning of hunting. Actually, that translates more to "shooting" when the quarry is Chukar, chiefly because they are almost impossible to hit unless one is a real pro with a shotgun. We had a fine time with the usual kidding of one another about missed shots. The man and his son turned out to be great sports, a lot of fun and very friendly. We returned to the ranch for lunch and went out again in the afternoon.

Hot and tired in late afternoon, we were invited to stay the night. This we appreciated, for we had hoped such would be the case and we then could forego rolling out our sleeping bags under the wings. We *happily* accepted.

Discussing hunting scheduled for the next day, it was decided that Ray and I would fly our plane out in the early morning to two or three locations, check those areas for birds, and then fly back to the ranch, from which we would all then drive back out to selected shooting grounds.

This brought up a small problem. My little ship carried only twelve gallons of fuel. We had used up most of it flying against headwinds on the trip over, plus used additional gas going the wrong way looking for the ranch. I wanted to use only the correct aviation fuel in my ship and the rancher had none. This would mean flying to the nearest airport to fill the fuel tank.

Ray and I talked over the situation and, after checking our chart, decided to take off immediately in late daytime and fly directly east to Lexington, about twenty minutes away…*under normal conditions*. According to the chart, the community had a small airport with a "fixed-base operator" who presumably could provide us with fuel. We fired up the plane and headed out on our mission. The sun was dipping low in the west as we flew east. "That shouldn't be a problem" we thought, as we would have just enough time to make it back to the ranch before dark. That is, *if everything went exactly right!*

Wishful thinking! We hadn't been in the air half the distance before the wind turned directly against us. Then, the sun moved a little lower, but we paid little attention while concentrating on navigation. Our destination town was *a very small target.*

With good luck, we flew directly to the airport...about ten minutes later than we had calculated because of the headwind...which was not necessarily a big problem…***yet!*** We taxied up to the fuel pumps and, when the prop stopped wind-milling, we looked around. *Not a soul in sight.* Hmmm! We walked quickly over to what appeared to be a sort of shop-office combination and looked in. *Locked up tight.* Hmmm *again!*

After shuffling around a bit, we noticed a small hand-lettered sign on a shop door. It directed customers to call the written number if no one was on the premises to provide service. We spotted a pay phone all alone on the edge of the hard surface area and I walked over and dropped a dime in (imagine that!). After dialing the number given, I was gratified to hear a welcome voice answer...the "gas-man" himself. Boy, was this good luck! Yes, *we needed fuel.* ***NOW!*** It was getting late quickly and we had to get back to the ranch. Sure, he would be happy to drive out to the airport. He said it would take him only a few minutes. I now noted nervously that the sun seemed to be sinking…like a rock!

The man showed up quite a few minutes later than he had implied he would. Tensely glancing to the west, I sensed that I could actually *see the sun move...downward.* And, it was right *on the horizon!*

The minutes ticked by ominously.

Now...why was I becoming so extremely fidgety? Well, my airplane was not equipped for flying at night, had no electrical system, hence no lights with which to see or be seen. Early on, very small planes seldom were built with electrical systems because they used up engine power and added too much weight. Plus, the systems are entirely unnecessary for the engine to run because "ignition" arrives from dual magnetos (a second one exists for "backup" safety) that create their own electricity to fire the spark plugs.

In our situation with no electrical system, the airplane had no navigation lights, no landing lights to light up a runway and no lights to illuminate the plane's instruments! Also, we foolishly had brought no flashlight with us and, even if we had, we had no instruments that would allow us to keep the airplane right side up if the night became so dark that we could not make out the horizon. And…it was going to be a very, very, black night. Need more be said? We just wanted to get back to an evening meal and warm beds...*pronto!*

Having paid the gas man, we started the engine and hopped in...all in quickstep motion. Holy mackerel, we *had* to get in the air! That sun-ball had now dropped to what appeared to be two inches plus below the horizon. I firewalled the throttle, turned away from the pumps and took off directly from the taxiway in one big sweep, banking sharply in the direction from which we had come.

Next, not only was the sun pulling a disappearing act, the wind now reversed itself 180 degrees and turned directly against us...again!

Consider how critical this can be! If a plane cruises normally at eighty miles an hour, as ours did, a thirty-mile an hour headwind reduces over-the-ground speed to fifty miles an hour net. This increases travel time considerably. Pilots who wish to live long consider these things in advance and plan each flight accordingly. Obviously, I still had much to learn…but, then, why hadn't Ray thought of this? *He was the expert.* Even sharp pilots sometimes make mistakes. Those...*you read about in the papers!*

I shoved the throttle forward much farther than the normal seventy-five percent power position to overcome the negative headwind effect… not a move that made me happy as that increases engine wear substantially and consumes a lot more fuel. Then…the sun slipped *completely out of sight.*

Perspiring, a clammy dampness swept over us as fear became our new companion! Interesting how two pilots in the same airplane have difficulty admitting to one another that they have made a potentially fatal mistake. As we journeyed toward the quickly darkening horizon, dead silence prevailed. We both knew we were headed for trouble, but neither of us uttered a word.

Of course, we could have been intelligent about this and used some basic common sense. We simply could have turned back immediately, landed at the same airport we had just left and solved the whole problem by calling our friends on the phone to come get us.

The beautiful orange sky still remaining from the newly-hidden sun began to darken very rapidly. The wind held steady in our face. The odds against us were increasing exponentially. The cold sweat of panic began to grip us! Still, neither of us voiced a word. And now, it was too late to turn back. We had used up too much distance and the airport behind wasn't lighted so returning there was not an option. Our options were diminishing! We peered ahead toward the dimming horizon and searched for the ranch. The night sky was now so dark that all the ranches for miles around had pale lights showing. But, which was our friend's? With no landmarks visible, we couldn't be sure. We could see absolutely nothing now except a few very dim lights to our left, right and directly behind us.

I finally broke the silence. "Ray, I see three sets of lights way up ahead to the left and right. Which do you think is the ranch?"

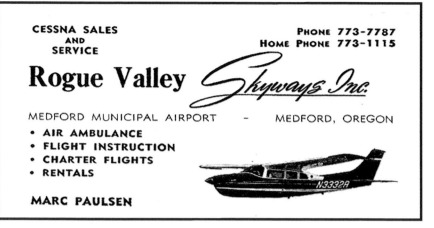

CESSNA SALES
AND
SERVICE

PHONE 773-7787
HOME PHONE 773-1115

Rogue Valley *Skyways Inc.*

MEDFORD MUNICIPAL AIRPORT - MEDFORD, OREGON

- AIR AMBULANCE
- FLIGHT INSTRUCTION
- CHARTER FLIGHTS
- RENTALS

MARC PAULSEN

My airplane salesman business card

Beginning the activity with only a "Private Pilot, Single-Engine-Land" rating, I took a job selling airplanes in 1969. Unfortunately, that was the exact time that a fairly long plane sales boom came to an abrupt end. Although it was a struggle to sell planes (Cessna did however, sell about 3,000 "150" trainers during this period), I found it to be an exhilarating occupation and met a lot of very interesting people in the couple of years of my sales activities...which I left when offered a challenging project management position in the timber and lumber industry.

An uneasy silence...it grew even darker.

"Heck, I don't know. I don't have a clue!"

"Well, pick one," I snapped back.

To this he returned abruptly, "***You pick one!***"

I responded sharply, "What the heck, we have to do something! Let's fly to the one ahead on the right."

"I think it's probably the one dead-ahead," was his growling response. Obviously, we weren't getting anywhere with this exchange. We could barely make out the ground by looking straight down. It was time for serious action! "Ray, I'm thinking of a number from one to ten," I yelled at him over the sound of the engine. "Pick a number and, if you're on the high side of it, we will go dead ahead. If you pick low, we'll head to the light on the right."

I thought number five. I guess he had the magnitude of the impending disaster pretty well plotted out, because he instantly turned his head to the side and yelled, "Six!"

I was surprised at his instantaneous response, because, in every other situation I had ever known him, it seemed he applied much time and thought to making careful decisions.

We continued straight ahead...both secretly praying.

As we arrived at the selected light, the sky appeared to be black orange, a hue that might have been considered romantic any other time but this. A few hundred feet from the light and the attached buildings, we could make out forms, fences and farm equipment…and *hot-dog!... it was our ranch!*

Banking immediately into a low, slow turn, we lined up with the outline of the barely visible fence we'd landed by earlier. Yanking back the throttle, we bumped onto the ground hard and rolled to a stop…almost sideways...miraculously *in one piece,* thank our guardian angels! With both of us still shaking with fright, I reached up and shut off the ignition switch and we sat *very* quietly for a *very* long moment. We then looked out of the plane toward the house.

The night was now as black as soot. Without saying a word to each other, we got out of the plane and looked again toward the house. Now, we couldn't see the fence from *fifteen feet* away.

We stood still for a while, waiting for our eyes to adjust to the now solid black night, felt for the fence, found it, climbed over, then groped slowly toward the dim lights of the house

Not for the rest of the trip, *nor ever,* did we discuss how close we imprudently had taken ourselves to the edge of potentially serious consequences that night on the desert. We knew that, if we had been just a couple of more minutes in the air, the situation would have made necessary landing the airplane in total blackness in the middle of nowhere with no reference points (assuming we could even keep it flying upright).

I'll guarantee you…my flight planning became much more intense and comprehensive after that extremely black night of nights!

28.62 Inches / 176 MPH

This title notes the second lowest barometer reading ever recorded in the state of Oregon and the highest wind speed recorded during the ill-famed Oregon Columbus Day storm of 1962. The wind speed is still an all-time record.

If Columbus had an accurate barometer on his ship and it read the same as on that historic Columbus Day in Northwestern Oregon (and he knew then what we now know about meteorology), he probably would have had a heart attack and dropped dead of fright knowing that extremely bad news soon would be on its potentially mast-smashing, sail-ripping destructive way.

There is still some debate over the wind speed. According to one weather expert, the strongest wind in the storm occurred on Mount Hebo in the coastal Cascade Mountain Range with the wind speed of 176 mph. That anemometer recording the event failed and came apart shortly after recording the super wind gust. The mph variations really didn't make much difference. The results were catastrophic! The wind gust velocity in the Portland area ranged up to 119 mph and that is where I had my pride and joy Piper Cub J-3/85 "tied down" at a private airstrip.

This storm was unusual for another reason. Portland's KGW radio station had a weatherman who was sharp enough, before anyone else, to read the importance of early signs of the massive storm. After hearing a report from a radar picket-ship off the Northern California coast stating a barometric pressure reading of 28.42 inches, he began to closely watch the teletype, our method of instant communication at that time. He noted Oregon coastal city radio stations stopped transmitting and correctly reasoned that they had lost power due to high winds in the early stages of the storm. Because the barometric readings were so significant, he did what few in his position had ever done. He made the forecast of his life!

"The worst storm ever known in this area is approaching Portland and the Willamette Valley right now," the weatherman told listeners. "I have never seen reports like this before. This is going to cause a lot of damage." The reader must keep in mind that he was making his determinations based on his education and experience…and had far less information to work with than modern meteorologists. But, he was spot on! The broadcast went out at 5:15 P.M. and soon the sky turned dark. Not long after, the "Storm of the Century" arrived with a vengeance.

I remember clearly the very unusual feelings I had the evening the storm broke. At about the same time the storm broadcast went out, as I stood outside a strange feeling swept over me, a feeling that my body had "loosened." In retrospect, that was somewhat factual because, with the rapidly dropping ambient air pressure, my body did change shape and enlarge slightly. It was one of the strangest feelings I've ever experienced. The ambient air seemed to warm considerably and, strangely, all was still and calm...as the pressure dropped rapidly and drastically. I remember exactly where I was when I remarked to one nearby that the weather seemed uniquely unusual and felt a little weird. That turned out to be a major understatement!

According to those who have studied the storm, a Pacific typhoon named Frieda crossed the entire ocean (against what should have been prevailing winds) and slammed into Oregon with unbelievable might…an event never recorded before…or since. Locally, fifty people were killed. Hundreds of thousands (possibly millions) of trees were blown down in the forests and more tens of thousands over, into and across roadways. Thousands of flat, tar-papered commercial building roofs were lifted right off their buildings by the aerodynamic forces of the relative wind. (Such a force creates a low-pressure area on tops of flat buildings and generates "lift" much like an airplane wing, simply raising the roofing right up and ripping it away.) Fifty thousand homes were damaged, many severely. Orchards were ruined. Livestock was killed when large barns with massive walls collapsed. The damage cost approached a billion dollars. Airplane owners learned first-hand what wind can do to a plane when it's not in the air. Even hangars thought to be safe proved less than effective.

Early the next morning (which was surprisingly calm after the storm), I drove my pickup to the private airstrip to survey my aircraft situation.

Aeronca "Champ" - more than 10,000 built

This cute little ship had a lot more front-seat leg-room than my J-3 Cub. The air seemed to be alive with these just after WWII.

Taylorcraft Model BC-12-D

I took a Taylorcraft like this in trade when I sold one of my planes. Although it came with a very desirable 85 HP engine, the cabin was so tiny I could barely fit in. After squeezing in, it was so difficult to operate the flight controls that it was necessary to sell the aircraft to someone of much smaller stature.

I grabbed my 35mm camera and a couple of rolls of color slide film and tried six different routes before finding one over which I could thread my way through many downed trees choking the road system. It was just pure luck that I finally worked my way through the road system at all. At that, I had to hook onto a couple of trees with a chain and use my pickup as a tractor to tug them far enough off the road to allow me through. The aftermath mess and the damage were plainly catastrophic!

When I reached the strip, it was apparent that no other plane owners had made it that far. No one was there! Even more surprising, the planes tied down there showed only very minor damage, if any. Hearing early morning news horror stories of death and devastation everywhere in the area, I had feared total destruction! Viewing the very limited damage on the strip, it became apparent that, because the airfield was located between two high hills, most of the vicious winds had skipped right over the entire field…a great stroke of luck for those of us with planes tied down there.

I rushed up to my little Piper Cub and immediately saw a problem. The plane was tied with the tail in the direction from which a few strong wind gusts had come and, as a result, the rudder was severely bent. Bad news! There was also good news! That was the only damage on the plane. Apparently, the field had experienced only a few serious gusts.

I stood disgruntled because my ship was disabled and could not be flown. Then I brightened after checking out the plane parked next to mine, a Piper Model J-5 of about the same vintage and, as I looked it over, it appeared the planes' rudders were identical. Upon closer inspection, it appeared to me that the J-5 rudder might fit right on my plane.

There were no other souls in sight. What I wanted to do was fly around the area and see what had happened to other planes on other fields. I figured, "Well, this is an emergency situation…if I am going to fly to other airports to see how they have fared, I guess I'll just have to borrow that rudder." The plane owner was a good friend and I figured would understand…and he probably wouldn't be as lucky as I to make it through all the downed trees on the highways. Fortunately, this thinking proved correct.

A pair of pliers, a couple of small tools and about fifteen minutes of effort and I successfully "borrowed" his rudder. The J-5 rudder fit perfectly and did the job admirably.

After an uneventful takeoff, I headed for the nearest large general aviation airport at Troutdale, Oregon, and saw that the airfield was a disaster area. From afar, I could see planes upside down on the tops of buildings, crunched-up planes in the middle of the field and building roofs collapsed on beautiful new and old flying machines alike.

The wind velocity at this airport peaked with gusts to 106 miles per hour. Pity the aircraft owner who had a sense of well-being from securing his ship for winds that seldom exceeded forty or fifty miles per hour. This storm was extremely educational for millions of people. This airport alone had more than fifty planes damaged or destroyed...and there were more than half a dozen moderately-sized airports and quite a number of private strips in our area.

I took a number of photos of planes and some very sad owners doing their best to salvage what they might. Although I'd started out quite early on my sojourn of viewing and photographing, many plane owners had rushed out (those who could make their way through roads dotted with downed trees) even earlier to check out the condition of their prized possessions. In quite a few cases, they had already acquired help in righting upside-down ships and rolled them back into tie-down positions. Most of the photos I took were of planes still outside of their hangars and those with the most damage.

For my next two visits, I crossed the Columbia River into Washington State and first landed at Evergreen Airport, a few miles east of Vancouver. The situation was the same...massive damage with airplane owners wandering around in a daze as they surveyed ship after ship after ship ripped apart by the powerful forces of nature. Flying from there to nearby Pearson Airpark in the city of Vancouver...the situation was much the same. There, I fueled up my Cub and took photos of more scattered damage.

Then, I flew back into Oregon and visited two more airports, Beaverton and Hillsboro. Again, devastation! On the way, I was shocked to see large half-acre warehouses here and there with their entire roofs unfrocked and their interiors exposed to the elements. This exposure caused tremendous damage because the next day a wet front moved in and blanketed the whole area with driving sheets of heavy rain. Anything still exposed that could be damaged by water...*was!*

Although my plane escaped major damage, I sustained a serious loss at another small private strip (the old Virgil Buroker strip) where I'd been given space in a hangar to store tools, equipment, personal gear and business records. The hangar was blown down and next day's heavy rain damaged materials I didn't have time to rescue. Fortunately, there had been

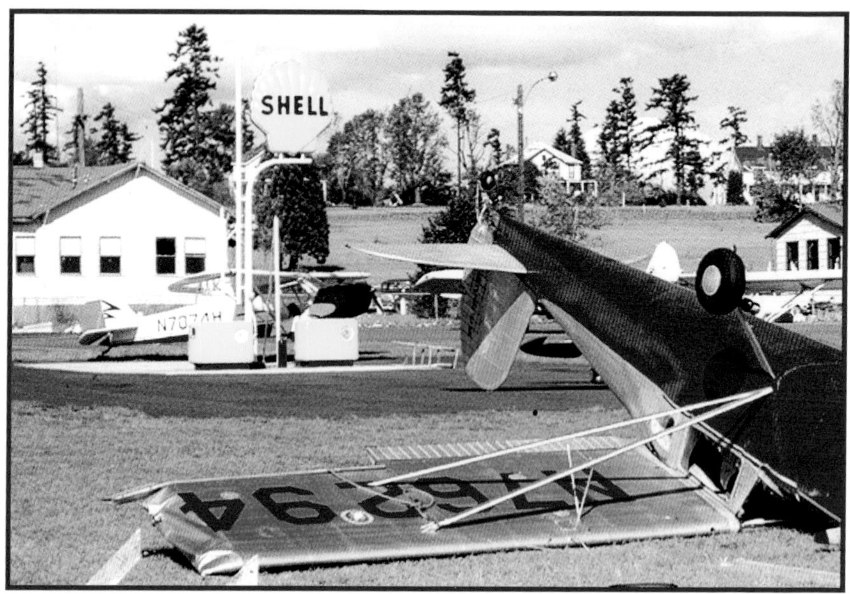

One Result Of The Great Columbus Day Windstorm, 1962

My J-3 Cub is in the background at the gas pumps (with the blue rudder). Years later, the Pearson Air Museum was established here in Vancouver, Washington. I then donated my color slide photos of the widespread windstorm airplane damage to the museum.

no airplane in the hangar and no airplanes on this field sustained major damage, perhaps due to a small forest of large Douglas fir trees upwind a couple of blocks away that acted as a windscreen.

In all, that morning, I took sixty-three color slide photos of major airplane and hangar damage. The storm's effect resulted in the biggest aircraft damage disaster in Oregon history.

Happening across the photos a few years later, I called the Oregon Historical Society and asked if they had a good photo history of airplane damage caused by the great blow. Surprisingly, they did not. I let them copy my slides for their records and later donated the originals to the Pearson Air Museum in Vancouver, Washington, the site of much damage during the epochal storm...and the location of the photo illustrated above.

The massive damage suggested a couple of thoughts. Airplane owners should monitor weather reports and be prepared to take quick action... such as moving a plane's location when extra-large storms are predicted. Second, if that isn't possible, make sure an airplane is in a very strong hangar or most certainly, "tied-down" exceedingly well. Many times I have watched as plane owners tied down a plane with inadequate rope or chain, poor knots and what might be called a lack of attention to detail. In this case, those types of action turned out to be disastrous for a great many plane owners. My bet is that those same people won't make those same mistakes again. On the other hand, there is always a new generation coming along who hasn't yet witnessed good ol' Mother Nature in a bad mood. They might be wise to study some history.

Hugh Hefner's "Big Bunny" Playboy DC-9

Imagine the surprise of our flight office staff when we came to work one morning at our Rogue Valley Skyways flight operation in Medford, Oregon, and found this massive new airplane (of *airliner* size) parked among our smaller airplanes. It was *rumored* that Playboy Corporation had set up a leasing company in Oregon to avoid paying sales tax...and simply took "legal delivery" of it at our airport. (Oregon had no sales tax.)

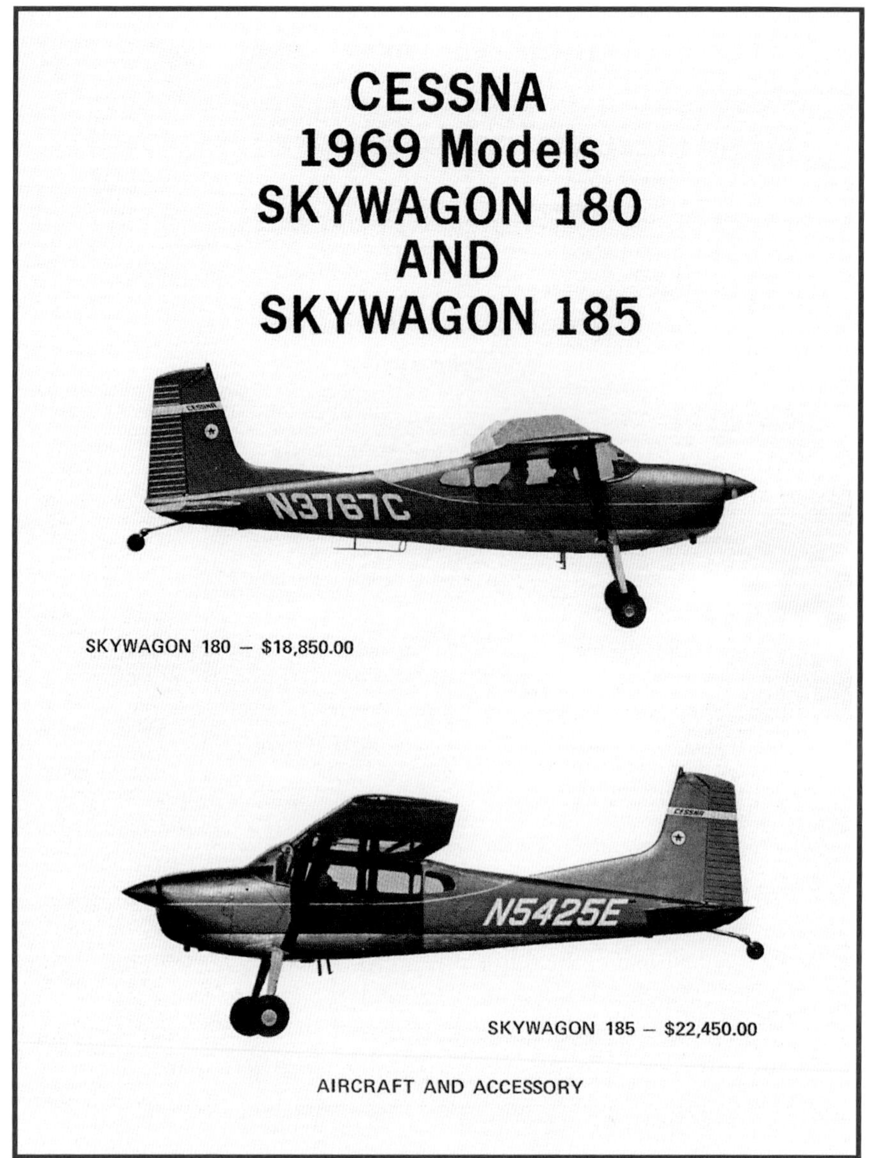

CESSNA
1969 Models
SKYWAGON 180
AND
SKYWAGON 185
N3767C
SKYWAGON 180 – $18,850.00
N5425E
SKYWAGON 185 – $22,450.00
AIRCRAFT AND ACCESSORY

Cessna 180 / 185

When I was selling these ships in 1969, little did I imagine that in future years the same airplanes (some now with very high flying times on their airframes) would command prices well into six figures.

Fantasy Takes Wing

In eastern Oregon, solo cross-country flight in a Piper Cub can be described as the closest thing to heaven for a new pilot. The weather is clear and bright much of the time and there is little or no air traffic out in the wide-open spaces of America's western high desert. As a result, it is possible to drop down low and cruise along a few feet off the ground, giving one a feeling of brotherhood with the jackrabbits and coyotes. Flying so close to the ground generates an experience of exhilaration like that displayed by the happy-go-lucky aviators in the movie, "Those Magnificent Men in Their Flying Machines"*...a sensation of mastery of the universe.*

The freedom of movement in so much three-dimensional space adds to the thrill of flying there and of being the pilot in command. When you are way out in the sparsely-populated country, you can waggle the stick back and forth, up and down, any which way you wish and get an instant response that gives you a little of that feeling the birds must have. Then, you can sit back, relax and dreamily gaze in a trance straight ahead through the little vertical wire with the half-inch ninety-degree hook that serves as the gas gauge (in a Piper J-3 Cub) and stands tall just in front of the windshield. *Just don't go to sleep!*

I had a close acquaintance I'd known for years who started a flying service in Alaska. He worked hard and the business grew rapidly. First, he had two planes, then three. Things went well and he would visit the "lower forty-eight" occasionally to buy planes. One day I asked a mutual friend why I hadn't seen him for a while and was jolted by the news that he had fallen asleep while ferrying a new plane up to Anchorage. The trips were so long and tedious that it was very difficult to refrain from falling asleep and, in his case, *he did only once!*

The time was November, 1962, and here I was with time on my hands, an airplane in my control, plenty of fuel in the tank, money in my pocket and flying along over the desert with no firm destination in mind and adventure in my soul. Winter was a time of intermittent activity in my line of masonry work, so being able to fly about during this quiet period was a great pleasure. Ah, *life was sweet!*

After a long day of flying and making stops for gas and food, first at Madras and then Burns, I found myself near the southeastern Oregon/Nevada border where one can look toward the horizon and see only desert for miles and miles and miles. In a few places, low mountains will appear in the distance, reflecting a beautiful hue of hazy blue in a dream-like setting.

This balmy fall afternoon was beginning its soft transition into evening and it was time to find a place to land and get lodging for the night. It wasn't my style to get concerned about a place to sleep. In a pinch, I could land anywhere in the desert since I had along a sleeping bag and camping gear. "But," I thought, "It might be more enjoyable to visit a town, have a little more comfort and find someone with whom to have conversation and dinner."

I had a full complement of charts with me for the entire region and knew approximately where I was, even with the dearth of landmarks in the desert. Thinking the situation over, I realized I was still quite a few miles from any town large enough to have an airport. Interestingly enough, some minor headwinds had appeared earlier and, when flying a relatively slow airplane, this can change flight planning considerably. Sometimes v*ery quickly* and *very considerably.* With a slow airplane, sudden unfavorable winds can bring up little problems like running out of fuel short of your destination...not a keen situation.

My initial plan had been to arrive at Lovelock, Nevada, a small town about 60 miles south of the Oregon border. I'd show up there about five in the evening of this crystal clear fall afternoon, giving ample time to get my bearings and secure the airplane. At this latitude at this time of year, darkness began to fall about five-thirty. I had no lights on the plane and the small airports in my flight path were unlighted, with no electronic navigation aids to help. As a student pilot with just one night landing to my credit, I didn't think it very wise to end up searching for an airport in the dark. This was not to mention my apprehension at possibly being forced to attempt my second night landing at a strange field...a scary thought for a relatively inexperienced pilot.

I now stopped thinking about jackrabbits and the beauty of the landscape and concentrated on determining if my direction and fuel was going to get me to Lovelock, Nevada, where I needed to land before nightfall... the only nearby airport in my path illustrated on the aeronautical chart. The timing would be close! At twilight, I made out some ranches which were noted on the chart landmarks and felt comforted knowing that the small town targeted was near. It was going to be almost dark as I arrived so there wasn't a minute to spare. Soon, the early evening lights of the town came in sight. I had planned my timing about right and now was over the town…but *where was the airport?*

The airport was depicted on my map so all that should be necessary would be to fly over the town to that general vicinity...and the airport would appear. I circled and circled and looked and looked but couldn't see it anywhere. Darkness was approaching fast. Where had I gone wrong? Where was that airport? My fuel was getting low. The sky was darkening rapidly. Panic threatened to get a choke hold on me. Damn those changing winds!

While circling, I saw a giant cattle feedlot used for preparing animals for market which appeared within walking distance of the town center. From above, I could almost read the neon signs on the taverns downtown. In the middle of the feed-lot were two of the biggest, longest stacks of baled hay I had ever seen, maybe five or six hundred feet long and twenty or thirty feet high. On closer scrutiny, it appeared that between the stacks was a space wide enough for my plane, but with only a little room to spare...and the only place in sight where there were no cattle or other obstacles. This was the moment of truth. Banking the plane around in a tight turn, I straightened it out, reduced the power and sideslipped (a maneuver done by manipulating the controls to slow the plane) down between the stacks.

The surface was relatively smooth and, luckily, I was able to hold the plane straight down the middle between the stacks of hay. While shutting down the engine, a pickup drove up with a cowhand at the wheel.

"Howdy," he greeted me.

"Howdy," I replied.

"What can I do for you?" he offered pleasantly.

He didn't seem as surprised as I thought he should be by my aerial arrival. Apparently, a lot of flying ranchers landed much the same way… maybe on a regular basis. I explained that I'd wanted to land at the town's airport but hadn't been able to find it and asked if he knew where it was. At this, he chuckled and explained that the "airport" I was referring to was nothing more than a grass field somewhat overgrown and little used. He did know where it was and gave me directions. By now, it was almost dark but, like the gambling man I am, decided it better to gamble and try to find the airport quickly than run the risk of getting the plane shoved around by curious cows nosing about the big stacks of hay.

Have you ever noticed how rapidly light turns to dark in the fall? Doesn't evening sometimes seem like there is a hidden force controlling the level of darkness? Well, that's how it seemed this night. I no sooner took off from between the hay bales, whisked over to the landing field, touched down on the strip and darkness moved in. Fortunately, the strip had been easy to find. Because of the conditions, taxiing was impossible.

Shutting the engine down, I got out of the plane and walked around for a while as my eyes became accustomed to the darkness...then picked the plane up by the tail and walk it to what looked like a parking area. I couldn't find a tiedown location, wasn't sure there were any...and figured that, if getting back early enough in the morning, I could fly out before a wind came up and blew my little cloth-covered machine away for lack of an adequate tie-down arrangement. A Cub weighs only about seven to eight hundred pounds empty, thus a problem with high winds.

Leaving the plane and taking my chances, I threw my gear on my shoulder and hiked across the end of the field for town. ***And that is when I saw it!***

On the far corner of the strip, I spotted a large object. Drawing closer, my eyes widened. In the darkness, I could just barely make out the shape of a biplane with silver fuselage and rudder. Though dark, the wings and elevator appeared colored. The plane looked to be in flyable condition. More importantly, visible in the profile were two neat little curved plastic windshields indicating two cockpits. It was hard to see well, but beyond a shadow of a doubt, this was not a typical military surplus WWII trainer-plane made into a cropduster! This was a real-life aerobatic two-cockpit antique biplane!

The unusual significance of this can be explained with the story of what happened to almost all of the many thousands of WWII biplane trainer planes and most other historic biplanes which existed up to and after WWII. The end of the war made thousands of biplane trainer ships available at bargain prices. After the war, agriculture boomed and there was a tremendous need for equipment to efficiently spread newly-developed herbicides, pesticides and fertilizers on expanding farms all over the U.S. To fill this need, the big ubiquitous Boeing Stearman "trainer" biplanes (thousands and thousands were made) with their super-strong structures and large beefy wings were re-powered with larger 450 horse-power engines and fitted out as crop sprayers and dusters. As the 1960s came along (when I became interested in flying), almost all of the surplus biplanes from the military had been utilized for this purpose, and many of these had by now crashed or been cannibalized for parts leaving their numbers greatly diminished. Many more were snatched up inexpensively by sportsman pilots or ex-airmen who tried to make a living giving flying lessons to what they thought were going to be droves of postwar pilots. That didn't happen. When people realized that flying a plane is not as simple as driving a car, the postwar flight instruction boom collapsed and most of the biplanes used for that form of training then were converted to "Ag" planes.

Of the few "pure" antique biplanes remaining from the thirties and earlier that were still airworthy, most also had been converted to "crop-dusters." So, seeing an intact two-cockpit biplane sitting all alone on what was otherwise a deserted and little-used field really piqued my interest. The fellow who owned the private airstrip where I based my plane had owned a Stearman for a few years, and had romanticized to me about it so much that I had developed a terrible case of the "*I wants.*"

It is important to understand the lure of the air from the point of view of a novice pilot thrilled with every aspect of the aviation world. By the late sixties, the Red Baron image of flight was drifting into distant history and very large, very fast, very heavy and very expensive flying machines were rapidly becoming the norm. These were quickly moving up in price and were mostly beyond the financial reach of the average person of modest means. The kids who built model airplanes during and after the "stick and rudder" era (and who grew up dreaming about flying and maybe sometime owning a plane) had grown up to the reality that the open-cockpit hero period was definitely over. Reality now meant one had to have lots of money to fly expensive airplanes. And when one did, such flight most likely would be in a very mundane modern craft lacking the romantic scarf and goggles of the bygone epoch. However, buying a relatively inexpensive slow mundane plane such as mine was still possible.

I had my first ride in a Piper Cub model J-3 the year after WWII ended. My cousin was just out of the Army Air Forces and gave me the ride as a birthday present. I was 12 years old. The thrill I felt during that ride as I left

Mother Earth for the heavens then returned to earth can be described only as about ten steps beyond mere exhilaration. I never forgot that exciting ride on a warm summer day. The cost was two dollars and fifty cents for a short flight. I remember clearly that the plane was bright yellow. Almost all the Cubs were yellow then. It was a stock machine with a sixty-five-horse engine and had a minimal instrument panel with only the very basic gauges. Easily remembering all that, plus learning much more about airplanes, I never got over wanting to repeat the experience. That flight made me feel like I was soaring with eagles...and it seemed that the absolute ultimate way to soar with them...would be...*in an open cockpit biplane!*

Walking around this biplane, I checked the machine out as best possible in the dark. Talk about romance! This plane had a radial engine with five huge exposed cylinders and the longest wooden prop I'd ever seen. There weren't many props like that left. The propeller was indeed a giant that appeared to be at least eight feet from tip to tip. The landing gear looked to be about eight or ten feet between wheels and the rudder looked like the shape of a Douglas DC-3 rudder. Never having seen anything like this plane, I couldn't figure out what make and model it was…but I knew for sure that this was the type of ship that a lot of guys would kill for.

Compared to my Cub, the plane was truly a giant but, then, almost any airplane seems giant next to a Cub. I could visualize myself at the helm of this ship doing aerobatics and landing and taking off while wearing the de rigueur helmet and goggles, windblown scarf, flying suit, parachute and the other accoutrements that make for a dramatic exhibition. My thoughts raced with the imagined glamour, "What was this plane doing here all alone? What if, by some fortunate stroke of fate, this intriguing ship might be available for purchase."

During the short walk into Lovelock, I envisioned what might be and was consumed by the possibilities. At town center, I searched out a restaurant, having in mind both eating dinner and asking about the plane's ownership. Surely, in a town this small, everyone would know the owner.

Not remembering the food, I certainly remember that the *first* person I conversed with knew all about the plane (plus almost everything else one would need or want to know about the plane's owner, this little burg and its people).

Imagine my awe when then told that the owner had recently died at age seventy-eight, had flown the plane until very recently and had owned the plane for decades! A local character, everyone in town knew him and of his plane. The old man had few relatives and, as far as was known, no relative or other party yet had laid claim to the plane. My source also knew the name of the lawyer handling the estate so now I was set to go in search of this flying "holy grail" by the shortest route possible. At the only hotel in town, I got a room and took a long time closing my eyes in sleep.

Upon rising the next morning, I rushed to breakfast, gulped down my food, then found the nearest phone. I called the lawyer's office but was too early. Later, his secretary told me that he had a prior appointment and to wait for a couple of hours while he finished some work with a local rancher. Finally getting him on the phone, he said, "Yes, I am the attorney for the estate," and "No, there are no claims on the airplane as yet."

Would he meet me for lunch to discuss this? "Sure. Be happy to!" I could think of absolutely nothing to do to kill the time so simply paced about town looking in meagerly-stocked store windows while waiting for the zero hour. Then, finally, it was noon.

EVERGREEN FLYING SERVICE, INC.
TAYLORCRAFT
CESSNA
INSTRUCTION — CHARTER SERVICE

PHONE OXford 3-6271 VANCOUVER, WASH.
ROUTE 1, BOX 2940

Date 9-16-62 195

M

Address

SOLD BY	CASH	C.O.D.	CHARGE	ON ACCT.	MDSE. RETD.	PAID OUT
	✓					

QUAN.	DESCRIPTION	PRICE	AMOUNT
3.7	#80 AVIATION	30	1 11
			1.15
WASH.	STATE ROAD TAX EXCLUDED		
METER	READING		
METER	READING		
	NET GALS.		

ALL claims and returned goods MUST be accompanied by this bill
2587 Rec'd by

Yep, that's thirty cents a gallon! My J-3 Cub's hourly fuel cost was less than the price of a latter-day-LATTE!

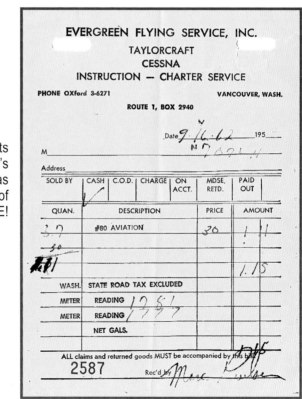

The attorney arrived wearing a suit that seemed out of place in this tiny western town, and gave the appearance that he hadn't been in the area for long. Out here in ranch country, I had expected to see him wearing cowboy boots like almost everybody but me.

At once, I worried that he might act like a big city lawyer and try to squeeze as much cash as he could from me, if, in fact, the plane might be available. If he knew how many pilots would do almost anything to own a biplane, there would be no question as to how negotiations would go. Thus, I was very surprised to hear him indicate that he didn't know much about airplanes and wasn't very interested in them. Also, he said, "Yes, there is a very good chance that you can buy the plane if we can come to an agreement on value. I am the executor of the old gentleman's estate and would like to find a buyer." Evidently, his main interest was simply in doing his duty of settling the estate and clearing up all details. I was dying to find out what type of plane it was.

Upon learning the details of the plane's existence, my delight knew no bounds! Already, in my imagination, I could smell the oil smoke in my nostrils from the starting of that great big radial engine. I almost could feel my white silk scarf whipping about my neck from the glorious open cockpit breeze blown back from that giant spinning prop. I was well on the way to becoming a "*Magnificent Man in a Flying Machine!*"

The attorney told me what he knew of the old gentleman's story, and I was amazed to hear that the old man had flown the plane one week before he died at his age of seventy-eight. From reading the man's records and from family members, the attorney had learned much about the story of the biplane. The family even had the man's Private Pilot Log Book and would be happy to let me go through it. According to the lawyer, the old man had purchased the plane as U.S. Government surplus in 1946, the year after the end of WWII and had been the only owner after the military. The plane had been a "primary" trainer and was manufactured in 1943. He had flown it for eighteen consecutive years. The pilot's logbook told the story of a very stable, constant flyer. Entries in the book showed that he had flown weekly or bi-weekly for most of the eighteen years of his active life of flight. The engine log books indicated a history of good maintenance and showed a fairly recent engine major-overhaul. The attorney wasn't acquainted with the make of the plane but, to me, that didn't matter. My prospects sounded better all the time. As good as this story was, the attorney saved the best part for last.

Not only did this unique old WWII trainer have an unusual and interesting ownership history, very recently it had been leased for a period of time by *MGM Studios* for movie work. And, *would you believe it*, the movie it was used in was "*The Misfits*" with *Clark Gable* and *Marilyn Monroe,* the last movie each one of them played in before their deaths ended their illustrious careers.

For proof, records came with the plane that indicated in writing beyond doubt that a movie role had been part of the plane's history. Amazing! Sitting in this plane would be to sit where Clark Gable had leaned over to chat while the cameras rolled with Marilyn contributing her enigmatic aura as well. This was too much…I had to see those logbooks! We left the restaurant and walked to the attorney's office, where he produced them and left me alone to read in amazed fascination.

The plane was a Meyers OTW and, sure enough, there was an entry where MGM had taken temporary possession of the plane, and then subsequent entries noting flying in the desert in search of and rounding up mustang horses, a part of the movie. An interesting entry showed that a major fuselage airframe repair had been made after a movie company truck had damaged the plane by backing into the side of it. Unfortunately, there were no personal signatures of the stars but, still, this was solid documentation of a fabled past with two of the most important movie stars in the history of cinema. What a fabulous association! But, *down to business.*

I had to admit that I had never heard of a Meyers OTW but I had been reading magazines like Trade-A-Plane, an aviation-only magazine advertising planes, parts and accessories for sale. From that reading, I had a very good idea of what a biplane in decent condition should be worth under various circumstances.

The engine logbook stated that the Kinner R-56, five-cylinder, 540 cubic inch displacement radial engine had been major-overhauled only sixty hours of flight time earlier. The "airframe" logbook had a recent entry indicating the fabric wings and elevators had been newly re-covered. The information available looked like all good news. So, I asked to be taken out to the plane to see it in daylight.

The lawyer agreed and out we drove. In the daylight, the plane looked even more romantic and wonderful. In fact, fantastic! Inspecting the plane thoroughly, I admired the bright polished aluminum fuselage and rudder and noted a section on the side of the fuselage that was shinier than the rest…apparently the spot where MGM had damage repaired. I inspected the big lower-wing single elevators, about eight feet long, and marveled at the large amount of wing area in the two wings. The engine and the visible carburetion system drew my attention. They both looked exceptionally clean and tidy. I gazed lovingly at the beautiful laminated and varnished wooden prop with the colorful “Sensenich” manufacturer’s decal that looked almost new. I never had sat in a biplane so now I took the liberty. *I had found my destiny!*

The attorney drove back to town with my brain churning. Could I negotiate a super low price and own this outstanding plane? Could I be that fortunate? YES, this could happen! It was clear that the lawyer didn’t know or care about planes. Apparently, he had no one knowledgeable about planes advising him.

I didn’t have much cash on hand so I’d have to borrow from the bank. I knew a bank wouldn’t lend money to me to buy a plane, but I felt sure I could talk them into loaning some to me as working capital for my modest contracting business. *I just had to have this plane!*

Broaching the subject of price, the attorney said he didn’t know much about plane values but anything reasonable would be considered. My heart pounded. This was too good to be true!

Did the estate have a price in mind? He said not as far as he knew. If I would make an offer, he would take the offer into consideration and discuss it with the heirs.

I asked how long he needed to consider an offer. He said about two weeks. My heart sank. I knew that, given a time period of two weeks, the chances were strong of being out-bid by another desirous buyer. But, the attorney wouldn’t shift the time element so it would be necessary for me to arrive at a figure, then pray.

He agreed to let me know if another buyer made an offer within the time period, and would give me another chance to talk price. If it did happen, it might create a bidding war and the price probably would escalate quickly beyond my ability to pay. I couldn’t see how the plane could be worth less than three or four thousand dollars, but I decided to take a monumental risk and offer one thousand seven hundred fifty. I reasoned that, if the plane had sat out here in the country and nobody in town seemed to have more than a passing interest, then the chances of someone else showing up to outbid me were minimal and, anyway, the lawyer had agreed to let me know if someone did. I knew the price I planned to offer was far below market and I was ready for the attorney to be insulted when I suggested it, but, to my astonishment, he said "Fine" and offered to write up the offer to make it official.

Almost breathless, I signed a tentative purchase agreement, we shook hands old-west style and he drove me to the airport to my Cub. We had become quite friendly in the short time we'd been together and I hoped we had built what might be some lasting rapport. I flew home in my Cub on "cloud nine" and began the almost interminable wait necessary until I heard from the attorney regarding the status of my "low-ball" offer.

At one point in my life, I had been involved in a sales situation that called for dealing with company executives at a fairly high level of decision-making. I will never forget a solid lesson given me by my employer. After I had almost lost a sales opportunity by appearing too eager, he explained the sales process from the point of view of one who had learned from experience. He had learned the hard way about over-zealousness in pursuing a transaction and said that, after one makes an offer, the best thing to do...is to say nothing and wait for the other party to respond. So, I waited, but not without a lot of trepidation…and *perspiration!*

Time inched along and, finally, the day I had waited for so impatiently arrived. And, surprisingly, the answer came by mail. Jeez...he could have called me. Astoundingly, ***the news was positive! The plane could be mine!*** All I had to do...was *come up with the cash.* I don't remember my creative plea given the banker but I secured a short-term loan! If you remember the first time you drove a car, your first date, your first kiss, your high school graduation, your first real job, your walk down the aisle and *your first time to "solo" in an airplane*, then you have a faint idea of how I felt as I contemplated the thrill and excitement of piloting an "antique" open-cockpit biplane for the first time.

As they say, "The rest is history." And...what a history flying this plane would turn out to be! Later, I would learn from reality what the phrase "cheating death" could mean in actual flying situations! I also would learn how questionable the terms "major-overhaul" and "recently-re-covered" can be when used in aircraft logbooks. However, I had numerous wonderful flying experiences with the ship and, as in my entire "flying life," met some outstanding people in the process.

One other thing; this first flight in the biplane would be in chilly November across some very high snow-covered mountains in an open cockpit.

Oh, did I mention earlier? At this time, I was a student pilot with only *85 hours total flying time.*

My 2nd plane, a World War II
1943 Meyers OTW ("Out To Win") biplane - 104 built

In anticipation of a demand for training aircraft in which civil flying schools were to provide primary training for the military, Allen Meyers designed the "OTW" and formed the Meyers Aircraft Company to build it. The OTW was a conventional biplane with tandem seating for two in open cockpits with a fixed tailwheel landing gear. The prototype was powered by a 125hp Warner Scarab engine and it first flew on May 10, 1936. The aircraft originally was produced in two main variants; the OTW-145, powered by a 145hp Warner Super Scarab engine, and the OTW-160 powered by a 160hp Kinner R-5 engine. In later production units (like mine shown above) Kinner R-56 160hp engines (w/automatic rocker-arm oilers) were installed.

Marc on an early OTW flight

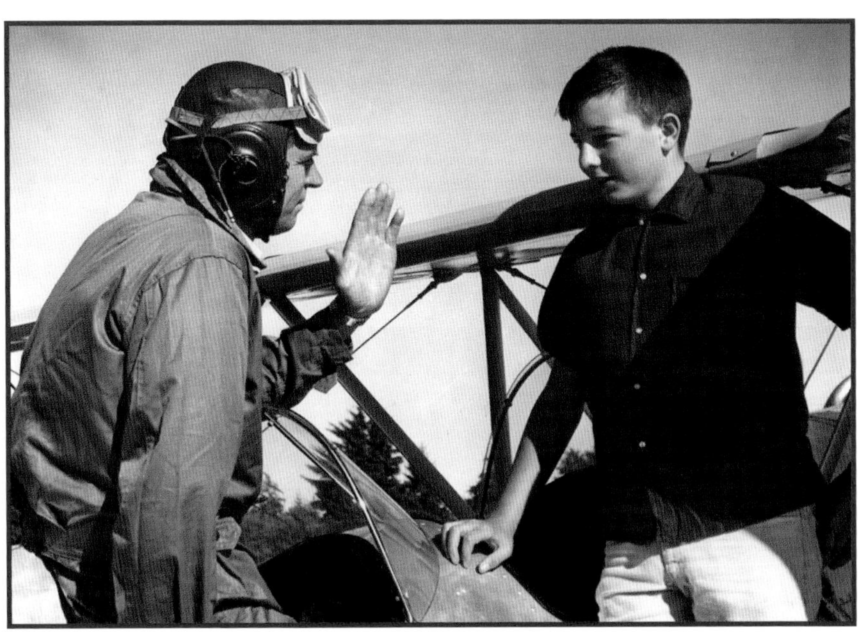

Marc and future aviator go over aerobatic routine before flying... always done to minimize surprises for the uninitiated.

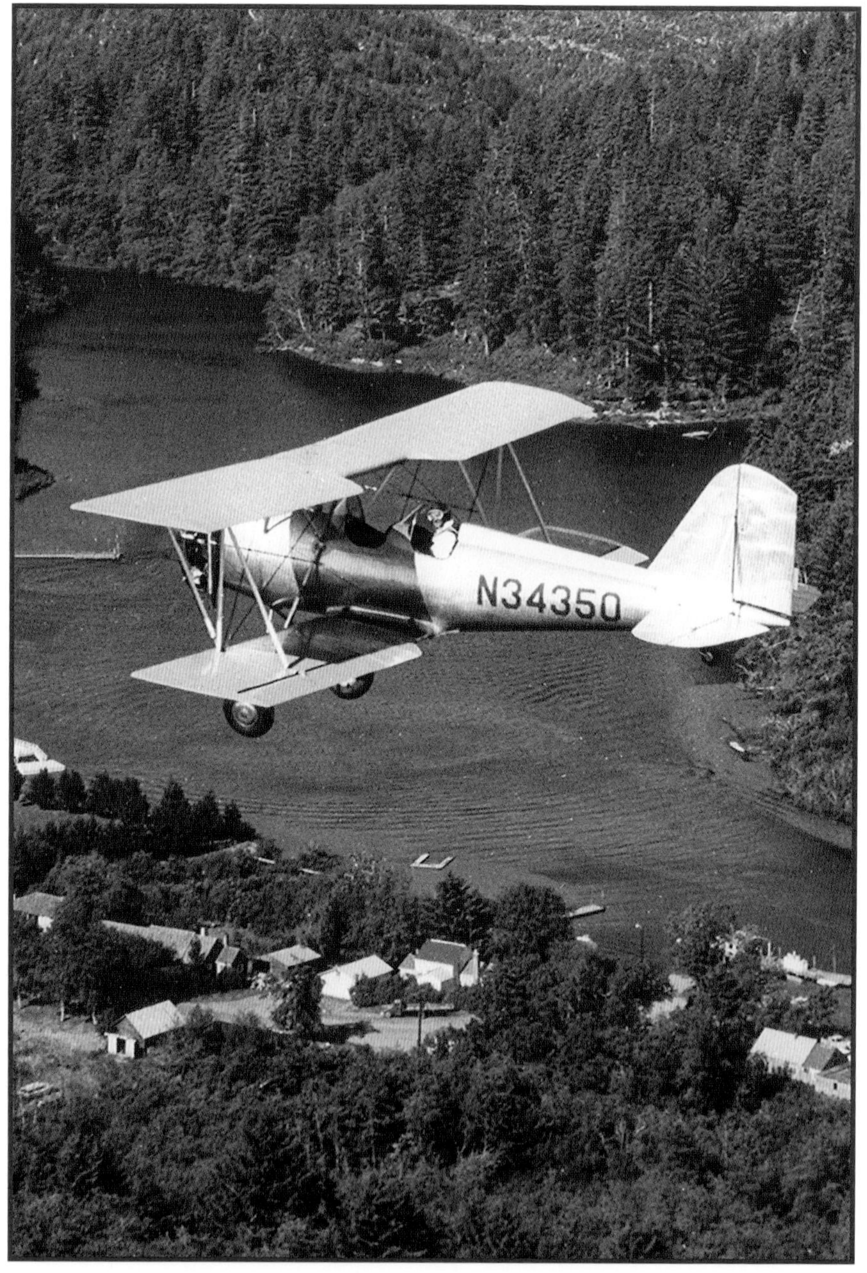

In my Meyers OTW near the Oregon coast, 1968

A Fable: Hands Across The Border

On a flight with our Cessna 180 into Old Mexico, my wife and I carried a 1965 Honda "Trail 90" motorcycle. The "bike" separated into two pieces utilizing a "split-kit" purchased via mail order. It was a neat setup and made possible carrying our own ground transportation with us. We crossed the U.S-Mexico border and landed thirteen miles inside Mexico at an airport having Mexican customs inspectors. After making our plane available for inspection on the tarmac, an official showed up to inspect the plane and cargo and review our documents. He poked around for a bit and suddenly exclaimed in alarm, "You can't bring THAT into our country!" He had spotted our little motorcycle and acted as if we had attempted to smuggle contraband.

Continuing to harangue us over our unique conveyance, he finally stated there was no alternative for us other than taking the pieces out of the plane, assembling them into a complete machine…and then driving it back to the U.S./Mexican border where we must check it into the country "legally." Much wrangling and foot-dragging on our part did nothing to deter this guy from attempting to make our life needlessly miserable.

When the situation seemed unresolvable other than doing his bidding, I suddenly remembered a trip to Mexico a few years earlier with a friend. He had studied medicine there and the trip was for the purpose of his acquiring paperwork for his medical degree. We carried a giant load of medicine samples (considered contraband) picked up from various medical facilities in the U.S…to be given out free of charge to poor people in a country clinic he and others had established to gain extra school credits. From the border all the way to Guadalajara, during which we encountered at least six tourist checkpoints, my friend was forced to bribe guards with modest sums of cash. It worked EVERY time. I thought we might end up in jail but my friend said, "Don't worry, such underhanded activity is 'business as usual' in all of Mexico." So...to resolve our customs problem, I slipped the official a $10 bill…big money in the 60s...and he waved us out to the active runway!

RADIO AERONAUTICA MEXICANA, S. A. de C. V.
Melchor Ocampo No. 469 Tel. 25-33-36
1er. Piso México, D. F.
AVIADOR PARTICULAR
CREDENCIAL No. 60D-142.
A los Jefes de Aeropuerto:
Por medio de la presente certificamos que
MARC ELLIOTT PAULSEN
piloto de la aeronave marca CESSNA-180
N-3361D
con matricula
es un AVIADOR PARTICULAR registrado en Radio Aeronáutica Mexicana, S. A. de C. V. y tiene derecho a que se le suministren gratuitamente los servicios de radionavegación, control de tránsito aéreo, meteorología y comunicaciones aeronáuticas, con sujeción a las condiciones que se especifican en el reverso de esta credencial, que el interesado firma de conformidad.
México, D. F., 09 de Novbre de 19 65.
Radio Aeronáutica Mexicana, S. A. de C. V.
1M-9-65
VALIDA POR 60 DIAS.- PRECIO $ 100.00 M. N.

PHONE LI 8-2332 P. O. BOX 667

LISTON AIRCRAFT

CESSNA

SALES – SERVICE

ROBERTS FIELD REDMOND, OREGON

Customer's Order No.______ Date 10-17 1962

M. Cash

Address______

SOLD BY	CASH	C.O.D.	CHARGE	ON ACCT.	MDSE. RETD.	PAID OUT
G	✓					

QUAN.	DESCRIPTION	PRICE	AMOUNT	
Rudder horn			1	00

Thank you

ALL claims and returned goods MUST be accompanied by this bill

Check that price for a J-3 Cub "rudder horn."

I suppose something like $20+ ***might*** get one now!

Well...
The Wright Brothers *Did It!*

I had just become the only person to bid on a biplane offered for sale by an estate in Lovelock, Nevada. Now in Portland, Oregon, I had only to show up where the biplane was located, pay my money and fly the plane home. It was in great condition...or at least it had appeared so when I had inspected it (with my limited expertise) and all negotiations seemed fairly simple.

There was a hurdle or two to overcome. The first was that I had never flown a biplane or any plane larger than my much smaller Piper Cub (the only plane I had flown *solo*). Much later, while talking to a "crop-dusting" plane operator and ex-Marine "Corsair" pilot, I learned that during WWII (according to the pilot) the U.S. Navy didn't let any pilot fly solo without close to one hundred hours of check-out time in a plane. Good thing I didn't know the ramifications of that at this time…the whole show would have been spoiled because my total logged flight time in six or eight different model trainers (none of which I was overly familiar with) was eighty-five hours.

To me, having only a student pilot's license and a very modest amount of total flight time didn't seem to be an issue worth losing much sleep over. What was the most that might happen? According to the flyers I had consulted, maybe a little ding or two to the plane or, at the very worst, a simple relatively damage-free ground-loop was possible.

Also presenting a bit of a challenge might be that, close up, I'd never even seen a radial engine, run let alone try to start one. For darn sure, I hadn't tried to start anything with a giant eight-foot long propeller that looked like it could do windmill duty in Holland.

In hangar talk with a pilot friend who had owned a biplane, he convinced me that all I had to do was observe a few simple mechanical rules applying to the operation of a radial engine (that is, if I could remember them at the appropriate time) and I would do just fine. Easy for him to say! He had owned and operated his biplane for over eight years. Standing in the hangar, he patiently explained to me how it is necessary to turn the engine over slowly with the prop (first making sure the ignition switch is *off*) to pump out any accumulation of engine oil that might have settled in the bottom cylinders. This, to avoid the possibility of "blowing a jug" on startup...as the old pilots say. ("Blowing a jug" is essentially a "hydraulic cylinder "lock" resulting from oil non-compressibility...with possible damage resulting.)

As to my actually flying this biplane to ferry it from the purchase location in Lovelock, Nevada, to my home base in Portland, Oregon, the hangar guys and I had a lengthy discussion over my ability (or lack of) to do that. My natural inclination is toward frugality, and I certainly didn't want to hire a ferry pilot at great cost. It was a shock to learn that the nearest FAA designated check-pilot to Lovelock was sixty miles away! To have him check me out, I would have to pay him to fly to and from Lovelock, the cost of his airplane use and the actual check-ride charges.

This would never do. There had to be a less expensive way. Also, there was the distinct possibility that this check-pilot might not be amenable to checking out and signing off a student pilot with little logged flight time in a fairly large and tricky-handling airplane. After much discussion over the fine points with my pilot friends, we arrived at the ultimate solution. Since my one friend had much time logged in a biplane, why not simply have *him* give me *verbal instruction*. I calculated...that by using my sharpest basic-pilot brainpower, I should be able to assimilate the information and execute an operation like this after only a few serious conversations.

And so...*that was the plan.* My friend explained just how the Wright brothers must have done it and, hey, it made sense. After all, we reasoned, they didn't have FAA "designated check-pilots" to contend with! *We had the solution!*

According to my friend, the secret to mastering flight in a biplane lay in high-speed taxi practice. In detail, he described how I could begin (after I figured out how to start the engine) the process by taxiing slowly back and forth, and then in circles. I would then graduate to moving slowly down the runway and, little by little, increase my speed with each successive run until I actually took the weight of the plane off the wheels…then reduce the power, settle down again and repeat. The idea was to do enough of this close to the ground "activity" to get a comfortable feel of the ship…then finally lift the airplane off the ground a few feet, then higher and higher on successive flights, and, when the feeling of adequate mastery of control arrived, just fly away. Yep. Sounded possible!

These conversations with my friend took place toward the end of November and the weather would be plenty cold at the altitudes I'd be flying (over some very high mountains). At one of the last war surplus stores in the Portland area, I purchased a neat leather WWII helmet that looked exactly like those worn by barnstormers of old, a pair of leather and sheepskin Army Air Corps overalls, a pair of sheepskin-lined flying boots with Air Corps insignia and goggles that looked exactly like the ones Eddie Rickenbacker wore in the early days of flight. Together with two pairs of insulated underwear and three jackets, I could bundle up as need be. Hey... I was ready to play the "barnstormer" role!

I carefully slipped a cashier's check from the bank for the airplane purchase into my pocket, had a friend drive me to the Portland Greyhound bus station and...I was on my way!

Upon arrival in Lovelock, the attorney handling the estate from which I was to buy the plane picked me up at the bus station and drove directly to his office. I gave him the cashier's check and, after signing the bill-of-sale papers, he handed me ownership papers, we shook hands and he congratulated me on my purchase. His estate people were apparently happy and, secretly, I was ecstatic! Thankfully, no other buyers had appeared to out-bid me and, therefore, the heirs apparently thought they were getting an adequate price. My thoughts? At a price this low, I felt like an airplane thief. My exit from the attorney's office...was in pure joy!

Taking off instantly was my real desire, but there wasn't enough daylight left. It took all of my willpower to resist the urge to go right out to the plane. The attorney graciously agreed to drive me to the plane very early the next morning and see me off. *Little did he know!*

The following morning my eyeballs snapped open at the crack of dawn. The lawyer and I had breakfast at a restaurant, during which I explained to him he would be needed for few extra moments at the airport to help start the planes's engine. We finished breakfast...and he then drove us to the airport.

It was a crystal clear, chilly, late fall morning and our breath made us look like steam engines as we got out of his car and approached my new treasure. Getting out of the attorney's car, my heart was hammering excitedly and my blood flowing fast enough to make me completely forget the cold. The attorney also got out of the car...but he immediately began complaining about the cold.

My first order of business was to inspect the plane carefully and then determine how to pack my gear. Starting the plane would take only a few moments and my gear needed to be stowed because, with the lawyer's lamentations about the cold, I figured he would leave the instant the engine started. He continued to show surprisingly little interest in anything connected with the airplane. However, his lack of interest had been a contributing factor that allowed me to buy the plane for so little, so I gave that little thought. Now, I just needed enough help from him to get the airplane's engine started.

With my small loose belongings placed in the minuscule baggage compartment behind the rear cockpit, I then cinched down my larger pack on the empty aluminum front bucket seat (which was made deep to contain "seat-pack" parachutes used as cushions). Looking again into the small baggage compartment, *a spray can of "ether starting-fluid" was spotted...*resting all the way to the rear. Why such an item would be there, I wasn't sure.

Next, the oil was checked in what appeared to be a two-gallon tank (that's what was stated on an attached placard). The oil tank was full. That seemed a heck of a lot of oil compared to modern aircraft engines. Checking the gas, I was surprised to learn the tank held just twenty-four gallons, only twice as much as my Cub...not a lot of fuel! However, that seemed enough to make the flight to Reno, my first planned stop. Considering the size of the engine, though, twenty-four gallons didn't seem to be very much fuel, a factor that would later proved to be *only too true.*

This type of plane having no self-starter, I'd informed the lawyer at breakfast that his help was necessary in starting the engine, because one person had to manipulate the fuel "boost pump" and the throttle in the rear cockpit while the other "propped" the engine…(the process of turning the engine over by swinging the propeller around by hand until the engine starts). He had expressed reluctance when agreeing to assist and that hadn't done much for my confidence in his help.

Finally...I gave the "non-mechanical" lawyer the world's fastest lesson in throttle-handling, an absolutely critical element in this process…and one typically never trusted to someone with little or no experience. But, I had no choice!

With the attorney on the wing leaning into the cockpit to handle his assigned task, I jumped down to *start it up*…figuring this should take about 30 seconds maximum. However, that optimistic estimate turned out to be...dead wrong!

Per the earlier instructions from my hangar friend, I yelled to the lawyer "*switch off*," to make sure the engine couldn't start accidentally...and pulled the prop through a few times (turning it as per instructions) to pump any accumulated oil out from the bottom cylinders. Noting no oil coming out from the exhaust pipe (where if there was any, it would appear), I proceeded to call up to my helper...and instructed him to manipulate the boost pump to move some fuel from the tank to the carburetor.

I'd never seen a "boost pump" before this and wasn't sure exactly how it fit into the process. My hangar friends hadn't mentioned *this little item*. Upon discovering the pump which was located to the left side of the rear cockpit, my assumption was that it should take only a few minor movements of the little boost pump's back and forth "wobble" lever to transfer enough fuel for engine starting.

The nervous lawyer worked the boost pump lever, then turned the ignition on at my yelled instructions…and my fingers gingerly grasped the tip of the giant propeller (certainly *giant to me*). Then, with all my strength, I gave the prop a very hefty spin, making my body swing back and away from it as my biplane pilot friend had illustrated for me. Then, a second spin and a third spin. A fourth time, I hurled all my energy into it. And so it went for quite a few minutes with absolutely *no ignition fire!* The engine *would not start!*

Leaving the prop, I climbed back up on the wing to see if the lawyer was following instructions. He appeared to be. Certain everything had been taken into consideration, I jumped down and went back to the propeller. When all again appeared ready, my call of "contact" gave him the message to switch the ignition on. "There really shouldn't be much to starting an engine like this," I thought, so was puzzled as to why it didn't fire right up.

More spinning. More nothing.

Putting about six times more energy into spinning the prop than was required to get the job done, I apparently didn't fully understand the process. As a neophyte, I obviously didn't have all the right information regarding this ship and its engine.

After about twenty minutes of very high-energy frenetic "propping," and it was clear we were getting *nowhere.* I was puffing and perspiring a lot in my ultra-thick cold weather togs, and the lawyer was freezing-cold in his business suit...and complaining about it. So, we had a conference. My helper informed me that he had places to go, things to do and had to leave. I pleaded. He said, "OK, I can only stay for only a little while longer!" He suggested getting an airplane mechanic to help. Easy for him to say…he wouldn't be paying the serviceman!

After working the "wobble" lever on the boost pump some more...still *no start!* Then, after double-checking the switch...still *more nothing.* A triple-check of the fuel lines. Nope. Stumped, I walked around the plane and scratched my head. What was the problem? No fuel to the carburetor? Faulty ignition system?

Now, heavy perspiration was making my inside clothes damp, a situation that would not be pleasant when finally ascending into very cold air. Almost an hour had passed and the lawyer was getting seriously perturbed. He wanted nothing more than to leave...*now!* ***I begged.*** He replied, "O.K... *Just a little while longer*...but very soon, I have to get back to the office."

At this point, a "light bulb" thought struck me. Maybe that can of *ether starting-fluid* in the baggage compartment was what the old man had used to start the plane. Never mind that I knew starting fluid to be extremely flammable (and that it was seldom used to start gas engines, only diesels). But…*I was desperate!* My good sense deserted me here and *I went for it!* The plane couldn't be safely started without an assistant, and my assistant was about to leave me.

Was luck changing for the better? There was ether in the can and it still sprayed. No telling how long the can had been there. I 'd never heard of anyone using ether starting-fluid to help start an airplane engine, but what the heck was that can doing here anyway?

We got all set up again, my helper ready to adjust the throttle and keep the engine running. Then I gave the carburetor a mighty shot of one of the most potent chemicals used in the business of transportation... and spun the prop.

With a tremendous "*whooooosh*" and ***a great ball of fire***, the massive carburetor at the bottom of the engine burst into flame. I stood thunderstruck and dumbfounded as the flames shot into the air up and around the cylinders.

An *instant solution* was needed! This was a speedily developing ***catastrophe!*** The lawyer jumped down and came running to see what was happening and, as he approached, I decided on the only action that came to mind. In a sweeping motion, I reached down to the ground, scooped up loose sandy soil with my hands and threw it at the aluminum carburetor. Then…*again and again and again*…all in only a few moments! It was either this drastic action or risk far more serious damage to the plane. One thing I knew for certain, aluminum melts quickly!)

The dirt put out the fire! Now, however, the area around the carburetor was scorched and the whole fuel induction system might be damaged.

Upon closer inspection and, after about a half hour of hard work cleaning the scorch marks and dirt out of engine recesses with a tiny stick and every piece of rag (found in the baggage compartment), my conclusion was that the engine and carburetor were undamaged. I couldn't have been happier about that fact!

However, ***the lawyer was not happy.*** He was getting *seriously irritated* with the entire process. He'd figured out I was an obvious rank-amateur and this was a losing cause. He'd stayed longer only because of the magnitude of the disaster which momentarily had shocked him into feeling a little charitable and somewhat sorry for me. He started for his car.

I stopped him and begged, pleaded...even groveled...and he agreed to stay for just *one more tiny-bit-longer...**no more!***

I could think of nothing different to do, so we tried the same "propping" routine as before the starting-fluid debacle, but again to no avail. By this time, I was absolutely "falling-down" tired, and could barely move. But I knew that if I didn't keep at it, my helper would disappear, so I summoned all my willpower and continued.

At about the two and a half hour point of this fiasco, I knew I *had* to do something different. (The lawyer was fuming mad...and COLD!)

Numerous checks indicated that the carburetor seemed to be receiving fuel but there was no way to be certain.

As an absolute last resort, I got up on the wing, leaned into the cockpit and wobbled the pump handle like a madman *for quite a while*…much more than my aide had been doing.

Jumping down and running back in front of the engine to resume spinning the prop, I was horrified to see gas running out of the bottom of the carburetor in a steady almost pencil-thick stream. Praying the carburetor wouldn't explode again in a ball of flame and fire taking me with it, I pulled on the prop ***one more time!***

With a deafening roar, the engine ***came to life!*** *I couldn't believe it!*

Holy smoke! (No pun intended!) Seconds earlier, I had just about given up and decided I'd call in a mechanic from sixty miles away and…here the engine was, sputtering and huffing and chuffing and acting like it wanted to continue doing so…even after damn near being destroyed by the dirt I'd thrown.

There was only one problem. The engine was racing at high speed. Fresh panic began to set in as I realized the plane might break loose from its tie-down ropes and jump its chocks if the lawyer didn't reduce throttle immediately.

A takeoff in the Meyers

Checking myself out in this ship (Meyers OTW) was a real thrill. Going from my Cub's 85 horsepower to 160hp was a big move for even an experienced pilot. Not wanting to spend the money to get the nearest commercial pilot to fly 60+ miles to perform a flight "check-out," I figured I could do my own check-out...a feat the Wright brothers managed to do successfully (as I reassured myself).

The attorney was ***FROZEN*** in fright at the sound of this powerful, roaring machine. Like a wild man, I raced around, jumped up on the wing in one bound, shoved him unceremoniously out of the way and lunged into the cockpit in a frantic grab for the throttle...just in time, as the plane's tires began to rise over the chocks.

With a great heave of relief on my part, the engine throttled down and settled at 300 rpm. I could now think. And, now…was ***ecstatic!*** How's that for a quick mood change? The lawyer was totally indifferent (and cold) and more than ready to leave...immediately! Would he stay just enough longer to hold the throttle in place while I walked around the plane to see if everything looked O.K.? He very reluctantly agreed and I checked the plane out as quickly as possible and pulled the chocks. Wiping heavy sweat from my brow, I adjusted my flying clothes, squeezed into the cockpit and waved good-bye to the lawyer. He quickly disappeared down the road leaving me all alone in a very large, very strange, very unique and foreign-to-me flying machine, with only my extremely limited experience and the need to start learning immediately. Fast…***right now!***

The throb of the great five-cylinder radial engine was like music to my ears. I worked the throttle and thrilled at the strong response. Easing the throttle forward a little, I released the brakes and felt the exhilaration of forward movement.

The airfield was large and smooth and taxiing practice proceeded without a problem. Following instructions from my biplane-flyer friend, I moved through a series of ever-more-demanding ground maneuvers. After a half hour and four trips up and down the runway, real flight seemed the next logical event. I had the "feel" of the ship and this taxiing routine couldn't go on forever. ***It was time to FLY!***

Rolling down the field, I turned and lined up at the end of the strip aimed into the wind. I checked the gauges, "ran up the engine," checked the magnetos, checked the controls, checked my clothing and gear and breathed deeply. I pushed a long forward stroke on the throttle and the plane was on its way to the wild blue yonder. With 278 square feet of wing area (a hundred more than my Cub), the wings generated aerodynamic lift like nothing I'd experienced before. It didn't need any nudging…it just *levitated vertically* when flying speed was reached.

In raptures, I now knew clearly how the Wright brothers felt that cold December day at Kitty Hawk!

Well, *what the heck…**they were student pilots, too!***

Student pilots

Wright Brothers' first flight, Kitty Hawk, N.C., 1903

Hughes 500 - 4,700 built

When I was selling airplanes, Bill Lamatta, pilot-brother of legendary "Columbia Helicopters" founder Wes Lamatta, stopped by our operation while on a visit to demonstrate his machine to a nearby sale prospect. He invited me along...and gave me an hour of dual flight instruction in the process. I was shocked when he put the ship down in his customer's back yard...which was only fifty-feet-plus in diameter!

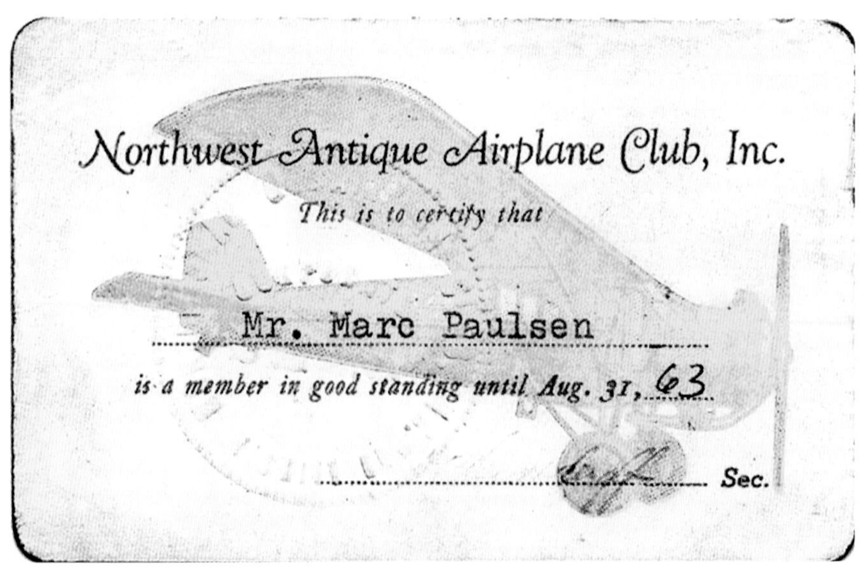

Northwest Antique Airplane Club, Inc.

This is to certify that

Mr. Marc Paulsen

is a member in good standing until ***Aug. 31,*** 63

Sec.

The Ultimate Pit-Stop

If you haven't experienced the exhilaration of open cockpit flight, it's high time you rush to the nearest airport boasting a "biplane" and buy a pleasure flight in one. You will thank me for the suggestion, guaranteed! The thrill received will not be forgotten as long as you live!

My purchase of a unique WWII "primary trainer" biplane had been successful. What made the plane unusual (even among biplanes) was the fact that it had been flown in a famous movie.

Owning one of these planes had been a longtime desire…and now, finally, I was roaring along in my very own biplane, the pilot in absolute command with every nerve in my body tingling with glorious elation. The goal of this flight was to "ferry" the plane to Portland, Oregon, where I planned to tie it down (park it) on a space negotiated earlier with Hank Troh, pioneer pilot and an airfield operator.

The day was clear and beautiful. It was "**CAVU**" (**C**eiling **A**nd **V**isibility **U**nlimited in pilot lingo)…with the long ferry trip ahead to give me much-needed experience...fervently desired in this type of plane. The only negative was that this was the very end of November and cold, cold, cold! The cockpit was so small that moving around in it with the necessary triple-thickness clothing was nearly impossible...and the clothes so bulky that it was difficult to manipulate the controls.

While flying along, I pulled the control stick back, then rocked the wings and pushed the stick forward while waggling the ailerons and alternately pushing on the rudder pedals. The ship darted up, down…sideways. The response to the controls was instant and positive and, to me, truly amazing when compared with reactions of single wing planes. My thought was: "So this is ***nirvana?***"

Leveling off at two thousand feet above ground level, it was possible to see quite clearly everything happening on the ground. My flight plan was simple enough...follow the same highway the bus had taken delivering me from Portland, Oregon, to the sleepy little town of Lovelock, Nevada, where the plane had been purchased, then make the first fuel stop plotted out earlier, at a small private strip at the east end of the city of Reno. The engine seemed to like the throttle setting of about 1600 rpm and, at that setting, the airspeed indicator needle pointed at ninety miles an hour. The fuel supply was enough to make Reno quite easily.

This plane had fewer gauges than my Piper Cub, so there wasn't much to keep an eye on except the oil pressure. The gas gauge, located dead-center ahead of the front passenger wind-screen on top of the engine cowling, looked very much like an old Model A Ford auto gauge and this made for a quaint effect like that of a true antique…even though this airplane was a 1943 model. The plane felt very much to me like flying a bomber must feel. That is how much heavier this plane was than my little Cub.

Settled down to comfortable cruising, everything seemed to be going beautifully when, about thirty minutes west of Lovelock, a tiny speck appeared on the front windshield. Straining to see exactly what it was, I leaned forward. Was the speck an insect? Not likely. It was too cold for insects to be out.

Whup….***another speck!***

Hmmmm…strange. Wonder where that came from?

Then ***another*** and ***another*** and ***another!***

They were "brownish"…and they sure looked a lot like oil. But that couldn't be! According to the log books, the engine had been major-overhauled only sixty flying hours ago and my walk-around inspection had indicated everything to be clean and tight. These specks surely did look suspicious, though.

Then the specks started to multiply. ***Fast!***

Half a dozen…then fifteen or twenty…then fifty or sixty and more. As a matter of fact, they had to be oil! But where was the oil coming from? I'd been only thirty-five minutes in the air and a tailwind now had developed, which would mean a headwind if returning to Lovelock. The "point of no return" was only seconds away…wasn't sure I'd have enough oil to fly back to the airfield.

Now the heavy specks elongated and started to whip around the front windshield and deposit on the rear windshield! Yep, it was...***oil!***

My response was to do the next logical thing. Or at least until doing so, the reaction seemed logical. I leaned out and tried to see forward to spot the exact location where the liquid was coming from. Upon poking my head out beyond the side of the windshield, the ever-increasing flow of substance into the "slipstream" immediately covered my goggles…so not only was it impossible to see what was going on up front by the engine, `now all forward vision was blocked! The substance ***was definitely oil!***

Hurriedly removing my goggles, I couldn't find anything with which to wipe them clean. The cockpit was so small and tight that turning to get at the luggage compartment directly behind my head wasn't possible.

It was abundantly clear...this was rapidly becoming a very precarious situation! Without goggles, my eyes were beginning to tear up, clouding my sight. A couple of ominous visions flashed in my mind. The first was of the plane's engine stopping, then the plane spiraling straight down to earth and crashing. The second was almost as forbidding. This involved attempting a "forced-landing" in the prairie sagebrush and sand, with a total of forty minutes of flight experience in this bird while having severely limited vision. Not pleasant thoughts. The engine was now pumping oil out in such significant quantity that most likely, there would be not enough remaining to get me back to my starting point without it "seizing."

The oil leak continued to increase in volume and, at the rate of loss, it became obvious that landing soon would be my *only* viable option. Oil now completely covered both windshields, my goggles, the inboard wing sections and the entire tail of the plane…and was still pumping out. My very limited overall experience flying a plane (a total of 85 hours flight time and still a student pilot) now forced me to contemplate the potential loss of this airplane even before getting it to home base.

When riding to Lovelock on the bus, I had observed massive new highway construction. Work crews were building what ultimately would become the "Winnemucca to The Sea" Interstate Highway. They were building a second two-lane highway parallel to the first. Just maybe…I could find salvation in this project. I put the plane into a sharp bank…and looked both out and down.

Lo and behold, work was going on directly beneath me. What's more, the work being done was the new side-by-side two-lane roadbed. On closer observation, this appeared to be a stretch of perfectly straight road about a mile long.

The roadbed looked like an almost perfect landing place…with two important exceptions. First, it looked frightfully narrow, not even the width of the plane, and the only prior landing experience I had was the few short "hops" up and down a few feet from the ground when checking myself out on the wide open field from which I had just flown. Second, there was a lot of equipment moving back and forth on the road...***a lot of equipment!***

I could see myself landing reasonably successfully (if I were so lucky) and then either colliding with large pieces of equipment…or having one crunch me under with its ten-foot-tall tires when I unexpectedly popped up in front from the sky! Great things to think about for this student pilot...trapped in a fast-failing airplane inescapably committed to doing something immediately...because of this grave quirk of fate.

I circled for a while, sweating out the situation while pondering the possible ways my prize possession now might be destroyed. I imagined how warplane pilots must feel when they've been shot-up and are going down in flames. What an overwhelming feeling of helplessness and frustration that must be!

By now, there was oil on the plane everywhere the slipstream could deposit it, so my only option was to do what was necessary to salvage the situation. I set up a descent with the limited knowledge I had of the glide-ratio of the ship and made tight orbits while searching for a place to land the plane. That place would have to be on the new roadbed between large pieces of moving equipment, with the operators completely unaware of the drama taking place in the sky above them, a drama in which they were soon to play a critical part.

After about three circles, a fairly long opening existed between a vehicle and a piece of earth-moving equipment that, thankfully, were moving slowly toward one another. Hopefully, they would continue slowly for at least a few more looong moments. All the while, I felt as if the plane was dropping like a lead brick…lower and lower in a power-off glide.

I was now absolutely, positively…committed to landing! There was no other choice!

Lower and lower, closer and closer.

The opening held.

Oil covered both windshields so I couldn't see directly ahead. If I attempted looking around the windshield, my eyes immediately would be blinded. I couldn't wear the goggles because they were covered with oil. Now I was thanking my lucky stars that I'd been forced to gain my first flight experience in my J-3 Cub on an extremely short strip and had been forced to learn the art of radically side-slipping an airplane to slow the speed and abruptly lose altitude. A fringe benefit of this maneuver is that, while in this configuration, the violently "skewed" attitude allows a pilot in the rear seat to see forward along the side of the plane and, if ever such sight was needed, it was here and now in this hair-raising real-life dilemma. Only a movie crew filming would have added more drama!

From the sky, a typical two-lane road appears very narrow to an amateur pilot, and this road seemed even narrower because of the presence of grade marking stakes jutting up on either side. But, as the earth rushed up to meet me, my luck held and the opening between the two construction rigs appeared to leave just barely enough room to land (if I made no mistakes).

During my descent, I hadn't realized how fast this plane lost altitude with the power shut down, but now, as I waited to hit the ground, I was gratified to feel it drop rapidly the last distance.

I glided over the first machine (a giant earthmover)…clearing it by maybe eight or ten feet. We were going in the same direction and I prayed the driver would see me immediately after I passed over him…and slow his rig to a halt before running over me. But, I had to concentrate and didn't dare look back.

I held the plane in the slip until the very last moment, then straightened out with a snap and pulled the stick back all the way into my gut for a full stall landing.

Almost miraculously, the biplane settled to a perfect three point touchdown and rollout while I tapped the toe brakes as gently as possible. Luckily, good fortune continued and I was able to keep the plane straight and on the center of the road by rapidly snapping my head from one side of the plane to the other...which made possible clear sight forward.

The driver of the other large rig which was headed toward me gasped in amazement at this apparition: a big twisting meat-grinder propeller appearing as if from nowhere moving directly toward him. He quickly applied his brakes…just in time to meet me as we both rolled to a stop with not more than fifty feet remaining between us.

When my prop stopped "wind-milling," both drivers hopped out and rushed up to the side of the plane to greet me and ask what in the world I was doing landing here. I was shaking like a leaf…but greeted them as cavalierly as possible. They addressed me as though I were LINDBERGH! *If only they knew!*

Trying to appear nonchalant, I drawled, "Looks like I have an oil leak, so I thought I'd better land immediately and try to locate the source."

The driver who had been coming toward me was driving a large enclosed-van service truck and he asked, "Is there anything we can do to help you?"

"Well, I don't know," I replied. "That's probably doubtful. It looks like I'm in big trouble, because the nearest airport with service facilities and airplane parts is a long, long way from here."

They were exceptionally friendly and very willing to help me if they could. Obviously, this new development with an *airplane* (and not just *any* airplane, but this "historic" biplane) had produced an astonishing diversion for them. The man driving the service truck said, "How about I back my rig up to your engine and we take a look?" I replied, "Fine, I'll be happy for any help you can give me," and, at that, he hastily turned his truck around and backed his lowered tailgate right up under my engine…and in just minutes from the time I touched down, I found myself standing with a mechanic on a solid platform on the rear of the truck at exactly the right height to work on the radial engine at belt level. ***Unbelievable!***

The top cylinder of my aircraft engine was now about chest high and as we inspected the tops of the cylinders the mechanic spoke authoritatively, "Looks like your top cylinder 'rocker-cover' gasket is permanently damaged."

I had a sinking feeling. This was going to be a major problem.

His next statement stopped me cold!

He asked, "Would you like me to make a new gasket for you?"

More unbelievable! My reply: "Sure, but how can you do that?"

He returned, "Not a problem, just give me a minute."

At that, he turned, reached three feet back to large double doors that opened into the innards of the boxy truck and disappeared inside for a few seconds. Not more than a few seconds!

He came back out almost immediately carrying a large sheet of gasket material, a small ball-peen hammer, and a tool with the correctly-sized socket to fit the rocker-cover cap-screws. No more than maybe three-plus minutes had elapsed from my touchdown. Now, *I was the astonished one!*

As he put his wrench on the first nut, a half dozen other workers appeared on the scene to gaze at this surprise visitor from the heavens...murmuring that this must be either an experienced crop-duster or an aerobatic pilot to be able to make such a difficult landing.

As the amazed workers arrived, they realized the problem was serious when seeing the plane covered its full length with oil. A couple asked if they could be of help and I answered that it surely would be great to figure a way to get the oil off the plane and the windscreens. With that, they immediately piped up almost in unison, "No problem, we'll be happy to help. If it's all right with you, we'll wipe it off with clean gasoline-soaked rags."

I was overjoyed! That would work just fine, as the plane's fuselage and "tail-feathers" were mostly aluminum.

One of the group crawled up into the service truck we were standing on, came out with his arms loaded with clean rags and distributed them to his fellow workers, while another got cans of gas from a tank located elsewhere on the truck. Together with even more workers who had now arrived, they **all** proceeded to clean every last drop of oil off the plane in very short order. For them, this was a uniquely memorable break from the daily routine and they all thought it great fun!

Meanwhile, the mechanic busily tapped out a new rocker-cover gasket for the top cylinder. He finished this in a matter of minutes because the work platform was at a perfect height for easy access and he was able to stand conveniently right up against the front of the engine. From inside his truck, he brought out a tube of gasket sealing material, applied some to the gasket, set the gasket in place, put the rocker cover on and spun all the nuts on with his speed wrench. The whole operation took him less than five minutes.

At this point, he queried, "You need some oil?"

Again, I was sure this would be another serious problem. I replied, "Yes, but the airplane uses only a heavy-weight aircraft oil."

He returned, "How heavy?"

"Well, we use 50-weight in airplanes."

To my utter and complete amazement, he replied, "No problem."

Again, I couldn't believe my ears.

Could this be true?

When I quizzed him about having the oil, he replied, "In our equipment, we use a lot of 50-weight motor oil out here and I don't suppose there is much difference from the oil you use in your airplane. We use only the best. I have a barrel right here on the truck, so we'll fill your tank from the platform."

I was amazed! And…if all that wasn't enough, one of the workers filled my fuel tank from the regular-gas supply carried on the truck. Their fuel wasn't "aviation" fuel, but my hangar flying buddies always had said that is was OK to use "regular" gasoline in an emergency...and this definitely qualified.

The plane was clean, the leak fixed, the oil tank full, the fuel tank full, and I was ready for take-off just fifteen minutes from the time I had touched down. ***These guys amazed me!***

I shook everyones' hand, thanked them profusely and climbed back into the cockpit.

The men moved their trucks apart far enough to allow comfortable margin for takeoff, then held back construction traffic so I would be clear of any of their giant machines. By this time, there were about twenty workers on hand for the next big show…my (hopefully) professionally-appearing take-off. Then, (to add to their stories as well as mine) I gave some very flamboyant waves to those "saviors"… and, with a theatrical adjustment of my helmet and goggles, eased the throttle forward and roared back into the wild blue...***a grateful student pilot with only 85 hours total flying time, a "self-check-out," and 40 total minutes of oil-soaked flight time in a much bigger and heavier aircraft than he'd ever flown before!***

Author's note:

On the flight back to Portland, Oregon, there were four more forced or very difficult emergency or semi-emergency landings: one due to a radical wind shift which reduced range dramatically…one because of a surprise November cold wave at high altitude…then, a second wind-shift range-reducing incident due to the limited fuel supply…and the last because of vicious very high unpredictable direct crosswinds at The Dalles, Oregon, airport…all very problematic landings!

Author (rear cockpit) and friend going up in the Meyers OTW to perform aerobatics.

Piper Cherokee
32,778 built (all variants)

Although a very nice airplane, I really never enjoyed flying these neat looking ships because the view is necessarily obstructed by the low-wing design. "High-wing" pilots joke to low-wing flyers, "Have you ever seen a low-winged bird?" However, it has proven to be a very popular airplane with owners, pilots and flight-training facitities...witness the mumber built!

Cessna 402 "Business Liner" - 1,535 built

After selling airplanes I worked as a sawmill project manager. The mill company had a "402" like this which we used to ferry workers to and from assorted projects. (*Classy smooth flying!*)

Cessna 177 Cardinal - 4,295 built

This plane was designed to look "*futuristic.*" The early models we flew lacked adequate performance...and, when they were improved with more horsepower, they still were outsold by the good ol' reliable 172 Skyhawk, thus this model was relatively short-lived.

Cold Weather Sweat

The ferry flight from Lovelock, Nevada, to Reno in my newly purchased 1943 Meyers "OTW" biplane continued uneventfully. The airplane handled beautifully. I was pleased at the instant response of the ship to only the slightest movement of the controls and now understood why biplanes were so well thought of when used for aerobatics. All the extra cold-weather clothes necessary for open-cockpit flight in November made movement in the tiny cockpit space almost impossible. This make of plane was a military trainer in World War Two. "How in heck were instructors and students able to jump in and out of the small cockpit quickly...and how did they manipulate the communication gear," I wondered...when I could hardly move a muscle when inside the cockpit? One answer is that most were smaller than my two-hundred-twenty pound frame.

In the 1960s, before highly exotic semi-conductor-charged electronics became the norm, most small-airplane pilots more or less followed the road systems and, because we flew so low and slow, it was almost as easy to follow an auto road map as an aeronautical chart. Of course, we carried both and read both, but generally we could see visually from town to town and distinguish landmarks well enough to easily get where we wanted to go with either.

My plan for this ferry trip was to continue on to Reno following the "Winnemucca-to-The-Sea" highway.

In the very early years of flight, when almost all planes were slow-going biplanes like this one, pilots followed the "Iron Beam"*...the railroads!* Before we had the great interstate highway system, flying the railroads worked out very well because they led almost everywhere long before cars or airplanes were invented. As long as the weather was clear enough or, at least, not "socked-in" (heavy clouds and fog) to the ground, that made a lot of sense. On sunny days, the light reflecting off the "iron beam" would cause it to sparkle far into the distance much like a silvery thread. Even on darker days, reflections off the shiny rails were still visible for miles ahead. Pilots don't follow the "iron-beam" much anymore but, occasionally, doing so comes in handy for simple planes with minimal instrumentation. Because rails never make sharp turns like country roads tend to do, following rails is much easier.

Cruising along, I had plenty of time to study the airplane. Glancing at the flat brace wires between the wings that were holding them together, I wondered…"Hmmm, are those skinny little bracing wires strong enough?" They sure didn't look so great!

The Meyers OTW biplane has two "landing" wires and three "flying" wires. The flying wires hold the upper wing in place and the landing wires, the lower. I remembered seeing photos of WWII Stearman trainer biplanes which had more and much heavier wires. It is a much bigger plane so that must explain the heavier wires, I thought. Still, it bothered me somewhat as I viewed the OTW wires a little nervously. But then, I reasoned, aeronautical engineers must have thought about that a long time ago.

The landing gear on an OTW has an enormous spread between the wheels. The big long hydraulic "oleo" (oil-filled) shock struts stretching above from the wheels are the longest I remembered seeing. With wheels so far apart and the airplane very short, this plane could be a potential instant "ground-looper" (to lose control upon touching down when landing). My figuring was that I better be very careful on landing, because it might be easy to damage or destroy this ship in a split second if I let my attention wander for the least moment.

The machine hummed along at 1600 RPM (engine crankshaft revolutions per minute) which is a far slower engine speed than I was used to. The low RPM reminded me of engines I'd heard rumbling on very large machines. I thought of ferryboats I'd ridden that made the same thrum-thrum-thrum drone, a very heavy, plodding, satisfying sound. The OTW's "radial" engine with its big cylinders was like that. It gave me the feeling that it would run forever. As any hot-rodder (which I have been) will tell you, high (RPM) engines don't always last very long, and sometimes come apart when least expected. I knew I was going to like this plane and its engine.

Arriving over the outskirts of Reno, I scanned the road ahead for the little airport that was depicted in my "flight guide"…and there it was, dead ahead. I set up a standard traffic-pattern approach but didn't see any traffic so, at the last minute, changed and decided to make a long "straight-in" approach. That would allow time to get well stabilized for a slow, easy touchdown and landing. The landing went surprisingly well. Spotting a tie-down location on the tarmac, I taxied over there, and wouldn't you know, one tie-down rope was missing... and I didn't notice it until out of the plane. That was typical at low-traffic airports. It made me very nervous to have a plane tied down inadequately (especially when I had to leave it for the night) but it was too much trouble to get the big engine started again, so I tied down one wing and the tail and let it go at that. Because of the large wing area of biplanes, moving air (wind) has a greater effect on them than single-winged planes. There was no wind, so I felt a little better about the risk. That was a mistake because I spent the whole night worrying about the plane's security and got little sleep. It was going to be a while before the "new" of this airplane ownership would wear off.

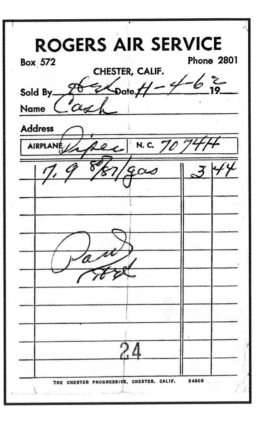

ROGERS AIR SERVICE

Box 572 Phone 2801

CHESTER, CALIF.

Sold By [illegible] Date 4-4-62 19

Name Cash

Address

AIRPLANE Piper N. C. 70744

7.9 8/87/gas	3	44

Paid

24

THE CHESTER PROGRESSIVE, CHESTER, CALIF. 34806

Searching for a flightline attendant, I found an airplane mechanic working in the shop on a Stearman biplane crop-duster. Busy, he hardly looked up, as, just for fun, upon entering, I effected a biplane-pilot swagger. I greeted him and he returned it...but not much more, and didn't even take notice of my "salty" winter flying outfit! I guessed he possibly saw this kind of thing every day here. The pilot of the Stearman on which he was working likely wore the same authentic old-time stuff regularly! I asked him if he could fuel my plane and he nodded yes. We walked out to the plane and he was astounded! He asked, "Where did you get this ship?" He acted like he had seen the plane before. I replied, "I just bought it from an estate in Lovelock."

"I thought so!" he responded. While holding the gas nozzle, he explained that the plane used to come to Reno every so often. He used to fuel the ship on occasion and he had talked many times to the old gentleman who had owned it. "Quite a character!" he exclaimed. Then said he was sorry to hear that the old man had died and added, "You'll probably have a great time with the plane." I nodded agreement. He asked if I knew the story of the old man.

"Yes, the attorney who wrote up the sale papers knew part of the man's story and a local man I met in a restaurant told me the rest. I have the old flyer's personal flight-log book and that tells even more. His was a fascinating story. Of all the flying stories I've heard, this one rates right up there for unusual and unique!"

The old gentleman had died at the age of seventy-eight just a few months earlier. When I was given the airplane log books, his personal flight log was along with the aircraft and engine logs. In going through his flight log, it was astonishing to see that he had been flying the plane right up until a week or so before he died. In fact, he had flown on a very regular basis, if not for a lot of hours, for the previous eighteen years. According to the local man who told me about him, he bought the plane as Army Air Corps "surplus" for very little money right at the end of the Second World War and, at the time he bought it, *he didn't know how to fly.* There was nothing too unusual about that. A lot of people bought war surplus planes for very little…but, not a lot of them who were sixty years old and couldn't fly! *He must have been one sharp old boy!*

We went into the office to settle the fuel bill and I used the phone to call my sister, Diane, who lived nearby in the city. I hadn't taken the effort to call her earlier and tell her I'd be coming through because I wasn't one hundred percent sure that a purchase of the plane would be successful, so had decided to wait for the outcome to contact her.

She was welcoming, indeed, so I asked her for a bed. She was very surprised to hear from me and even more so when told what my mission was. She was used to my doing wild and crazy things and drove to the airport to pick me up. We had a good time discussing this and that and she told me all about her business activities. Her husband was in San Francisco on business so she and I ate dinner then spent the rest of the evening discussing old times, trivia and…"What the heck was I doing buying this airplane when I already had another one?" As I told her, a pilot never can have too many airplanes. She always had been quite adventurous herself so she understood.

I left my sister's home early in the morning in a state of excitement! This was going to be another big day in my life...the continuation of a very long ferry flight home. Diane was all questions. She and her husband were not mechanical types so she wanted to know all about the plane, how and where I got it and the various details of the acquisition. She was as awed as I over the age and the storied activities of the late owner and sensed my anticipation and impatience to get to the airport so we hopped in her car and drove quickly back out to the field. Diane was thrilled to see the plane and I helped her into the cockpit to get the feel of sitting in it.

Looking forward to enjoying what began as a beautiful clear but moderately warm day, I would learn that such short warmish days in winter can breed a complacency that can turn fatal.

While Diane watched in amusement, I bounced around the plane in an obvious state of exhilaration giving the plane its "walk-around" inspection and checking the oil and fuel. Again, I loaded my meager gear in the front seat and in the minuscule compartment directly behind the position of my head. While flying it was physically impossible for me to reach into this tiny rear compartment and there was no way of reaching anything stored in the front cockpit, so it was necessary to have everything I needed right in my lap. Why in the world hadn't the manufacturer designed some type of small compartment within easy reach? It must have been because the cockpit was so small there plainly wasn't room.

I'll say the cockpit was small...getting in and out because of my large frame was a real "shoe-horn" job. However, in time I got used to the difficult process. At that time, when the plane was still new to me, sitting in the small cockpit bordered closely on psychologically claustrophobic.

I untied the tie-down ropes, grabbed the big prop, pulled it through a few times, then hiked into the hangar to find the mechanic to help me start the engine.

He was happy to help and this time, after climbing into the cockpit and getting settled, I reached over to the wobble pump and pumped briskly. I asked him to let me know when a steady stream of fuel was pouring from the carburetor. I may not always learn quickly but I learned that lesson well. I explained that on the very first try at starting the engine, I learned that it wouldn't start unless fuel was running out, a point he found hard to believe. At any rate, after fuel began to pour out from the bottom of the carburetor, he gave me the high sign to turn the magneto switches on and I replied loudly, "Contact!" He pulled the prop smoothly like the expert he was and I thought, "I wonder how long it will be until I can do that...and I sincerely hope the big prop doesn't cut my head off before I become an old hand at pulling it through."

The engine started with a roar! I thrilled knowing it truly was me sitting there relishing the magnificent machine with its thundering engine. And, *it was all mine* (well...and *the bank's*)! But only I knew that. What would the bankers have thought if they had known that the cash they loaned me was about to join the birds over high mountains in the form of an antique plane with a pilot of very limited experience and familiarity at the controls?

Waving goodbye to my sister and the mechanic, I "gunned the engine," moved out onto the taxi-way, went through my takeoff checklist and lined up on the runway. This was only my third take-off in the plane and my heart was beating like the first time. Would I ever get over that feeling?

I fed power to the engine slowly and accelerated. Flying speed came quickly and the ship did its almost vertical "levitation" again. It needed no help from me…it just *flew*…no assistance necessary! The large double wing area created so much lift that the plane just rose up as if by magic. With only one person on board and the resultant light weight, the plane got off the ground in a hurry and, by the time I passed my sister standing in front of the hangars, I had gained a hundred feet or so of altitude. I looked down, my heart and soul fluttering with pride, spotted her, and waved. She waved back and I was off to meet my future.

Flying north from Reno toward Stead Air Force Base on the northwestern edge of the city, I became concerned that I might be too close, possibly infringing on air base airspace. I cursed myself for not being more knowledgeable about these fairly basic rules of flight. Concerned, I didn't want to get in trouble with Air Force traffic control. But then, I decided to steer right through the airspace like an experienced cropduster...who isn't about to move over because he doesn't want to burn unnecessary fuel.

The overall plan was to follow Highway 395 up to Susanville and then on to Alturas. My flight-guide showed good airports with fuel available at both towns. At this late time of year, the smaller strips most likely would have unattended fuel pumps, if they had them at all, so I figured it best to land at the largest airports on my route.

Approaching a highway junction below, suddenly I had to relieve myself…and I mean *fast!* Now, why in God's name hadn't I covered this in Reno? Man, oh man! This was irritating. *I had to go. Pronto!*

Desperately, I tried to remember the nearest airstrip on the chart. Wouldn't it be great if there were room to spread the map out now? I could forget that! Boy, I thought…when I get out of this predicament, I swear I'll slip a folded chart under my rear even if doing so causes damage to it! I'd have given ten bucks for a chart in my hand about then. Simply, I didn't remember the indicated airports I'd checked earlier. So...where to put the ship down? And quick! *Damn!* I was two-thirds sure I'd seen an airport on the chart up Hwy 70 to my left. I didn't want to go that direction but there were none up Highway 395 for a long way. That, I was sure of.

Under major urinary duress, I turned westerly toward Beckwourth, California, about fifteen minutes away. That is, fifteen minutes before I realized I should have calculated for climbing over Beckwourth Pass! It turned out to be more like twenty minutes plus. *I was in agony.* Non-pilots don't have a clue about crazy situations in which pilots can find themselves. One more detail... just through the pass, the wind increased *considerably*. And then *increased even more!* Below, I saw what looked like log-slash burn smoke blowing *briskly.* That meant a "high wind. How in the world could the wind increase this much in such a short distance? In Reno, there was *no* wind. But…not now! And...the wind was mostly from my left, causing the plane to point left while continuing in a straight line forward. That situation puts the plane in a position of flight called by pilots, "crab" angle. How many things could go wrong at the same time?

I had plenty of fuel but I wasn't happy about landing on a field I hadn't checked out. Shouldn't be too much traffic. Spotting the field at Beckwourth a couple of miles ahead, I aimed directly for it, hoping to make a quick straight-in approach and landing. I couldn't hold out much longer and wet pants (through three pairs) was not a pleasant thought.

I set up for the straight-in approach to land on what looked like runway 25. Fortunately, the runway was directly in my path so this should be an easy landing. It looked like I'd be on the ground in only a few moments.

At that moment, I was jolted by a new and unpleasant awareness! The windsock in the middle of the airport was *absolutely straight out…but* ***ninety-degrees*** *to my flight path!* I knew it was plenty windy because my "crab angle" had increased while getting closer to the airport. I simply hadn't realized *how much* the wind had increased!

Getting my Piper Cub safely down with only a *modest crosswind* had been giving me problems. How in the world was I going to land this ship successfully, a plane with twice the Cub's wing area (which gives wind much more surface area to act on...*just like a big sail*)? And how would I be able to hold it in one place on the ground and keep it there with what must now seemed about a forty to fifty-mile-an-hour direct crosswind... with me *still very uneasy about my abilities to fly this ship*. I leveled out

CESSNA
1969 MODELS
177 and CARDINAL

Rogue Valley Skyways, Inc.
Medford Municipal Airport
Medford, Oregon - Ph. 773-7787

AIRCRAFT & ACCESSORY PRICE LIST

EFFECTIVE SEPTEMBER 16, 1968

177
$15,775.00

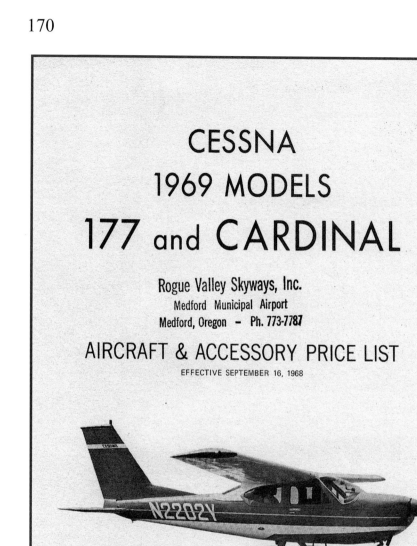

CARDINAL
$16,995.00

SUGGESTED LIST PRICE
FAF WICHITA, KANSAS

and began a 360 degree (a circle) turn to the left for time to think the situation over. And man, did I have to go!

After thinking over the wind conditions for a few moments, my conclusion was that it would be impossible for me to put the plane down on runway 25 in this high crosswind without great worry about losing control. There was just too much wind! That was definite! I could visualize what the plane would look like after the wind had blown it into a hangar or whipped it upside down. A new plan was necessary!

While circling just above pattern altitude, a possibility struck me. There was no traffic whatsoever. No one was in sight anywhere on the strip or around buildings. I'd just land it *across the runway directly into the wind* instead of down the runway. There appeared to be exceptionally wide shoulders of gravel on both sides...slick plan...should work.

I brought the ship around smartly and lined up headed directly at a spot between two buildings just the other side of the runway. With the power reduced, the plane settled down to a very slow forward speed over the ground. It was surprising how *much* wind there was and how very slowly I was going over the ground. In fact, a little less power and the plane would be stationary in the air (as in a "hover"). A small push forward on the throttle brought the ship forward ever so slightly. I was astounded. If I was going to get on the ground, I'd have to add more power. I eased the throttle forward. As such a new pilot, I hadn't yet had to fly onto the ground under power. But, if I was going to land here, that is exactly what I'd have to do.

Two hundred feet, one hundred feet, fifty feet. I was approaching the runway very, very slowly under power…on a path directly across what looked like a total of maybe one hundred feet of width on which to set down the plane...and *that* included the gravel on both sides. Well, what the heck, it should work. "How in the world did I get myself into this one?" (One more predicament...this one caused simply by neglecting bodily priorities!)

Finally, the ship touched down. The windsock was still straight out and I had essentially just de-levitated. In fact, with this amount of wind, I could have stopped directly over the center of the runway and, with the low landing speed of this plane, descended straight down like a helicopter.

But, now there was another serious problem. I didn't dare turn the airplane. Sitting in the middle of the runway pointed directly across it and having to hold power to stay in place, there was no question that, if I tried to turn, I'd lose control and the plane would blow away for sure. The giant wing area made it extremely vulnerable to high gusts. So, what to do? My instructors talked about crosswind landings but, until now, I hadn't really paid much attention. I should have.

The hangars looked to be deserted…not a soul in sight. I had figured my engine noise would roust someone from inside the buildings who could come out and help by holding my wings while I taxied to a tie-down. I figured wrong! No one appeared!

Sitting tight, I held the power. At least, the wind was smooth so holding power and the plane in place in the center of the runway was not difficult. Think, think! I didn't dare turn. The wind seemed to be almost fifty miles an hour...maybe more. This airplane would fly at thirty-five.

Through my mind flashed the recall of a classic story I once read about... a typhoon hitting a small WWII bomber base island in the Pacific. In the evening, winds came up and rain started falling. By late evening, the atoll was bombarded with higher and higher gales until the commander could imagine potential disaster. The typhoon's force had started to tear the planes from their very strong moorings and it was evident they couldn't hold out against it. The commander sent all pilots and copilots to their ships with instructions to start their engines and power them up to hold them against the wind. In effect, the men "flew" their planes all night long "on the ground" to counteract the winds. The strategy worked. They saved their planes!

Snapping back to reality, that true story wasn't going to help me. There was no ground crew or person in view. My plane would simply run out of fuel in a short time...and *then get blown away.*

Searching my mind for a quick solution, I tried to remember how far it was to the next planned fuel stop. I'd considered the airport at Chester earlier...but had then done a calculation and figured my fuel should take the plane further to Alturas. "Now," I thought, "maybe I should head for Chester and by the time I get there, the wind shouldn't be a problem."

That's it! I eased the throttle forward. The plane rose vertically directly above the runway. I used *zero* runway (just shot straight up), added more throttle, then banked left and headed back along the runway from where I had just come.

Leveling out at about a thousand feet above ground, I set up for cruising speed and aimed in the direction of Chester with a plan to follow the road. The plane, the engine and I settled down to an uneventful droning rhythm, *except, however...*I *still* had to relieve myself*!* ***And how!*** The urge now came back to me with a vengeance. What to do? As I recalled from the chart I'd tried to memorize (because of not being able to open it in the small cockpit), heading due north from this point would put me over Highway 395 and, with lower winds, if I were fortunate, the plane could land on any large usable field. There were some minor ranch strips indicated along that route so they should be suitable for landing. I turned the plane and headed north and would either hold my liquid…*or let go!* There *was* no other choice.

There was another major problem…climbing over peaks ahead would slow me down somewhat, but, as bad as I had to go, it appeared the lesser of evils. I forged ahead. Unfortunately, the wind changed to almost directly toward the plane so, with the climb added to that, my forward progress was snail-like!

It's downright astounding how many things a person has to learn to be a truly competent pilot. The number of difficulties which can accumulate seems astronomical. Right then, I was looking down and remembering what my hangar friends told me about always having a landing spot in sight. I didn't have one! I was in the middle of high mountains with both forests and logged-over "stump lands" below. Neither are compatible with landing planes. Too far beyond the "point of no return" to Reno, I couldn't see anything but more rugged territory ahead, and I wanted to keep this ship in one piece so I could become a senior birdman.

All of a sudden, it seemed to be getting really chilly. "Jeez," I thought, "*that's odd!*" I had on so much clothing that I could barely move a muscle…longjohns, double trousers and shirts, sheepskin-lined flying overalls and two jackets. How could I be getting cold? The altimeter read just over ten thousand feet. I had climbed that high to overcome my nervousness at being too close to those infernal trees and stumps below. Now, it really wouldn't make any difference if the engine quit at ten thousand or two hundred feet above the terrain below, I'd be just as dead either way. There was no way I had enough altitude to glide to a safe landing place. I didn't need lessons in what happens when planes go down in trees or stump pastures. I'd read enough about them in aviation magazines.

Then, it got *even colder and colder*. "My God," I thought, "It must be way below zero. All these clothes should be keeping me warm as toast but, *they're not doing the job!*"

I sat thinking this over as the engine rumbled along. It got much colder yet! For the moment, I'd forgotten about how badly I needed to urinate. Now the realization came over me that I was rapidly losing the ability to move my body because of the intense cold. Not able to see over the mountains ahead, I fought to control my thoughts. This is about the last thing I thought would happen. Then, *it continued to get even colder.* I was freezing! No place to land, getting colder…*I was in deep trouble.* If I wet my pants, the wetness might begin to freeze and accelerate the cooling of my body temperature. Should I turn back? And how much farther to the crest of the mountain ahead?

Moving my arms was almost impossible now, but they didn't have to move very much to make an effect on the controls. However, if this went on much longer, I wouldn't be able to control the plane. I thought how "un-hero-like" if I crashed simply due to cold. Somehow, that wouldn't seem dramatic enough! I strained to see ahead. It appeared that these high mountains ended beyond the pass up ahead. *Could I hold out?*

With supreme effort, I gave the control stick a shove forward. I was so cold that I couldn't reach over to the throttle, so I left the setting untouched. Calculating my distance, I aimed the ship down to descend and barely cleared the pass upon reaching it. Somehow, I had to get to a lower altitude as fast as possible and hope to have both higher temperature *and* less wind. At about a hundred feet above trees, I shot over the pass edge. The land dropped off fast on the other side and I could see Highway 395 a few miles beyond. I was so awfully cold, I barely could move. I began to pray. (Most fliers and passengers excel at this when facing possible doom.)

The temperature needed to increase considerably before my limbs could manage the controls adequately and get the plane down normally... thereby avoiding an inadvertent graveyard spiral (an uncontrolled downward circling...ending in a crash). I gave myself about five minutes until losing all control due to cold.

The airplane was really moving down fast now because I had leaned my entire body forward against the control stick. It was aimed sharply downhill with cruise power, over "red-line" speed. The wind blowing over my face was warming up a bit. Down to six thousand feet, the temperature was definitely warmer. The insulation of my clothes was now making it hard for warmer air to get to me and I was still bitterly cold, but now it seemed that, if I could make it to the ground, I might be able to control my landing…and de-pressurize my bladder.

At this point it didn't make a bit of difference where I landed the plane. Any reasonably flat spot would have to do.

Then…*glory be!* A rancher's strip appeared up ahead a bit to my left. I eased my entire body to the left. It was the only way I could move the stick. The ship responded and veered left. With much effort, I leaned back the other way to straighten out the plane. I felt very weary. It was bad enough almost wetting my pants, freezing my bottom and being almost totally out of control. I was now forced to make another difficult landing on an unfamiliar field and, I still had next to no practice in this plane. *Incredible!*

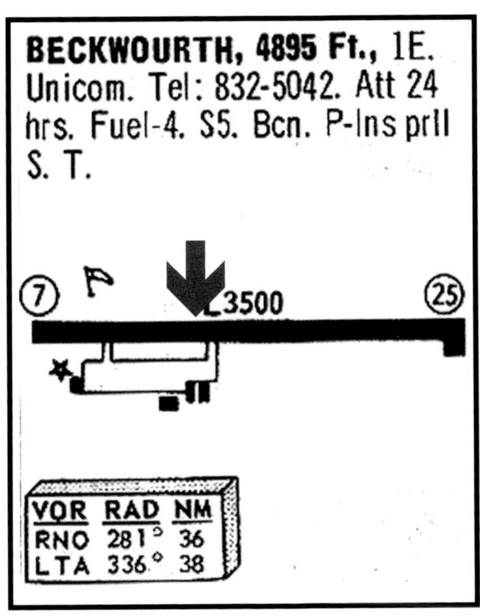

The Beckwourth airport layout as illustrated in a Flight Guide. The red arrow indicates the point at which I aimed my OTW (across the field) in an attempt to land during an exceedingly high "crosswind." After "hovering" over the strip for some time and seeing no one about to assist holding the plane after touching down, I gave up due to the excessive wind and flew instead to a ranch airstrip a few miles east...just off HWY 395.

This was a labor bill for work on my Piper J-3 Cub at the same airport a couple of weeks earlier. Today, one can only dream of aircraft repair labor bills this small.

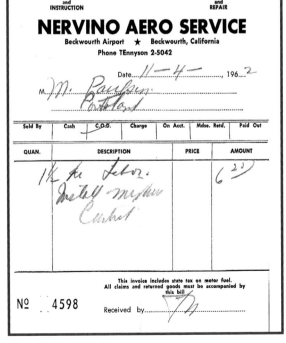

CHARTER and INSTRUCTION — AIRCRAFT RENTAL — MAINTENANCE and REPAIR

NERVINO AERO SERVICE

Beckwourth Airport ★ Beckwourth, California

Phone TEnnyson 2-5042

Date 11—4—, 1962

M. M. Paulsen
Portland

Sold By	Cash	C.O.D.	Charge	On Acct.	Mdse. Retd.	Paid Out

QUAN.	DESCRIPTION	PRICE	AMOUNT
1½	hr labor. Install mixture Control		6 20

This invoice includes state tax on motor fuel.
All claims and returned goods must be accompanied by this bill

№ 4598

Received by

Here goes! I came up on the tiny narrow strip and banked the plane over to line up with the runway. The airspeed was still reading "red-line" (over recommended aircraft speed), but I had to get there in a hurry. Now on final approach, I was forced to reach over with my right arm and lift my stiff left hand onto the throttle, but I couldn't get my hand solidly on the knob. No way could I get my gloves off! I could barely squeeze my fingers shut. I hooked the back of my glove on the throttle and turned my body to the left to drag the throttle back. Fortunately, *that worked.* So far, so good. The engine slowed and the airspeed began to decrease. Lined up with the runway, the strip didn't look like much but I just wanted back on solid ground, relieve myself...and *get warm!* I couldn't remember ever having been so cold in my life.

The strip came fast up to meet me. Darn! It wasn't yet clear that I'd make it all the way to the field. The plane was descending too rapidly. Then I remembered the old pilots' adage, "If you want to go up, pull back on the stick. If you want to go down, pull it back further." For non-pilots, this simply means that if you don't have enough speed and pull the nose up too far, you will stall and go straight down into the ground. What a spooky thought as I now approached with questionable airspeed and altitude. There was no choice! I forced both hands to come together over the top of the stick and started easing it back...but only a little. The drag increased, the airspeed lessened.

The plane made it over a rock pile and almost landed "short," touching down right on the very end of the strip*...but...made it!* I'll bet the plane didn't clear the rocks by more than ten feet. And this field was ROUGH...plus looked seldom used. I shifted my body around, the only way I could get my arms to move the stick, and strained to hold straight. Then the plane veered to the right and to the edge of the field and, with what little effort I could muster, I pushed on the brakes. The plane settled down and came to a stop only five feet from a barbed-wire fence. Breathing a giant sigh of relief, I still couldn't move and felt practically frozen in place. I couldn't even move enough to shut off the engine! I just sat in the bright sunshine with my feet on the brakes and let the engine run. But...*I was alive!*

The temperature was definitely warmer now. The sun was a great help. The altimeter read a little over forty-two hundred feet. As my brain thawed out, I realized there was no wind here. I hadn't even considered that before landing. That wouldn't have made any difference. As close as I had been to losing total control because of cold, I would have had to fly straight in…even *downwind.* In retrospect, I knew I'd have crashed for sure if that had been the case.

Fifteen minutes elapsed before I moved my body enough to shut off the engine…and ***get this***…*my body had even forgotten about needing to urinate!* After thawing a tiny bit, I exited the ship and spent ten more minutes warming up by flinging my arms around and jumping up and down. Finally, I warmed up enough to start shaking from fright. About that time, I did relieve myself and tried to calm down.

The returning warmth is something I'll never forget. Maybe this experience is one reason why I've liked fires in the fireplace even more since then. Contemplating my next move, I thought about the world of flight and was reminded of the many wild flying stories I'd read when I was a young boy. Now a thought struck me...that the end of many of those stories was death.

I looked over at the airplane and realized that an immediate new adventure was facing me…the rest of this ferry journey back to Portland, Oregon, and…*I was going to have to start the engine all by myself!*

Discussion before the flight

A friend and I go over basic aerobatic maneuvers we are going to perform in my Meyers OTW. It's always a good idea for the passenger to know exactly what is going to transpire in the air. I was almost shocked to death once when, as a passenger in a biplane, the pilot, with no warning, shoved the stick forward, shot straight down...and pulled out inverted ...about a hundred feet from the ground!

Pressurized Cessna 414 - 1,070 built

Selling airplanes had some great advantages. One day a distributor's pilot came through with one of these outstanding ships and stopped for fuel. After "airplane talk" with him, he invited me to fly the plane to his next stop. He had an instructor's certificate so I jumped at the opportunity and was able to add another interesting airplane flight entry in my pilot's logbook. The ship was fast, large inside, smooth and quiet. It was easy to see that the pressurized Cessna "400" series of planes were going to be big winners. In later years, that proved true...and they became the choice of many operators and pilots when they entered the "secondary" market.

Checkpilot/Checkpilot

During my ferry trip north from Nevada to Portland, Oregon, I landed my newly-purchased 1943 WWII Meyers OTW biplane at a large former WWII auxiliary airfield located near Lakeview in sparsely-populated southeastern Oregon. Already having had two odd-ball forced landings enroute, I wasn't in the least interested in another due to simple fuel starvation.

Darkness was approaching as I taxied to the gas pumps. The "fixed-base operator" pleasantly inquired as to my wishes. Please fill my tank while I check the oil," I responded. "It looks like I'll have to spend the night here. How does one get to town?"

It seemed he hadn't heard me...and he began talking. I pulled my helmet off so I could hear clearly and cocked my ear.

"I took my Army Air Corps training in one of these when I was a Cadet," he happily bubbled. "Great airplane! Had some fun times in one of these planes," he continued.

"The heck you did," I said. "I just bought this ship down in Nevada and I'm ferrying it home to Portland." Looking around, the place seemed somewhat deserted...only a couple of airplanes parked on the tarmac and a very few closed hangars. A lonely outpost, I wondered if he had many people to talk to. I repeated, "Is there a way to get into town from here?"

"Well," he replied, "I usually have an old car here for pilots to use but it isn't running at the moment." That made me a little nervous because my chart indicated the distance to town about six or eight miles. I had no sleeping bag nor camping gear and not enough extra money for private transportation…even if it was available. He rambled on congenially, warming up more and more to the wonderful fact that my ship brought back many pleasant distant memories to him. It was as if old friends had come to visit…the plane and I! He introduced himself as "Buzz."

As he described some of his Cadet activities, it was like a transformation came over him and he offered, "It's almost dark and I don't think you are going to find a way into town. *You're welcome to stay here tonight if you'd like."*

Secretly, I was overjoyed and happily accepted.

He showed me where to tie my ship down and helped me with the process, all the time chatting on about his exploits in the same type of plane. Upon my asking him about his other flying experiences, he told that he had been a B-24 bomber pilot in World War II, that he was a "CFI" (Certified Flight Instructor), now gave occasional dual flight instruction and, in addition, did some "charter work." It became clear that he was quite an accomplished man of the sky!

As we tied down the OTW, I asked him about a shiny Aero Commander twin-engine plane parked over to one side. "Oh, that belongs to some guys from down south who come up here goose-hunting every year." I walked over to take a look. The plane was very new and beautiful and I knew it to be the very same type that President Eisenhower had flown in. In fact, this model Aero Commander was the first small airplane any "sitting" president had ever flown in. Buzz had serviced the ship and was about to taxi it to a permanent tie-down for the night and the entry door was still open, so I peeked inside. There was a small owner's placard just inside the door that read, "Del E. Webb Construction Company." I thought, "Man, oh man…some people have all the luck. Imagine being able to fly to your goose-hunting in a great ship like that!"

It appeared that Buzz lived alone in the small quarters he led me into. They were clean and neat and he showed me to a small bedroom which was perfectly adequate. As I stowed my gear, he invited me to have dinner with him. We had a great time talking flying and began a warm friendship. (If pilots are at all compatible, it doesn't take long for this process to jell. There are so few pilots per capita in the population that, when they connect, a meeting can seem like "old home week.")

He recounted a number of his "bomber-flight" experiences and I tried hard not to seem over-awed, *but I was.* How must he have felt to be flying through clouds of deadly "flak" while watching close friends nearby blown to smithereens by direct hits or wiped out by fighter plane skirmishes? We talked into the early morning hours. He seemed to relish the chance to go on and on. Perhaps, with passage of time, wartime events were easier to talk about.

Offhandedly, I mentioned that I was only a student pilot and that I'd checked myself out in the OTW before I left Nevada…because the nearest qualified check-pilot was sixty miles away. I pointed out that a former biplane-owner friend had instructed me verbally on the fine points of a "self-checkout" and the concept had worked just fine. Further, I explained that I wanted to have a legal entry made by a Certified Flight Instructor in my Pilot's Flight-Log book indicating that I'd been ***legally*** "checked-out" to fly my OTW. He sounded skeptical about that but replied that he would be happy to talk to me about a check-out in the morning. I said, "Sounds good to me" and we both retired.

Before sleep, the thought came to me that this pilot might not be as handy in my plane as he was in the planes he flew daily, and the last thing I wanted was to give control of my new purchase to someone who might get in trouble with it. Well, I would have to address that when daylight came!

The smell of eggs and bacon frying aroused me and I hurried when my new friend called to me. I had slept soundly because the previous day's forced landing had produced heavy stress.

During breakfast, I hung on Buzz's every word as he answered my questions with fascinating tales of flight under astounding circumstances and pressure in warring Europe. This guy had done some very, very wild and dangerous flying.

Finally, my situation came up...that I'd like to be legally signed off in my biplane. Admittedly, I'd had very little flight experience in it but it was as recent as could be, having acquired it in only the last two days. Plus, I'd accomplished two successful forced landings already which I managed to live through and complete without damaging the ship. Explaining all of this to Buzz in detail…he finally seemed reasonably satisfied.

He asked to see my Pilot's Logbook and was visibly taken aback when he realized it accounted for only ninety hours of total flight time…and I was still a student pilot! He said, "This is all the time you have?"

"Yep," I meekly responded and threw in the fact that I also had my own Piper Cub J-3/85…in which I had logged all my previous flight time and, in my opinion, the planes were somewhat similar in flight characteristics.

"Hmmmm," he murmured, as he turned the few pages of entries and was lost in thought for a few moments. "Why haven't you gotten your *pilot's license?"*

Weakly, I could reply only, "Well, since I own the J-3 Cub and I've had so much fun flying it, I just haven't gotten around to taking my private pilot license 'check-ride.'"

"Weeeaaalllll," he finally said, "We have a problem here. I haven't flown an open cockpit plane for a long time and certainly not a short-coupled plane like yours." I later learned that my OTW was considered by *other pilots* to be a bit "squirrelly" on landings and takeoffs. This was due to a relatively short distance between the front wheels and the rear tailwheel, hence "short-coupled" (as mentioned in an earlier story). But, by now I had already become used to flying the J-3 Cub which was also "squirrelly" so flying my new acquisition didn't make me overly nervous.

"I'd like to help you with a check-out but I'm afraid I truly am not qualified in the strict manner of speaking." He went on, "Tell you what. You may be only a student but you've gotten this far safely so let's do this: *You check me out first...then we'll fly awhile...and then I'll sign you off in your logbook for solo flight in your plane."*

This was bizarre! I, the student, check out the check-pilot??? And…*a veteran military bomber pilot at that!* Unbelievable! But it did make a fair amount of sense. I darn sure didn't want anyone inadequately familiar with my new acquisition to roll it up into a ball of bent metal, wood and cloth. So…off we went, into the blue…the student monitoring very closely, every move of his much more experienced senior.

Probably because he was an experienced instructor, he handled it well, and, after just one landing, felt quite comfortable with the plane. Then, after a couple more takeoffs and landings, we headed for altitude to introduce me to some aerobatics. He had offered to begin with some basic "gyrations" if our initial flights went well…and they had...and I must say... this guy could *really fly*!

He executed loops, barrel rolls, slow rolls, snap rolls and spins. Then we did hammerhead stalls, Immelmans and split Ss. These were all maneuvers one will see in a typical airshow...usually done by professional pilots. In just a little while, he was feeling comfortable with the controls and I could see that he was enjoying the flight. *We both were!*

Back on the ground, I got out my logbook and handed it to him. He joked as he made the important mandatory legal entry I needed, signed it and handed it back to me, then chuckled, "In all my years of flying, that is absolutely the first time I have ever been checked out in an airplane…***by my student."***

Author's note: The fixed-base operator was **Myron (Buzz) Buswell**, a man later honored by Evergreen Aviation Museum, McMinnville, Oregon, as one of the state's noteworthy "Pioneer" pilots.

DATE 19 62	FLIGHT FROM	FLIGHT TO	AIRCRAFT MAKE AND MODEL	CERTIFICATE NUMBER	ENGINE	H. P.	CLASSIFICATION ASEL			DURATION OF FLIGHT	
							81:30			84	10
10-4	TULE LAKE	BEND	PIPER J-3	7674H	CONT	65	2:10			2	10
10-5	BEND	PORTLAND	"	"	"	"	2:45			2	45
10-5	PORTLAND	LOCAL	"	"	"	"	:30				30
11-6	"	"	"	"	"	"	2:15			2	15
11-7	PORTLAND	LOCAL	PIPER J3	7074H	CONT	65	3:45			3	45
11-8	"	"	"	"	"	"	:45				45
11-15	"	"	"	"	"	"	1:15			1	15
18 Nov 62	Lakeview	Ore. Local	Meyers OTW	34350	Kinner	160				2	00
19 Nov 62	"	LOCAL	"	"	"	"	3:15			3	15
11-19	"	THE DALLES	"	"	"	"	2:50			2	50
11-20	THE DALLES	HOOD RIVER	"	"	"	"	:30				30
THE RECORD ON THIS PAGE IS CERTIFIED TRUE AND CORRECT:							101:30			106	10

PILOT__________ ATTESTED BY__________

CARRY TOTALS FORWARD TO TOP OF NEXT PAGE

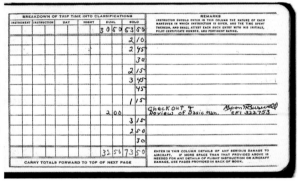

My flight logbook indicating 1st "official" OTW flight...this so anyone checking my logbook would not know I'd *checked myself out* 4 flight hours earlier in this ship.

INSTRUMENT	INSTRUCTION	DAY	NIGHT	DUAL	SOLO	REMARKS
				30 50	53 50	INSTRUCTOR SHOULD ENTER IN THIS COLUMN THE NATURE OF EACH MANEUVER IN WHICH INSTRUCTION IS GIVEN, AND THE TIME SPENT THEREON, AND SHALL ATTEST EACH SUCH ENTRY WITH HIS INITIALS, PILOT CERTIFICATE NUMBER, AND PERTINENT RATING.
					2 10	
					2 45	
					30	
					2 15	
					3 45	
					45	
					1 15	
				2 00		Checkout & Review of Basic man. Myron H Buswell CFI 322753
					3 15	
					2 50	
					30	
				32 50	73 50	ENTER IN THIS COLUMN DETAILS OF ANY SERIOUS DAMAGE TO AIRCRAFT. IF MORE SPACE THAN THAT PROVIDED ABOVE IS NEEDED FOR ANY DETAILS OF FLIGHT INSTRUCTION OR AIRCRAFT DAMAGE, USE PAGES PROVIDED IN BACK OF BOOK.

CARRY TOTALS FORWARD TO TOP OF NEXT PAGE

Note the 4th line up from the bottom... that's the "official" OTW flight-checkout "signoff" entry by Myron "Buzz" Buswell, WWII bomber pilot.

PAINTING - UPHOLSTERY - WAXING - AIRCRAFT SALES

694-8971

AIRCRAFT SPECIALTIES

213 E. RESERVE "PEARSON AIR PARK" VANCOUVER, WASH.

Customer's Order No.____ Date 6/2 1966

M Mark Paulson

Address

SOLD BY	CASH	C.O.D.	CHARGE	ON ACCT.	MDSE. RETD.	PAID OUT
CCK						

QUAN.	DESCRIPTION	PRICE	AMOUNT
:30	C310 dual		25 00
	To be logged at		
	later date		
	pd - Check		
	CCK		

ALL claims and returned goods MUST be accompanied by this bill

1130 Rec'd by

Check that hourly figure for Cessna 310 twin-engine flight instruction...$50 an hour for one very sharp flying machine (1966).

Stealth Aerobatics

When selling airplanes, I met some truly spirited individuals. On one occasion in our flight lounge, I overheard a couple of visiting professional pilots chuckling to themselves about one of their recent flights. Joining them at our coffee bar for a cup, I mentioned overhearing them discussing what sounded like a very unique experience.

Obligingly, the command pilot explained: "We fly a Cessna 421 'Golden Eagle' twin and recently were on an instrument night flight carrying a full load of executives while flying in smooth solid klag (opaque clouds). Jim here...my copilot, brought up the old story of Boeing's test pilot, 'Tex' Johnston amazing a mass of people at a Seattle Gold Cup hydroplane race by doing a barrel roll over their heads in the giant newly-developed 707 passenger ship. He did so to impress prospective buyers with its capabilities. Going upside down in such a plane is a very unusual stunt and we got to arguing over whether or not it could be done as easily with our ship.

Cessna 421 Twin-engine "Golden Eagle" 1,901 built

At the 1970 Cessna International sales meeting in Wichita, Kansas, this ship was introduced to us as the "Belle of The Ball."

The more we talked about the maneuver, the more intrigued we became with the idea. Jim said to me, 'I'll bet you can't do one right now with a full load of passengers without them knowing. As pilots know, a 'barrel roll' is a 'coordinated' maneuver in which, if done correctly, people in the plane experience no unusual effects. The key is to do the roll perfectly!

Not a guy to pass up a challenge, I disengaged the autopilot, took a deep breath and pulled the plane up, completely over (upside down) and around back down to normal flight. It worked out flawlessly. Shortly after, looking back to our passengers through the privacy curtain, I inquired of them how they were enjoying the flight. "Going great," said one. "Smooth as silk." Jim and I have been laughing about that flight ever since!"

Logbook Fantasy

"You see these little scallops between the ribs?"

"Yes."

"Well…they indicate the possibility that there may be serious problems inside which may call for a lot of reconstructive work."

"Are you sure of that? According to the airplane logbook, the fabric cover on the wings and ailerons is only *a year old*."

"Well, of course, you can't be sure until you've looked inside but, from my past experiences and how it looks to me, I'm inclined to think there is a serious problem."

This is something I was not at all happy to hear. It had been my amateur pilot's assumption that the information entered into an aircraft's maintenance logbooks was essentially sacrosanct. From my very careful reading of the logbooks, my interpretation had been that this airplane was in like-new condition. The work had been "*signed off*" as airworthy and safe by a certified aircraft mechanic, the type of person I assumed was beyond reproach in airplane repair matters. Now, here was a very knowledgeable old-hand pilot suggesting that my recent purchase was far less than pristine…not a consideration that overjoyed me! His statement aroused alarming consternation!

"Just how bad do you think the situation is?"

"Can't tell without opening it up."

"You mean that to determine whether or not it needs work, the fabric cover has to come off?" was my incredulous response.

"Yep, that's the only way."

"You're kidding. Do you really think that is necessary?"

"Yep. I'm deadly serious. Don't think the plane will *license* without some corrective repair. Could be wrong, but I don't think so. In my experience and from what I see, the *inspector* will want to look *inside*."

He was referring to an inspector who would soon have to check the airplane over thoroughly for the purpose of renewing the airplane's "air worthiness" certificate. This is absolutely mandatory to continue flying, an annual ritual that all general aviation private airplanes must be subjected to by iron-clad mandate of the Federal Aviation Administration. The usual name applied is "***The annual inspection***."

I proudly had led this old-hand pilot, a new acquaintance, out to my prize possession, a 1943 Meyers OTW biplane...to show it off, and all I'd achieved was learning the strong possibility of serious hidden airplane damage inside the wings and ailerons. Surely, he must be wrong!

Sadly, not only was he *not wrong* about this one specific item, I would get a sound education from the long drawn-out scenario that followed. I would learn well the valued lesson from that old maxim, "If something sounds too good to be true, that might be the case!"

As with many epochs in the passage of time, there appear occasional windows of opportunity during which those with foresight (or those who happen to be lucky with accidental timing) take great advantage of situations that, ultimately, prove highly beneficial both financially and inspirationally. In the world of aviation, one of these fortuitous windows emerged for many aviators during the late nineteen forties into the fifties and sixties. I was lucky enough to be able to take advantage of a great opportunity during this period.

Less than twenty years after WWII, there still existed a great number of airplanes that the U.S. Government was selling as "war surplus" which were not yet regarded as objects of high value. There were too many of them! On airports and odd places scattered around the U.S., one could see them pushed off to one side, forlornly aging. At the time, most of these ships required a lot of restoration and/or maintenance while modern small private aircraft were still priced within the reach of people with relatively average salaries. Pilots or aspiring pilots hadn't yet gone totally crazy with desire for the surplus planes. However, that situation changed dramatically as the sixties progressed. Antique and classic autos, along with unique and antique airplanes, became objects of high desire, and prices for them escalated accordingly. I found and purchased my OTW biplane just in time... *before the full rush!*

According to the Meyers' clearly written airframe and engine logbooks, the wings and ailerons had been recently recovered with new fabric and the engine completely major-overhauled.

Then a new student pilot with just ninety hours total flying time, I had learned enough to know that all airplanes are required by law to have logbooks that ***are supposed to represent*** the plane's true condition. Because pilots (unlike auto drivers) do not have the luxury of simply pulling over to the side of the road in the event of serious mechanical emergencies, it is clearly understandable why such records of maintenance and alteration are required. A pilot must (or most certainly should) know the exact condition of an airplane before he risks his life or anyone else's when leaving Mother Earth in a heavier-than-air flying machine. Thus…after reading the logbooks very carefully and determining that this aircraft (***according to the logbook entries***) appeared to be in outstanding condition, I wrote a check for the plane and handed it over to the seller.

In retrospect, I should have been more curious about the ship's overall condition when, minutes after my initial takeoff headed for home, I had a very close call because of an almost immediate oil leak serious enough to cause a forced landing. This discovery took place only thirty minutes after takeoff…too far from my point of origin to risk turning back and possibly ruining the engine for lack of oil. The fact that I luckily was able to land on a brand new highway bed under construction possibly gave me a false sense of basic well-being. Although I had three other forced landings on the way to my home field, upon arrival I considered my purchase to be an absolute dream machine because the plane flew so well.

The plane was a Meyers OTW biplane, serial no. 94. According to the owners of one of these ships now displayed in a museum, "OTW" stands for "*Out To Win.*" The model designation is a bit like the one given the famed Howard "DGA" which informed pilots know stands for "*Damned Good Airplane!*"

Now, the "old-hand" pilot's implication that my newly-found treasure might not be the "airworthy" gem I thought it to be unnerved me considerably. I'd learned enough of his background to know that, without doubt, he was exceptionally knowledgeable about airplanes and their foibles and, when he made a statement as significant as the one he had, I knew I was in for some serious difficulty. Before making my journey by bus from Portland, Oregon, to Lovelock, Nevada, to fly the ship back home, I had consulted him because he had owned a WWII surplus biplane for the preceding eight years, in addition to having extensive mechanical involvement with various other planes.

"But…what about the logbook entries?" I uneasily inquired later of a local aircraft mechanic. "They state clearly that much work has been done on the ship and it should be in first-class condition."

"Well, not every mechanic sees things the same way," apologetically replied Randall, the pleasant middle-aged aircraft technician I had engaged for the inspection process.

"You mean to say that shoddy work could be done on an ***AIRPLANE*** and signed off as ***ACCEPTABLE*** in the logbooks?"

"*It happens all the time.*"

Astonishing! Was he correct? My naïve impression was, that, because of the very serious and potentially deadly results of work they performed, all aircraft mechanics did outstanding and unquestionably superb work. Isn't that logical because of the obvious possibility of human death that could result from anything less? Now it was being strongly intimated that there are a number of mechanics out there who lack sufficient knowledge, ability and principles to always "do the job right."

"How can a shoddy mechanic *retain his license?*"

"Well…how many times have you had your car repaired and had to go back and have the same work corrected?"

"I see the point but I thought that airplanes were unique enough and their safety critical enough that their mechanics would be a few cuts above auto repairmen."

"Unfortunately, we have a few in our midst who could be a lot better than they are…and probably a lot more honest as well. But, right now, the next step is for us to look inside the inspection points and see if the skin and structure of the ailerons will, in fact, pass inspection."

Darn…I had not counted on anything even remotely as serious as this. This did not sound good. And the logbooks indicated this plane was absolutely "airworthy!"

"Hello?" the aircraft inspection mechanic opened when I picked up the phone on the second ring. "I'm afraid my news is not what you want to hear." That would be the first of far too many such calls I soon would be hearing. Upon receiving each call, I'd be in shock for a week. The first call was to inform me that the plane could not be signed off as airworthy without completely disassembling and rebuilding both ailerons from scratch…***at considerable expense***. My immediate reaction was total disbelief but, after a mechanical "show and tell," it was obvious earlier woodwork repair on the ailerons indeed had been grossly inferior...plus other lousy workmanship had been covered over with a brand-new equally inferior fabric job.

The next call from John, an aircraft and engine mechanic with whom I had become on a first-name basis. He stated that an FAA ***"Airworthiness Directive"*** regarding required work on the engine's master rod had not been entered in the logbook when, according to the logbook, the engine had been recently major-overhauled. With strong incredulity, I asked for clarification on the question of just what in the heck could that mean for an engine which the logbook showed just sixty-plus hours total flight time from brand new?

"Well," he began very slowly and deliberately, "With this particular engine, there is supposed to be a logbook entry showing that special work has been done to the master rod at the time of engine overhaul. If such an entry is not in the logbook, I cannot sign the airplane off as 'Airworthy.'"

"Jiminy," I thought. "What in the world else can be mechanically wrong?" I had figured that by now I'd be up in the sky above earthlings learning fantastic aerobatics. And here I was getting nothing but bad news after bad news after bad news. Will even more unfortunate problems be found? Good news: there were no more surprise discoveries as were those first two…however, there were *plenty more lesser jolts!* Another call informed me that there would be a three-month wait for engine parts…and then those three months turned into six months.

A major problem was that John (the recommended airplane mechanic whom I hired to work on my plane) worked for the Forest Service on their planes as a regular job and, as a result, could spend only a modest amount of his spare time on my plane. Both the aileron work and re-majoring the big five-cylinder radial engine were very time-consuming projects. John said he would do his best to get these jobs done, but couldn't really make any time guarantees. Hey…just what I didn't want to hear! And me with every nerve in my body crying out to be in the air in that flashy biplane…what crummy luck. But, choices were extremely limited. Even though the process would take longer, John would charge much less than a typical large aviation repair facility, thus I'd be better off having him do all the work. Reluctantly, I gave him the go-ahead. Little did I know what would transpire!

Even more structural work was required than first indicated. Soon the entire wings were removed. They also needed remedial work. Jeeez! I just couldn't believe that the mechanic who had signed off the earlier work in the logbooks could still be in business, but John assured me that there were plenty of aircraft mechanics out there who somehow hung onto their licenses by "thin margins."

As long as the wings and the engine were off, I decided it would be a good time to clean and polish up the rest of the plane. I knew of a young fellow, Ken, who had a job working for an aircraft outfit that rebuilt old Grumman Widgeon amphibians. Recently, he had mentioned he'd been laid off for a substantial period of time because his company ran out of immediate rebuild work. Since the work he did was somewhat menial in the realm of airplane cleanup and elementary mechanical tasks, I reasoned that he might be interested in working temporarily on my biplane fuselage. I gave him a call.

Ken definitely was interested and, if we could come to agreement, he would work on the fuselage until he was called back to work or found another job. He agreed to work for a modest amount above the minimum wage…on the condition we would tow the airplane fuselage to his home so he could work on it without the expense of driving his car to work.

He was called back to work about a month later, so he continued to work on it only in his spare time and, as a result, it took him ***over a year*** to complete the project. As he worked, we continued to discover instruments, fittings, and metal that needed attention. By the time he finished and presented me with a shiny polished aluminum fuselage that looked like new, the work had all cost quite a bit, although, by today's standards…*a very modest figure.*

Back to John…during this time, he had built what were essentially brand new ailerons from scratch in his living room on a sawhorse table! His wife had toyed with the idea of killing him a few times but he somehow managed to calm her down and get the job done. He re-major-overhauled the engine in his double garage, leaving his wife's car out in the rain, another gambit that annoyed her immensely. The amazing part of the whole scenario was that John took longer to get his work done than it had taken Ken to complete the fuselage work. Finally, I got the reassembled airplane back and in the air…just short of ***two years from the day*** I handed it over to John to rework the engine and Ken, who shaped up the fuselage. And all of that for an airplane which the logbooks had indicated was in absolute first-class condition at the time of my purchase.

Did I learn anything? You bet! As mentioned earlier about maybe "too good to be true," I received a sound lesson. And, believe me, the next time I bought an airplane, I exercised extremely careful judgment. I double-checked with a mechanic first, then double-checked his references before having him double-check the plane, double-checked the logbooks myself and personally conducted a detailed inspection. Then, after all that, I got a "second" mechanical opinion. With airplanes, mechanical correctness ***is that important***. If all that isn't enough, from my biplane purchase forward, I learned always to look upon airplane "logbook entries" as highly questionable and, if they stated that an engine had been recently overhauled, I simply assumed the worst and made deals accordingly to allow for the possibility of poorly performed work, or work not done at all.

It is fascinating in this life we live how two people (such as two different aircraft mechanics) can work in a way which each considers reasonable, logical, fair and diligent...and end up with some wildly different results...and ***both think they have done a fine acceptable job***.

In the intervening years I developed a little "saying" of my own regarding workman of all types. It goes like this: "I have never met a workman or craftsman who, when asked about the quality of his work, replied, 'Oh, don't hire me...I do terrible work.'" *Au contraire*...almost every workman, no matter how fantastically good, mediocre or just plain god-awfully bad, ***thinks he is good!*** Mull that over *the next time you check your logbooks!*

Kinner R-56
"radial" engine

5 cylinders
540 cubic inches

According to the Kinner engine logbook for *my "OTW,"* it had been recently ***major-overhauled***. Unfortunately, the mechanic overlooked an important "***Mandatory Airworthiness Directive***" requiring an expensive master-connecting-rod revision.

The scenario simply proved ....***that no two airplane mechanics think alike!***

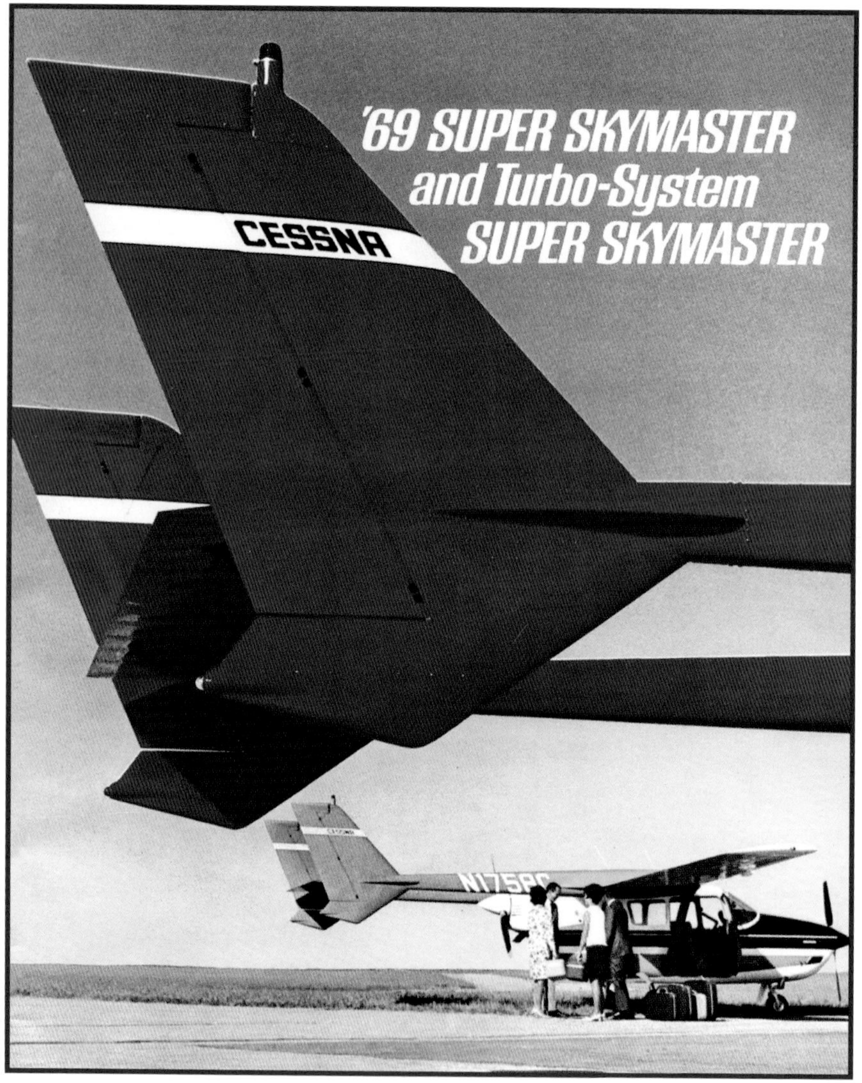

Cessna 336/337 Skymaster - 2,993 built
336 with fixed gear - 337 with retractable gear

The Skymaster handles differently from a conventional twin-engine aircraft, primarily in that it will not "yaw" (pull) into the dead-engine if one engine fails. Without the issue of "differential" thrust inherent to conventional (engines-on-wings) twins, engine failure on takeoff will not produce potentially dangerous yaw...away from the runway direction.

Del's Dream

Soft spoken! *Really* soft spoken. Why do I run into so many people who are "soft spoken?" And me…a type-A noisier than the devil. I've tried to improve myself but I still wind up making a lot of noise. Too late now. The way I am is the way I'll leave.

Del, though, was the epitome of "soft spoken." Just one heck of a nice guy and easy-going. I don't believe Del would have said boo to a butterfly! Everybody liked him. Oh, and one more thing: *Del had a dream.*

We met as apprentice bricklayers. He worked for one contractor and I worked for another. In all the time we were friends, we never did work together. We didn't become the closest of friends but we were in contact on a lot of occasions because of mutual interests and necessity. As apprentices, we were required to attend a school every other Saturday for the entire three and a half years of our apprenticeships. (That sure interfered with a lot of days of otherwise potential fun.) I met some outstanding people there and Del rated at the top. He was quiet and thoughtful, quite intelligent and very accommodating when time came for pitching in and helping with an activity.

Toward the end of apprentice school as we neared journeymanship, Del became engrossed in skydiving. He also acquired his pilot's license and bought a very nice four-place single engine airplane. I always was amazed when he would tell me how many skydiving jumps he had in his logbook. I was surprised to see such a soft-spoken guy doing such an unconventional thing as skydiving, and he surprised me even more when he acquired a Certified Flight Instructor rating. That rating was hard to get. It allowed him to charge for flight instruction in his own plane and make extra money on weekends. This guy was sharp *and dedicated.* You had to be one heck of a student to gain a "CFI" rating.

About then, I bought my Piper Cub. The Cub had brand new fabric covering but the engine needed an overhaul. It was purchased from a young aircraft mechanic who agreed to provide a major engine overhaul at no extra charge. When purchased, the plane had a sixty-five horsepower engine but what I wanted was an eighty-five horsepower engine. It was also about then that I found what fulfilled one of my long-held desires…*a biplane.* Hey, not just any biplane! A 1943 Meyers OTW! This one had appeared in a well-known movie! Now I was the proud owner of two planes, the Piper J-3 Cub and the biplane (and still a *student* pilot)!

Some time went by and I found myself working toward earning my own pilot's license. Del had been flying and jumping a long time before I got around to this. In fact, when I received my license at the age of twenty-nine, Del had already made six hundred parachute jumps and had over a thousand hours of flying time. That's a substantial amount of flying time for a private pilot. *A substantial number of jumps, too!*

I'd see Del once in a while and, on one occasion, we had a long lunch. That was when he told me of *his dream.* Del desperately wanted to be an "Ag" pilot…a "*Crop Duster.*" The one thing he wanted to do to move his dream along was get some flying time in a *biplane.* At that time, most cropdusters were using converted WWII surplus Stearman biplane primary trainers for their work. There were a lot of them available for relatively low cost and the "dusters" could have a much more powerful engine installed. Due to the great lifting capacity of their two big wings, those planes could carry very heavy loads. Del was anxious to get into a biplane to get the feel of such a different airplane from his Cessna 172. I wanted to do some parachute jumps so that, if I were doing aerobatics in my biplane and something drastic happened to the plane, I wouldn't be nervous about "bailing" out of the ship and pulling the ripcord to open the "chute." I always flew the biplane wearing a "seat-pack" parachute (it took the place of a seat cushion), in the unlikely event it might be necessary.

Del and I made a deal. He'd get to fly in my biplane to get some familiarity time, and he would take me skydiving in his airplane to satisfy my desire for the parachute experience.

My first two jumps were made near Hillsboro, Oregon...and the third

NO.	DATE	LOCATION	AIRCRAFT TYPE	LICENSED PARACHUTIST OR PILOT SIGNATURE AND LICENSE NO.	BACK CHUTE	
					TYPE	NUMBER
1	18 JUL 62	HILLSBORO	CESS 182	George F. Mitchell C447	BALGARIAN CUT	52-01-25005
2	3 AUG 62	Hillsboro	Cessna 172	[illegible]	T-10	
3	[illegible] 2 1964	Western Spot	172 Cessna	[illegible] CS01228	B-4	

My very modest parachute log book

My friend Del took me skydiving in his Cessna 172 Skyhawk for my second jump (of only three total). Del had two airplanes, one heck of a lot of flight time...and had jumped over six hundred times in "sky-diving" mode.

jump from Battleground, Washington. They were made on bright sunny days with almost no wind. I was surprised at how many other skydivers were taking part in the activities. It was easy to see that the sport was going to be big in the future.

The jumps were made at a time when much war surplus equipment still was used. My chute was military "surplus" and I was too big and it was too small...too small a diameter "canopy!" I hit the ground so hard the first time, that I felt the "after-effects" (bruises, sprained ankle, etc.) for two weeks.

Back then, almost no one owned a "custom" parachute...almost all were military surplus. Most skydivers weighed much less than I, who hit the ground with a thud that could be heard from twenty feet away. I lived to tell about it...and made two more jumps to be sure *I really had jumped...* and to feel confident about the whole procedure. That was enough for me! I wasn't interested in skydiving because, as heavy as I was and as small as the chutes were, I figured I'd just be constantly bruising my body!

Del was in heaven at the controls of my biplane. He sat in the front (student) cockpit because the pilot in command always sits in the rear cockpit. I could see him thrilling to the moment. Every time he looked back at me, his joyous countenance indicated that he might even be having palpitations of the heart from his excitement! After the flights, he said he knew he would somehow get his hands on a Stearman cropduster and be in business before long. He could feel it in his bones.

A couple more years went by and every time I saw Del, he would say he hadn't gotten into cropdusting yet, but he had more money saved up and a lot more flying experience, both of which he would need to be an Ag pilot. I had purchased a wrecked Piper Cub with an engine bigger than the one in my present Cub. The plane mechanic who sold me my Cub had agreed to overhaul the engine as part of the deal and said he'd be happy to overhaul the one from the wreck in place of it (which gave me twenty more horsepower). Then, I had a surplus Cub with a small engine. Del bought both from me and rebuilt them to do limited aerobatics and continue improving his skills in preparation for the big day when he would be behind the controls of his own cropduster. This guy was dedicated totally to his dream like no one I've known before or since.

We got another year older and saw less and less of each other. I wasn't sure what Del was doing now…didn't know if he was still laying brick or doing something else. Then one day we connected and he excitedly described how he had finally (after all these years) put together the outright "sole" ownership of a complete cropdusting outfit: airplane, tank truck (cropdusters apply *mostly liquid*) including the accessories, a pickup and every miscellaneous item needed for the operation. Some good ol' boy in Texas had decided to retire. By this time, Del religiously had saved enough money so that he could make a substantial down payment and then pay for enough necessary insurance to cover the seller's worries about equipment damage on the unpaid balance.

I said, "Texas? You gotta go all the way to Texas just to get a cropdusting business?"

"Well, that's kind of the way it is," he replied. "I couldn't find a darn thing here."

"I wish you well…hope you make a million bucks."

"The business won't be *that* good but I've wanted to do this for the last fifteen years. I even had to sell both my planes to make this happen, but it's going to be worth the effort." He meant he'd sold both the Piper Cub he'd bought from me and the Cessna 172 he'd used to fly skydivers. It took that much money and more to buy this going business. Bidding him goodbye and again wishing him great success, I was inwardly jealous...because he now would be a highly respected Ag pilot and I was a mere contractor. (Agricultural cropdusters are much respected by other pilots because of their highly developed skills.)

Another year rolled off the calendar and I ran into another bricklayer I hadn't seen in years. We visited a club for a drink and to talk over old times and the construction business.

We'd been visiting for a half hour or so when out of the blue he inquired, "Did you hear about Del?"

"Del?…golly, I haven't seen Del since he went to Texas a year or so ago."

"Well, you won't see him anymore. *He's dead!*"

"You've got to be kidding. *Not Del?*"

"Yep, *sure as hell!"*

"What happened?"

"Well, I'm not a pilot so I don't know the details, but a friend of mine knows all about the accident and he gave me the story. He knew Del well and he's really shaken up. I think I've got this right. Down in Texas where Del was flying, the crops he was working on have bees pollinating all day long so the dusters have to apply their 'stuff' at night to keep from killing the bees. That is close to what my friend said. Well, if it wasn't bees, it was something like that. Anyway, he was flying at night and flew right into his own tank truck…*dead center!*

Dear God…all I could think about was what a nice guy he was and all his years of dreaming, planning, scheming, saving, practicing, manipulating…it was just too much. I actually teared up in front of my bricklayer friend. Guess he thought that a little strange but, then, he hadn't been there when I had wished so hard that I could be *just like Del.*

Cessna 195, 1947-1954 short-term forerunner of the revered "180" - 1,180 built.

Forget seeing forward over the cowling on takeoff!

A "Walk-around" inspection before flight

My Cessna 180 raring to go!

Just A Day At The Beach

You've heard the old saying "A little bit of knowledge can be a dangerous thing." I can tell you it didn't mean much to me. I don't remember paying much attention to many of those old wise sayings such as, "A penny saved is a penny earned" or, "An ounce of prevention is worth a pound of cure." (I guarantee you that I've since learned the value of them, especially the last one!) Some of the things I did before the age of thirty and maybe even a little after, leave monumental question marks regarding reason!

My "little bit of knowledge" turned out to be a hefty supply of overconfidence and an inflated opinion of my technical flying skills…mated with extensive lack of experience. With only a limited number of flying hours, I felt I was getting pretty comfortable controlling my airplane...and this false confidence led me to perform a few imprudent activities which made for some dangerous, wild experiences. Did I want to be able to tell great hangar stories? Sure, most pilots do…but, on this occasion, bad luck struck.

A great mid-summer weekend day had me at the airport inspecting my Cub for a day of flying. The weather was glorious…one of those days when it's great to be alive. Not a cloud in the sky and the temperature moving up to tropical degrees. No special place to go or see…just the anticipation of a pleasant day sharing airspace with birds in the open skies. After a leisurely airplane "walk-around," I unfastened the tie-down ropes.

Each time arriving to fly the plane, I felt a secret inner excitement and thrill. That's how I felt this day as I stood alongside my little Piper Cub, reached forward to the propeller and prop-started the engine. As the engine surged to life, I knew that this day would be different from others and that, in some way, it would be a great adventure. Yep, this day was full of promise!

Basing my ship at the airport of Troutdale, Oregon, radio contact was necessary with its recently constructed "control" tower. I'd purchased a used Hallicrafters TRV-128A portable VHF radio (actually a "luggable" due to its 12 lb. battery pack) for the purpose...and now called "ground control."

Upon receiving "clearance" to move from ground control, I taxied to the end of the active runway, then called the "tower" for, and was given, take-off clearance. Applying power to the ship, the plane turned and straightened out looking ahead to forty-six hundred feet of blacktop. Helping the ship with a bit of control-stick back-pressure, it rose into the air with a bit of headwind help after using only a hundred-plus-feet of runway,

I then requested from tower control a mid-runway departure. I'd used only about one fifth of the usual takeoff length and thought: "When a greater little ship than this is made, that will be the ship to buy! Or, at least, *dream about!*" It was fun emulating "bush pilots" ways of flying.

Leveling off at traffic pattern altitude, the little ship headed up over the great Columbia River. My plan was to check out the various beaches along the river plus some sightseeing then, maybe, visit some friends on a wheat ranch south of The Dalles on the Oregon side of the river. I'd been a charter member of a fun group of carefree water-skiers who called themselves the "Sons-Of-Beaches." To see if any of the boys were out and about, my thought was to skim the water near Rooster Rock along the river on the Oregon side, one of our favorite haunts. This group had a grand time swaggering around in clothes that had our flashy double-entendre name embroidered on the shirt backs. Chuckling at the beach crowd ogling our spirited demeanor, we were perfectly harmless. Our activities were all in fun!

Dropping the little ship down near the water, it cruised along at about ten feet above the waves. That was legal as long as such flying put no one at risk other than the pilot! Every chance possible, I'd fly low and feel the exhilaration of the land mass rolling toward me as if in accelerated motion. Sometimes I would pull the stick back at cruising speed and climb steeply until running out of airspeed. Usually, that would give me around eight hundred to a thousand feet of altitude and then the plane would level off…always experimenting.

This day, to make things even more interesting, the plan was to pass by the nude beach near our usual water skiing location, flying right past the men to check out the ladies! Few below can escape being viewed from a plane above. Unfortunately, the plane is at a speed or altitude that doesn't offer the pilot much detail.

Everywhere below, people appeared to be having the times of their lives enjoying the warmth and water. Boats were moving in every direction with water skiers zipping this way and that. There must have been a few thousand people in a few miles of water and beach.

Alas! The nude beach was somewhat disappointing with only a dozen or so people. There were so many boats and people below me that I decided to use prudence and not get too close to any human bodies. Surely I didn't want my plane numbers reported for flying overly close, an infraction of FAA rules.

Proceeding east, the ship continued on toward nearby Bonneville Dam. I checked out fishermen in anchored boats trying their luck at catching the famous Columbia River Sturgeon, and then flew over to the Washington state shoreline on the other side of the river. Nothing much happening. Not much air traffic either, so a 180-degree turn was executed and the plane headed back downriver.

Continuing west, I flew directly out from a tiny sand island that, as water-skiers, we used occasionally as a temporary base of operations. I noticed that the east end of the isle had a flat open length of sand that looked like an interesting place to land. No special reason for landing except for adventure.

Pulling into a tight bank, I straightened out and drifted over to the downwind end of the minuscule make-believe airstrip, then, turning upwind, eased back on the throttle and executed a slow pass to get a closer look to see if a landing could be made. A small sand mountain maybe fifty feet high blocked the downriver end. At the upper end a very large assemblage of pilings was lashed together about thirty feet above the water, this grouping known in the river business as a "dolphin." The pilings were located just out from a tiny sandy point. The entire open patch of sand amounted to about two-hundred-fifty feet between obstructions and about thirty or forty feet wide from a sand bank that sloped upward into willow brush. Jokingly, I thought, "This teeny island would look like LaGuardia International to an aircraft carrier pilot."

It was settled! *I'd land here!* I'd landed in places a lot smaller (or, at least, a ***little*** smaller).

Nervously circling six or eight times and checking over the landing site in detail, there appeared to be no apparent challenges I couldn't overcome. The sand looked damp and hard and the beach was perfectly clear of flotsam.

The spirit of wild adventure had overtaken my senses. A thinking person might ask, "Why in the world land here and risk my precious little ship?" Well...why did Amelia Earhart challenge the Earth and try to fly all the way around? Why did numerous early pilots challenge the Atlantic in attempted solo crossings? The answer? As mountain climbers say, "*Because it's there!*"

The strip was so short it would be necessary to fly in easing the ship over from the river on an angle, then quickly reduce the power and drop the Cub on the sand while still in a slightly-turning configuration. The plane would be lined up with the landing site for only the last hundred feet. Gross weight of the plane was relatively low because of minimal fuel and no extra baggage. There wasn't enough room to make a normal landing so it would be necessary to fly back out the same way. This would be a very *"tight"* landing and takeoff situation!

Setting up and entering an approach, my heart throbbed as the plane got closer and closer. This was definitely a challenging operation and had to be made *on the first try*. Coming around smoothly in a gentle arc, I straightened, reduced power and joyously landed on the sand perfectly.

Slowing down, it didn't clearly register with me that the brakes weren't needed to lose groundspeed and, that extra power was needed to keep moving while taxiing to the far end of the strip to turn around. It seemed no problem. Upon turning, I aimed the ship down the strip...and then decided to stop, get out and relax for a bit.

Shutting down the engine, I deplaned, stretched and looked around. Boats were now nowhere in sight.

I poked around the beach area for a bit and then, looking toward the plane, noticed the wing on the water side drooping a little toward the river. The plane had been on the ground for only a few minutes. Was this my imagination?

While walking about on the sand, second thoughts about this venture had begun to enter my thinking. Now, I was developing serious "second and *third* thoughts." Yes, the wing *definitely was drooping*. And, *much lower* than the other wing. In fact, moving toward the plane with anxiety, it was clear the river-side tire was sinking into the sand.

How could this be? When I got out, there had been no sinking while standing alongside the plane. On a dead run, I rushed up to and around the plane. The right wheel had sunk a third of the way into the sand and the axle was nearing the surface. What had appeared to be damp *hard* sand was damp *medium*-hard sand, a hazardous difference! Why wasn't the soft sand noticed the moment I got out of the plane? Probably because my weight had been widely distributed when stepping out and pausing for the few moments on the beach. I hadn't stayed in one place long enough for the problem to be evident.

The plane appeared to be sinking into the sand rapidly. In panic, I quickly reached inside, turned on the ignition switch and started the engine by spinning the propeller. As the engine came to life, I jumped in with one large motion and, without even fastening the seatbelt, pushed the throttle as far forward as it would go. ***The plane didn't move an inch!***

Shutting off the engine and jumping out, a cold sweat prickled like nettles around my neck and ears. The plane had to be extricated from the sand quickly before it sank so far that it couldn't be flown out. Surely, boatloads of people would see my situation and stop to help me in this dire time of need. Dozens and dozens of boats had been upriver. Now, not a boat in sight. Not even one! By this time, the "masses" apparently had all gone home. ***Disaster loomed!***

The plane appeared to have sunk a little bit more...the drooping wing had drooped even lower. This was fast becoming a potential catastrophe. Mentally, I began castigating myself for making this landing at all. Why get myself trapped like this? Did I really need this experience?

Now I reached down under the tail of the airplane just ahead of the rudder, grasped the tail handle there and, with a giant bear hug, put my arms all the way around the tail to distribute the pressure so the fabric wouldn't rip. Next, I lifted up and pulled sideways with all my might, hoping to wrench the little ship free with applied leverage...and then wig-wagged the tail back and forth sideways. Well, good luck, fella! It moved a few inches but not enough to wrench the sinking wheel out of its rapidly-developing tomb as the plane still slowly sank. About the only thing of major note that this super-straining effort produced was a feeling of bulging out in my lower extremities near a hernia repair of many years ago. Great! Just what I needed…to pop my innards through an old hernia hole while trying to get out of a situation I shouldn't have gotten into in the first place.

This whole scene wouldn't have panicked me if I hadn't been in such an isolated area. By myself, there was just no way to get this plane out other than to fly it out. The island and my challenging situation were hidden from the main highway by groves of mainland trees, and, even ***if*** the plane could be seen by the many cars passing nearby, any help would still have to come by water so no aid from autos would be forthcoming!

Again, I scanned the giant river for someone to help me out of my predicament. Still...not a chance! Too late! All those on the water who could have been of help had disappeared!

Beginning to feel an astonishing charge of adrenalin due to the seriousness of the situation, my will to succeed increased...as this state of affairs had now reached crisis proportions. Only one pursuit now...save the ship at all costs! If not, most certainly my life would be lost in one of the most awful ways known to civilized man: ***death by humiliation!***

Desperately now, I searched up and down the beach at the driftwood line looking for something flat. Anything! *There was nothing close.*

Up the beach, nothing. Down the beach, aaah...a few driftwood boards at the far end. Odd sizes (long, short, narrow, wide) but, nonetheless, rays of hope. Grabbing them up, I raced back to the ship.

My years of varied mechanical experience took over. On my knees, I scooped at the sand behind the sinking wheel. Jamming the smallest board in under the wheel...then jumping back to the tail, I grabbed the tail handle again and heaved to one side with all my might. My repaired hernia area was still bulging…but, hey, the plane moved a little.

But, *not enough!*

Back to the wheel, I jerked the board out, then scooped sand out boring a trench as long as the board. By this time, the axle was lowering to touch the sand and, if success didn't come soon, it would be time to somehow get outside help and let the whole world in on my foolishness, a thought which gave me another temporary shot of muscle.

Zipping to the rear of the plane again, I quickly took up my position of leverage and gave one immense thrust to the side. And hurray…the wheel moved onto the board! A little. But…it was a start. Holding on with all the power that comes from facing total mortification, I gave one more powerful heave and moved the plane up a little farther sideways onto the plank. Another bowel-breaking strain and, lo and behold, the plane's wheel was lifted halfway onto the board. Leaning into my effort at a forty-five degree list to retain the gain made, I stood resting for a few moments. But man, oh man, now the other wheel was sinking! Holding the tail for a bit proved the plane would stay in place. Great!

Rushing, I dug rapidly under the second wheel, then slipped a board under that wheel and ran back to the tail again and heaved in the opposite direction until thinking I might be inventing the quadruple hernia. Good news! On this side of the ship, getting the wheel on the higher board worked the first time!

The ship was now floating atop the boards on the sand as if wearing snowshoes. A direct pardon had been received from the spirit of destiny that sentences fools like me to death by that terminal embarrassment I feared. My fortunes were improving!

The next hour was spent finding and hauling more driftwood boards and building a plank runway in front of the plane. I carefully placed them one before the other in front of each of the main wheels of the plane in a straight line. Then, I managed to jack the plane up one more plank to level ground by working the tail back and forth. At last, all was ready for the one shot I'd get at a take-off on my makeshift runway!

By this time, extreme fatigue was setting in and I was falling-down tired, but didn't dare let up for a moment and wanted only to get the heck out, go home, lie down and pass out for about a week.

Ready now, I propped the engine and it fired instantly! Dead-tired and feeling like a zombie, I sat for a few moments to let my remaining energy accumulate for my escape from what still could become sands of doom!

Finally, I held the brakes, shoved the throttle forward, raised the tail to get a clear picture of the perilously *narrow board track* and, with one last silent prayer, released the brakes.

If anyone ever wondered why ol' William T. Piper was able to build and successfully sell tens of thousands of Piper Cubs, the answer lay in the ability this flying machine exhibited as it surged forward very quickly on this unique airstrip of driftwood Douglas Fir boards, achieving the speed necessary to soar back into its domain in the sky.

Yep, by only the thinnest of foolishly self-imposed margins, stupidity was cheated...*once again!*

"Iconic" best describes this legendary airplane rudder (technically, the vertical stabilizer...the "rudder" is the movable part). Instantly recognizable to all intrepid pilots who fly in and out of the most formidable destinations on the planet, this is an airplane component which remains significant to aviation after 58 years in the sky.

(The vertical stabilizer belongs to the illustrious Cessna "180.")

Check Pilot Chills

Before becoming an airplane salesman, I didn't have a clue as to the multitude of wild stories the typical "check-pilot" can tell. (A check-pilot is a highly-experienced pilot designated by the FAA to examine and determine the abilities competency of a student and/or advanced pilot for a "rating" or to safely fly a "type" of plane.) Some of their tales indicate that they face challenging flight situations considerably more often than basic fair-weather private pilots. A few check-pilots have some stories they would rather not tell...and this is one of them.

After flying around the sky for about a year and logging a couple of hundred hours in my little Piper Cub, it was time (actually...about a hundred hours past time) to get my private pilot's license or I might spend my years flying alone. The license is required to carry passengers, and I was getting over the initial raptures of the sky and looking forward to flying around with other people. Owning my little Piper Cub outright and in the air almost daily, I'd become quite proficient at flying this little jewel.

I enrolled in a sophisticated ground school program and, after a few intense weeks, passed the course with a reasonable score. In addition to completing ground school, flight proficiency had to be proven. Along with demonstrating basic aircraft handling skills, it was required that students show ability to perform elementary "blind" flight using "instruments" only (no visibility through the windows). My Cub had few instruments... and those it had were very basic, but *just barely enough* for (most) of that portion of the "check-ride." I was not remotely interested in renting an aircraft with more instruments if it could be avoided. However, I would have to rent a more sophisticated plane for the "radio communication and radio navigation" portion of the check-ride.

I'd earlier learned the basics of instrument flight by having a vacuum-generating "venturi" installed which powered a "turn and bank" indicator, a requirement for "in the clouds" flight. Then I practiced instrument flight by flying into clouds, making climbs, descents and turns and simply flying back out. Although this routine had produced a couple of extremely hair-raising events, I did become moderately proficient at maintaining control of the aircraft and keeping it straight and level when flying "in the clouds." The earliest pilots must have learned "blind" flight much the same way, thus it seemed to make sense and…after a fashion, it worked, so I planned to take the "instrument" part of my check-ride ***in my own ship***.

Presenting myself to Western Skyways at the Troutdale, Oregon, airport to take my "Private Pilot, Single-Engine Land" license check-ride, I filled out the necessary papers and, after much discussion about procedure, those in charge finally agreed to my terms. Because I owned my own plane and my flying costs were very little, I wanted to take as much of the check-ride in it as the law allowed. I'd spent time looking into this and concluded that, because I had a "Turn and Bank" indicator which allows blind flight (although on a limited basis), I should be allowed to take the "Instrument" part of the check-ride in my own plane.

The flight operation opposed me on this issue but acknowledged that it was legal to do. Their objection was that my airplane had a very limited instrument panel and the plane they'd like me to rent from them had much more sophistication. A basic Piper Cub with a turn and bank indicator is indeed somewhat limited, but *it is possible* to stay alive in the clouds with the plane. They reluctantly gave in but forced me to rent one of their ships for the "radio-work" part of the checkride because of my lack of equipment. For tower communication, I was using my Hallicrafters TRV-128A portable VHF (very high frequency) radio that had only one crystal (frequency).

The day of my flight checkride, we had a disagreement over the issue of using my plane for the instrument flight-check. The commotion attracted the attention of the company's Chief Pilot, "Fred."

Fred apparently heard me raising my voice, came out from his office, stood by the end of a counter and listened in. He was surprised to hear that an aspiring pilot wished to take the instrument part of a check-ride in a basic

J-3 Cub. He hadn't run into that before and this definitely got his attention.

He was anxious to jump into the conversation and pointed out that he had taken his first flight instruction in the very same type of plane. He went on to relate experiences flying in World War II. Everyone knew that he was one of the select Army Air Corps pilots who had flown the "Hump" in a "Gooney Bird." Air-minded people know the Gooney Bird to be the famed Douglas DC3 ("C-47" in the military) of early air transport fame, and the "Hump" to be the difficult and dangerous wartime flight path over the massive high Himalayan mountain range on the "ICB" route (India, China, Burma...later changed to "CBI").

This mention of the DC3 and the Chief Pilot's "Hump" connection most certainly got our attention. Of all the superb pilots who flew in World War Two, the comparative few who flew the Hump could lay claim to many of the greatest flying stories of all time. Those pilots and the illustrious Flying Tigers of fighter pilot legend rate as many of the finest flyers ever! Just to live through flying the Hump made a unique tale. And we could actually reach over and touch this Hump pilot whose presence now graced this very room. It was like rubbing shoulders with one of the Gods of Flight. To say that we were impressed would be an understatement of major proportions.

His next utterance gave me goose-bumps. He very casually remarked to the man setting up my flight: "John, I have a little extra time and I think I'll take this part of the check-ride. It will be to my advantage to get the time in this gentleman's Cub because I haven't been in a 'tail-dragger' (usually, older planes having the third wheel under the tail) lately and this is as good a way as any to do that."

I was stunned! I'd been around Troutdale airport a lot and everybody talked about what a fantastic pilot this man had been in the military and ***how exacting*** he now had become as a "Chief Pilot."

I was torn between two realities. First, if I actually got to fly with Fred in this situation, I'd develop my own minor claim to fame and bragging rights. On the other hand, if he really did this, I would now be in the position of having to perform exceptionally well to satisfy what I'd heard was his predisposition toward absolute perfection. He was known to have flunked students for very minor procedure infractions.

Sure enough, true to Fred's statement, he became my check-pilot. He looked directly at me with an unflinching gaze, (probably developed from years of tolerating lesser pilots) and commanded, ***"Let's do it!"***

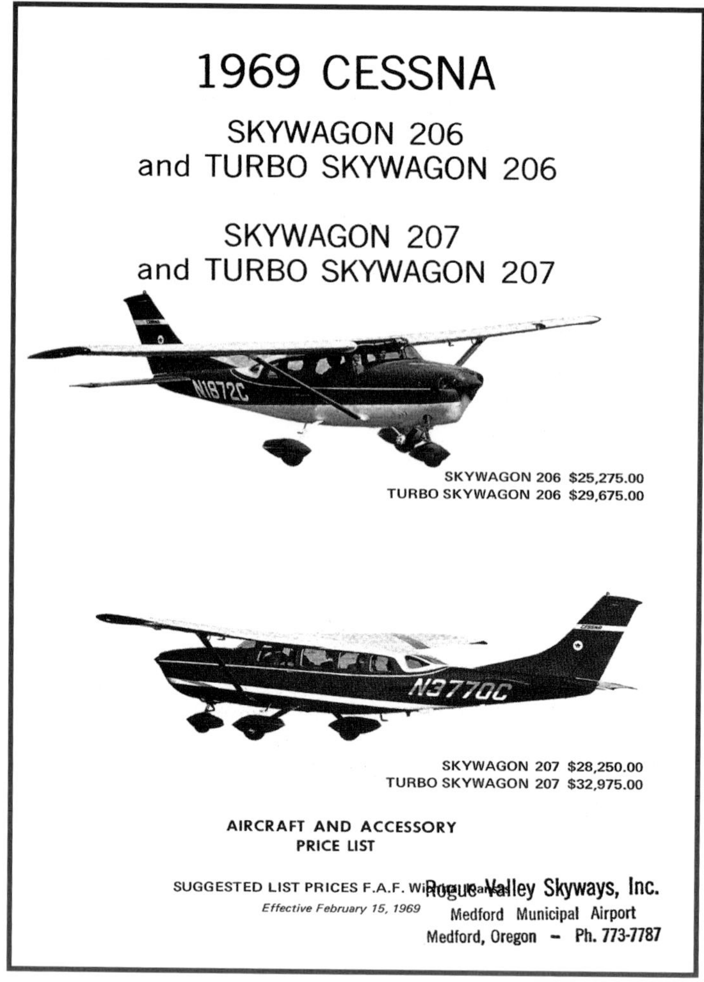

He explained a few details and then we went directly to my little ship parked out on the flight line.

He watched me intently as I went through my airplane "walk-around" inspection and officiously monitored my every move. This did, however, appear to be one of his good days because he actually began joking with me as I went through the routines of checking the plane's flight-readiness. He tried to hide it but it appeared that he was yearning to climb into this small ship and bring back memories of his youth. By now, he had become congenial! I calmed down…but only a little.

During preflight briefing, we discussed exactly how we would proceed to simulate “Instrument Flight.” We decided that I’d fly from the front tandem seat with the windshield and my side windows covered with newspapers taped in place to block my outside view and, therefore, simulate “blind” flight.

Most of my flying experience in this plane was from the rear tandem seat. When flying solo, which is how I had accumulated most of my flying time, that is the correct location to pilot the Cub due to weight and balance considerations. Flying now from the front seat had me a little worried because my large physical size made it somewhat difficult for me to manage the controls comfortably. I simply would have to do my best!

Fred seemed to chuckle the whole time we attempted to achieve a reasonably full coverage of the front window areas with uncooperative newspaper. The work was a struggle and took an inordinate amount of time to get the job done, but he didn’t seem to mind at all. Maybe he would use this unusual and out-of-the-ordinary flight to add to his already long list of unique aerial escapades.

We finished our paperwork and I climbed…or, more correctly, *squeezed* myself into the front seat as good ol’ Fred, the super pilot, awkwardly entered the much roomier rear seat. It was obvious that he was aging and working with diminished mobility.

He took quite some time “scrunching” around to get himself in and situated. I thought, “I wonder if this old boy with all his late-model big-airplane flying time, can still fly this little old-fashioned tail-wheel puddle-jumper?” I hoped so! I didn’t have a nickel’s worth of insurance and I doubted his flight operation would cover any damage costs in a situation like this.

I prop-started the engine and climbed in, then settled down, called ground control, received taxi instructions and taxied to the end of the active runway. After checking the pre-takoff list, I called the tower and was given takeoff clearance. We flew to a practice area and then began the usual required air maneuvers involved in the pursuit of a Private Pilot license.

When Fred called for “recovery from unusual attitudes” and other basic blind-flying “instrument” work, I apparently performed to at least his minimum standards because he touched my shoulder and nodded approval. He yelled up to tell me to remove the newspaper from my section of the windows. I pulled the paper off and handed it back to him, which he stuffed behind his seat into my recently installed baggage compartment (a very small thin-plywood-lined area).

After executing more required basic flying maneuvers, he yelled up...“Give me a ‘short-field’ landing,” and motioned in the direction of nearby Sandy airport, a very small airstrip that allowed transient flight activity.

Generally, there is no big mystery to making a successful “short-field” landing. The reason they are considered important is because, in an emergency situation, it might be necessary to land in a very small patch of ground where a pilot might have few options and little decision-making time. They are also used in the normal course of flying at short airfields.

The process is to pick a spot on the field at which you wish to touch down, slow the aircraft to very low airspeed, bring the ship over the runway threshold (or over a fence and into a farmer’s field) as low and slowly as possible, reduce all power at the appropriate time...allowing the plane to settle down precisely where you had planned and brake to a quick stop…using very little distance. Such a successful landing can save a pilot’s life.

Nearing the airport, I pulled on carburetor heat, reduced power and began my glide to the field. I crossed the runway’s end with just a little too much airspeed and overshot my planned touch-down point by a bit less than a hundred feet...which, ordinarily, would have been considered pretty darn good. However, ***that wasn’t good enough for Fred.***

With a low muffled growl, he grabbed at the “stick,” took control away from me and yelled over the noise of the engine, “Here, let me show you how I like em’ done.”

I was crushed! I had been trying my very best to appear as much as possible like an accomplished young future master of the skies… and apparently had failed in one of the very important tests…at least to Fred’s thinking. Interestingly, Fred did not give the impression that he was overly displeased with my short-field landing performance. It was that he seemed to want to show me what ***absolute perfection*** really looked like.

Now with the ship under Fred’s full control, he shoved the throttle forward to full power and the little Cub rose into the air and clawed for altitude. Fred seemed almost in a blissful trance as he leveled the plane out on its downwind leg (to me, though, his piloting technique in my precious little jewel seemed a little lacking). I shrugged it off as his unfamiliarity with the machine.

Turning on base leg, Fred applied carburetor heat and pulled back on the throttle. Turning final, the plane wobbled around a bit as Fred attempted to get in direct line with the runway but finally got the plane headed approximately in the right direction...albeit a little off to one side from a perfect alignment.

I thought, "Well, he seems rusty but, with as many hours of flight in his logs, he should be able to handle this little plane."

The airfield was all grass. The runway was simply a mowed strip of moderate width right down the middle of a very large field. The remaining field (sides and ends) was tall grass...*very tall grass*. In fact, more like potential hay. This very tall grass began right at the edges of the mowed strip close on both sides and was maybe three feet high. Very tall and **dense!** ***Airplanes do not like tall grass!*** "Dense" tall grass presents a veritable barrier to airplane wheels and, if a plane attempts to land in tall grass, it might very possibly be slowed dramatically to the point of tipping over forward.

The plane was now aimed not down the center of the strip but a little to the right side and we were now almost over the runway threshold. I nervously wondered just when he was going to get the ship centered for touchdown...on the *very narrow strip.*

Closer and closer we came to touchdown and still the plane lingered off-center dangerously to the right, just over the long line of tall grass. I waited for his final correction…and waited...and waited…and waited. ***The correction never came!***

Later, I would conclude that Fred had not been in a tail-wheel airplane for so long that he had apparently forgotten how obstructed the visibility is from the rear seat, the usual seat of the pilot in command. It is impossible to see directly forward, only forward at an angle to the sides. Without a vigorous side-to-side movement of the pilot's head and direction-correcting actions just before touchdown, holding straight forward motion can be difficult. This old "vet" had been flying late-model tricycle gear planes with great forward visibility from very large, long and wide solid paved strips for so long that he clearly had overlooked the potential pitfalls of a poorly-executed landing with a "tail-wheel" plane on a grass strip.

We collided with Mother Earth at exactly the meeting point of the mowed strip and the much too-tall grass! The right tire caught in the high grass and began to twist the ship to one side with a sickening lurch that warned "***Immediate disaster imminent!!!***"

That put us in the first stage of the dreaded "ground loop," a characteristic of airplanes which presents itself when one wheel or the other has its forward movement abruptly hindered. This results in the plane whipping around into a sharp spin on the ground at high speed frequently causing expensive damage.

In that same nervous instant, my brain rolled over about six different scenarios of outcome…all of them ugly in the face of this swiftly unfolding situation and my subservient student pilot position. As the next one-hundredth of a second elapsed, it was obvious that Fred had completely lost control and, if the situation were to improve, the unthinkable must now rear its head...specifically, ***someone*** must regain control. In this case, the only answer I could think of was that…***the student must wrest control from the veteran!***

"*Save my ship*" was all that raced through my head and, although I had second thoughts, my third thoughts automatically directed my hand to the controls. With a lightning move, I made a mad grab at the control stick, jerked it out of Fred's now shaking hands and, with my other hand, wildly shoved the throttle full-forward. At the same time, I pulled the stick back to hold the plane on the ground so it wouldn't nose over and pushed hard on the left rudder to try to stay straight and upright. We slowed dramatically…fate was on our side…and after mowing a big strip of the very tall grass, the ship bounced back out onto the runway. *Whew!!*

Not a word was uttered. Now shaking, I looked forward and kept the plane straight with full power on. We left the ground and I trimmed it up for a normal climb to altitude. The little ship hummed along neatly. Still, not a word was exchanged. Continuing to look straight ahead I wondered who would say what, next.

All was very quiet for what seemed an inordinately long stretch. I never once turned to look back at my superior. After making a few shallow turns and leveling out at two thousand feet, I heard what sounded like a grunt and turned my head to the side. Fred cleared his throat a time or two and muttered barely over the sound of the engine, "You can take her back to the base now." Not another word was spoken until we were back inside the flight office.

Fred quietly asked for my logbook and made his entry affirming my achievement of earning an "Airplane, Single-Engine Land" private pilot's license. He silently, but pleasantly, shook my hand, then congratulated me, waved me over to the desk clerk to pay my bill…and (wordlessly) shuffled away to his office.

Short Landing Lunacy

Landing *across* an aircraft carrier? Well, not really. But, it sure seemed like it at the time. The space couldn't have been much more than fifty feet total between obstacles. You say, "Landing in a space that small can't be done with an airplane." As a matter of fact, *it all depends on the circumstances.*

The event began on one of the windiest early fall days in the Portland area for some time. I headed for the airport after discovering my contract job for the day wasn't to start until later in the week. The airport was my destination whenever I could think up even the weakest excuse, an indication of how "taken" I had become with my new-found love of flying. One happy year I accumulated 200 flying hours. Now, *that* was a vintage year! *I flew almost every day the Northwest's weather allowed.*

Today would be a good day to fly over to visit my friend, Eldon, on his family's farm. Arriving at the Troutdale, Oregon, airport...I hiked over to my trusty J-3/85 Cub, which was tied down on a blacktop apron, gave it a careful pre-flight inspection, then started the engine and climbed in. After calling ground control and receiving taxi clearance, I taxied to the active runway.

Awaiting take-off clearance, I queried my amateur pilot brain for any unique activities I could get involved with this day that I hadn't done before in my little ship. Listening to pilots claiming to have seen or done magnificent feats, I'd heard talk about flying activities that could be done in high wind, but many seemed far-fetched! At the very least, some of this talk sounded like a sure-fire way to risk destroying an airplane.

The wind this day was only fifteen mph at the airport but much higher a few miles up the Columbia Gorge and in other nearby areas. I'd called the Troutdale Flight Service Station to check the weather earlier and up the Gorge the wind was gusting about thirty to fifty miles an hour and sometimes holding steady at the high end. In our area, this big autumn "blow" is titled the "East Wind" and we can expect it early every fall. The wind blows westerly so hard and steady at some points in the nearby Columbia River Gorge, that the limbs on giant Douglas Fir trees there grow on only one side of the tree.

Calling the control tower, I requested a straight-out departure having decided that the Columbia Gorge directly ahead looked like a good place to start searching for the day's adventure on the way to Eldon's place. The request was granted and I eased into a cruise directly into the increasing wind ahead.

After a number of minutes airborne which had taken me a few miles up the "Gorge," the first thing that struck me as unusual was that, at my standard cruise airspeed, the cars on the freeway below were all passing me. This was a new experience, for I'd never flown into a wind condition this severe. It was surprising how greatly the wind had increased in only a short distance traversed.

When pilots flying very small airplanes see cars below passing them, it is a shocking revelation. Most new pilots naturally assume that airplane travel will always be much faster than travel by auto. *Not necessarily.* That impression is soon dashed by the first automobile below that leaves you behind when a really strong headwind is pushing against the plane. The only solution for this is a plane with more horsepower or one that is much more aerodynamically efficient.

I was surprised how long it took to cover the relatively short distance east from Troutdale to the venerable Columbia River Highway landmark, "Crown Point," an almost vertical precipice a thousand feet above the water and topped with an historic viewpoint building named "Vista House." Approaching Vista House, I began to get the feel of how slowly I was moving by using the building as a point of reference. It seemed that I was only creeping toward it. So slowly, in fact, that a quaint idea popped into my head. There were a number of tourists standing at the edge of the cliff looking over a stone wall appearing awed at the *thousand foot drop* beneath them. Here, then, was a golden opportunity to play barnstormer!

Flying out in front of the tourists with the thousand feet of space below me, I moved my ship slowly over toward them, almost stopping a couple hundred feet away. My ship could fly in slow flight at thirty-five miles an hour in such a wind *remaining suspended and absolutely still,* so a forty-mile-plus wind made the gambit easy. I even had to increase power considerably above typical slow speed rpm and was surprised at how smooth the wind was. I *hovered*...without moving so much as an inch forward, backward, up or down. People came running out from the building and formed a small crowd watching this unusual phenomenon. I held the plane in position and waved back to children waving to me.

For variety, after a short period of holding my position, I pushed the stick forward and plummeted straight down about three hundred feet. I "parked" there in space for a few moments directly below and looked up through my roof window to see many faces peering down at me over the wall. Next, I pulled the stick back and shot straight up like a rocket passing the building level and "stopping" in midair about three hundred feet above the awed groundlings. Didn't Leonardo da Vinci say that man eventually would fly like a bird?

Repeating the up and down production a couple more times, I then dropped back down level with those watching and held the plane motionless...as from a "skyhook." Contemplating what other foolhardiness I could perform, I saw a man writing in a notebook; maybe, just maybe, *my registration number!* My memory now was jogged by something I heard in ground school about an FAA ruling that prohibited planes from flying closer than so-many-feet to humans. Having forgotten exactly how many feet, I knew for sure the distance was way over a couple hundred…more like a thousand plus, near ten times more distant than I now was. In the thrill of the moment, I'd been carried away. Pulling back on the stick with alacrity, the plane shot skyward...to get out of close sight of any would-be informers. This time I flew up to about two thousand feet to quickly hide my registration numbers and then banked sharply southward. It was high time to make a quick getaway and speed over to Eldon's farm.

I mentally censured myself for showing off so blatantly, knowing full well that such activity might lead to a license suspension and embarrassing exposure to the rest of the aviation community. How would this look in the newspapers! How could I be so foolish? The good news is that, apparently, nobody reported my number. At least, nothing came of the "incident."

As I approached Eldon's farm, the wind direction changed to blow directly across tall cane-berry (boysenberry) vines located to one side of a large barn. The now-dead berry vines had been strung on rows of wires about four feet high between wooden posts. Crossing the berry field, I then flew over Eldon's house and pulled up into a steep wingover, then leveled out holding a couple hundred feet of altitude, circled for a bit, then saw Eldon and his brothers and sisters come running from the house.

Ah, ha! A space about fifty feet wide was visible between sections of rows. With the "East Wind" still blowing about forty miles per hour directly across the berry rows, it appeared that I could pull over to the open slot crossways and simply *de-levitate* straight down onto the fifty-foot space between the four-foot-high vines and then shut down the engine. Lined up for descent, I slowly pulled the throttle back and the little ship gradually settled straight down.

I had overlooked only one thing. Arriving at the four-foot level (top of the vines), the wind was slowed to a large extent because of a vine wind-break effect. The plane had descended the final four feet like a rock...with a major bounce and a big "thud." Then, with little wind to inhibit forward motion and still some power on the throttle, the Cub shot forward before I could get the throttle retarded. By the time I hit the brakes and stopped, *less than three inches* separated the plane from the row wires. But those three inches saved wiping out a gleaming new metal propeller, plus much loss of face!

I crawled out of the plane and greeted my friends who were fascinated for no airplane ever before had landed on the property.

From the moment the engine shut off, I was thinking about my chances of getting back out without difficulty. I chattered with the group as if in conversation but, had they noticed the glazed look in my eyes, they would have known that I was looking right through them...figuring a discreet way out of this tight spot. Even if the wind died, there still wasn't enough room for a safe takeoff along the rows, plus there would be some direct crosswind. Problem was, there wasn't enough wind below vine-top level to levitate back out vertically with power. The alternative of taking the plane apart and hauling it out in pieces by truck definitely was not appealing. Mulling this over, I continued conversing with the enthralled group... trying to look engaged, but puzzling over how the heck I was going to get out. Finally, a thought struck…a possible out!

Having to own up to my miscalculation, I explained to the gathering that there was a problem and *what it was.* And...would they mind getting me some shears? They would be necessary to cut some upwind vines (and a few downwind) from their wire holders to permit enough wind through them. That would make it possible for the wings to gain the "lift" needed to fly out. Luckily, the vines were dead and had served their purpose, so cutting them down would cause no harm. However, the vines had a plethora of long sharp thorns usually removed by specialists in that work using very thick leather gloves.

I grabbed the shears and began cutting away like a wild man to finish before the wind died. If I didn't get out *now,* no telling when the wind

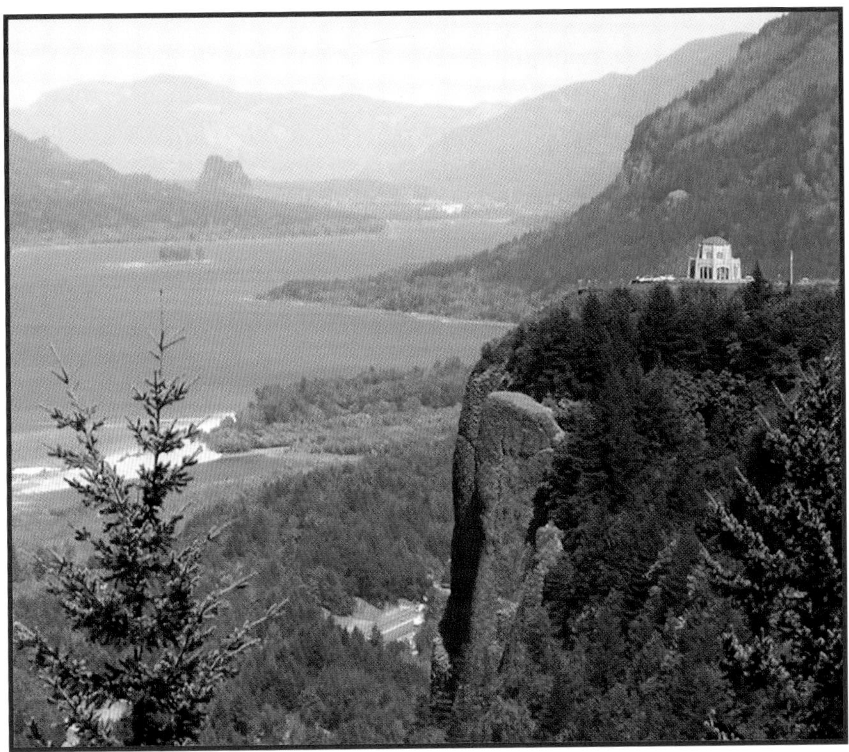

Vista House in The Columbia River Gorge

When winds blew in excess of forty miles per hour through the deep canyon in front of famed Vista House, I occasionally "hovered" my Cub in the air there level with the Vista House. Tourists viewed the plane in awe...which appeared to them to be hanging in midair as if stationary from an invisible skyhook! (Sadly, a photo never was acquired of the plane "parked" above the chasm.)

again would blow here this hard. The group watched my actions until the cold wind drove all but Eldon back into the house.

After about forty-five minutes of heart-pulsing effort and many bloody scratches on my arms, enough vines were cut down to allow the wind through the rows close to ground level. While I perspired, Eldon, much to my chagrin, watched while chiding me about the whole affair. When finished with my vine cutting, he helped me pull the plane backward until the tail was in the rear vine row.

Goodbye, Eldon! (I couldn't say it fast enough!) Having prop-started the engine, I hopped in, pressed down hard on the toe-brakes to hold the plane in place, and revved the engine to high r.p.m....to blow enough air back to raise the tail. Holding the ship level in place with locked brakes and the engine at full power, I stared intently forward at the wires almost under my nose. Anxiously, I waited for what would feel like an even higher gust than the high steady wind presented. There would be a forward run of only *about* twenty-five feet toward the wires.

At last, I felt a high gust and, with one of the deepest breaths inhaled in my body's history, I released the brakes and eased back on the stick...all in one smooth motion. Buffeting somewhat, the little plane elevated. Straight up! *Hallelujah! It worked!*

With knees knocking like a snare drum, I flew straight to my home airport. Did I learn anything from this predicament? Yep! For the rest of my flying career, I treated the wind as cautiously as I would a wounded tiger! And...I vowed to be much more astute in selecting activities for demonstration!

Flying rule #33: To avoid near-fatal embarrassment, never do anything that clearly exposes your stupidity to anyone but God!

BARR AIRCRAFT SERVICE

FLIGHT INSTRUCTION
CHARTER SERVICE
MAINTENANCE - REPAIR

Municipal Airport — Susanville, Calif.

Telephone 257-3410

Customer's Order No. ______ Date 11-17 1962

M ark Tilsom

Address

SOLD BY	CASH	C. O. D.	CHARGE	ON ACCT.	MDSE. RETD.	PAID OUT

QUAN.	DESCRIPTION	PRICE	AMOUNT
1	8.00 5 c tube	6.88	6 88
7.1	gal 80/87	.44	3 12
1	lite pare	1.00	1 00
	Sales Tax		28
			11 28

ALL claims and returned goods MUST be accompanied by this bill

548 Rec'd by

MOORE DEALER-COBEL'S, SUSANVILLE CALIF.

Aviation prices used to be in line with average paychecks.

This receipt includes a tube for one of my "Cub" tires. Try to buy one ***now*** for that price! Notice the fuel attendant spelled by sound alone. That is supposed to be my name...but, *how about those prices???*

Lend You My Airplane? ...*I Don't Think So!*

Model "T"s were all the rage! No, I'm not talking about the early 1900s when Henry Ford sold over fifteen million of them. No...I mean they were the rage in the 1960s. But this time, they were sought after by many neophyte devotees of the antique auto hobby. Other car buffs, those with more resources, went after the rare and exotic cars such as early Locomobiles, Stevens Duryeas, Duesenbergs and the like.

I also became interested in old cars at that point in time but my interests fell in line with those of the former group. In my late teens, my age group was deeply into the "hot rod" hobby. Then we aged out of hot-rodding as the "Soaring Sixties" came along with its great economy and increased earnings for many. Along with quite a number of other former hot-rodders, I matured into the antique auto restoration and ownership pastime.

The key reason the hobby was taken up by a great many people (most went after old Fords)...was that, as late as the nineteen sixties, there were still tens of thousands of junker Model T Ford bodies and assorted parts scattered around the country in barns and fields. Also, some long-time car dealerships had "NOS" (**N**ew **O**ld-**S**tock) remaining parts still in inventory.

My own involvement in the hobby began strictly by accident. As a contractor, I enjoyed getting jobs out of town so that I could drive my big truck and trailer, one of my secret pleasures. On one job at the south end of Bend, in central Oregon, a builder was putting together an antique auto museum and had a whole collection of antique cars he had hauled out from the Midwest. Most of the old cars were fairly unique and valuable but he also had a few less desirable cars stored behind one of his buildings. He turned out to be really frugal when parting with money and, when I gave him my bid for work on his museum, he began immediately to complain about what a monumental sum it was. Then, he continued to grumble about how hard it had been for him to save enough to build this museum and he really couldn't spend that much cash so…would I take an old unrestored antique car as part trade in payment for my work?

Mulling that over, I thought about how he accidentally had dropped the fact that my bid was lower than one his cousin had given him. I'd been considering lowering my bid but now, on second thought with this new surprise offer, I responded, "Sure, I'll take a car, if the value works out with my bid." Happily, I ended up with a "free" antique car. If he had been a little more hesitant, I would have felt forced to drop my price. But I certainly enjoyed my "free" unrestored but drivable…*1927 Model T Ford roadster!* That's what started me on the road to becoming a Model T hobbyist. Little did I know that my positive reply to him would ultimately lead me to some unique adventures in the world of aviation.

Even though the car he gave me was a beat-up semi-junker, it ran! Eventually, I decided to do what many other "T" enthusiasts were doing: search out enough individual parts at modest prices to assemble a complete and more desirable *early model.* That's how the hobby works….start out small and try to end up with something more imposing. I had the advantage of working away from the "big city" on my out-of-town jobs where I could search for old parts in areas which hadn't already been canvassed heavily for them by every Tom, Dick, and Harry "*flatlander*" (people ***from*** the "***big city***") in the hobby.

About then, I fortuitously rediscovered airplanes! Earlier, I had attempted a number of times to learn to fly and given up each time because of the expense (although flying was far less costly than in later years). A motorcycle-racing compatriot of mine took me for a ride in his Piper Tri-Pacer, a small four-place ship. My latent airplane enthusiasm was aroused! The Wright brothers were right on target…***flying really is magic!*** Anybody can drive a car, ride a bike, rollerskate, operate a boat, ride a horse, get on a train or bus...bu***t very few people can fly an airplane!***

Everybody loves a biplane!

Flying the Meyers OTW biplane was always great sport. Friends and bystanders usually materialized in sizable numbers. It frequently became necessary to give rides until time to refuel. (Marc is closest to plane...parachute “D-ring” is visible on his chest.)

SHELL
AVIATION CREDIT CARD INVOICE

SOLD TO: MARC E PAULSEN JR

CITY & STATE:

AIRCRAFT LICENSE NO.

CARD NO.: 387 151 251

58746

THIS COPY CANNOT BE USED FOR TAX REFUND PURPOSES.

SOLD BY: MADRAS AIR SEV
MADRAS ORE

DATE: 10—9-62

The charges shown are hereby transferred to SHELL OIL COMPANY

SHELL PRODUCTS	QUAN.	PRICE INC. TAX	TAXES STATE	TAXES FED.	AMOUNT	
Shell 80 Aviation Fuel	8.3	.42	--		3.	49
AeroShell Oil Grade						
SALES OR LOCAL TAXES						
	TOTAL			$	3.	49

The amounts shown include all taxes which the vendor or any prior vendor must pay or is obligated to collect.

CUSTOMER'S COPY

RECEIVED BY X

Peering out and down from my friend's airplane window, I was reminded that there were no trees, fences, hills or buildings to block lines of sight from a plane and almost everything on the ground could be spotted readily. Now in the old-car hobby, I suddenly recognized the potential of flying to search for old cars and parts deposited behind ranches out in the Pacific Northwest's high desert country. Due to low desert rainfall, old cars and parts likely would be in good condition with little rust. Thus, I bought an airplane and finished learning to fly.

To locate Model T cars and parts, a brilliant plan emerged. I'd had a modest contract on a huge new paper mill which required purchasing two portable low-frequency handset radios for jobsite communication. For hunting "T" cars and parts, I enlisted the help of my friend, Dave. Dave drove my truck on the ground while I flew my airplane (like an iron-hungry buzzard) circling over ranch after ranch checking out their "back-forty" (usually acreage out of sight of the home) surplus scrap piles. Many of the "piles" were so old that they harbored complete antique autos which were long obsolete.

Dave and I communicated via the radios and, when I made a find, it was easy to either direct Dave right to the "treasure"or lead him to a landing spot where we could meet and then both drive in the truck to the find. We found enough auto parts this way to acquire what I needed for my own project, plus a lot of "extra" parts that we sold quite profitably. The activity was great sport and a truly exhilarating treasure hunt from the sky!

Ranchers are some of the most fiscally conservative people ever. Over time, I learned that a rancher never discards a piece of metal of any kind. They just plain don't! The farther out in the wild they live, the more conservative they are, thus the more scrap iron there is to be found on their back forties! The lucky part about searching dry-country ranches by plane was that the owners stashed their junk piles far behind their buildings, almost always completely out of sight of anyone *driving* thus those *drivers on old car searches* would ***never*** spot this stuff. Most ranches are miles apart and one wouldn't think pride to be much of a consideration but I suspect the wives spoke up about where all that ugly iron was piled: "Fred, you get that junk outa this yard *right now!*" So, out to the junk pile in the ravine it went. *Waaayyy out!*

Another great advantage of this parts-hunting program was that, during this era of farm history, these people had not yet been overrun by hobbyist "flat-land furriners." This was before many people had four-wheel drive vehicles, campers, and motor homes which allowed them to traverse and spend time in "back-country" areas more easily. The benefit to Dave and I was that the land-owners were still happy to see and talk with strangers, plus easy to deal with because they saw no useful need for what we were searching out. Because no competing old-car hobbyists could see the ranchers' hidden old-car "gold" from the road, most of it remained undiscovered until we flew over with the trusty little red and white Piper Cub.

Dave and I worked this operation very successfully for a couple of years until we tired of it but not without getting ourselves into some very "sketchy" flying situations.

I had a Flying-Farmer Association member friend, "Erwin," (actually, a wheat and cattle rancher) who lived on the east side of the Cascade Mountain Range in dry wheat country. Erwin had his own airstrip and a Piper J-3 Cub like mine so we had that in common.

Irwin had a thirteen-year-old son named Marvin who was one very quick-thinking farm boy. Marvin and I made a deal. From time to time, Marvin would search out old car parts which I would then buy from him. When I once asked how much he wanted for some car parts he had discovered, his *lightning quick* reply was, "***Cash is King!***" *Thirteen years old!* I've never forgotten that one and still use that "line" myself.

One long weekend, Dave and I drove over to visit friend Erwin and check on what old car parts Marvin may have scrounged up. Upon our arrival, young Marvin rushed out to my truck and excitedly described a "find" he had made for us at an abandoned homestead ranch. He had asked the owner for the "find" and been given permission to remove it.

There was only a minor problem. In earlier years, the homestead property had been turned into a massive wheat field leaving all of the buildings abandoned in the center *right where these desirable old items were located.* Unfortunately, there was no road leading directly in to it. If that wasn't problem enough, the owner had recently *disc-plowed the entire field.*

In many situations, "disc-plowing" leaves the soil "relatively" firm because the process typically doesn't dig down nearly as deep as "mold-board" plowing, which leaves the earth soft to a greater depth. Of course, soil conditions can vary a lot from one field to the next. Smart farm kid that he was, Marvin knew all about such field conditions so he described to me what he thought was the ultimate solution for getting to these desirable items...and retrieving them from a difficult-to-reach location.

Since Dave and I had driven over to eastern Oregon, my plane was back at home, so Marvin would get his dad to loan me his plane for an hour or so. Then, he and I would fly in with tools, land, remove the best of the old car parts and fly out. According to Marvin, his dad flew in and out of fields like this all the time. Elementary, hmm?

Dad Erwin agreed, knowing that I flew a plane like his and said, "Sure, take the plane." We had it made! I could almost feel the parts in my hands already!

With minimum fuel in the tank (allowing the carrying of more cargo) for this short flight, Erwin's pretty little yellow Cub lifted off the ground quickly and, in a matter of minutes, we were circling our quarry over the plowed field.

We flew low over the abandoned ranch buildings several times to get a reading on the wind direction from tall grass growing near them. The wind appeared to be very light and I got ready to set up for a landing. As I looked down at the freshly-plowed field, I had a momentary twinge of trepidation. Raising my voice, I bellowed up to Marvin in the front seat, "Marvin, this field *looks awfully soft!*" He turned and shouted back, "My Dad lands in fields like this all the time!" That was all I needed…a little reassurance.

Of course we could land there. His dad was an outstanding pilot, wasn't he? And, *he landed planes in places like this all the time*, didn't he? Of course he did! He lived right in the midst of fields like this. And Marvin flew in and out of these types of fields with his dad all the time, didn't he? Obviously, then, *the plane could land here*. Hey, it made sense to me!

The fact that not only ***did I not*** do this all the time and I was still a fairly "low-time" pilot flying someone else's little jewel, didn't seem to register any great consternation to me. To get those old car parts, we would have to land on that *plowed* field. *We had to get that stuff!* My final decision? ***I would listen to the wisdom of a thirteen-year-old!***

Calculating the direction of the light wind, I powered downwind, banked around in a tight turn and set up an approach that should put us right alongside the buildings when we stopped rolling.

As the ground came up to meet us, I could swear the plowed furrows seemed to grow in size. As we neared touchdown, the furrows visually had grown into giant bulbous rows like so many large sections of pipe laid side-by-side, and a flashback gave me pause for thought! I remembered a dilemma in which a fellow with whom I once worked trapped himself. For $500, he had just purchased a J-3 Cub like the one we were now flying... and had taken a friend for a ride. Over the Sandy River canyon at about 600 feet above the water, the engine quit. In panic, he discovered he didn't have enough altitude above the canyon sides to glide over them onto terrain which might offer better opportunities for a safe landing.

He then took the appropriate action for this type of emergency and set up a landing glide. His only landing option then was directly beneath him. He reassured his passenger that they would be able to land safely way down below on that narrow strip of "gravel" alongside the river. Only when the plane was irreversibly committed to land did he realize the strip consisted of stone boulders up to eighteen inches in diameter. "***It sure looked like big 'gravel'*** from way up above!" he later recalled. Amazingly, they "walked away" (no injuries) from the "landing" but the airplane was not so fortunate. The propeller was bent, the gear ripped off and most of the rest of the plane damaged beyond help. The only parts worth saving were the wings so the next day the two of them went back, took off the wings and, when nightfall interrupted their work, laid them aside the plane. Upon returning a couple of days later to get the wings, it was learned that some vandal-types had discovered the wreck and floated them down the river. (They probably ended up in the Pacific Ocean circling toward Asia in the Japanese Current!)

Back to my landing in the "plowed" field:

I braced myself for touchdown! The wheels ever so lightly touched the tops of the plowed "furrows." We skipped along on top of the plowed earth toward the buildings as the wing's "lift" diminished...due to the slowing airspeed. O.K. *so far!*

The next event *happened in an instant!* One moment we were flying... and the next instant we were hanging in our seat-belts and looking almost straight down at a very dark dirty-brown swirl! The plane was perched on its nose with its tail pointing at the sky.

We must have come to a complete stop in no more than fifty or sixty feet when the plane finally slowed enough to stop flying and the main wheels sunk into the soil! I couldn't believe we hadn't tipped all the way over to upside-down! I couldn't see a thing through the cloud of enveloping dust. The engine had stopped abruptly at precisely the same instant the cabin went dark in the cloud of dust. We hung there motionless for a few moments in the almost vertical airplane...in total shock!

Checking out the airport on downwind...

"Through the wires" of the OTW biplane - Seaside, Oregon, 1967

CARD NO. 747 738 156 5 1959

STANDARD OIL COMPANY
OF CALIFORNIA,
WESTERN OPERATIONS, INC.

SOLD TO MARC E PAULSEN JR
OCT 1962

X REC'D BY

SCAPPOOSE FLYG SER
SCAPPOOSE OREG 740 10 21 62

SOLD BY

BRAND	QUANTITY	DATE PRICE	AMOUNT	
AVIATION GASOLINE (NO. 80-87)	7,0	36	2	52
AVIATION TURBINE FUEL TF-1 (NO.)				
RPM AVIATION OIL (GRADE)				
LUBRICATION				
C801840	SALES TAX			
	TOTAL		2	52

70 74 H
AIRCRAFT LICENSE NUMBER

DUPLICATE

PRICE INCLUDES MOTOR VEHICLE FUEL TAX (IF APPLICABLE) WHICH HAS BEEN OR WILL BE PAID WHEN DUE.

S-28-AV-CHEVRONMATIC (7-61) (A)

The first thing out of my mouth was, "Marvin, dammit!…***you** said we could land here!*" Was I blaming ***him**?* In this shocked state of mind, I somehow had overlooked who was***...pilot in command!***

Marvin's response? "Hey, my dad lands in places like this all the time. *What did **you** do wrong?*" Immediately, I knew that I wasn't going to be able to talk my way out of this one!

After a few minutes, we and the dust settled enough to check out the situation. We managed to unfasten our belts and swing out onto the ground. No wonder we crashed! Our shoes sank into the soft earth six full inches. The soil was like quicksand! Planes don't land on this...***They crash!***

Man, oh man, had this kid steered me wrong! Well, another needed lesson…*learned the hard way.* Silently, I wondered how much cash this one was going to cost me. Amazingly, there was no damage to the stopped metal prop now mostly buried in the soft ground. Usually, the slightest little hit and it's *good-bye propeller.* Whew! Was that lucky!

Grumbling at the kid for a bit, I knew full well who was at fault here. Calmed down somewhat, I surveyed the damage. Surprisingly (no, *amazingly*), there was no damage to the plane. Together, we pulled the plane back down to earth by gently grasping the wing struts…and then the tail fuselage handle.

We trudged around the ship through the too-soft earth and examined it closely. Not a visible scratch anywhere…astounding…because this really had been a violent landing. We felt the length of the beautiful shiny metal propeller. Not even a nick! This was too good to be true. Had the engine been damaged by the sudden stop? *We hoped not.*

We studied our predicament. By now, we'd completely forgotten our reason for coming here. To salvage wounded pride, I wanted only to get out of here. *Forget the car parts!*

I asked Marvin, "What do you think?" After all, if he flies in and out of places like this with his dad, he should have some ideas...even if he is only thirteen. He replied, "I think we should try to...***fly out!***"

"How the heck can we do that if we can't even walk in this "quick-sand-like soil?" I growled. He shot back, "Well, do you have any better ideas?" "Well, maybe we should give it a try."

But, how? We could barely budge the plane in any direction. The wheels wouldn't move. They were immobile in the soft earth.

We discussed the situation for a while and concluded that we ***might*** fly out ***if*** we could flatten down and compact the earth with our feet well enough in front of the ship to emulate a landing strip. So, we started "stomping." ***Posthaste!***

1919 Model T Ford "Touring" Car
15,007,033 "Ts" built

After getting involved in the old-car hobby due to a fortuitous trade deal made for a 1927 Model T Roadster (in rough original condition), I sold the first car and bought this fully restored car...which firmed my interest and expanded my desire to acquire more cars and accessories. Flying my Piper Cub and later the Cessna 180, a friend and I searched out truckloads of hidden "T" and other antique cars and parts hidden behind ranches all over the Pacific Northwest high desert country. The airplanes made possible finding many of the very last remnants of junked early 20th Century automobiles.

I wanted to get out of there before we were missed so no one would find out about this dumb maneuver. So did Marvin. He didn't want to face *any part* of his father's wrath!

So…we stomped and we stomped and we stomped…***like crazy!*** We worked as fast as possible to flatten out two strips of earth, one in front of each tire about two feet wide and stretching ahead of the plane about 200 feet. Stomping until our bodies were heaving and gasping with fatigue, we continued with no stop for rest.

After an hour of one of the most intense workouts ever, we had mashed the earth down for what I thought to be the absolute minimum which would allow us to get up enough speed to fly at this elevation above sea level. We were so tired that we didn't even talk…just nodded to each other. Embarrassed, I desperately wanted to get back to Erwin's ranch as quickly as possible to avoid having to explain our long absence.

Barely able to stand, getting into the plane was almost more than I could manage but, with a supreme effort, I pulled myself up and in and collapsed in the rear seat. Marvin was in great physical condition from farm work...good news for us. He still had enough energy remaining to prop-start the engine.

The engine came to life with a noisy burst and blew a giant cloud of dust from the engine cowling area and the rest of the plane, momentarily plunging us into darkness once again. By a major stroke of luck, the engine didn't appear to be damaged by the almost instant stop (an event that often can be very costly). Marvin pulled himself into the front seat. Soon, the air cleared up and I shoved the throttle all the way forward...and the plane *inched ahead!*

We moved ahead a little more and then...*out of the hole* the wheels had been in...then forward with increasing speed leaving a massive dust-cloud behind. By the time we reached the end of the two-hundred-foot-long double path, we were generating just enough wing lift to float along...barely skimming the plowed furrows that followed. Finally, like that hulking plane in the classic aviation movie, "*Flight of The Phoenix,*" we broke free of the earth and staggered along in free-flight. Our airspeed increased...and we both heaved enormous sighs of relief. As our airspeed climbed, almost all of the dust blew off the plane and the little Cub's yellow color returned very closely to its natural state.

It looked like I wouldn't be out any cash for plane damage and, if Marvin would keep his mouth shut, we wouldn't lose any face either. Plus, Marvin wouldn't have to endure a father's fury. *We were two lucky guys!*

Landing back at the ranch and asked what took us so long, we "mumbled" about doing a little extra touring over the general area. When Erwin wondered how we had enough fuel for that, we simply changed the subject as quickly as possible.

Erwin didn't find out about our escapade in the dust until many years later when I told him the story... but I could not get him to believe it happened. He swore that couldn't have happened without damaging the plane.

I absolutely can guarantee that I never again attempted a landing in anything that even remotely resembled a plowed field!

PRINEVILLE, OREGON — PHONE HI 7-5300

AIRPLANE DEALER

DICK BALLANTINE

FLYING SERVICE

INSTRUCTION - CHARTER - AERIAL SPRAYING

Customer's Order No. 7074H Date 10-2 196

M.

Address

SOLD BY	CASH	C.O.D.	CHARGE	ON ACCT.	MDSE. RETD.	PAID OUT

QUAN.	DESCRIPTION	PRICE	AMOUNT
11	gasoline	.41	4.59

ALL claims and returned goods MUST be accompanied by this bill

Rec'd by

MOORE DEALER - OREGON STATIONERY, INC.

When Dell and I visited this flight operation after landing with a severely damaged right-wheel landing strut, the airport operator offered to do a quick repair job. Usually, work on aircraft is done with extreme "finesse" and careful manipulation. Imagine our surprise (and shock) when he grabbed a giant hammer and an acetylene torch from a messy workbench...then proceeded to wildly whack away at the heated tubing to bend it back into a semblance of partially bent-up usability!

Of course, we realized the need for temporary improvisation...which would allow us to to be on our way...but still, that was something we hadn't seen done to an airplane!

Never Let Your Passenger Talk To The Reporters

One hundred hours! That was his flat, cool answer. I had asked an older crop-dusting pilot friend about WWII military aircraft "pilot-in-command" checkout requirements.

"*One hundred hours* ***in type***" was the number he gave when asked how many hours Marine pilots were required to log in "trainer" planes before being allowed to fly them ***solo*** (alone).

One hundred hours!

That really got my attention. In answer to my question to him about what he thought a reasonable number of hours for a private pilot to check out in an airplane, he described the strict rules (according to *HIS* memory) of airplane "solo" flight-time requirements during his WWII Marine pilot years. He'd heard about my latest flying misadventure (*and wasn't impressed*). The story had either sneaked out in my conversation with him or maybe he had read about it in the newspapers. I wasn't sure which.

He droned on and on about his one hundred hours in a primary trainer, then a hundred in a basic trainer, a hundred in an advanced trainer and graduation to the legendary Corsair fighter plane. Until this conversation, I had no idea that the military required that many hours of checkout time in each different type of ship.

Earlier, I had joined a local flying club when informed of their low hourly rental rates. The club was planning to add a used A35 Beechcraft "Bonanza" retractable-gear ship to their existing Cessna 172 and Piper 135hp Tri-Pacer fleet.

I was interested in expanding my flight horizons by learning to fly this early model of the fabled "Bonanza," an airplane highly revered to this day. Added to my zeal was the fact that this one was going to be a very early model without a modern automatic "constant-speed" propeller (a propeller that retains the same RPM regardless of the power setting). The more primitive "controllable-pitch," or "variable" pitch propeller was controlled in the cockpit by a toggle switch, with the pitch change mechanism an electric motor. It seemed to me a great opportunity to better learn the rudiments of propeller pitch change effect, an important element in utilizing airplane engine power efficiently.

After flying the two smaller club ships and waiting with barely-restrained patience, my opportunity finally arrived. I could already imagine taking passengers up in this more complicated flying machine, a bird considered by many aviators in the world of flight to be an absolute *"classic"* ship.

I had signed up early for the privilege of flying the plane. When the time came for Karl, the club member-instructor to give check-rides, I was close to first in line. Other members also had been looking forward to this event. Consequently there were quite a few signed after me waiting for their turns at the controls.

In later years, I often wondered if I should have contacted Karl and apologized to him profusely for my pushing the implication that I was more proficient than I actually was. Ahhh...well, the folly of youth!

Karl was a typical flight instructor having a tremendous love of flight and a very steady disposition. He had quite a lot of flight time but not very much in the Bonanza. Here, we had something in common.

Things went beautifully right from the start. I had just over four hundred hours total time in my logbook, but only thirteen hours in anything more complex than Piper Cub types and no flight time in aircraft with retractable landing gear. This was to be a checkout with three giant milestones. First, that of learning to retract the landing gear (and remembering to put it back down at the right time), then learning to operate the electric variable-pitch propeller and, finally, gaining a very basic understanding of the aerodynamics of a laminar-flow wing. In addition, I would be flying in my first plane with a low wing and also the first with a "manifold pressure" gauge. All in all, quite a few *firsts* with which to become comfortable.

I had no difficulty understanding and operating the retractable gear and it didn't take long to figure out the variable prop. In retrospect, I do recall that I was somewhat impatient and seemed to have a short attention span when the laminar-flow wing was discussed. To fully understand all there is to know about the aerodynamics of such a wing, one would have to spend a heck of a lot of time on this feature alone. We didn't take that time. The total check-out consisted of four flights, all from the Troutdale, Oregon, airport.

The first flight was uneventful. The weather was great, there was little air traffic on and around the airport, the plane functioned perfectly and my airplane operation was acceptable to Karl. The flight went so well that Karl might have been lulled into a false sense of well-being considering my abilities. I asked if it was all right to take passengers on the second flight and he was so assured of my apparent abilities that he replied, "Sure, O.K." He even agreed to the second flight taking place at night.

On the second, third and fourth flights, I brought passengers along and all flights were flown very successfully at night. On the third flight, potential disaster reared up! With only four hours of time in the ship (as I was changing propeller-pitch immediately after takeoff at about two hundred feet of altitude) *the engine quit…**dead!***

With instant reaction and without hesitation or looking at Karl, I lowered the nose quickly to gain even more airspeed (which was already quite adequate), began a sharply-banked one-hundred-eighty degree turn back to the runway, called the tower at the same time and told them I was coming back due to loss of engine power…and rapidly was given clearance to land.

This all happened in a matter of seconds. In moments we were safely back on the end of the runway with just the right amount of airspeed remaining...and the plane coasted to a comfortable halt. The incident happened so quickly, nobody had time to get nervous...and we then all exited and pushed the ship over to the nearest parking space.

I didn't have to say anything to Karl. He knew that the situation had gone the best possible way. He was very impressed with my handling of the airplane in the emergency. What he didn't know was that I operated in this situation much like I would have with my J-3 Cub and, as I'd maintained an extra margin of airspeed on climb-out with this more critical ship, the whole episode turned out to be simple and successful. For this reason, no one in the plane had any "after effect" feelings of queasiness from the crisis.

The next day mechanics found the problem in the carburetion system, corrected the issue, and we were ready to go flying again. The last two check flights were uneventful. I'd almost been living in my Piper J-3 so I was very comfortable in the air and I managed to handle the Bonanza's more complicated systems to Karl's satisfaction. I do believe that he had been so impressed with my handling of the one serious night flight emergency that he may have overestimated my abilities.

With a little less than six hours total flight time in the aircraft type, Karl signed me off to fly as "pilot-in-command" of the famed "Beechcraft Bonanza." I was ecstatic!

Just two days later I was at the controls of the Bonanza flying over the Oregon Coast Range mountains, having just left the Seaside airport and headed east for the small town of Beaverton which is located on Portland's western outskirts.

A few months earlier, a friend of mine in the construction business had worked in Beaverton on a sixteen-unit apartment building. I visited him while he was at work there and I liked the design concept. It had appeared so simple to build that I thought I would attempt to get some investors together, duplicate it and join the ranks of apartment house owners. The outcome of this flight is what ended my short-lived attempt to become an apartment building mogul.

I had managed to interest three potential investment partners who lived at the coast (all physically large men) and, as a result of their size plus my two hundred twenty pounds, the airplane was heavily loaded as we winged our way inland toward Beaverton. However, I'd carefully calculated that I'd have flown enough fuel out of the ship to make the next takeoff safely.

Two of the men had flown a couple of times in light planes and the third was on his first flight (somewhat nervously). It was a glorious late spring morning with bright sunshine. The temperature moved well into the sixties before ten o'clock.

Arriving at Beaverton, I flew the plane in a circle over the small airport to determine the wind direction from a windsock located at mid-field and prepared for a landing. We touched down softly on the grass strip, taxied to a tie-down, got out, and cinched the plane to ropes fastened to steel loops in the ground. We then walked about three quarters of a mile to the apartment building I wanted to show them.

I now had found a legitimate way to use an airplane for business. Walking along, I dreamed about the type of private jet I soon would have to buy to adequately service the fifty apartment buildings we would build all over the west. Dang! *How sweet this was going to be!*

Reaching the apartment building, we all walked to and fro and around… and then around again, and I waxed eloquently on the tons of money we

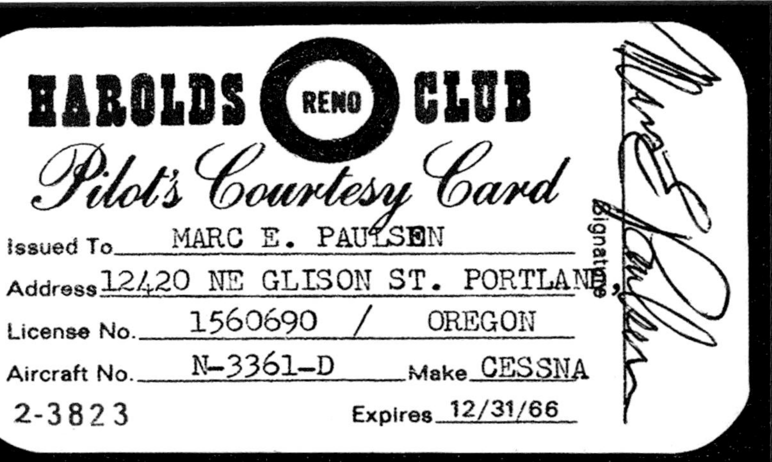
HAROLDS RENO CLUB

Pilot's Courtesy Card

Issued To MARC E. PAULSEN

Address 12420 NE GLISON ST. PORTLAND,

License No. 1560690 / OREGON

Aircraft No. N-3361-D Make CESSNA

2-3823 Expires 12/31/66

Signature

There was a time when a surprising number of "freebies" were offered by Las Vegas and Reno, Nevada, casinos to lure private pilots into the cities. This card and a fistful of coupons were issued to just about any pilot who landed at the Reno airport in his own airplane and intimated that he and his party were open for a night on the town.

AIRCRAFT OWNERS & PILOTS ASSOCIATION

MARC E PAULSEN
P O BOX 485
JACKSONVILLE, OR
97530

is a registered and fully qualified member entitled to receive all rights and privileges thereunder until

MAR 31-78 *Original Affiliation* 1963

237952 *Signature*

See overside for addresses and service hours

"AOPA" magazine performed good service for airmen by including a section each month describing airplane accidents and their causes...or probable causes. *Maybe I should have paid more attention.*

DATE	CHARGES AND CREDITS	BALANCE
4-14-71	9.2 hrs. Apache 3173P rental @ $45.00 per hr.	$404.00
4-27-71	.58 hr. Cessna 180 N4600U @ $28.00 per hr.	16.24
4-29-71	5.10 hrs. Cessna 180 N4600U @ $28.00 per hr.	142.80
	TOTAL DUE	$563.04

Partial 1971 statement for airplane rentals

These are rates pilots now only can dream about! (Rates included fuel.)

could reap from this venture. The prospective investors asked questions which I answered...trying to sound knowledgeable. They listened and nodded...doing their best not to openly commit themselves (I was beginning to suspect they just wanted the pleasure of a free plane ride).

When we couldn't justify walking around the building one more time, we agreed that we would all think about what we saw and discuss the venture in detail at a later date. Time to return to the airport. As we walked back, the temperature was rising enough that one of the men took off his light jacket to refrain from perspiring.

At the airport, I looked more closely at the runway. It was relatively short compared with many and canted down a long moderate slope. I guessed the strip dropped maybe thirty or forty feet in twenty-five-hundred, so that didn't appear to be significant. Checking the windsock, I noted a very light wind blowing...*downhill.* Four hundred hours of my total logbook-time of four hundred and eight hours were in planes with high-lift wings, in which we almost always took off *into the wind.* With that background, I now reasoned that the right thing to do was...take off *into the wind.* Hey...isn't that how you fly an airplane? Of course! Every pilot takes off "upwind" (toward the wind). If aircraft carrier pilots didn't do that, they would never get off the carrier.

We all entered the plane, buckled up and I started the engine...then taxied down the very slight grade to the end of the lush grass strip. The ship sounded great on "run-up" and, finishing that, I eased the throttle forward and turned into the wind for takeoff.

Let's see here...let's add this up. According to the flight manual which I had briefly scanned, the plane would carry four one-hundred-seventy pound people (but, with very little fuel). We had four two-hundred-plus pound people, a very modest amount of fuel, the sun had warmed up to about seventy-five degrees, we were at about two hundred feet of elevation, we were headed somewhat uphill and the strip was grass and twenty-five-hundred feet long. Hmmmmm! Before this, when I had taken off with more fuel at sea level on blacktop in a cooler temperature, the airplane had left the ground very quickly in a short distance…and that takeoff was still fresh in my thoughts.

Pushing the throttle control in, the plane began to move. *Slowly.* I shoved the throttle all the way forward. The plane didn't seem to accelerate as rapidly as in the morning. It had *lunged* forward when I'd flown out alone early in the morning, and then, when we'd taken off from the coast with less than "full fuel" at sea level, The plane had literally jumped into the air (planes fly much better at sea level).

We were picking up speed *very slowly.* I could feel prickly sweat rise on my neck as valuable runway disappeared behind us. Somewhere in the recesses of my sub-conscious, I could hear the old saying, "***You can't use the runway behind you!***"

Still the acceleration lagged. Now, my concentration sharpened considerably and I glued my eyes to the airspeed indicator. ***It was not indicating enough airspeed!.***

As we approached mid-field, I decided it was time to fly. ***Big mistake!*** A pilot doesn't decide when the plane will fly...***the plane does!*** This is how it works. When the plane is going fast enough, the wings will create the amount of lift the plane needs to fly and it will rise into the air by itself. In fact, if a plane goes very fast over the ground, it cannot be held on the ground. There's an old pilots' saying: "If you can make a plane on the ground go fast enough, you can use a two by twelve board for a wing." That simply implies that almost anything will create enough "lift" and fly if it goes through the air fast enough. ***Airspeed is the key!***

This plane would normally rotate (leave the ground) at around sixty-five miles per hour. We were indicating a little more than that, maybe seventy or so, and not creating much lift at all. I eased back gently on the control yoke. The nose came up. I eased back a tiny bit more.

There is another old-pilot maxim worth noting here: "To make a plane go up, you pull back on the controls; *to make it go down*, ***you pull back further.*** " It means that if you pull back too far on the control wheel or stick, the plane will lose the ability to climb up in such a steep attitude and will then "stall" and fall out of the sky.

The nose came up a little more. Now we were past mid-field!

Oh...did I fail to mention the very busy road across the end of the field in front of us...with *no separation fence?* The runway ended right at the edge of a street that was exactly level with the it and, as we were approaching, I could see a number of cars driving across in front of us.

Suddenly the ship swerved a little to the right. I corrected with rudder but then the plane swerved sharply back to the left. The reaction felt strange…as if the gear was collapsing or something else equally ominous.

At this point, I knew I was in serious trouble. The plane wasn't going to get off the ground before we met the road...with all its traffic. I momentarily envisioned us colliding with a vehicle at eighty or ninety mph...and *I pulled on the throttle to reduce power.*

At least, in this now terror-filled instant of swiftly growing panic, I *thought* I did. What *really happened* came back to me later. The throttle refused to budge. The problem was the throttle's "***Vernier***" control!

For the uninitiated, the "*Vernier*" throttle control needs some explaining. The "Bonanza" had some very advanced mechanical devices for its time, and the "Vernier" throttle control was one. It is a knob on a shaft that fits nicely in the hand and projects out from the center of the control panel about three or four inches when in the off position. The knob can be slowly turned and, therefore, *screwed* in and out slowly. This assists in making very fine throttle adjustments for cruising.

In the center of the knob is a push-button release. If the pilot grasps the knob and pushes the button in at the same time with his thumb, the control can be moved all the way back and forth...*very quickly to either power up or power down almost instantly.*

Later, I remembered with crystal clarity precisely what I had done (*and not done*) that was to change some people's lives for a long time. But for now, *I was in big trouble!*

As we careened down what remained of the strip, the ship bucked like a bronco "stalling" its way along the strip and trying to fly (partly because I had increased its "drag" by trying to "help" it fly...which in fact, was inhibiting flight).

At this point, I realized *for certain* that we were not going to make it into the air and aborted the takeoff. That is, I ***thought*** that was what I was doing. And that is certainly what I wanted to do. Actually, what I did was jam on the brakes and pull the throttle out. But...the throttle didn't pull out. *Because...**what I was doing** was **unscrewing**...*and it unscrews only *very slowly!* In the extreme heat of the moment, as my eyes grew the size of golf balls, I saw the cars on the road converging with my still-speeding plane, I panicked! Because most of my experience was with a simple push and pull throttle in a Cub, my mind went blank on the correct concept of punching the end of the knob with my thumb and, therefore, instantly reducing the power. So, with probably three-quarters engine power still on and the locked tires skidding on the slippery fresh green grass, the plane continued on its merry way... slowing down only little by little.

With only the six hours of checkout time, I hadn't adequately become acquainted with that "blankity-blank" Vernier control. In this moment of frozen panic, with my eyes riveted to the oncoming cross street, I didn't mentally register the mandatory requirement to push in the release button. The plane roared toward a questionable fate as I almost unconsciously continued unscrewing and trying to pull the unwilling throttle...while the plane *slowed very reluctantly.*

The ship was doing close to sixty mph as we hit a small drainage ditch perhaps six inches deep and bounced across the road between two cars, so close that we could almost read the numbers on their license plates.

Mercifully, the field beyond was large, flat, unoccupied by buildings, and open enough to allow the plane to go into a smooth skid and put itself into a giant sweeping left hand turn...*still at thirty or so miles an hour!*

Finally, the plane did slow down. However, it took a pile of earth about ten feet high to get the job done. As the plane made a big self-directed turn through one-hundred-eighty degrees, the right wing poked heavily into the pile of earth and curled up three or four feet in the air with a snap. So, the end was not without serious airplane pain. Then, with one last half-left-hand loop, we came to an unceremonious halt. Fortunately, there was no physical pain on the part of anyone in the plane.

The engine was still rumbling so I shut it down. For a moment, all was still. But then, as I looked out ruefully at the bent wing in my view to the right, my passengers *abruptly came to life* and *panicked!* They had been shocked into motionless stupor by the suddenness of this catastrophe. But, in a flash, they regained their senses and decided that, if they didn't get out immediately, they might burn to death (*or something...they weren't sure what!*).

A word to the wise pilot: Don't take people on their first plane ride *and crash.* If they live, the stories they will tell about what happened will be bizarre beyond belief. ***And,*** the stories will ***all*** make you look like a totally incompetent pilot, which, unfortunately, may be the case, and in this situation (which I hate to admit)...was sadly true. ***"Accidents"*** ***<u>are not accidents</u>!*** They are ***All*** due to carelessness or inadequate knowledge, incorrect operation, improper maintenance, inadequate preparation or inattention to detail.

As we scrambled out onto the soft earth, the usual hundred people who always appear out of nowhere to further embarrass the pilot...*showed up right on cue.* Zounds!...*where in the devil do <u>they</u> come from?*

Of course, before I could make my escape to avoid even more humiliation, the police showed up, halted my progress…and took my name. That fact allowed the newsmen who came shortly after to make sure they had the pilot's name spelled correctly for the front page dramatic photograph that appeared the next day in 300,000 newspapers issued all over the state. The picture in the paper was taken from an angle that made incident appear as though we had spun in like a mortally-wounded space shuttle from ten thousand feet at four hundred miles an hour. Of course, the cub reporter implied that it was indeed a miracle that we were not all ground into bloody pulp.

We're talking way beyond major mortification here! To add even more insult to injury, one of my passengers (naturally, the one with no light-plane flight experience) was the only one interviewed by the press and his account was *really a doozy!*

This was actually in print: He stated that the airplane had climbed to an altitude of *fifty feet and more* when it suddenly stopped flying and crashed straight back down to earth!" I would say that the ship never <u>bounced</u> more than *one foot off the ground*, if that. If stalling from fifty feet at sixty or seventy miles an hour, we would have ended up flying with St. Peter. So much for "*first-hand*" newspaper accounts.

There is <u>more</u> to this dreary tale than my complete shame and gross humiliation! Hard to believe, but I was the only person in the flying club

This is the model Bonanza that got away from me.

The Beechcraft Bonanza is an American general aviation aircraft introduced in 1947 by The Beech Aircraft Corporation. More than 17,000 Bonanzas of many variations have been built.

Engine Controls

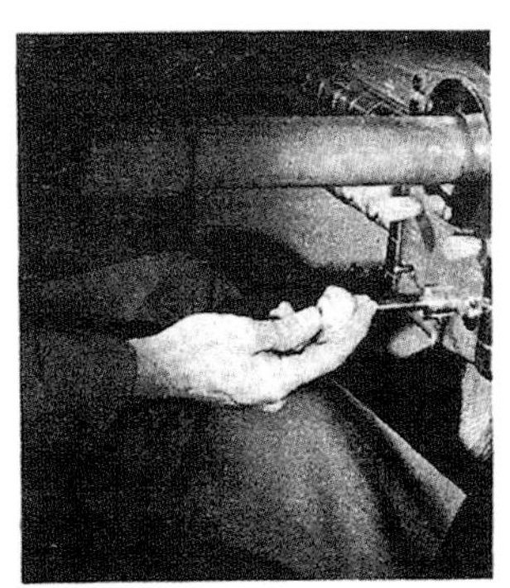

THROTTLE — The throttle control has a micrometer adjustment feature for fine adjustments of the throttle. This adjustment is operated by turning the knob clockwise to increase the engine rpm and counterclockwise to decrease it. The micrometer adjusting feature can be released by pressing the button in the center of the knob, and the throttle may then be opened or closed without turning the knob.

The throttle control that did me in.

The "Engine Controls" panel illustrated here is from an early Bonanza Flight Manual.

who actually had enough cash to pay the insurance deductible (a sizable amount). So, I promptly wrote a check to cover my ineptitude, thereby reducing my life savings at the time to something in the neighborhood of zero. At least, I covered my agreed-upon obligation. Beyond that, it turned out that the club finances were very weak and, insurance-wise, the Bonanza turned out to be "totaled" because of the one bent-up wing. The sum result of all this was that the club went out of existence because of my screw-up and lack of funds. I felt badly about that but I guess it's that sneaky "destiny" at work again.

Later, reviewing the incident with understanding and knowledgeable flying buddies, I was to learn what I had done wrong on that fateful day. They pointed out that with what all the things I had working against me in the form of overload, warm weather and uphill run, the one thing which might have saved me is the one thing I hadn't learned clearly at checkout time. According to them, I should have taken off downhill and downwind. (There wasn't much wind.) Even though that is rarely done, such action probably would have worked in this situation because of the airplane's "laminar flow" wing. According to my even more knowledgeable pilot friends, I would have gained ground-speed much faster downhill with this particular ship, and most likely would not have stalled it on the ground as I apparently did when I attempted to coax it into the air (although *any* "coaxing" is incorrect procedure).

After my good ol' boy crop-duster friend said: "I don't think that private pilots ever spend nearly enough time in the cockpit for their checkouts," ***"Understatement"*** was the first thought that struck me!

Needle, Ball and Airspeed!

Those were the words drilled into student pilots for many of the earlier years of aviation. The instructor would say, "Remember...when you find yourself in an 'unusual attitude,' think 'Needle, Ball and Airspeed!'"

What he meant was...if you find yourself in clouds, fog, haze or any condition or situation that causes or allows the plane to go into an "unusual attitude," the plane can be righted back into straight and level flight by first centering the "needle and ball" with ailerons and rudder...and then returned to normal airspeed with forward or backward pressure on the "stick" or "yoke" (as required).

That was the crux of a hangar discussion when one of the guys piped up regarding flight in the clouds: "You can fly with only three instruments! With a needle and ball, altimeter and a compass you can fly across the ocean in solid klag without ever seeing the ground! And...you can stay alive with only two of the above!" To a fledgling birdman still working hard at learning to hold altitude, airspeed and heading on a perfectly clear day with no turbulence, this sounded like a rather extreme situation to contemplate.

Elaborating, he explained that to do this with such a minimum of equipment, the absolute key item you needed on a tiny plane was an externally-mounted air-driven venturi tube. That was needed to create power to drive a gyroscope connected to a vertical indicator called a needle, or "turn indicator." When flying blind, the needle can tell you which way the ship is turning. The ball is the second part of the "needle and ball" indicator instrument. The "ball" is a small three-eighths inch or so diameter sphere immersed in clear liquid and placed in a partial-circle glass tube with the bottom of the circle located directly under the needle. As the ball moves side to side it

When I first climbed into my **Piper Apache "twin,"** the instrument panel (shown here) seemed to my single-engine eyes to be as big and magnificent as those in commercial airliners.

indicates "yaw" or "skid" showing visually whether or not your turn is "coordinated." The name for the two instruments (usually combined) was "Turn and Bank Indicator" or Turn and "Slip." The more recent name is "Turn Coordinator," and modern units are electrically powered. This instrument can indicate if the wings are level. That is very important because, in clouds with no outside reference and no instruments, it isn't possible to know this for sure...a situation that will lead to disaster.

The altimeter is also critical to "instrument" flight, most certainly if one were attempting "instrument" flight with minimum instrumentation. When in a solid overcast, the altimeter will indicate when you are going up or going down by the direction the indicator needle is moving. Very simple! If the altitude indicated increases, you are climbing. If it indicates a steady number you are flying level and maintaining altitude. If it indicates a declining altitude, you are descending. The compass, as most know, indicates which direction the plane is headed.

"Just these three! That's all you need. It's as simple as that!" It was also stated that you can fly and stay alive with only two of the above.

That would be the "turn and bank" and the "altimeter." Sure, you could stay alive with them...but without the compass, you wouldn't have a clue exactly which direction you were going.

The three instruments, used properly according to basic flight theory, will

Early "Needlle & Ball," then also called a "Turn & Bank" indicator...which is similar to the one installed in my Piper Cub.

Basic flight instruments arranged in a "T"

From top left: airspeed indicator, attitude indicator, altimeter, *turn coordinator* (turn & bank) heading indicator and vertical speed indicator. Most aircraft are equipped with this "standard" set of flight instruments which give the pilot information (critical while inside clouds) about the aircraft's airspeed, attitude, altitude, turning condition, direction & speed it is going up or down.

allow you to fly safely out of foul weather flight assuming you don't hit a mountain...you are supposed to have planned carefully so that won't happen. Without these instruments, there is a very good possibility you will exit clouds headed down and possibly over "redline" airspeed…a condition not conducive to favorable outcomes. Also quite possible, is your coming out of the bottom of the clouds in a number of disconnected pieces due to the overstressing of the ship while making incorrect and frantic high "g-force" turns.

My Piper Cub had come to me having an airspeed, altimeter and compass but no "needle and ball" instrument. While having my plane rebuilt after a minor crash (I "walked away" from the incident, so technically, it was just a hard landing), I had the mechanic install instruments until we couldn't fit another one anywhere into the modest little instrument panel the plane had come with from the factory.

In the small space available, the panel looked (to me) much like that of a Boeing 747 airliner, relatively speaking. No matter that some of the instruments served no seriously useful purpose (does a J-3 Cub really need a G-Meter?) or at least no useful purpose for my level of expertise. Why would one need a "rate-of-climb" indicator in a Piper Cub?

While the mechanic was working on the instrument panel I said to him, "Aw, what the heck, if we can get a used venturi and needle and ball setup inexpensively, let's install one." Little did I know at the time what the ultimate significance of this decision would be. All this took place at a time in my flying adventures when I had become enamored with the ultimate expression of airplane flight, aerobatics.

How well I remember my first loop. Before learning to fly, I purchased the Piper J-3 Cub and asked a licensed-pilot friend to take me for my first ride in my own ship. We took off into the blue and when we were headed home, my friend leaned forward (a Piper Cub is flown from the rear tandem seat by the "pilot in command") and spoke loudly in my ear, "Hang on!"

He then pulled back on the stick...and straight up, up, over and back down around we went. I was shocked and hadn't realized that even the simplest airplane can perform such maneuvers safely. After we leveled out, my companion patiently explained to me that he really hadn't overstressed my poor little plane but, that in fact, the plane was designed to do that type of maneuver all day long without damaging the plane. Somewhat skeptical, I checked out what he had said and found that, yes indeedy, I could do quite a few aerobatics in that model ship and live to tell about it. But, now the plot thickens…

After a year and a half of flight enjoyment in my plane, I decided to put on a newly acquired seat-pack parachute and try some unusual and exciting flight: "aerobatics!"

Out to the Sandy, Oregon, airport to the plane and up into a cloudless bright morning sky I went. Clearing the airport, I set up a course to the northwest to the village of Battle Ground, Washington. En route, I mulled over which aerobatics to attempt and concluded that the most prudent approach to executing them would be to go up to high altitude and first do simple stalls and spins. With a substantial amount of altitude even the most inept pilot has a chance to recover from "unusual attitudes" if he lets the airplane get out of his control. In fact, most small planes, if left to their own devices and if there is enough altitude, will straighten out and fly by themselves (that is, "up to a point").

Arriving over my planned area of activity, I had acquired only about six thousand feet of altitude…not enough to put this pursuer of thrills completely at ease. Continuing in a spiral climb, the next twenty-some minutes were spent increasing my altitude.

Upon reaching eleven thousand feet (finally, after quite a bit of time due to my plane's slow "rate of climb"), I leveled out the plane, relaxed for a moment to decide my next move and concluded that the only logical maneuver would be a spin. With this much altitude (I assumed), no matter what maneuver was done, recovery would not present a challenge, so a spin...it would be!

After reducing all engine power and slowing the ship, I pulled back on the stick smoothly, pointed the nose up sharply into the sky and, as the rest of the airspeed bled off, pressed hard on the left rudder and quickly pulled the stick all the way back at the same time. The little plane shuddered for just a moment...then the wing dropped and entered a left hand spin downward.

The result was amazing! A typical spin will find the nose of the plane pointed down in a very steep attitude. Not so, this spin. Obviously, I had overlooked a couple of minor details.

There is a very important item involving flight which every pilot learns…or he may encounter serious flight problems. That item is called "CG," meaning "center of gravity." It involves calculating the load the plane will carry as related to its "rated" capacity and how that load is distributed in the ship...to safely balance the craft fore and aft. And…you do this before you take off.

The details overlooked were basic. This type of airplane, a Cub J-3, is always soloed from the rear seat, a fact that moves the CG somewhat aft (back) if you are as heavy as I am. Number two, my fuel supply was low. My fuel tank was just forward of the front seat so the light fuel load exacerbated the situation moving the CG even further aft. In addition, I was wearing my seatpack parachute which is heavy...and that was also behind the CG...along with me. All in all, my loading was considerably aft from where it should have been for any slow flight configurations...and some other maneuvers. The way my weight was arranged meant the plane was very "tail-heavy." Such a condition was not so critical at airplane takeoff speed and during cruise speeds (in this plane) because the higher speed allowed "compensation" for the weight condition simply by adjusting the leading edge of the tail's "horizontal stabilizer" upward with "trim." At any rate, I was now to learn the serious degree to which my ship's operation could be altered by a "far aft" CG.

As the ship settled down into a mature spin (one in which the plane usually will remain for quite a few turns), I immediately realized that this was a very strange spin indeed. The plane was rotating but, where the plane should have been pointing steeply down, it was spinning in what was very close to a level attitude, with the nose pointed only very little down. As the plane went round and round in a big wide circle, all was ominously quiet, the only sound an intermittent rippling of the fabric on the rear fuselage of the plane. It was eerie!

For the first couple of turns, I sat frozen in surprise. Admittedly, this was an exhilarating feeling...sitting there in an almost level configuration but soon the thoughts came back of what a flight instructor had warned me never to do. I had taken some student instruction in a sailplane and the instructor had cautioned me never to get into a "flat" spin in a sailplane because, without an engine it is impossible to fly out of the spin. He said that, try as one might to recover from such a spin, the ship would continue to spin right into the ground...and what would be left...would not be a pretty sight.

Now I found myself in what appeared to be just such a "flat" spin and, without much experience as a pilot, I began to wonder if this flat spin might not result in an odd situation. Could it be that centrifugal force might keep fuel from properly feeding the carburetor and, after starving the engine of fuel, the plane remain in a flight configuration from which recovery may not be possible?

Fortunately, easing the throttle forward caused the engine to come to life ...which then allowed me to push the stick forward and gain enough forward aircraft speed that the plane then recovered to normal flight.

Now a bit spooked (not all low-flight-time pilots seem to have the knowledge to adequately understand the true meaning of fear), I decided to try another spin. Climbing back up to start the maneuver again, my altimeter read just about ten thousand feet. After "stalling" off to the left again, the plane began a downward spiral...and this time the stick was pushed a bit forward (after entry) to force the plane into a very steep downward attitude. The result was a more natural nose-down spin "attitude" and the plane continued down...tightly spinning.

Ahhh...a much better entry and a more correct downward attitude. Nice and tight…and the steep attitude held. I began counting off the turns and watching the altimeter unwind. Three, four, five, six. Fifteen, sixteen, seventeen. Twenty eight, twenty nine, thirty. Thirty one....

Descending rapidly, my instruments indicated the plane was losing about one-hundred-eighty-plus feet per revolution. The altimeter indicator needle was twisting wildly around in reverse. The plane continued down turn after turn as the blood in my veins throbbed with excitement. This was living on the edge! There was something about all of this that held me spellbound… glued to my seat and glowing all over with the thrill of the descent.

Deciding to recover from the spin back into normal flight, I came to the stark realization that...I could not move! After so many turns, I had gone way beyond mere dizziness and simple vertigo and had become seriously disoriented. I could look only straight ahead, my body unable to move.

I tried desperately to move! It was as if my body was like a block of granite, frozen and able only to look straight ahead at the instrument panel. Then, miraculously, I remembered my "needle and ball" instrument recently installed.

Pulling my thoughts together, I tried to remember lessons about the very basics of instrument flight. I'd done some in-flight practice and remembered from ground school a line related to instrument flight that had been repeated a number of times by the instructor. That banged away in my head as the turns of the spin ticked off.

Needle, ball and airspeed! Needle, ball and airspeed! Needle, ball and airspeed! At about the third repetition, my brain began to function, even if my body wouldn't. As my monotonous counting of turns hit forty-four, my thought processes centered my eyeballs on those critical instruments directly in my gaze; the needle and ball and the airspeed indicator.

With a rush of adrenaline, I pushed the stick forward and shoved hard on the right rudder pedal to stop rotation...then concentrated my view straight ahead and, as the airspeed increased, centered the needle and ball with the ailerons and rudder pedals. When the airspeed passed seventy, I pulled back on the stick to even the airspeed out at eighty miles per hour, my usual cruising speed.

Stabilizing the airspeed and holding the needle and ball centered, I could not believe my eyes or my senses! The airplane seemed to be motionless! It appeared to have achieved suspended animation! Highly disoriented, I couldn't detect any outside motion of the plane with my peripheral vision. Attempting to turn my head to look out the window came to no avail. I was still frozen in place from the dizzyness-producing descent. Blue sky above and earth below indicated the plane was definitely upright. Clearly, the airspeed read eighty, the altimeter held an altitude and the needle and ball remained centered. The airplane had to be flying in perfectly level flight because that's what the instruments indicated but seemed more like it was hanging from a skyhook.

Seconds passed and normality began to return. . .after a while, I could move my head a little and the airplane appeared to begin to move. Another few moments and all my senses returned enough for me to move my body, look around, move the controls more easily and recover from my multi-spin-induced trance.

In the years after this exciting and strange episode, I performed many spins in many different airplanes. Ask me how many turns I'd make in these spins and, assuredly, the number would always come out in single digits!

Peering through struts and wires during OTW landing, Seaside, Oregon, 1966

If my very first landing in this plane (which was a forced-emergency landing on a narrow new-highway roadbed) had been on a field this big, I'd have felt like space shuttle pilots approaching Cape Canaveral.

I. UNITED STATES OF AMERICA XI.
DEPARTMENT OF TRANSPORTATION – FEDERAL AVIATION ADMINISTRATION
THIS CERTIFIES THAT IV. MARC ELLIOTT PAULSEN
V. 10220 SW MELNORE STREET
542321710 PORTLAND OR 97225

DATE OF BIRTH	HEIGHT	WEIGHT	HAIR	EYES	SEX	NATIONALITY VI.
07-26-33	75 IN	215	BROWN	GREEN	M	USA

IX. HAS BEEN FOUND TO BE PROPERLY QUALIFIED TO EXERCISE THE PRIVILEGES OF
II. PRIVATE PILOT III. CERT. NO. 1560690
RATINGS AND LIMITATIONS
XII. AIRPLANE SINGLE & MULTIENGINE LAND<

XIII.

VII. SIGNATURE OF HOLDER X.
X. DATE OF ISSUE 11-01-90 VIII. ADMINISTRATOR

My "Re-issued" pilot's license (after losing the original with my wallet).

No Engine, No Airspeed, No Altitude, No Hope

Airspeed is like cash,
Altitude is like money in the bank.
You can't have money in the bank
Without first depositing some cash.

The useful old aviators' maxim above is about paying close attention to the basic physics of flight. In a nutshell, it means one better have either airspeed, altitude ***or both*** any time airborne...or success in flight may be highly problematic. And...having ***both*** is decidedly better!

The theory is that with airspeed, the airplane can be can transitioned into a climb and altitude quickly gained to rise above obstacles…and, when an airplane has altitude, the nose can be lowered, airspeed gained... and the plane flown (with or without power) to safety. Either way, having one or both provides a number of favorable options which will allow flying safely and increase a pilot's chances of survival in a crisis. Improper flight management technique or unusual mechanical situations that occur with an airplane at low airspeeds and low altitudes can put a ship into a flight configuration that offers little or no chance of recovery to normal flight...frequently ending in a crash. So...when it comes to airspeed and altitude, it is best to have one or the other, or both! And...remember, ***both*** are better...and ***I*** was destined to learn...***exactly how much better!***

"***CAVU!***" The acronym "**CAVU**" (**C**eiling **A**nd **V**isibility **U**nlimited) is desired by all pilots. It denotes a day that has absolutely no clouds and is usually brightly sunlit and clear for long distances. It is every pilot's dream day! I drove to the airport on just such a day at the end of summer... and it was so bright, clear and beautiful that my thoughts of flying raced with delight.

The masonry contract work I was engaged in at the time was intermittent and I couldn't have been more pleased. During this young and single period of my life, I was seldom nervous about not bringing in money on a regular basis. Having recently spent two years in the Army as a draftee earning less than a hundred dollars a month, I now felt financially comfortable even if I didn't have big sums in the bank. Hey...I had learned the value of dollars and could really make them stretch so I would just as soon spend as much of my time as I could in the solo seat of my airplane as spend the time working.

My J-3/85hp Piper Cub was in perfect condition and ready to fly. I picked up a young friend, William "Butch" Richards, who worked for me in my contracting business. On the way to the Sandy airport, we stopped to pick up Butch's brother Mike, who also thought airplanes intriguing.

The airport at which I had my plane hangared was perched on the very edge of a river canyon about four hundred feet deep with densely-wooded almost cliff-like sides. The airstrip was green grass well kept. All in all, it was quite a picturesque setting. There was never a lot of traffic and, when we arrived this day, we had it all to ourselves. *Life couldn't be better!*

The boys helped me pull the ship out of the hangar for my usual walk-around inspection. As I inspected the airplane, they took turns sitting in the plane getting the feel of it and day-dreaming about their own future flight possibilities. I then checked the fuel and remarked to the boys that the supply was low. The airport owner was nowhere in sight. The gas pumps were locked thus all flying would have to be done with what fuel the tank now held. I'd flown this little ship with many different take-off fuel levels in the tank so I understood clearly how much time I could fly and still be safe.

"Let's see some fancy aerobatics," suggested one of the boys, excited at possibly having their own personal air-show. Sometime before, I had performed for them directly above this same isolated airport when there was little traffic and it had been a lot of fun for the three of us.

"OK," I replied, moving toward the plane with a measured pace much as I imagined an accomplished stunt pilot might...while the boys perched on the lowered tailgate of my pickup to observe the show.

I went through my routine of starting the engine by hand swinging the propeller from the rear with my right hand as I controlled the throttle inside with my left. It was quite a contortion but my eighty-two-inch armspread allowed me to pull it off. The engine had only about 300 hours of flight time on it and it always started promptly. This day was no exception and it came to life with a gentle roar. Putting one foot up on a tire, I swung up over the wing struts and dropped into the tiny rear cockpit.

Pushing the throttle forward, I eased the plane onto the runway then taxied to the end and turned and pointed the ship at the strip. Locking the brakes, I performed the pilot's "***C-I-G-A-R***" pre-flight safety procedure... that is almost as old as aviation.

"**C-I-G-A-R**" is an easy to remember "mnemonic" for checking (just before takeoff) the ***Controls*** for freedom of travel, the ***Instruments*** which (in the Cub) include oil pressure and atimeter barometric pressure-correction adjustment, ***Gas*** (fuel quantity and/or correct tank with fuel selected), ***Attitude*** or "trim" (a manual control, the adjustment of which levels the plane fore and aft compensating for variations in the location of the load within the plane), and ***Runup***,) "revving" the engine up to medium-high RPM...revolutions per minute) while checking carburetor-heat for operation and how the dual magnetos perform individually. Performing the "**CIGAR**" on a "light plane" achieves a complete assessment of the plane's "flight-ready" condition (***after*** having done a complete "walk-around" inspection of the airplane on the ground). Prudence demands the "CIGAR" check be done ***every time before take-off*** and is generally accomplished prior to takeoff to one side of a runway end in a "***run-up***" area. The plane engine makes a lot of noise during this process...which is music to a pilot's ears.

The CIGAR check indicated the plane was in good flyable condition so I pushed the throttle forward and began my takeoff. With only me in the plane, it rose from the runway in about two hundred feet. Climbing steeply, I planned for a 1500 foot altitude above the field. That always worked out well for the type of junior-grade "aerobatics" I performed. The altitude was close enough to be seen...and high enough to recover from any poorly-performed maneuvers or an airplane malfunction.

I leveled out at just over 1500 feet and, flying back to the strip from the same end from which I'd left, began my routine thusly: I executed a snaproll (a quick sharp rotation of the plane) just over the runway threshold and, upon recovery, pulled up into a cruising speed loop; out of the loop and over the center of the runway into "slow roll" (a slow rotation of a plane on its "longitudinal" axis) and out of that pulled up into a vertical climb until the plane stopped midair (a "hammerhead" stall), then dropped left out of the hammerhead into a one-turn spin and recovered into level flight, reversing my path back to the runway end from which I had begun…then made a 180 degree turn and repeated the same program. Following that, I cruised back to the center of the runway and executed a dozen or so consecutive cruising-speed loops while holding exact altitude and hitting my "slipstream" (a "vortex" disturbance left behind after a plane's movement through air) on the bottom (point of beginning of maneuver) of each; a few more maneuvers such as steep wing-overs, more hammer-head stalls, short tail-skids, vertical reversements...then I shut down the engine, the prop stopped turning and I flew "dead-stick" (engine stopped) down onto the field...touched down... and rolled right up to the tailgate of the pickup and ***braked to a stop!***

The boys were overjoyed! They yelled! They clapped! They were thrilled! ***Life was good!***

Hopping out of the plane, I walked over to the boys and we talked about aerobatics for a short time. Butch couldn't contain himself. "Go up again! ***We want to see some more***."

I replied, "Well, let me check my fuel supply first. It's getting low."

I stepped up on a tire, twisted off the gas tank cap and peered down into the tank. "Well, guys," I said, "the plane has only enough fuel left for a half-hour maximum of flying time so the program will have to be short."

"That's great!" they trilled in unison...*they just wanted more!*

I picked up the plane's tail, turned the plane around and away from the pickup, then walked to the front and propped the engine to life and climbed back into the rear "solo" seat. I taxied back to the end of the runway, curved around onto the strip at full power like a bush pilot, then left the ground and pulled up into a ***very steep climb-out at a very low airspeed (to add a little extra pizzazz)!***

Big mistake!!!

At one hundred feet of altitude, with barely enough airspeed to stay in the air, ***the engine quit dead!***

Now...those of you ***who are pilots*** are thinking, "We pilots were taught to hold the plane ***straight ahead*** in such a situation, ***no matter what!***"

Yeah!...***I was taught that, too!*** But...how many of you would hold to that theory when the ship you are flying is your pride and joy, is an exceptionally neat and highly-modified airplane in brand-new condition...and is completely paid for…with *zero insurance*. Plus, in addition…there are big threatening fences, chicken coops and barns directly ahead.

Well…that was my situation! And, yeah, I know I should have taken out the fences and chicken coops. I promise to do that…***next time***.

I jammed the stick forward and instantly began a (forbidden) left turn...at the same time figuring (in the panic of the moment) that I somehow might be able to complete a 180 degree turn and fly back to the field. ***Another big mistake!!!***

Ninety degrees through the turn, I knew that wasn't going to happen. I could feel the plane starting to "go over the top"! That meant if I continued the turn, the airplane would go upside down...and then *straight into the ground to certain death.* The only good news in the situation was that I had very good "feel" for the ship (a very good understanding of the plane's basic flight characteristics developed from flying the plane almost every day). That "feel" for the ship caused me to shove the right rudder pedal hard just before *it went over the top (upside down)*, and, as poorly effective as the rudder was due to lack of airflow because of low airspeed, my action leveled the ship out at treetop height…unfortunately...going straight out over the canyon wall, which was about a hundred feet directly away from the strip.

At the time the ship leveled, I already was almost at the canyon crest *without enough flying speed...*which meant that the plane then began mushing down quickly.

Over the edge and down into the canyon the plane and I went...***very steeply***... with the plane still maintaining a fairly level configuration and simply skipping down on the tops of hundred foot high deciduous trees as if bouncing along on their tops, one by one. We're talking serious ***rapid de-elevation*** here!

What was I thinking as this was happening? You've got to be kidding! A person doesn't think sanely while in this kind of situation. You do that later (if there is a later). I don't remember exactly what I was thinking but *my* ***imminent death*** *was right up there in front*. I can tell you from experience, this sort of thing happens so fast you can't believe it. That is, if you have anything left to "can't believe it" with when it's all over. But then, you'll notice...I am writing this so my case has to be one of the better ones. But, back to the almost vertical uncontrolled descent in my pride and joy.

The plane skipped down murderously across tree after tree, ripping off uppermost leaves. After a woefully long period of this (which I imagined ...but actually took very little elapsed time), an opening in the tree-top canopy appeared beneath the plane...about three-fourths of the way to the canyon bottom. The opening was not quite the size of the plane; probably the size of only *one large missing tree.*

Dropping down like a rock, the plane had very little forward airspeed. When it got to the opening between trees, the plane simply slipped down into the hole and went ***straight down***. I braced myself to shake hands with the Grim Reaper. *Death was less than eighty feet away!*

Well, I'll be darned if the "Reaper" didn't get distracted by a text message just as I was about to drill a big deathly hole in the ground with my plane and body. The result??? The opening in the trees turned out to be big enough to let the plane's fuselage through...but small enough that the outboard sections of the wings caught many tree limbs projecting from surrounding trees. As the ship's nose headed straight for the ground, descent was slowed significantly by tree limbs on each side and instead...the plane went in upside-down and landed on its back with what could almost be called a gentle "thud," and ***the ride to hell ended!***

Almost gentle…***but not quite***. Hanging upside down in my harness, I saw bent metal and fabric which appeared beyond salvage.

Checking my body, I couldn't feel a scratch. No Blood. Didn't feel a thing. No pain. Everything seemed OK. <u>***I was still alive!***</u>

Did that make me happy? You better believe ***it did not!*** I'd checked the fuel correctly, knew the capabilities of this airplane, had run low on fuel on purpose in the air a number of times just to see at what level the engine would quit, thought I had it all figured out…and, **obviously**, was ***dead wrong!***

After crawling out of the ship, I looked it over for a few moments and distressfully realized that I had just written off a major chunk of my hard-earned life savings. Then it dawned on me that if I didn't act quickly, I could write off yet another chunk.

I knew that the boys must be not only in a state of shock but they naturally would call an ambulance to cart out my remains. No way did I want to pay an unnecessary ambulance bill. I already had lost enough.

I charged uphill through the brush. As I ran, I yelled, "***Don't call an ambulance, don't call an ambulance!***" Butch has never forgiven me for that! He said he had never run anywhere so fast and hard in his life as he did to get to me (of course, <u>***after***</u> he had called an ambulance). And then, I arrived alive and well meeting the group halfway up the hill, all the while still screaming at the top of my lungs for them to not order an ambulance. Later, Butch told me that I swore at him when he said he had called one and, to this day, he says I was an ingrate. Yeah, he's right! But ***he*** hadn't just wiped out ***his*** most prized possession with one of the dumbest maneuvers known in the world of aviation. I didn't want to lose one more nickel for an unnecessary ambulance. Not only had I been humbled into oblivion by my widely-exposed stupidity, I had just cashed myself out financially.

It took me a while to get over that one. I gave the remnants of the airframe to an airplane mechanic living nearby for hauling it up out of the canyon. I didn't follow up on exactly how he got those pieces out, but Butch told me later he and a friend manhandled a wheelbarrow up over a defunct overgrown logging road with the engine. Today, the plane simply would be lifted out by a helicopter. The mechanic, no doubt, retrieved the parts by a vastly more difficult process.

The mechanic kept what was left of the airframe, instruments, landing gear, etc., and I sold the almost-new engine for somewhere around four hundred bucks, a "give-away" compared with how much engines later went up in value.

For some reason, the FAA did not "write me up" for reckless flying or whatever they usually charge a pilot with for doing such a dumb trick. Maybe they figured I'd been punished enough. I surely thought so and I decided that it might be in my best interests to make that my last crash in an airplane ...and by golly, ***it was!***

The moving finger writes...and having writ, moves on...
Nor all thy piety nor wit shall change a line
Or all thy tears wash out a word of it.

Omar Khayyam

An Alarming Ascension

One weekend, I was invited to help at a charitable auction event. Upon my arrival, which turned out to be on an extremely windy day, I was asked to be the auctioneer of a hot air balloon ride (ostensibly because of my aviation connection). I accepted, and when the balloon ride came up, I stepped forward and began chanting for bids.

Not getting adequate bids, I bid on the ride myself...and won! The auction (and the balloon) was located in front of a big home in the center of a grove of high trees. I invited the auction chair-lady to ride with me and, together with the balloon pilot, we climbed into the wicker basket.

The pilot noted the wind velocity was right at (or maybe above) safe flying speed. However, because 300 attendees were waiting in breathless anticipation to see the balloon-ascension, he felt obligated to go. He called for release of the balloon's tethering ropes held by volunteers and up we went! The moment the balloon envelope cleared the trees, higher winds above blew it rapidly against the nearest greenery. The balloon continued to ascend, dragging us in the basket through leaves and branches. By only a thin margin, our basket managed to escape through the trees without getting entangled...and then the high wind took over in earnest.

It was obvious the pilot had grossly miscalculated the speed of the wind. He immediately (with much embarrassment) explained to us that there was way too much wind for a safe ride and we needed to land at the first favorable spot. Less than a mile from the auction, he pulled a release rope that let air out of the bag...and our basket began skipping along the ground at an alarming rate.

Finally, skipping along for another half mile, the pilot was able to jump out and bring the balloon and basket to a stop. Our lady passenger was beside herself with fright but, after a bit, as the flapping balloon deflated to a manageable condition, we all heaved sighs of relief. My only balloon ride did not turn out very well, but the fact that we weren't dumped out of the basket at treetop level...plus the customary champagne the pilot poured after landing tempered my disappointment!

Smoke and Fears

It was one of the most awesome sights I'd ever seen! Four giant black smoke-trails pouring out of one of the biggest airplanes to ply the skies. *I couldn't believe this was happening!* I waited for the crash.....

The episode began innocently enough. In the summer of 1967, I flew my Cessna 180 to the small Troutdale, Oregon, airport to pick up a brake disc I'd ordered earlier from the regional Cessna distributor/dealer.

The single Troutdale runway is situated at 007/250 degrees (4600 feet long at the time) and is aligned in a similar direction and slightly out of direct line to two much longer runways (about 2 miles each) located on the nearby, much larger Portland International Airport. Portland's north main runway (there are two, parallel) is 100/280 degrees and only about ten miles from Troutdale. Approaching Troutdale airport from the east at night, a pilot can usually spot both airports at the same time...if there are no clouds or haze.

In the early 1960s, this close configuration of airports played a significant role in the following major aviation incident: One dark night a United Airlines pilot (and his co-pilot) flying a giant fully-loaded DC-8 four-engine jet passenger plane, mistook Troutdale's much shorter runway for a Portland International runway. After twilight when runway lights are on, the two airports appear almost directly in line and, when arriving from the east at altitude, *a "beginner" pilot* might possibly confuse the two airports (for about two seconds until reality corrects the situation). For seasoned airline pilots to make such a gross mistake…is ***unforgivable***. Such a colossal "faux pas" might happen to a small-plane "student" pilot but is never expected of airline pilots.

The upshot of this astounding momentary lapse of attention was that, by the time the two DC-8 pilots realized they were landing at the wrong airport, they were totally committed and had to complete the landing. That is the way flying works with very large airplanes. Fortunately, they screeched to a halt before overrunning the end of the runway and everyone lived to tell about it...(and other pilots to joke about it). That is, everyone except the crimson-faced pilots, who were severely reprimanded.

The Troutdale runway was too short for even a partially-loaded DC-8 takeoff so the passengers had to be unloaded and bussed to Portland International…a very embarrassing development for the airline. The giant plane was parked in Troutdale for the night (incongruously in a small space ordinarily occupied by a half dozen or so light planes).

Because Troutdale runway was at the time only 4600 feet long, far too short for ordinary DC-8 operation (takeoffs generally require much more length than do landings), a crew had to come from Portland the next day, take out all removable equipment from inside the plane and most of the remaining fuel (they needed only enough to fly the ten miles to Portland) and prepare the big ship to fly out. To the cheering of many amused onlookers and private pilots lined up at the fences, a different pair of professional pilots flew the plane out clearing the end of the runway with a modest amount of room to spare. I don't remember the fate of the two unfortunate "wrong-airport" pilots…but I can guess it wasn't pretty.

One hilarious result: a local airport wag assembled and posted in the Troutdale flight lounge (for all private pilots to see) a cartoon illustrating the goofy-looking head of a grizzled old wild-eyed tobacco-chewing buffoon wearing a fancy gold-plated space helmet. Appearing totally befuddled, the geezer gazed into the night effecting a bewildered, quizzical expression innocently inquiring in the caption beneath…***"Troutdale???"***

To continue my story...I picked up my brake disc and hiked back to my four-place Cessna 180. I'd flown in from my home about a hundred miles away and, for convenience, had agreed to meet a man at the Portland airport on business. It would be easy for me to fly the mere ten miles to save much time, complete my business and then fly home. Simple!

I hopped into the plane, started the engine and called ground control. The controller directed me to runway 25. Taxiing to the end of the runway,

One of few remaining photos of the giant DC-8 jet that landed by mistake at tiny Troutdale, Oregon, 1967

I turned onto the "run-up ramp," gave the plane the usual engine "run-up and controls checkout, changed radio frequencies and called the Tower for takeoff clearance.

"Troutdale Tower, this is 3361 Delta (my aircraft registration and identification number) ready for takeoff. My destination is PDX (Portland)."

"Roger, 61 Delta. Cleared for immediate takeoff runway two-five. Upon clearing the field, call Portland Tower on (radio frequency) 118.7."

My simple reply that I had heard and understood was: "61 Delta."

Powering up, I roared down the runway, reached flying speed, elevated and was on my way. Upon clearing the departure end of the runway, I switched radio frequencies to Portland Tower 118.7 and checked in.

"Portland Tower, Cessna 180 3361 Delta just clearing Troutdale airport, landing Portland."

"Roger, 61 Delta, continue approach, report five-mile final 28-Right."

In other words, I was to call Portland "tower" when approximately five miles from the end of the Portland airport runway or about halfway between the airports.

Portland has two major parallel runways and they are designated "Left" and "Right." As mentioned, the runway I'd land on is almost exactly in line with Troutdale's Runway 25. All very simple. I had to fly over a tiny bit to the right and I would be lined up directly toward PDX Runway 25-Right. So far, so good. The Portland air controllers knew I was coming and knew exactly where I was. Of course they did! I would show up clearly on their radar, so they could be absolutely sure of my location in relation to other aircraft. No problem. That's why we *have* aircraft traffic "control."

About seven miles out from Troutdale runway 28R, I looked over to my left. To my alarm, I could see a very large commercial jet plane at my same altitude at what appeared to be four or five miles south and moving fast directly toward me. This shouldn't have been a problem but I also was astonished that the Portland aircraft controller hadn't seen fit to make me aware of this rapidly approaching ship. Traffic rules mandated a three-mile separation between landing airplanes to allow plenty of time for the plane on the ground to get out of the way of the next coming in…and this giant ship was going to end up a heck of a lot closer than that required separation distance.

My usual runway final approach speed "over the threshold" would be about 80 miles an hour, or a bit less. Large commercial jets don't stay in the air at much less than 130+ mph, so the situation clearly should have been obvious to the aircraft tower controller that one of us would have to execute a "holding maneuver" to allow the other adequate legal space to land. When these situations arise, generally it's the small plane that has to move to give the larger craft the right of way. The only case when this isn't true is when a motorized "lighter-than-air" craft such as a "blimp" (or balloon) is involved. They always have the right of way.

Man, oh man, this big ship was closing in on me fast from "eight o'clock." It was clear that something was definitely wrong in the tower… most likely a "trainee" tower controller misdirecting this action.

Airplane people are a de facto "fraternity." Within reason, they will help each other as much as they possibly can. I decided to try to help this apparently somewhat befuddled air controller.

Via a radio call, I volunteered: "Portland Tower, 61 Delta seven-mile final. I'll be happy to do a 360° to the right over the river" (which would have taken me out of the way and given the big ship time to land first).

The great Columbia River runs close beside both the Troutdale and

Portland airports. To help shake the controller up and get him out of this rapidly-evolving potential disaster, I thought my offer would come as a great relief to him. To my *everlasting shock*, he hesitated for quite a few moments (all the time both airplanes were closing rapidly) and finally, stuttering, called me back.

"Uh….er….ah….61 Delta…..continue final, (runway) 28-Right."

Unbelievable!

We were on a COLLISION course! Surely, he could clearly see us both on the radar screen. By now, he even could see us easily with field glasses…almost *with the naked eye!* Surely he could see this giant Boeing 707 four-engine jet rapidly bearing down on me!

It is a fact that, almost without question, no pilot ever disobeys an aircraft controller. What in the world was this controller thinking? Or, was he thinking at all?

Something had to be done. ***Right now!***

I called again.

"Portland Tower, 61 Delta."

"61 Delta, go ahead."

"Portland Tower," I repeated, "I'm prepared to make an immediate 360° (complete circle allowing time tor the 707 to land) to the right."

I waited for a response. Nothing!

Radio quiet!

I looked over to my left….the 707 was getting much closer. I called again.

"Portland Tower…*how about a 360 to the right???"*

Finally the controller called back. I couldn't believe what I heard!

"61 Delta…uuhhh…aaahhhh…..eeerrrrr….uuhhh….*Continue approach two-eight-right (continue to the runway)."*

All that stuttering had consumed enough time to let the 707 get *much closer.* Soon, I'd be able to see the two pilots! What in the world were ***they*** thinking? They could hear all this on their radio. Were they talking to the controller on a frequency I couldn't hear? Was something else going on that I wasn't privy to? Why weren't they taking some type of last-minute action? They continued to roar along directly toward me and the airport.

Enough! I had to do something…***instantly!***

I firewalled the throttle and continued straight ahead. In a couple of moments my airspeed indicator was reading *one-hundred-fifty…and moving up!* I figured I'd better get onto the ground pronto and get off the runway as quickly as possible.

180 -182 Check List

BEFORE ENTERING AIRCRAFT

1. Check ignition switch "OFF"
2. Remove control lock
3. Master switch "ON"
4. Check fuel gauges
5. Drain gasculator
6. Master switch "OFF"
7. Extend flaps
8. Visual check of aircraft
9. Check fuel & oil supply

STARTING ENGINE

1. Adjust & lock seat
2. Cowl flaps "OPEN"
3. Fuel selector on "BOTH" tanks (no take-off with less than ¼ fuel level)
4. Check brakes & set parking brake
5. Radios "OFF"
6. Mixture control "Full Rich"
7. Carburetor heat control to "Cold"
8. Propeller "High RPM" (Full In)
9. 2 strokes of primer (if cold)
10. Master switch "ON"
11. Crack throttle ½ inch
12. Ignition switch to "BOTH"
13. "CLEAR" propeller
14. Engage starter (no longer than 30 seconds)
15. Radios "ON"

TAXI

1. Call tower
2. Set clock & altimeter (tower information)
3. Set Directional Gyros
4. Check brakes, fuel, directional gyro, turn & bank, artificial horizon and magnetic compass

BEFORE TAKE-OFF

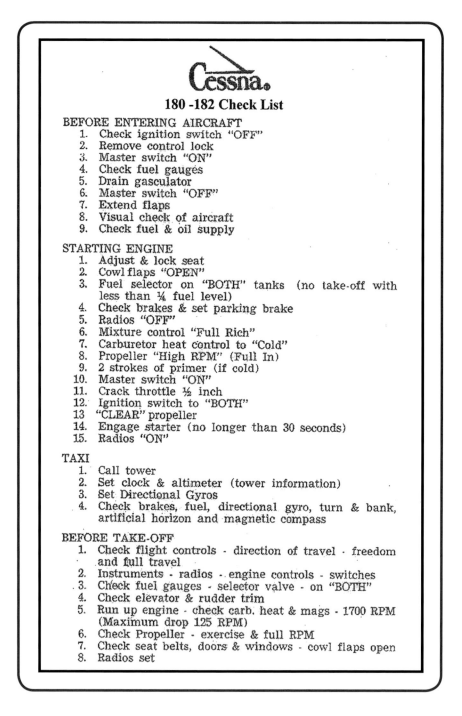

1. Check flight controls - direction of travel - freedom and full travel
2. Instruments - radios - engine controls - switches
3. Check fuel gauges - selector valve - on "BOTH"
4. Check elevator & rudder trim
5. Run up engine - check carb. heat & mags - 1700 RPM (Maximum drop 125 RPM)
6. Check Propeller - exercise & full RPM
7. Check seat belts, doors & windows - cowl flaps open
8. Radios set

TAKE-OFF

1. Apply full throttle smoothly to avoid propeller surging
2. Avoid braking
3. Raise nose wheel at 60 mph indicated - let aircraft fly off the ground
4. Maximum flaps 20° for take-off

CLIMB

1. Air speed 100 to 120 mph
2. Power at 23 inches & 2450 RPM

CRUISE

1. 22 inches and 2300 RPM (normal)
2. Close Cowl flaps
3. See cruise charts in owners manual

BEFORE LANDING

1. Mixture full rich
2. Carb heat "ON"
3. Gas on BOTH
4. Prop full forward on final
5. Glide 70-80 with flaps (see owners manual)

AFTER LANDING

1. Flaps up
2. Cowl flaps open
3. Carb heat "OFF"

STOPPING ENGINE

1. Mixture lean
2. AFTER engine stops turn ignition "OFF"
3. Master switch "OFF"
4. Set parking brakes
5. Tie down aircraft

OTHER DATA

Useable fuel 55.0 Gal. Gas 80 octane.
Oil 12 quarts capacity. Use 40 RPM compounded
In the event of electrical fire, turn Master Switch "OFF"

OPERATING LIMITATIONS

Gross Weight 2800 lbs.
Never exceed (Glide-Dive or Smooth Air) 193 mph (red line)
Caution range 160-193 mph (yellow arc)
Maximum structural cruising speed 160 mph
(Level flight or climb)
Normal operation range 67-160 mph (green arc)
Maximum speed flaps extended 110 mph
Flap operation range 60-110 mph
Maneuvering speed 128 mph

A very few moments passed….they seemed like an eternity.

Then…from the tower, "61 Delta…. aaahhhh…. errrrahhh…. uuh-hh…. ***CLEARED TO LAND!***" he blurted out. This controller was seriously out of control.

As I approached within about a half mile of the runway, I called on the radio to no one in particular to make everyone aware of my high approach speed. I hoped that both the dizzy controller and the 707 pilots would figure out what I was doing (*speeding up* so I could get down and off the runway before the 707 reached touchdown behind me). The rule is that no two planes can be on the runway at the same time.

I called the Tower: "61 Delta one-mile final indicating 180 (mph)." I had gained so much speed that the airspeed indicator displayed over the "redline" (the speed the airplane is not supposed to exceed). This speed for a small Cessna on final approach is unheard of and leaning somewhere toward illegality. Surely, both the controller and the 707 pilots were bright enough to figure out what I was doing and take appropriate measures to ensure a completely safe outcome. I didn't want to be overly explicit on the radio because the transmissions are all taped and a playback would expose this dimwit controller to possible punitive action. Maybe we could work this out without a lot of unnecessary drama. I just wanted everyone to land safely and get this scene over!

The Portland runway is about two miles long and I shot over the threshold at the 180 mph speed I'd been holding for the last mile. That was a little over 100 miles an hour more than my usual approach speed, and I held that for a bit more...and then yanked the throttle all the way back to reduce power. As the little ship slowed to around 140 mph, I put the ship sideways in a slight "skid" to bleed off more speed and then lowered the flaps to the first notch while still moving over "safe" flap-lowering speed, all in an effort to get far down the runway, on the ground and onto an angled "high-speed" exit quickly…***before the 707 arrived over the threshold.***

I touched the wheels down in a level attitude well above stall speed and applied the brakes. The Cessna 180 is a "tail wheel" airplane and cannot normally be landed at as high a speed as a "tricycle gear" plane. Tricycle gear planes can simply fly onto the runway, touch down above "stall-speed" and hit the brakes, but tail-wheel ships must execute a complete slow speed "stall" to settle down into a typical correct "3-point" landing. I had hurried the process along by

The NORTHWEST FLYER Monday, April 27, 1970

This airplane? - Sales Chief Marc Paulsen studies his stock; and if you're flying a J-3, Bonanza, Meyers OTW, 180 or LearJet, he knows what you want - because he's been there.

Caption a bit exaggerated by a journalist.

touching only front wheels down in a level attitude at a much higher than normal 60 mph touchdown speed. Operating in this fashion is very hard on the plane's brakes...but this was imperative to get off that runway speedily.

All this time the radio remained dead silent. ***Amazing!***

Two-thirds down the runway I swerved (still at a very high speed) toward an angled exit lane and, just as I turned, the bewildered controller almost screamed over the radio to the 707 now behind me, ***"GO AROUND...GO AROUND...GO AROUND!!!"***

I was dumbstruck at what I was hearing! I knew the giant 707 had to be almost over the threshold and committed to landing and, in big airplanes, pilots don't change their minds at the last minute. They plan their maneuvers *well ahead*. I couldn't imagine that the 707 pilots would try a "go-around" at such a late stage of their approach. The big ship was almost on the runway. In a situation as delicate as this, the pilot in command will take over and apply appropriate action to minimize danger.

To illustrate the danger of attempting to regain safe flying speed after almost touching the runway, a lesson learned from what happened to a few of the first Boeing 727 tri-jet passenger planes is in order. They were manufactured with exceptionally large landing "flaps" to assist in reducing landing speed. Larger flaps allow a plane to fly slower, a benefit that makes landings easier. Although pilots seemed to be thoroughly "checked out" to fly these big planes, the reality was that the ships were exceedingly "squirrelly" (tricky to maneuver) when the flaps were fully extended in a landing configuration. Pilots learned (after some fatal crashes killing all aboard) that flying these planes with their much larger-than-typical flaps set up a situation in which they could easily get behind the "power-curve," (a situation in which adding more power is done too late) a condition that makes regaining flying speed impossible.

That fact was what now concerned me greatly when I heard the controller almost yell to the now slow-flying and very low 707 to ***"go-around!"*** Because I was not quite off the runway when the big plane crossed the threshold, the controller apparently decided to not allow the 707 to land, most likely so he (the controller) couldn't be accused of the controller-infraction of allowing two moving planes on a runway at the same time...which is against flight rules. Another half second and I was off the runway.

The big plane began a "go-around!"

As I turned my plane into the high-speed exit taxi-way and eased it to a smoking-brake stop...the monster plane staggered the length of the runway trying to regain safe flying speed...with the tail almost touching the runway. As the ship desperately clawed back into the air, ***massive clouds of black smoke*** poured out of four big engines. The safest thing the pilot of the big plane might have done...would have been to put it down on the runway, let the chips fall where they may and not worry about what might happen to the errant controller. Attempting to abort a landing at such a late stage has proven fatal in many well-documented cases. The pilots probably felt the same way I did about the controller's incompetence because ordering such harrowing maneuvers easily could have cost a lot of lives.

I wondered later what in the world the plane's crew told the passengers about the unusual flight antics. They must have explained something because that type of thing seldom happens and is alarming for the uninitiated. I also wondered if the controller's superiors ever heard the highly unorthodox conversations recorded from our radios. If so, there could have been serious consequences in the control tower!

In all the commercial flights I've taken and continue to take since that day, each time (when safety-belted into a plane on landing approach), I rerun that precarious landing situation through my memory…and sincerely hope that every single body up front in the cockpit is wide awake and paying serious attention to the smallest detail.

Boeing 707

This 707 is like the one that struggled to regain flying speed after a befuddled airport tower controller issued a very late "Go-around" (*do not land*) command when the plane arrived too closely behind me while I was still on the runway after *having just landed.* The 707 in my story didn't touch the runway...but came perilously close.

Preparing a Cessna 182 "Skylane" for flight - 23,237+ built

After I was diagnosed as having a high-pitch hearing loss, this model plane was the last type of ship I flew as pilot-in-command. That was a sad day for me after many years of high-flying excitement in the sky!

Swiss Pilatus PC-6 Turbo-Porter

One of these wild-looking ships stopped at our facility for fuel (1970). The Swiss Pilatus "Porter" may have looked unorthodox (to say the least) but the plane proved to be an outstanding performer in high mountains.

As Close As It Gets!

A two-hour flight that morning had been a lot of fun and my passenger and I had covered much territory, done some great sight-seeing and counted many magnificent elk on mountainsides. As we approached my home airport at coastal Astoria, Oregon, the fuel gauge clearly indicated it was time to land. I always thought it wise to land with at least a half to three quarters of an hour (or a shade more) of fuel remaining. Pilots calculate the time they can fly a plane by dividing the quantity of fuel carried by the amount-per-hour the engine consumes.

I landed the plane and taxied toward the fueling location of the "fixed-base operator." As we got close, a ***very unusual*** crystal-clear message sounded on our radio. The transmission was from the Coast Guard Station headquarters, which were located only a couple of hundred yards from our position.

I turned my ear directly toward the airplane's cabin speaker to listen intently, and motioned my partner to do the same. *The radio sounded again* and ***with a strong sense of urgency,*** the person on the radio repeated the call. The "call" was to notify all Coast Guard aviation personnel on base and in the air that a helicopter had just been reported late for arrival from a nearby offshore oil drilling platform. The personnel were to man their ships immediately preparatory for takeoff and standby for further instructions. (It was 1965...Shell Oil Company was drilling an "exploratory" well from a platform located 25 miles offshore...directly out from Seaside, Oregon.)

The radio call had a special significance for me because I was personally acquainted with all the helicopter pilots involved with the oil drilling operation and knew them well…even knowing which local girls to whom the single ones had been making overtures. They were a great fun-loving group…all excellent pilots.

The call alarmed me! Then, ***the radio sounded again!*** The Coast Guardsman on duty gave the order for a helicopter to fly.

Two helicopters were employed by the drilling company to ferry workers to and from the platform; one, an old large military surplus Sikorsky "H-34" on "floats" for hauling crews and a small Bell "47G" two-place ship for transporting officials and special-purpose flights. I had kidded the pilots about their H-34 a number of times because I'd flown in them in the Army while in Europe and always thought they were extremely noisy plus they vibrated one heck of a lot. We (airplane pilots) also ribbed them, suggesting their strange-looking machines were just a bunch of loose mechanical parts "flying in formation!"

More radio calls came through the speaker. It now became clear that the big H-34 was missing…***with a full load of passengers.*** With the plane's engine still idling, I reached for the throttle, for I knew the oil company pilots needed all the help they could get!

It was wintertime in the Pacific Northwest and the cold ocean temperature would generally take a person's life in a little over twenty minutes (or less). If the oil operation's helicopter was in the water, the pilots and passengers were in big trouble! ***There was no time to lose!***

The Guard's helicopter (which had been nearby with engines running) moved out onto the taxiway and levitated in one big sweeping motion. I looked over at my friend somberly as the helicopter disappeared in the distance.

The troubled helicopter the fellows were down in had been fitted with giant black neoprene floats…supposedly with the idea that if it did have any kind of trouble, it could simply land on water. That may sound like a good concept on paper but, if their helicopter was down on the very cold northern Pacific Ocean in high wind, the odds of their ship staying upright were nil.

They could be anywhere in an area approximately twenty-five miles by twenty-five miles but, hopefully, only twenty-five miles by much less. I quickly calculated that the relatively slow speed of the Coast Guard helicopter would not allow them to execute a complete search of the area necessary in time to save lives if the crew was now in the water. The Guard's other helicopters were too far away on other missions to be of additional help, so I decided to do what I could to be of assistance.

There were no other planes nearby or in the landing pattern to inhibit our movement so we taxied rapidly toward the center intersection of the main runway and then took off while still on the taxiway. This was no time to follow inhibiting rules!

Keying my microphone, I called the Guard base radio operator informing him of my position and said we had heard his call and were off the ground and heading for the search area. He called back and replied, "Great, there will be only you and our helicopter in the air, so I'll call you back shortly with instructions."

The northern section of the search area was about five minutes away and I told the radio operator that I had an estimated thirty to forty-five minutes of usable fuel so could remain in the air for about fifteen minutes plus. I knew we would be risking running low on fuel but also knew how important it would be to search during the first most critical minutes. If we kept close track of time, we should be able to get back and land safely with a minimum quantity of fuel remaining.

Another minute went by and the Coast Guard operator called me.

"61 Delta, how do you read?"

"61 Delta, loud and clear."

"61 Delta, what is your position?"

"Just now over the beach and heading out to sea in the direction of the platform."

"61 Delta, continue and search the area directly north from the line between the platform and the shore. Our ship will search the area south of that line. Begin traversing to and from the shore and move north just enough on each pass to cover new territory but only high enough to still allow a good view. Look for fluorescent orange clothing or orange smoke."

We began our first leg out from the beach toward the platform. It's amazing how far twenty-five miles can seem when you are low on fuel and out at sea! I clearly realized how precarious this undertaking was, but the alternative was to let several guys die in the cold ocean very close to civilization. That just didn't seem right. I reduced power to conserve fuel and slowed to get a better view of the water. The wind was blowing almost directly across our path and the waves were blowing giant whitecaps, making thorough visibility highly questionable. The chances of being found at sea in rough water can be very slim! But there was no time to spare!

We continued and stayed out longer than we should have but, as the minutes ticked by, we knew life was probably ebbing as our engine droned...and we couldn't bear the thought of the fellows out there drowning if there was the slightest chance of helping.

Close to fifteen minutes went by and we now began to realize that, as we moved further north and the Coast Guard chopper moved south, even if we spotted survivors in our search area, the helicopter might not get there in time to save them. ***Time was quickly running out!***

Just as our limited fuel supply forced us to give up the hunt and we turned back for land, the Coast Guard helicopter radioed that they had found the lost fliers to the south and were putting rescue swimmers in the water. They said the found helicopter was upside down in the water and there appeared to be men struggling to hold onto the "floats."

With a big sigh of relief, we immediately aimed directly for shore to land at our nearer small Seaside airport located south of Astoria, and only a mile from the beach. My fuel supply was stretched as far as possible and *the gauges showed almost zero fuel.*

We approached the airport low and slow, made a smooth continuous final approach turn and quietly settled onto the short single runway. The main gear touched the blacktop first in level flight and then, as airspeed diminished and the tail wheel touched down, the engine QUIT DEAD…and the plane rolled to a stop in the middle of the runway. Out of fuel!

We had to get additional help to push the plane off the runway and over to the parking ramp. A couple of other pilots looked our way and wondered aloud to each other as to my sanity...or was I just a totally incompetent. To their way of thinking, anyone who would run out of fuel ***on the runway*** must be brain-dead. I attempted to explain that we had a little more fuel available when in level flight attitude but they were in a hurry to leave and didn't bother to listen. They are probably still talking about the nut who ran out of fuel on the runway.

Thinking back on the situation, I convinced myself that if I hadn't taken such a chance, the Coast Guard helicopter may well have flown a different search pattern, thereby missing the location of the men in the water. It was my calculation that the plane had ***just enough fuel*** to do the job…and I'm still here to write about the event and all the men in the water lived to tell their stories so I felt it was the right decision.

By what some considered a miracle, everyone in the downed helicopter survived. Hours later at the hospital, when they were able to talk, they said that when they were found they figured they could have lasted no more than another five or ten minutes before succumbing to hypothermia. All the involved doctors concurred.

It was that close!

Fueling up in Farmington

Fueling up my Cessna 180 at Farmington, New Mexico, on the way to Old Mexico. At a fuel-up in Guaymas, Mexico, a few days later, I handed the gas attendant a hundred dollar bill...and suddenly he didn't understand English anymore. Strange...he had understood me clearly when I requested that he fill my tanks. Astoundingly, we went through much wrangling before he finally gave up and returned the proper amount of change. (He tried about a half dozen lesser settlements before the correct figures were defined.) Then I flew nervously for the next few hours...wondering if the fuel might be as "questionable" as the fuel operator had been!

Beechcraft Debonaire - 1,297 built

This is one of the planes I got to fly when I was an airplane salesman. It's the Beechcraft "straight-tailed" retractable-gear "Debonaire," flying mate to its near-twin version, the famed V-tailed "Bonanza" model...one of the longest-produced private planes ever. The plane was so well built that pilots lovingly remarked, "It's built like a tank and flies like a dream." It was also one of the highest-priced single engine planes of the mid-twentieth century. A fellow ground school student (a middle-aged logging contractor) told me he had just bought a spanking new Bonanza with enough modern radio gear to almost double the cost of the basic plane to a final figure approaching $46,000... an amount large enough (no...astronomical) at the time to boggle the minds of us lesser mortal souls. (I recently had paid only $1,250 total for my little used Piper "Cub.") Additionally unique was that this fellow was not yet a licensed pilot...and planned to finish learning to fly in his own high-powered and relatively complex Bonanza, one of the more demanding ships of the day. But...logging operators are known to run a large variety of complex equipment in their work, so I figured his operating expertise would serve him well.

Destiny Gives A "Check-ride"

Tis all a Chequer-board of Nights and Days
Where Destiny with Men for Pieces plays;
Hither and thither Moves, and Mates, and Slays,
And one by one, *back in the Closet lays.*

Omar Khayyam

An airshow in Puyallup, Washington, seemed like an exciting way to spend a summer Sunday. On the morning of the show, my wife and I made an early start for the airport. We had talked over whether we wanted to fly up from our home airport in Astoria, Oregon, in our four-place Cessna 180 or in the Meyers OTW open cockpit biplane that I had acquired for pure fun flying. It was to be a warm day and the show would feature a number of similar aerobatic biplanes, so we thought it novel to take the open cockpit plane and join in the spirit of the activity.

Our planes were parked side by side inside a giant old blimp hangar that was a remnant of World War II. The enormity of the building made all of the planes inside look like toys. Some people say this type of building is so large inside that there can be a separate weather system within and it can actually rain inside. If that's true, it is probably more like a fine mist. Sounds interesting, though.

We had to gently move a couple of other planes to get to ours, something of an irritation we suffered somewhat willingly because of the low rent charged in consideration of this fact. Sometimes, an owner might have to move ten planes to get to his own. In our case, the maintenance costs of two airplanes was enough without having to pay an additional charge of high hangar rent. The space was a pretty good deal because much of the time our planes were up front and fairly easy to get out. The major difficulty was the necessity to push them into the hangar and carefully "fit them in" rather than taxi up and push in with nothing in the way, as is usually the situation with private hangars. A negative was the occasional "hangar rash" a plane might exhibit after a careless neighbor bumped your ship…not a pleasant outcome…but it was the price paid for low rent.

We had to wait for some thin low fog to clear before we could be on our way so we used this time to inspect the plane carefully and check for any deficiencies which might have gone unnoticed before. Everything appeared to be in good order and, by the time the fog had lifted enough for a safe departure, we were ready. We put on our seat-pack parachutes which, as the name implies, were also cushions we sat on, which would be our salvation in the event of disaster to the ship (that being very theoretical, of course). If an unfortunate event did occur, with the seat parachutes we would have the ability to step out of what might be left of a broken airplane and safely float down to earth. I had jumped three times earlier from Cessnas to become familiar with "bailing out" but still wasn't sure I could let my own plane whirl down to its demise while I hung in the "chute" shrouds as an unwilling observer.

Cruising up the southern Washington coast, we looked down to see people enjoying their morning ocean beach constitutionals on the peninsula of Long Beach, one of the longest uninterrupted straight sand beaches in America. The beach is about thirty miles long and a great place to drive. When I was *very* young, my family used to dig for razor clams here where the clamming was some of the best on the West Coast. When beach traffic was light, we would speed along over the sand in our cars at velocities of more than one hundred miles per hour. The sand was so smooth it felt more like thirty or forty miles an hour. This was at a time when the law was not a serious factor. Try that today and you'd soon be looking out through steel latticework windows. Now, realistic speed limits have been established.

When motorcycles were my interest (yes, I raced "motocross" with one for a time...albeit with limited success), groups of us would take our English "bikes" out on the beach sand and roar around in giant sweeping circles at seventy or eighty miles an hour in big controlled slides. Usually, if one lost control, the machine only slid and skidded harmlessly for a distance because the sand was perfectly flat. No more of that now but I did land my Piper Cub on this beach once just for the sport of it. Nope. None of that anymore, either!

Beechcraft "Muskateer" - 4,366 built

The plane salesman years: Marc with a 4-place single-engine semi-classic. This was Beech Aircraft Company's attempt to break into the light single-engine airplane business. The ship was very well made but suffered from market high-pricing due to Beech's stringent high-quality design and production standards.

Moving inland, we flew east to Olympia and then toward Tacoma. To stay out of the restricted flight area of Ft. Lewis (Army) and McChord Air Base (Air Force), we flew north of Olympia and out over south Puget Sound. Over Tacoma, we turned inland and cruised south to Puyallup, the site of the day's airshow.

Arriving over the field late in the morning, there were planes coming in from all directions. We stayed far from the traffic pattern until spotting an opening between planes entering the downwind leg. Apparently *too far* to see *exactly what* was transpiring. When that opening appeared, we headed in and when we arrived to turn onto the downwind leg, we realized that some AT-6s (WWII "advanced" trainers) had just left the field and were moving out in formation for a return sweep down the runway. The airshow had begun at just that time.

Instead of continuing to land, I held the ship at the edge of the traffic pattern and began to circle doing tight 360 degree orbits so I could view the airshow over my shoulder. I wanted to see every bit of the action and continued to fly the plane in the very high "G-force" configuration for quite a number of orbits. After about ten or twelve of these, my wife began motioning wildly to me that she was becoming seriously air-sick. I didn't have a problem with air sickness because I flew my other plane frequently. She made clear that if I didn't get down immediately, we would end up with a major clean-up job in the front seat.

Good news prevailed much to my relief. As my wife appeared at the point of throwing up, an opening in the program presented itself and I made an abbreviated approach pattern and landing. Luck was with us and we didn't get "chewed out" for what probably was a violation of the program rules. If we hadn't had an interesting biplane, the result might have been different. The biplane made us sort of "de facto" members of the aerobatic community.

This was to be a great day, because Charlie Hillard, who would later become a world-class champion aerobatic pilot, was scheduled to give his outstanding J-3 Piper Cub "dead-stick" performance (flying down from altitude with the engine turned off and the propeller stopped). Seeing his performance was one of my key reasons for coming to the airshow. Having owned, flown and even crashed a J-3 a few times, I had developed a love for the J-3 Cub and had wanted to see Hillard's performance for some time. This would be my first opportunity to see a truly stellar display of light-plane aerobatic piloting in this model of airplane.

Another "great" in the world of aerobatics to fly this day was to be well-known Harold Krier in a Great Lakes biplane. The Great Lakes is a relatively small plane, between the size of the famous Boeing Stearman and our Meyers OTW. Krier's airplane model was a highly desirable one for aerobatics before the arrival of such planes as tiny "Pitts Special" biplanes and others specially designed for the activity. Every pilot I ever talked to about the Great Lakes (used widely in WWII as a trainer) had an almost mystical reverence in his voice when he spoke of it. This was still the era of readily available surplus military trainers. It was also a time when there were still a lot of former WWII pilots around to tell stories of the old days when they trained in these planes as Army Air Corps Cadets.

Unfortunately, like so many aerobatic performers before him, Krier would meet his end in aerobatic flight while flight-testing a prototype aerobatic plane on July 6, 1971.

My wife and I had an exciting time viewing the unique aerobatics and the other program air features. For pilots, practically all flight comes under the heading of unique and entertaining. The day progressed with the usual adoration of daring and not-so-daring pilots by a mesmerized general public, pilots like me and many "would-like-to-be-pilots" and some student pilots-to-be.

Hillard's dead-stick Cub performance was the highlight of the day for me and I couldn't have been happier. The show ended around three-thirty in the afternoon, allowing us time to fly the long way back home to Astoria above Interstate Highway I-5 that runs through Chehalis, Centralia and Kelso, Washington...then follows the great Columbia River for a distance. We made a big sweep south around massive Fort Lewis and joined I-5 above Centralia, then down to Kelso where we landed and taxied up to the gas pumps at the Kelso flight operations.

Hopping out of the plane, we were pleasantly surprised to be met by a fairly large group of interested onlookers, among whom was a construction superintendent working for the general contractor of a new paper mill project in Wauna, Oregon, by the Columbia River. I also was working on the paper mill construction, but as a subcontractor. The project was large enough to have a temporary airstrip right on the property. The superintendent and I were well acquainted, partly because he was also a pilot and airplane owner. He owned a modern Piper Cherokee aircraft and he flew daily just as I flew my Cessna 180 each day to the project (weather permitting).

The superintendent's twenty-two-year-old son was there and he was totally taken by the fact that his father was on "good-buddy" terms with me, a biplane owner and pilot. The son hovered around me and the plane and, since I got along well with the superintendent, I thought to myself, "This is a great opportunity to 'make points' with his father." I could offer to take the boy for a ride and possibly further ingratiate myself with the 'super'...because he worked directly for the general contractor on our job and had a substantial share of influence on how my situation prospered (or didn't). Plus, I could treat the boy to some aerobatics!

The boy took about a hundredth of a second to say yes when I proposed that he go up with me for some aerobatics. He unabashedly displayed his excitement and anticipation at this unexpected good fortune.

Out to the ship with him I went, his dad following to get a closer look at the unique machine in which his son was about to ascend into the skies. At the plane, I got out a parachute and proceeded to go over the use of it with him.

We walked around the plane and I explained the points of a finely-restored antique biplane. I covered some of the history of the plane, mentioning that he would warm the very same front cockpit seat Marilyn Monroe had occupied (a conjecture) while making the movie, "The Misfits," for which the plane had been leased by MGM Studios to round up wild horses. As I described some of the maneuvers we would be doing above the crowd (actually, about 3,000 feet), he seemed electrified at the prospect of this unexpected opportunity.

An experienced pilot from the crowd prop-started the engine for us and it rumbled to life. I added power and we rolled out onto the taxiway and up to the active runway. In a big half circle, we swung around, straightened out on the strip and, with the engine chuggedy-chugging at full power, we levitated toward our place of action in the sky.

If I failed to describe the actual sound of the antique five-cylinder Kinner R-56, 540-cubic-inch radial engine earlier, I apologize. I'm sorry to say that the engine (unfortunately) really did sound more like a tired threshing machine than a sophisticated fighter plane. The saving grace was the fact that the plane existed at all and was operational…and for any biplane, that is enough.

There is an abrupt hill just to the east of the Kelso airport a little less than half a mile away…close enough that the kid's dad and others at the airport could watch as we performed our aerobatic gyrations.

With the nose pointed up in a maximum climb, we arrived at an altitude of about a thousand feet above the top of the nearby hill. I trimmed the ship out in level flight headed south in line with the hill...which paralleled highway I-5.

One little detail I might have overlooked mentioning earlier was the fact that I'd flown this plane only a couple of times in the last year. The airplane now had been in my possession for a few years and the "new" had long ago worn off. The plane mostly sat in the hangar and looked the part of the antique that it was. Digging out flying attire and parachutes, getting the plane ready to fly and flying it, were enough bother that I flew it these days only once in a *very* long while. I was not *"current"* in the plane! And...that is not "*good form!*"

Applying power to the ship, I pulled up smoothly into a perfect straight-up hammerhead stall (*very easy to do*). The airplane came to a dead stop correctly pointed at the galaxy of "Glurg" far, far away in the universe…and we hovered motionless for a split second…*suspended animation in the air.*

Then we slid down backward on the plane's tail and I pushed in left rudder. The plane twisted neatly one-hundred-eighty-degrees on its yaw axis and headed straight down. Pulling back smoothly again, the G-meter on the panel pointed to three and a half. Not bad.

Punching the little reset button on the G-meter, it went back to neutral, ready to record the G-force of the next maneuver. With enough airspeed saved from the hammerhead…I pulled up into a loop, another simple maneuver for any pilot...but very impressive-appearing to onlookers. Out of the loop, I hoarded enough airspeed to pull the nose above the horizon and moved the stick all the way left - hard. Feeding in right rudder and forward stick, the plane continued around in a slow roll. This airplane just didn't have what it took to make a really good looking slow roll. Well...I guess ***I*** didn't have what it took! I decided to stick with the easy maneuvers.

Out of the slow roll and nose down to pick up some airspeed, I then pulled the nose up a little…then a little more and, finally, a super hard jerk on the stick into the corner and full rudder at the same time. *A pretty good-looking snap roll…* even came out right side up! Can't beat that! Then dropping the nose, we gained speed again and pulled up tightly into half a loop...leveled out upside down...then rolled around into level flight. A fair "Immelman." *Just fair.*

Then, I rolled the plane over again into inverted flight and pulled the stick back for a "split-s" to return to right-side-up level flight. The G-meter read four and a half Gs....boy, I let that recovery go a bit long! The kid turned around and gave me a "thumbs up." He didn't know the difference. Obviously, he was thrilled. Good thing! I'd really have been embarrassed to have had a pro up there grading me on this.

Now, there's a personal secret that I'll not readily admit. These maneuvers, plus one more, comprised the extent of my repertoire. I know you won't tell anybody else and I want you to know that I appreciate that.

The "one more" I knew is one of the simplest, and yet one of the most dramatic aerobatic maneuvers of them all to observers on the ground, the illustrious "tailspin" (or simply "spin" to pilots). The final maneuver of the program, it looks spectacular from the ground. That's why it's usually saved for last!

A perfect spin is easy to do. In fact, a pilot can't do a *bad spin.* The spin essentially controls itself and, when you see one performed, it's the plane doing the performing.....repeat, you *can't do a bad spin!* There's just no way!

The spin is also a great way to lose a lot of altitude in a hurry, *a major hurry!* It's almost the next thing to going straight down in an airplane and a natural for finishing a routine, because you have to come down anyway...

so it might as well be with super *flair.* Checking my altitude, there was plenty…probably good for five or six exciting-appearing "spin" revolutions ...before *recovery.*

For the last time, I pulled the nose up steeply and the airspeed quickly decreased almost to a stall. Pulling back the stick and then pushing hard, sharp rudder, the ship staggered, the remaining airspeed fell off and the ship turned over to the left…then dropped off into the void of the world below...twisting violently like an angry whirling dervish.

"Spinning" an airplane is actually so simple a maneuver that, for the first fifty years of amateur flight training, all student pilots were *required* to learn spins. They were taught spins fairly early in the training schedule because it was thought that all students should know how to recover from them in case they somehow lost control to the point that their plane got into one inadvertently. (Not knowing how to recover from a spin usually meant certain death.) At first, spins seem a little scary to a new pilot but not for long. The great part about them is that they look so dramatic from the ground. A student pilot doing a spin can look to mortals on the ground like a master of flight. For modern flight, spins are taught only to flight instructors.

One...two...three tight rotations into the spin...and, whoa, I began to feel a bit nervous...probably because I hadn't been doing a lot of serious aerobatics for a long while and that can make one more than a little uneasy. The spin produces an exciting carnival-ride feeling from inside a plane... which is especially so in an open cockpit biplane. However, in this case... as the turns increased in number, it suddenly struck me that this particular spin *did not feel right.*

Three-plus turns were enough. I wanted to be out of the maneuver with altitude to spare and so nervously began pushing opposite rudder to stop the rotation. The rudder moved with a big sloppy flop and hammered against its stop. Nothing happened. No aircraft response! ***Unbelievable!***

I pushed at the rudder pedal like mad. The ship continued to twist crazily and roared downward in another very fast orbit! The ground was moving up quickly as the uninterrupted spin continued.

The kid must have frozen with his hands holding the control stick in the front cockpit...in a death-like grasp. I struggled to hold off panic and remain calm while working the controls with all my might. The kid must have a grip like iron. What the heck was wrong? Why didn't the plane respond? Why couldn't I override him? I mashed on the rudder pedal with all my might! Those giant two-hundred foot fir trees were coming up very fast now.

We were getting *really close* to the trees. Soon I'd be able to see the individual fir boughs…all the while it was *deathly quiet* in the rapidly-spinning craft...with only the rush of the passing air. *Was I dreaming all this?*

I often had heard that one's life passes before one's eyes as death is about to occur and have wondered about that. Now, here I was, getting a first-hand chance to learn if it were true.

About three hundred feet from the end of a fairly short life...with maybe three to five seconds left to live before it was all over, I now could almost make out the individual fir bough <u>needles</u>! We were that close! What the hell was that damned kid doing to my controls up front? What was going on? *Why wouldn't they work?*

In my addled brain...throbbing with chilled blood, I figured...what the hell...I'd tried everything so I'd give the controls one more shot. Don't ask me why....*I jammed the stick and the throttle forward* at the same time. The airspeed increased and the little bird screamed. I hit opposite rudder...and *Shazam! The rotation stopped!* But the trees were almost upon us. Were we going to hit? I pulled back hard on the stick. The G-meter looked like it would break its needle off (O.K…an exaggeration). Recovery?...Crash?... What?...Please God. Oh, please!

Roarrrr...right down to the very tops of the fir trees. Are we going to hit? No...*we're not*. No...No...thirty, *forty feet to spare*...and the *ship swooped back up*…and awaaaay!

Quite a few years have gone by since that day. (That is the only reason I am now admitting the truth). I still get a strange, empty feeling in the pit of my stomach when I think of how that father would have felt had destiny played a different hand. Fortunately, I wouldn't have had to face him!

And oh, yes, *you want to know what really happened up there?* Well, the truth is, I hadn't flown the biplane for over eight months and was sorely out of practice. The fact is...that the ***last*** desperate stabs I made at the controls were the accepted way to recover from a typical tailspin. I had simply momentarily ***forgotten*** how to correctly recover from a spin.

Do you suppose there is a message here for you pilots and "plan-to-be" pilots?

Cessna 337 Skymaster

When I was selling airplanes, my employer and I flew a plane like this to the Oregon coast one day to give a prospect there an airplane flight demonstration. I was on the ride so I could log left-seat twin-engine flight time. Upon approach, the coastal airfield was "socked-in" with a low thin layer of fog. The prospective buyer hadn't mentioned that when he called and asked us to fly the airplane to his home airport. The ocean was clear of clouds so we flew out to sea a couple of miles and circled. When we saw the thin fog layer dissipating over the field, we turned toward the airport and I was asked to lower the gear. The gear lights didn't turn "green"...which would indicate "gear down and locked." While trying to determine the problem, we circled and circled, gloomily anticipating the possibility of a "gear-up" landing. After about thirty anxious minutes, my companion noticed a switch on the panel that read "Generator." He switched it on...and voila! We had green gear lights. I had little time in the type...but he had a lot of flight hours flying this same ship on charter flights. I surely scratched my head over that one.

Cessna 206 Skywagon - over 8,500 built

An early encounter with this legendary ship took place when I, then an airplane salesman, heard that a company needed money and had to sell one. Upon flying to their operation (they had their own airstrip) and talking with their CEO, we agreed on a price. The price was so low that I brought out my personal checkbook and paid for the plane on the spot. (I didn't have a company check with me and didn't want to miss the opportunity.) Years later, in 2002, I was sitting with an auto dealer in an airshow tent sipping a libation and discussing airplanes. He said he had just purchased a new 206...and paid $320,000. Imagine his surprise when I told him I'd paid only $9,000 for a used ship of the very same model thirty years earlier. Of course, the value of money had changed a lot and the avionics (electronics) had improved immensely over that period but the basic "airframe" was little changed in all that time. The basic other elements were essentially the same. The plane I bought had a "run-out" engine (needing overhaul) and required a modest amount of work on leaking fuel tanks but it had three good radios and was otherwise in great condition. The plane stayed in our inventory only one week when I sold it for a modest profit and ferried it to northern Washington state.

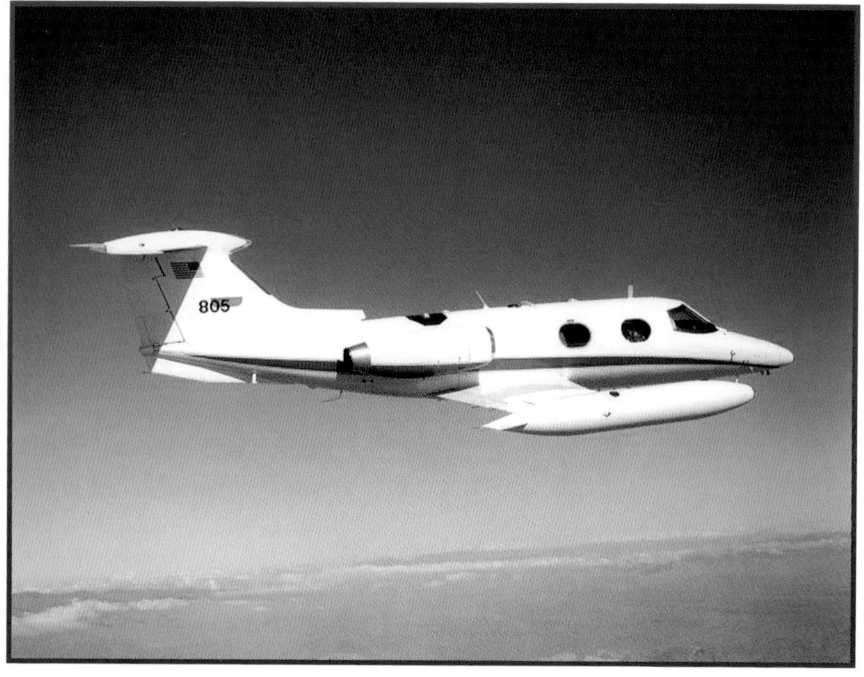

A Learjet "24" similar to the one I flew "right seat"

It was astonishing to watch the altimeter needle twist rapidly as the plane climbed to "flight-level four-one-zero" (41,000 feet). Initial rate of climb? ***7,000 feet per minute!*** 210 of this model were built.

Learjet, Right Seat

By quirk of situation, I found myself in a job with a company that operated not one, but *two*, Learjets. This, in 1968, a time when there were only a very few private jets in the entire world, and so it was an exciting time in a fast-moving operation. In fact, at that time in our state, Oregon, there were only three private jets: our two and a four-engine Lockheed Jetstar owned by a Fortune 500 company. (Consider that number and then mull over this one: I recently read that in 2011 approximately *1100 private jets* arrived in Dallas, Texas, for football's "Superbowl XLV." *Imagine that for a number!)*

I had met the company owner a couple of years earlier when he was learning to fly. I did business with his company, saw him there occasionally and, at one meeting, we discussed flying. When he learned I was a pilot and owned a couple of small airplanes, he invited me to be his "safety-pilot" while he flew in training. This was necessary because he was so busy that he did most of his flight training at night, and he and his instructor wanted another pair of eyes to watch for other airplane traffic. I accepted and was amazed that anyone would, or even could, learn to fly at night because at that time I had done very little night flying myself and still considered that somewhat exotic. He did it very matter-of-factly. Although he was still a student pilot, he had purchased a Cessna 175 "Skylark," a single-engine model with a "geared" propeller (the propeller was geared to run slower than the engine for enhanced efficiency) and planned to use the plane strictly for business travel.

He learned quickly and moved from single engine training to multi-engine…then became an instrument-rated pilot all in very short elapsed time. Soon, he purchased a twin engine plane and was flying all over the Pacific

Northwest on business. His business boomed. He was a very dynamic young man and when the opportunity presented itself, he decided to "go national" with sales efforts for his new innovations of automatic car wash equipment.

In one of the most rapid business expansions ever, he created a country-wide distribution network for his products by mapping cities having potential distributors and dealers, then leasing a Learjet Model 23 (the first Learjet model in production) with a 100-hour "block" of "dry" flight-time and used it for swift transportation. "Dry" meant the lessee furnished pilots, fuel and insurance. The plane's owner (lessor) provided 100 hours (use of the plane) and its maintenance.

With a five-man sales force, he visited *sixty cities in 28 days and set up 120 factory representatives, distributors and dealers.* It was a bold move that took the entire national competition by surprise. This aggressive action brought in enough immediate sales to warrant leasing the plane for a much longer period. Very soon his company was doing enough increased business for him to purchase a Learjet Model 24 to work with the leased Lear 23 (pioneer aircraft maker Bill Lear quickly had improved on the original Model 23). The young 29-year-old entrepreneur was checked out as "pilot-in-command" in the "24" not long after he bought the plane. He accumulated flying time very rapidly during this time of working and traveling to quickly build new business. The competition was left scrambling to catch up.

When I went to work for him, he'd had the second plane for a few months. At this time, there still were only a couple hundred or so private jets in the entire world. The airplanes then were considered so exotic that his customers would metaphorically kill to get a ride in one and, when they did, they usually were levered into buying many hundreds of thousands or millions of dollars worth of product (essentially, just for the privilege of private-jet-ride bragging rights).

He asked me to fly with him in the Learjet 24 to Chicago on the very first evening of my employment. I was overjoyed…no, elated…no, just plain thrilled to the absolute core! Imagine! Only a handful of private jets in the entire world and I was to ride in one.

I showed up at the Portland, Oregon, airport at five in the evening with my whole family in tow to watch the experience. The company had their own hangar large enough to hold both planes and, as we arrived, both were being rolled out majestically at the same time. We watched in awe as these beautiful gleaming white works of airplane art were gracefully eased out

Lockheed "Jetstar" - 204 built

When I bought an airplane and afterward received my pilot's license in 1962 (after running out of cash on each of my first three flight lesson starts), a Lockheed Jetstar like this (four engines) was the only private jet based in the state of Oregon. Even when I flew in 1968 as a "pseudo" copilot in a Learjet Model 24 which was hangared near the Jetstar, still there were only three private jets total in the state (two flown by our company, a Lear Model 23 and the 24). Compare those figures with present-day registrations. It is amazing how rapidly private business-jet aviation expanded worldwide...following Bill Lear's early visionary "Lear-Jet" production.

onto the tarmac. I felt more like royalty than a mere new employee. Then, four men piled into each plane...and *off we went!*

A winter day was growing dark as we left the runway and headed up directly toward a brilliant new moon that lit up the whole sky. Later, I would hear my five-year-old exclaim that he thought I had, in fact, left forever *to go to the moon.* He worried about that!

The Learjet's outstanding initial rate of climb was most impressive. I was used to something like a thousand feet a minute in my own Cessna 180. That was pretty good but the Lear 24 could climb *seven thousand* feet a minute (initial rate of climb). The angle of climb was so steep that a private pilot like me could be shocked into thinking we might stall at any moment...but this ship simply continued to climb. The Lear cruised at 41,000 feet back then...when the only other traffic at that high altitude was military (far above airliners and weather).

On this, my first private-jet flight, both planes flew to the Wichita Learjet factory and stopped there for service on the way to Chicago, the "Windy City." Surprisingly, we flew the two planes in formation, something I hadn't realized would be allowed. It was fascinating to fly along high above the clouds in the bright moonlight and look over to see the other ship flying along a couple of hundred feet away on our same level with navigation lights flashing.

When my new employer *invited me to sit in the right seat*, I was further amazed! His "rated" co-pilot obligingly moved out and offered me his seat. As I remember the event, the company owner had indicated when he hired me that he occasionally flew with just himself and a co-pilot and all that was necessary to make the insurance valid at the time was a pilot with a basic "Private Pilot, Single Engine Land" rating in the right seat. Not even an instrument rating was necessary. At least, that is what he told me at the time. The concept must have been that control of the plane was close enough to a "one-pilot" operation that, if trouble developed, an ordinary "private pilot" could probably bring the ship down (in an emergency). In my opinion, that was a lot more than highly debatable but, fortunately, I never had to prove the point. Not very long after my experience as copilot in the jet, the insurance folks realized (from the high number of early crashes and flight "incidents") that the Learjet was indeed an extremely complex ship to fly and they subsequently increased the standards for pilot qualification. Pilot "type" ratings accompanied by "instrument" rating clauses were then written into policies and lucky guys like me had to ride in the back seats from then on.

When I eased into the co-pilot's seat, the pilot pointed out and explained to me the many gauges, dials, levers and instruments to me. Compared to what I had been flying, this ship, with its many mechanical intricacies and large impressive panel of circuit breakers, etc., seemed to me as complex as a large airliner.

Later, I got to fly a number of times with just the two of us as pilots and that was most certainly a big thrill. I knew if anything happened to him, I would have a challenging time attempting to get this ship on the ground in anything less than a thousand broken pieces scattered over a couple of square miles. Amazing! Hadn't he considered that?

One fairly nervous landing with just the two of us in the ship took place on the relatively small Meigs Field runway located out in the water of Lake Michigan adjacent to downtown Chicago. The week before we landed, another Learjet had lost power and ditched in the water nearby. By a unique and very unusual gift from fate, that plane didn't break up or sink and all got off with only minor injuries, an extraordinary outcome for a private jet.

The day we landed, the wind was blowing in a direct crosswind *much higher* than generally recommended for Lear landings, but we had important business in the city so we landed anyway (of course, that "we" is editorial). It should be noted, however, activities like this one of "pushing the envelope" do, in fact, have the potential to produce negative outcomes. Fortunately, *we* didn't create any new headlines…only a few very tense moments.

Another notable moment was a time we returned from Oakland, California, and found ourselves flying in the high wind "jetstream." We crossed over the Medford, Oregon, radio navigation omni-range transmitter indicating ***735 miles an hour*** on our "DME" (distance measuring equipment). That is actually how fast we were going (over the ground) with the help of that amazing push of high-speed, high-altitude air movement. Faster than the speed of sound, such speed in "still" air would have broken the sound "barrier" and created a sonic boom. However, in this situation our usual flight cruising speed of about 550 mph was located *within* the volume of jetstream air which was moving at approximately 185 mph, thus the two were simply combined by our flight instruments to indicate a true groundspeed between points over land.

I never did "actually" fly the plane (other than a bit of "steering" at altitude) but when others were around, it was great to sit in the right seat and pretend I was a real co-pilot. I didn't tell anybody any different and acted the part.

Supposedly, one could call me a Learjet co-pilot at the time because that is what I was, even if allowed only to "tune the radios!" Always I've been unhappy with myself for not entering those flights in my pilot's logbook. That would be a neat thing to have! So…for you pilots reading this, let that be a lesson. *Always enter every last flight in your logbook, no matter what!*

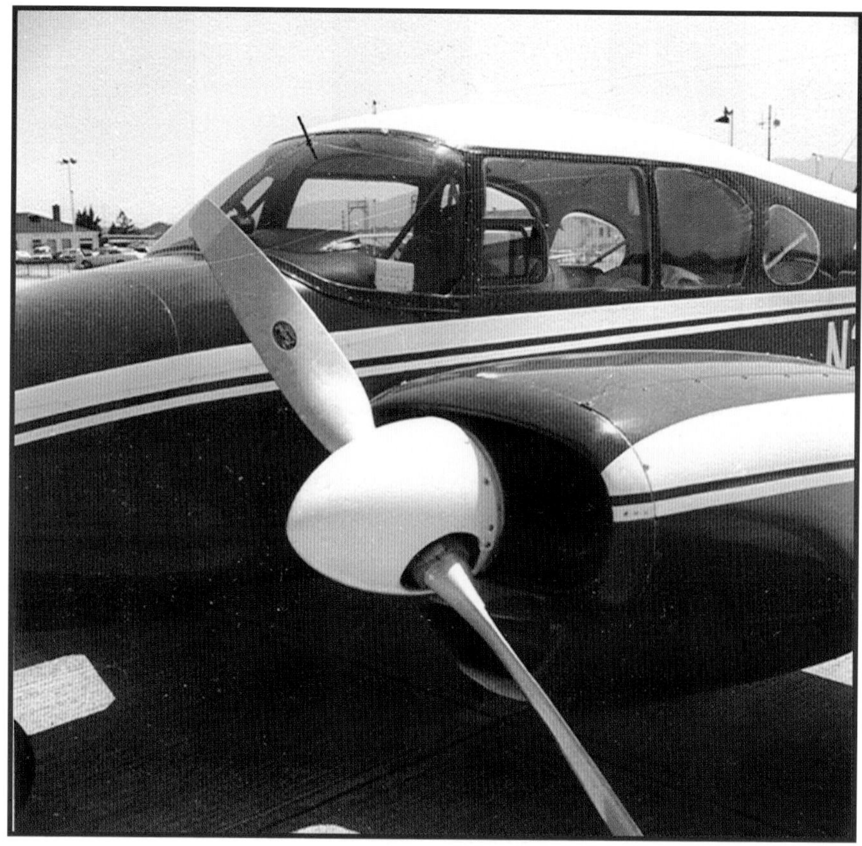

Limited visibility

My Piper Apache. One day we got word at our flight operation that a Ryan Navion was missing on a flight that was supposed to pass over our airport. I filled the Apache with observers and we hurried into the air to join the search. We flew out most of the fuel in the ship...banking constantly to allow unobstructed vision down into thick forests. Other than my biplane, this was my first attempt to view the ground seriously from a low-wing craft. The constant G-forces of steep turning made almost everyone in the plane sick. Because time was of the essence, we continued as long as we could, but the effort certainly made all in the plane aware of how useless a low-wing plane is for search and rescue.

Double Trouble

Pilots and pilot/plane-owners are never completely happy with their current situations. Most seem interested in getting additional flight proficiency ratings. Some enjoy acquiring additional pilot ratings (more demanding) for the sheer enjoyment of doing so whether or not they need them. I haven't met many pilots who were not aspiring to move up to larger, faster, more complex ships. Planes are much like boats in some ways. Each incremental move up the ladder in size, power and sophistication will cost plenty…*exponentially! Count on it!*

So, being a typical pilot, the time came when I found myself wanting something bigger and faster and more impressive.

With airplanes, the biggest early step up is from single engine with fixed wheels to more expertise-demanding "retractable" landing gear ships that fly a lot faster due to less "drag" (more aerodynamic efficiency). The next big step is to a twin-engine, usually a "relative" giant (by comparison). By the time this typically masculine desire overwhelmed my otherwise good sense, I found myself in an improved financial position and able to "pay the piper." In my case, I actually did "*pay the piper.*" I bought a "*Piper*" plane with *two engines*. However, mine was an *underpowered* twin compared with others of the time. My aviation operation employer leased the plane from me to give twin-engine flight instruction, a situation that tempered my personal flying costs.

Surprisingly, *yes*...a twin-engine plane can be "*underpowered,*" and many of the early "general aviation" type twins were very much so. The reason for this sometimes ominous condition (one which has been a contributing factor ending in many disastrous flying excursions) is that the early private twins cost a lot of money in relation to the cost of simple single engine planes which were the norm at the time. As a result, manufacturers installed only modest power to hold costs down until a few product cycles passed and more power was found necessary...and demanded by buyers.

My "twin" was the famous (and infamous) early version of the 150 horsepower-per-engine Piper "Apache." This was a five-seat model and had all the modern flight instruments I had dreamed of having. That I didn't know how to use them all too well didn't dampen my enthusiasm or penchant for spending inordinate amounts of time learning about them. This ship even had built-in five-port oxygen, one port to serve each of its five seats. The plane had one heck of a time climbing high enough to need that oxygen but surely looked impressive with those little fittings (ports) all around the ceiling.

Unfortunately, although it looked like a typical twin-engine plane with a large engine nacelles (engine enclosures) on each wing, the relatively low horsepower engines (150hp, small compared to other twins) led many a pilot into situations which wrote the final chapter in the stories of their enchantment with aviation. With the extra weight of the five seats, the oxygen system, a full instrument panel to allow flight in clouds and four fuel tanks in this plane, flight performance was limited. The plane looked about like most other twins but was only a marginal flyer, lacking both high speed and the ability to climb rapidly, especially when heavily loaded. The highest altitude I could hold with only one engine running and the propeller feathered (stopped with the blade-edges pointed into the wind to reduce "drag") was around five thousand feet and *that* was in dense air with a modest fuel load and only two occupants.

There is a major bone of contention between many light-single-engine pilots and light-twin pilots. The twin pilots wouldn't be caught dead in a single if there was any possible way to avoid it. Many single-engine pilots call light-twins "Double Trouble" when considering the fair amount of twin pilots who get into situations beyond their abilities to control.

After flying a twin for a while at night, plus over Pacific Northwest stump pastures (logged-over land), I can't imagine taking such chances in a single...unless *absolutely necessary.*

Beginning on one heavenly spring day, I headed for the airport to leave my home in Medford, Oregon, and fly to Washington, Idaho and Montana to visit sawmills to sell equipment. My airplane walk-around inspection revealed no surprises and, after double-checking all four tanks

MK 9609-2

RETAIL PURCHASE ORDER

"What's your need? Name your Cessna!"

PURCHASER'S NAME HALSTEAD EQUIPMENT CO.   DATE: December 5, 1969

ADDRESS   SELLER'S NAME Rogue Valley Skyways

CITY AND STATE   ADDRESS Mun.Airport, Medford, Oregon

I, the undersigned Purchaser, hereby enter my order for a Cessna aircraft as detailed below. The attached deposit of $ 3,000.00 is to apply against the total purchase price. I agree to complete this agreement, accept delivery of the aircraft at Medford, Ore. within 14 days after notification that the aircraft is ready for delivery, and pay the balance of the purchase price or make financial arrangements satisfactory to Seller at the time of delivery, subject to the terms set forth below and the terms, conditions, warranty and limitations of liability printed on the reverse side of this Purchase Order.

Model: CESSNA T210-0438, 1969   Exterior Color: #964 WH/RED/BURG   Interior Color: EL CLOUD GRAY

INFORMATION ABOUT AIRCRAFT (NEW)

1. Make: CESSNA

Model: T210

3. Serial No.: 0438

Remarks: N2288R
DEMO/with 150 TT

BALANCE TO BE FINANCED:

Balance in ______ monthly notes of $ ______ each, starting date ______

Remarks:

THE UNDERSIGNED PURCHASER AGREES THAT HE HAS READ AND UNDERSTANDS THE TERMS, CONDITIONS, WARRANTY AND LIMITATIONS OF LIABILITY SET OUT ON THE REVERSE SIDE HEREOF AND THAT THE SAME ARE INCLUDED IN AND ARE A PART OF THIS PURCHASE ORDER ALL AS IF SET FORTH ON THE FACE HEREOF.

PURCHASER'S SIGNATURE

[signature]

SALESMAN'S SIGNATURE

Insurance Coverage:

Kind:

Effective Date:

Name of Insurance Company:

HALSTEAD EQUIPMENT CO.
NAME IN WHICH NEW AIRCRAFT SHOULD BE REGISTERED

CECIL HALSTEAD
NAME WHICH TRADE-IN REGISTRATION CARRIES

ACCEPTED BY:

SIGNATURE OF SELLER

ADDRESS OF SELLER

DATE OF ACCEPTANCE

December 19, 1969
EXPECTED DELIVERY DATE

Optional Equipment (See Accessory Price List)	PRICE Dollars	Cents
Base Price F.A.F., Wichita, Kansas	$35,695	00
300 NAV/COM 360 CH VOR/LOC IND.	2,165	00
300 NAV/COM 360 CH VOR/LOC & GL SLOPE	2,165	00
400 NAV-O-MATIC Autopilot	4,850	00
KING KR85 Crystal-controlled ADF	1,295	00
300 TRANSPONDER	1,550	00
400 GLIDESLOPE	915	00
300 DISTANCE MEASURING EQUIPMENT DME	1,810	00
300 MARKER BEACON RECEIVER	395	00
INDICATOR, ECOMOMY POWER	105	00
ARMRESTS, SET OF (2)	35	00
DUAL CONTROLS	225	00
GROUND SERVICE PLUG REC.	67	50
HEADRESTS, (2)	50	00
HEATING SYSTEM, S.W. & PITOT	35	00
INTERIOR, ALL LEATHER	125	00
DETECT. NAV. LIGHTS	10	00
CONTROL WHEEL MAP LIGHT	25	00
LIGHT, ROTATING BEACON	105	00
LIGHTS, COURTESY	20	00
LIGHTS, INST. POST	175	00
PRIMING SYSTEM	85	00
THREE BLADED PROP. & vert. adj. seats	560	00
Price with accessories and equipment	$52,512	00
Gas, oil and delivery cost	52,894	64
State and local taxes, if any		
License, transfer and registration fee	25	00
TOTAL PURCHASE PRICE	$52,919	64

	Dollars	Cents
Cash deposit with this order	3,000	00
Trade value of used aircraft	12,500	00
Amount of cash to be paid on delivery	37,419	64
TOTAL CREDIT TO PURCHASE PRICE	15,500	00
BALANCE TO BE FINANCED		

Cessna 210 "Retail Purchase Order," 1969

The total airplane price illustrated here (which included all accessories) might not be enough to buy some communication/navigation "radio packages" for a similar airplane purchased after year 2000.

for full fuel levels, I loaded my gear and boarded the plane. After doing all the necessary cockpit checks, I started the engines. Then, I taxied the plane out to the active runway and was off into a glorious clear wild blue yonder which was good, because I was one of the few twin-engine pilots who had only a basic multi-engine license and no instrument rating to fly in the clouds…never did get one! No true need. But…I darn sure needed all that blue sky!

The flight was long with one business stop about halfway at a location where I had to land on a short dirt farm strip...which was unusual with a twin but fun to do because it happened rarely. A sawmill superintendent picked me up, took me to the mill, showed me his equipment, discussed ours and then drove me back out to the strip for my continuing schedule to Spokane, Washington.

Talking business and having lunch with the millman had consumed most of the day. The Piper Apache is fairly slow as twins go so, as I approached Spokane, I decided the time was too late to go any further and stayed the night there. Next morning, it was on to Kalispell, Montana.

At Kalispell, most of the day was spent visiting two sawmills. My plan then was to depart Kalispell and stay airborne until I returned to my base in Medford even if I had to fly late into the night.

At the Kalispell airport, I had line service "top off" (fill) the main and outboard fuel tanks...and climbed in for the trip south.

At this point, I had about one-hundred-thirty hours of twin-engine flight time, most of which was in my Apache. I still didn't feel one hundred percent comfortable as a twin pilot and kept wondering how many flight hours it would take for me to feel completely at home behind the controls. I thought, "Did other pilots take to these complex machines easier than I? And, with fewer…or more hours? Was this feeling natural?" Of course, a macho airman doesn't let anyone know about these feelings. Hey...we keep this stuff to ourselves…and *that* is something I ***always*** keep foremost in mind when flying with other pilots-in-command. I've had some unsettling experiences flying with ***other*** pilots and it is not considered good form to get so concerned that you reach over and take the controls out of their hands to save yourself (especially, in ***their airplane***)! But, it's nice to continue living so I'm always ready to make that mad grab should such an situation become a matter of life over death. That's in case someone turns out to be as lacking in depth of experience as I have been in earlier situations, which might have turned out differently but for the kind benevolence of fate and destiny. *This day was to turn fateful soon enough!*

I started the left engine, then the right...called ground control on the radio and requested and received taxi instructions to the active runway. The day was hotter than Hades so I left open the plane's only door (which was located far over to my right, a very long reach).

Manipulating both throttle levers with one hand, I eased the plane out onto the taxiway. Then I chortled to myself, "Man, these twins are really solid feeling. This is the *only way* to fly!"

My "run-up" checklist showed everything in a "go" condition. Calling the tower for takeoff instructions, I was given immediate clearance to the active runway. Reaching across the right seat (that very long stretch), I pulled the door closed then rolled out onto the runway and turned down the center line in one grand sweep. Pushing all levers forward (well…the two throttles...mixture and prop levers were already forward), I held the plane straight as the ship hummed along smoothly, picking up speed.

The initial climb characteristics of the Apache were reasonably good with a very light load so, when the plane became airborne, I rolled the trim-wheel back a little and helped ease it into a fairly steep climb. With the Apache's fat wing, this ship could lift tons at sea level but don't try it at high altitude on a hot day. On this day, with an already high temperature... but a very light load, the ship climbed out smartly.

Dreamily enjoying the scene and the super-smooth departure, I eased the throttles back...which reduces the "manifold pressure" (measures the pressure inside the fuel and air induction system of an engine) to set up a normal climb, and, at about four hundred feet of altitude and about a quarter mile from the runway, ***all hell broke loose! Something exploded with a roar.*** I thought the world had ended! Good God! What happened? ***Did a wing come off?***

No…I looked out and both wings were *still there*. The plane was buffeting wildly and was close to being uncontrollable. Holding the plane straight ahead, I instantly lowered the nose to increase airspeed and leveled out. Shoving all controls forward to gain more airspeed, I regained some control but not much. The plane was still buffeting and the noise level was awesome.

With the explosion had come a fantastic rush of air. It took all my presence of mind to concentrate on controlling the ship so, at first, I couldn't look for the source of the problem. Leveling out and holding the plane steady, I looked around to see that...***the door was open!*** About three inches! *That was the problem!* Nothing more…and all this commotion over something that simple!

My Meyers "OTW" fresh from major repairs

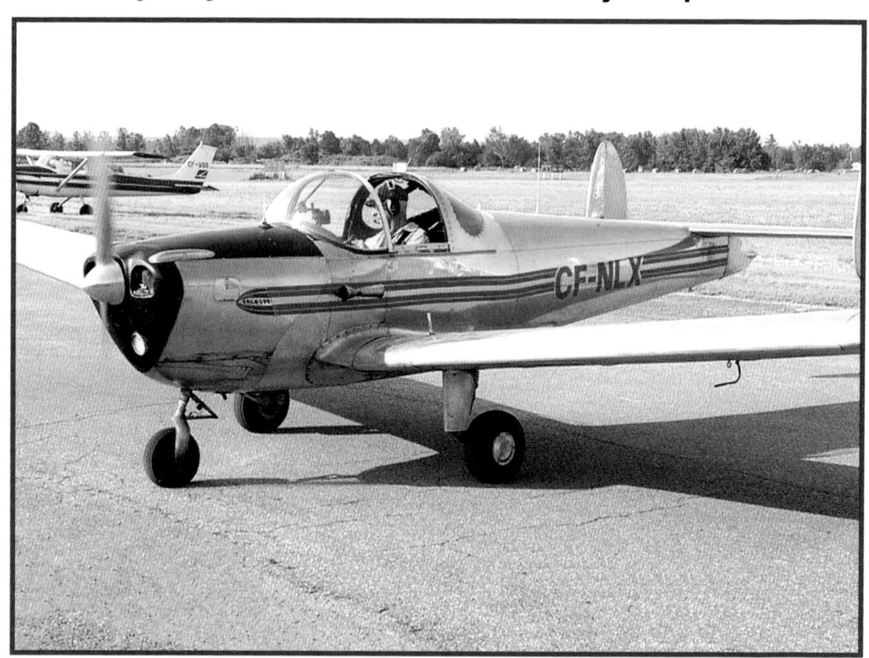

1956 Erco "Ercoupe," 5,685 built

I checked myself out in one of these when a rancher/owner asked to have one of our pilots drive to his ranch and fly his to our service facility. It was an odd feeling flying with...***no rudder pedals.***

Obviously, *I hadn't latched the door completely* by turning the handle fully into the locked position as per the takeoff checklist. So much for having left the door open to cool off while taxiing. The only explanation was that I'd gotten over-confident at a hundred and thirty hours of flight time and just skipped over the checklist at takeoff. When was I going to learn? And, would I learn before I killed myself? I had no idea such a simple oversight ultimately would make so much noise and confusion and seriously affect the control of the plane. Nobody, including my multi-engine instructor, had stressed how critical a "popped-open" door on some planes in flight might prove to be. I now knew such an event can cause serious interference with the effectiveness of some planes' rear control surfaces. Imagine this happening at night in a tight box canyon with a heavy load at high altitude in hot weather with a load of passengers. *Not a pleasant thought!*

But now, there were more pressing problems! I barely could hold the ship stable in a level attitude and I tried turning back to the airport but gave up that idea fast when the plane seemed extra hard to control after entering the turn.

I reached over and, with all my might, tried to pull the door closed. Nope! Pulling it back into its frame and locking it at this speed would have taken the strength of three. Humbly scared, I hoped that the terrific roar of the air and the jerking and shaking weren't tearing anything unseen off the ship which was needed to stay airborne. Could a ***simple open door*** be this threatening! Yes! Can only seconds of hammering vibration and reduced power with minimum control seem like an eternity? ***Yes!***

The plane did settle down to what might be called a semblance of straight-ahead stability. However, with that infernal continuing roar of rushing air, there wasn't enough altitude to be attempting turns as they might throw the ship into a spin, so I continued trying to reason out the problem. Airborne but unable to shut the door, it might be too dangerous to attempt turning back and landing with such reduced control so I decided to climb higher and gain time to think about the situation. Any pilot worth his junior birdman wings knows that altitude is a pilot's best friend. That is, *if you can get it.*

The air temperature must have been around ninety degrees, so climbing higher now became a fairly slow process. Ten minutes passed to gain much altitude because of the buffeting, the poor flight configuration and the struggle to keep the ship stable but, finally, little by little, the plane climbed higher. I began mulling over schemes for closing the door without losing airplane control in the process…and, now, was calming down.

"Holy smoke," I thought, "Just how many wild flying scenarios must pilots go through during their careers in the sky? Is this all mandatory in flying?"

At last, I had the answer! When reaching an adequately safe altitude, I'd perform a maneuver to remedy this open-door situation. An observer might think me timid, but I decided on four thousand feet above ground level as safe enough for the action. In the event of a spin, I wanted to have far more than enough room to recover and pull out, because I remembered old-timers telling me that twins spin into the ground fast...a lot faster than the single-engine planes in which I had most of my flight hours..

Reaching my planned altitude, I leveled out, took a deep breath, throttled the engines down, pulled all the way back on the control wheel and maneuvered the plane up steeply into a power-off stall. Jerking my seat belt loose, I lurched wildly over to the passenger side and yanked at the door to pull it closed. *The door still wouldn't close!* The apparent reason was still some forward speed.

The plane then lost flight ability...and plunged downward into a tight spin. The descent had all the sensation of going straight down...although that mostly was my overworked imagination. Gathering my wits, I fought my way back over into the pilot's seat, wedged myself in, and, after getting my bearings, recovered from the stall-induced spin...then reattached my seat belt.

The plane had lost a lot of altitude and the process of climbing back up to regain enough for another attempt took quite a while. The plane continued to shake and buffet while climbing to a safer altitude again. As it climbed, I talked myself into calming down...and concluded that the plane hadn't slowed enough the first time to cut the airfoil effect that was *holding the door open.*

This time, I pulled the plane up into a ***very steep*** power-off "stall." When the ship stopped flying, it stopped pointed almost straight up...and hung motionless there for a few very brief moments. And *talk about fast...* like greased lightning, ***I lunged for that open door!***

With all my strength, I yanked the door into its frame with a loud bang and moved the handle up into the locking position. Good thing, too, because that was about all the time it took for the plane to careen over and start a steep downward spiral. After that, recovery to straight and level flight was an easy maneuver.

For an old pro pilot, this situation might seem a very simple situation but, for a relative rank-amateur twin-engine pilot like I was at the time, the event was enough to dramatically improve the quality of ***my attention to check-lists!***

From that day to this, I am the guy in the plane who pipes up before moving out onto the active runway and says…

*"Let's give that door latch…**one final check!**"*

**My Piper "Apache" fuel-management panel...
(4 tanks, 108 gallons).**

1957 Piper PA-23 Apache 150 HP.
My Cost In 1969?....$13,500.

The first time I saw an Apache was 1959 in Oregon pioneer pilot Hank Troh's big hangar at his "Skyport" on 148th and Division St. in Portand, Oregon. Hank proudly explained he used it to fly "charters" such as Forest Service business, dedicated fishermen to isolated British Columbia lakes and many other activities. He allowed me to climb up on the wing and look in and I remember thinking, "Wow, what a great ship. I'd sure like to have one like it, someday." The cost of mine was eased somewhat because my flight operation employer agreed to lease it from me for the purpose of giving flight instruction to veterans utilizing benefits of the "G.I. Bill." I received $45 per hour for every hour the plane flew. With 150hp engines, it then was considered underpowered in the eyes of more sophisticated pilots, but it would hold altitude at 5,000 feet with one engine out and the prop feathered (with a light load). It was a joy to fly, quiet inside, had full blind-flight instrumentation, five-place oxygen and with 5 seats plus extra space, a very roomy cabin. Throttled back to a modest cruise, the cabin was quiet enough to allow conversations in normal tones of voice.

The Apache was developed in 1952 with two 125hp Lycoming engines. The plane performed poorly and the engines were quickly replaced with more powerful 150hp Lycoming O-320-A engines, which entered into production in 1954. 1,231 were built. Later, a model with twin 235hp engines was built but sold poorly and was discontinued. In 1958 an upgraded version with 250hp Lycoming O-540 engines and a swept vertical tail was built. The plane was designated PA-23-250 and was named "Aztec." I much rather would have liked to own an Aztec but at the time I bought my Apache, the Aztec's higher price was more than I could afford.

Twice a Day in The U.S.A.

As this new development rapidly unfolded, I looked quizzically at my passenger. He was looking back at me with the same strange questioning look. What in the heck was all ***this*** about?

The day had begun like most others, with nothing unusual expected and full of optimism and anticipation of success. I had taken a job not too long before selling large sawmill equipment throughout the West and my ownership of a twin-engine plane had been an important factor in this new employment. My company couldn't have been happier than to have a salesman able to cover a lot of territory very quickly and I certainly found flying to sawmills much more convenient than driving. Most mills had landing fields in or near their vicinities and provided ground transportation, thus air travel was proving valuable and useful. I got buyers' rapt attention when telephoning them in the morning and stating I could be visiting them in person a few hundred miles away by afternoon. Of course, I loved doing that because aviation was my great passion.

The young engineer riding with me had gone on a number of these trips and we had a lot of fun and got a lot of work done at the same time. He helped keep me alert when we worked many hours consecutively and assisted with minor flying duties with which non-pilots can be useful. We had flown all night long a few times and were quite familiar with each other's idiosyncrasies. He would josh me for not knowing as much as he about engineering and I would kid him about his lack of flying ability. We were a great team!

We had planned this trip very carefully, as we did all trips. We were to make five mill visits in four states, and estimated our total flying time to be about twenty hours in a day and a half…a fast, tightly-planned program.

We left from the Medford, Oregon, airport, and were off the ground at 5 A.M. and climbing over Crater Lake about twenty minutes later. It was always a thrill to break over the rim of that grand old spent volcano and peer down into the extremely blue water that is some of the purest in the United States.

This day, the engines purred beautifully and we continued to gain altitude as we cleared the opposite rim. Then, on across scrub pine forests with mixed Ponderosa groves and continuing over high desert. I leveled out at nine thousand five hundred feet so we had about four thousand-plus feet above ground level, a reasonably safe altitude in case of emergency. This mid-summer day was clear and warm and the views were spectacular. We had fifty miles of visibility in all directions with no haze and no forest fire smoke to inhibit sight. This is the type of day pilots live for…"CAVU"…(***Ceiling And Visibility Unlimited***)!

I really like a twin-engine plane because, with the engines out on the wings and, when throttled back to cruising speed, they are much quieter inside than a single engine plane. Conversation is possible without shouting above background noise and that makes for more comfortable and less tiring flying over long distances. A single engine plane with the engine close in front has much ambient cabin noise. To converse, it's almost a necessity to have an "intercom" system with a couple of pairs of headphones to hear another person adequately. The only negative of this plane we were flying, a Piper Apache, was modest horsepower. However, a big thick high-lift wing made up somewhat for that lack. If a pilot didn't overload the airplane or operate beyond the flight manual "rated" abilities, it performed quite well on short strips which could be a great plus and…the ship had a very roomy cockpit designed large enough for five people. Of course, reality would suggest those five people be made up of two average size individuals, two small people and one dwarf or troll (that is, *if you also wanted to carry fuel*).

We cruised along smoothly, thoroughly enjoying the bright day and discussing the mechanical aspects of the different mills on our route. *What a great way to make a living!*

Our first planned stop was John Day, Oregon, a small cattle and lumber town on the John Day River. The airport was located on a plateau across the river from the mill we were to visit. Casually, I mused about our destinations and the fact that we who fly frequently end up with the problem of ground transportation. My thoughts recalled the statement that an older pilot and plane owner had made to me about airplane travel when I had just become involved in aviation. He said, "An airplane is the greatest form of transportation known to man…*if you are going to another airport!*" I now had been a pilot long enough to understand clearly the "tongue-in-cheek" meaning of that statement. I have been known to do a lot of walking after landing. Fortunately, we had our ground transportation well-planned in advance for this flight.

As we neared our first stop, we discussed the fact that we had heard this mill may have violated patent law and copied our product. We were somewhat concerned about this but planned to visit and see for ourselves. If this was only rumor, which we thought must be the case, we certainly wanted an opportunity to make our sales presentation, thus we planned to arrive at the mill in spite of the rumor.

Arriving near the town of John Day, we could see our destination mill in the distance. I called "Unicom" (airport operator) on our radio to announce our arrival to the base operator and to any other planes in the area, a standard procedure when arriving at small airports lacking a control tower. There was so little traffic at this airport that, most of the time, there was no one available or in the air to answer a radio call. I could see the windsock clearly from a couple of miles away. It appeared that we would arrive on time and figured the mill personnel probably would be there as they had agreed. I throttled back and set up a long cruising-speed descent.

In preparation for landing, I went through my checklist: made sure the carburetor heat was on, set the full selectors on the fullest tanks, moved the mixture controls full forward, eased the throttle levers back and pushed the prop-pitch levers into flat-pitch position then lowered the landing flaps to twenty degrees. Scanning all appropriate instruments, I reached over and moved the landing gear handle to lower the wheels. The process all went well and the landing gear lights turned green, indicating "gear down and locked."

Turning final, I lined up on the center of the runway (which happened to be sloped uphill), lowered the flaps to their "stop"...and prepared for the airplane to settle down and touch the pavement. So far, so good!

I pulled the throttles back all the way and, just as I was easing back on the wheel for a perfect touchdown, my partner in the right seat leaned over and said in a very loud voice, "As we passed the mill, it looked to me like I could see a patent violation on the side of a large burner."

"Are you sure?"

"It darn sure looked like it from where I sit."

"Well," I shot back, "let's buzz back over there and take a look from the air while we're still up."

With just a few sweeping motions, I had the flaps begin retracting, the gear retracting, throttles full forward and carburetor heat off. With a modest roar, we flew along above the runway...slowly picking up the speed we had given away for the landing. *Very slowly.* The Apache is notoriously underpowered in this configuration, plus rising morning heat and high field elevation added to the reduction of available power.

With the flaps retracted completely and the gear up, we gained enough airspeed to make a safe right turn and head back to the mill. The mill was only about a mile and a half away so, by the time I had straightened out, we were over it.

I began a very tight orbit and we circled around the suspicious equipment unit at low altitude. After the fourth circle, we agreed that this definitely was not a patent violation, a fact that pleased us immensely, for now we had the potential to sell them some equipment.

As I eased the plane back into level flight and aimed again for the end of the airport's runway, we discussed what we had seen. We were both relieved that the situation looked much more favorable than anticipated.

To prepare for landing I pulled carburetor heat, throttled back, flattened the pitch of the props and lowered the flaps one "notch."

When passing over the runway threshold the plane was going like a bullet. It was a thrill sometimes to zip across the threshold at a hundred-plus mph with a small plane.

It now took a long, long time to bleed off enough airspeed to get down to a landing stall. That big thick high-lift wing just floated us along. Then, I eased back on the wheel ever so slowly and waited for touchdown.

Uhhh….what's *that*?

And…*what's my partner trying to say to me?*

Why is he shouting?

Man, oh man, *is he excited! What the heck is his problem?*

I yell to him, ***"Speak up, I can't hear you!"***

Finally, his voice cut through to me at precisely the same time the reason for his animation dawned on me. The plane was just inches from the runway and I had...***overlooked one little detail…LOWERING THE LANDING GEAR!***

Red! Red! Red! blazed on the gear indicator lights!

The gear was still fully retracted and nicely hidden from view in the engine nacelles under the plane. The reason I couldn't hear him very well was because the gear warning horn was screaming so loud it was noisier than heck inside the plane.

This was one of the times in my flying life when I actually remembered precisely what the instructor had told me to do in such emergencies with this ship. *Reality* hammered home! Hey... I bolted to attention...***instantly!***

The important words of my multi-engine instructor were: "When in trouble, shove everything forward!" And...for the second time in only a few minutes, *I pushed everything forward...*carburetor heat, throttles, prop controls and mixture handles. Now, the moves were***...to save the ship!*** We were so close to touching the pavement with the nice shiny recently-rebuilt props, I had a sinking feeling my actions might be too late. The little ship jerked and grunted and staggered...and was so close to a stall, that all I could do was hold it steady and pray.

It took *for evvvveeerrrr* to see that airspeed needle move up. But, finally it moved up.

How could I? Only idiots did this. The one thing every retractable pilot knows he never will do, **I darn near did.** Where was my brain? *What brain?* What I had failed to do...was ***again*** go completely through my landing checklist (*the correct procedure*)!

Holding the plane straight, my shaking hand grasped the little flap-shaped lever and very slowly worked the flaps up raising them inch by inch. (retracting the flaps too rapidly at the plane's low airspeed could be disastrous!)

Finally level and straight a half mile past the end of the runway, I was still working the flap handle up. That's how shaken I was over making such a recklessly fast approach (without ***again*** going completely through the landing checklist)...which almost ended with catastrophic results.

*I knew without being told...*that my passenger now felt he was riding with a defective pilot! If you were the guy in the right seat and you didn't know much about flying, how would *you* feel *now* about the pilot-in-command after this unique display of moronic ineptitude. And here you are, the passenger, trapped in this tiny claustrophobic flying machine with a character who has almost caused you serious bodily harm. I winced in shame and mumbled:

"Son of a gun.....I, I, I,....er....I, er...uh, uh, guess...uh....I sure screwed up on that one!"

No answer.

More shame consumed me. God, the atmosphere was quiet in that plane!

The next approach was absolutely perfect.

By the book!

You can bet that...***I followed the checklist!***

The landing gear snapped to attention and the indicator lights read ***"green, green and green."***

It took me a long, long time to get over that one. *Compliments to my partner.* He bravely continued the flight with me and we even had a couple more "interesting experiences" on the trip...like taking off from a field elevation of 8,600 feet on a 92-degree afternoon. He was most likely nervous about my abilities...but he continued with me for the trip. However, out of the corner of my eye I could see he was watching me with a very different look than when we began the trip. You would, too, wouldn't you?

There's a saying for almost everything that either has happened or might happen in the world of aviation. When it comes to "gear-up" landings, some of you may have heard it. If you're a pilot, you don't hassle other pilots about their gear-up landings...

You simply remember the old adage: "***There are those who have.... and there are those who will***" (and....keep your thoughts to yourself).

"Never *Compromise* A Checklist!"

Those were the very last words from the flight instructor who checked me out for my multi-engine ticket. To emphasize the importance of the above phrase, early in my training he told the following tale:

"I was a Navy multi-engine pilot operating in Alaska. We flew the fabulous 'Super Connie,' (nickname for the legendary giant Lockheed Constellation) with four big Wright-Cyclone 2000 horsepower radial engines and a monumental triple-tail that was then very distinctive when compared to other large planes. This is the legendary ship that Trans World Airlines (TWA) was flying when Howard Hughes bought the airline.

"On one forever-memorable flight, we arrived at the strip on the island of Adak in the Aleutian chain, and set up for a visual approach. We went through our sizable pre-landing checklist and, as we approached the runway threshold, an idiot in a truck rolled out onto the pavement in front of us. We scarcely could believe this was happening and it was either hit the truck or 'go-around,' so we shoved the throttles forward and retracted the gear and flaps when our airspeed was adequate. We spent the next few moments voicing obscenities aimed at the guy in the truck who had come very close to causing a major crash.

"Large planes require a lot of airspace to maneuver, and it took us quite a while to gain altitude and turn downwind. Coming around again for a second approach, we straightened out in line with the runway and eased the throttles back while gently adding flaps to bleed off speed. The truck had moved off the runway and all was clear but we all continued to yak away and berate the driver even as we flew down the glide path. We crossed the threshold with full flaps, pulled throttles to full-off and began to ease back on the controls to settle in for a nice, easy soft landing.

"At that point, the ***gear horn*** just about blew all of us out of the cockpit. We looked at each other for a split-second…then, realizing what was happening, we again shovelled the throttles forward. But, our efforts were***...too little, too late!***

"The plane was still settling…and continued settling until the tips of the inboard engine props actually hit the pavement! Unbelievably, Lady Luck was with us and that was as far as we settled. Astoundingly, the plane staggered along for a few sickening moments still barely flying and then, by a stroke of amazingly good fortune, moved back into the air. The sound of those prop tips hammering the hard surface was one of the wildest things we had ever heard. The propeller tips were bent over about six inches... throwing them out of balance and aerodynamic correctness which added a crazy new sound and vibration to the din as the damaged giant plane grasped for altitude.

Our hearts pounded and the ship vibrated as the airspeed slowly increased to flying speed…barely out of "ground-effect." Finally, we were able to retract the flaps, regain a reasonable airspeed (very low due to the vibrating props), reach some altitude and assess the situation.

There wasn't much to assess. We would have liked to stay in the air forever...because we knew we were in a heap of trouble. We were shocked to realize that, even with as much flying time as those of us on the flight deck had, we all failed at preparing properly for the second landing. No matter the circumstances, we had failed to ***go completely through the landing checklist again*** that second time around.

We later were chastised heavily by our superiors for our transgression and I can assure you the episode left all of us with '*an indelible lesson!*'"

Note: As most private pilots know…there is an average of about two "gear-up" landings every day in the good ol' U.S.A.!

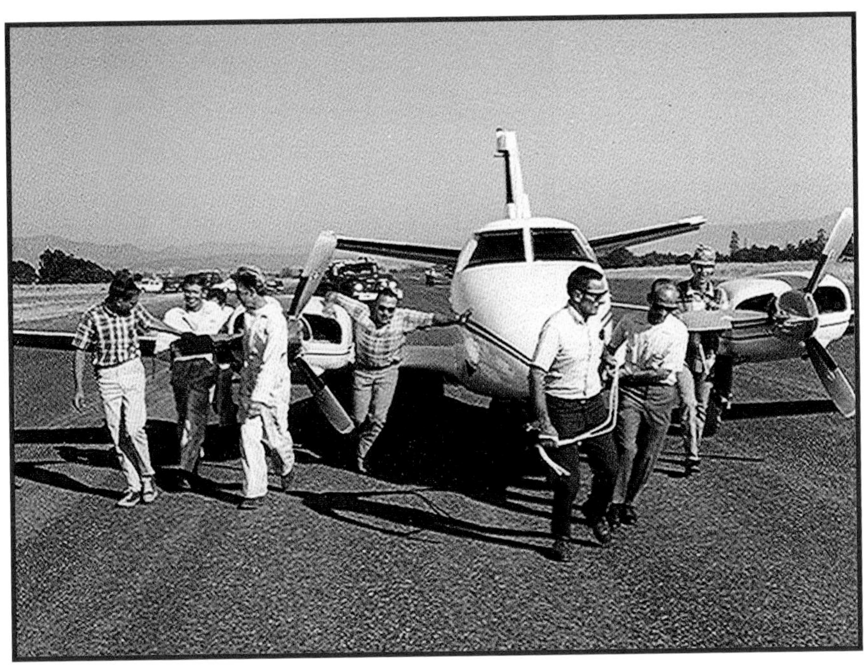

Wounded Beechcraft "Duke" - 596 built

The pilot of this beautiful brand new Beechcraft "Duke" (1969 model) is nowhere to be seen (due to almost terminal mortification). This helpful group pulling the plane off the runway was the assemblage in our flight office when we heard the pilot call the control tower stating that he couldn't get his gear lights to "go green" (down and locked). He had left his hangar a hundred miles away and overlooked the small detail of removing his little tow-tractor from the nosegear and after takeoff, moved the gear lever to "retract," which then jammed the tow-machine into the nosewheel compartment. He apparently flew all the way to our airport before noticing the situation (or recognizing its seriousness.) The tower controller brought out his binoculars, figured out what the problem was, then called the pilot and gave him the bad news. Landing partially "gear-up" cost him around twenty thousand dollars!

Piper Apache Twin Landing Check List:

1. Mixtures rich.
2. Propellers at high cruising R.P.M.
3. Carburetor heat off (unless icing conditions exist).
4. Electric fuel pumps on.
5. Fuel on proper tanks.
6. Landing gear down (under 125 M.P.H.), check green indicator lights on, landing gear warning horn off, and flashing red light in gear handle off.
7. flaps full down or as desired (under 100 M.P.H.).

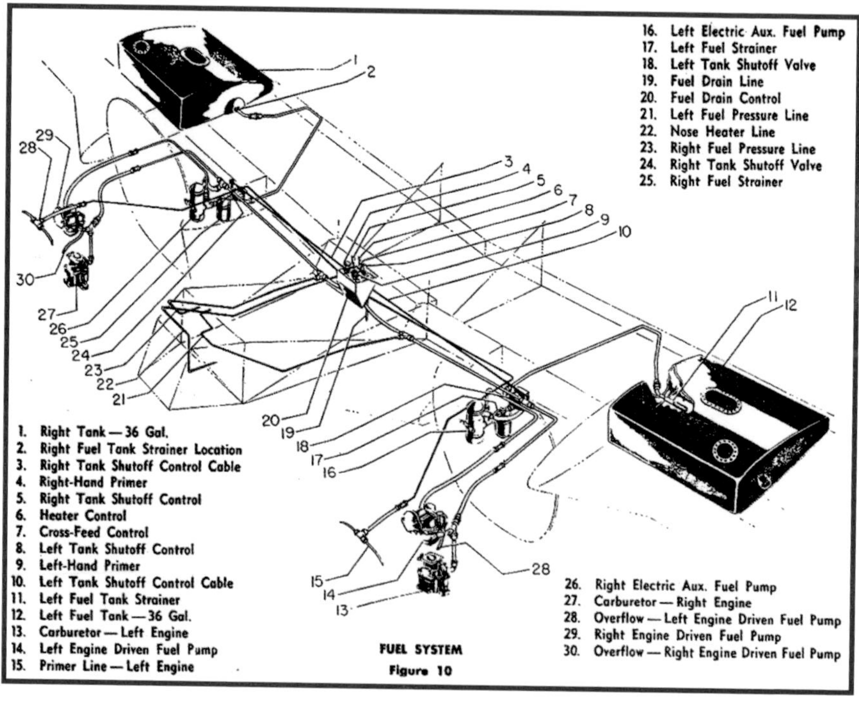

FUEL SYSTEM
Figure 10

Apache Fuel system - My Apache had 2 additional wing tanks.

The Cessna 210 "Centurion" - 9,240 built

The Cessna 210 is a pleasure to fly and a beautiful ship. It was my delight to own one (a 1967 model) if only for a relatively short time. The fixed-base operator I was associated with as a salesman at that time didn't have the cash on hand to make the purchase, so I wrote a check to purchase the plane myself to preclude missing a good deal. After flying the plane to my homebase my employer reimbursed me. After I gave a number of flight demonstrations (one as far as British Columbia), the plane was sold for a modest profit. It was only 4 years old when I bought it, was well equipped and the engine was "medium-time" (about halfway through its useful life), so there still was a lot of flight left before major repairs would be needed. A very desirable retractable-gear ship, our asking price of $24,000 at the time still was priced far below what the same plane would bring in later years.

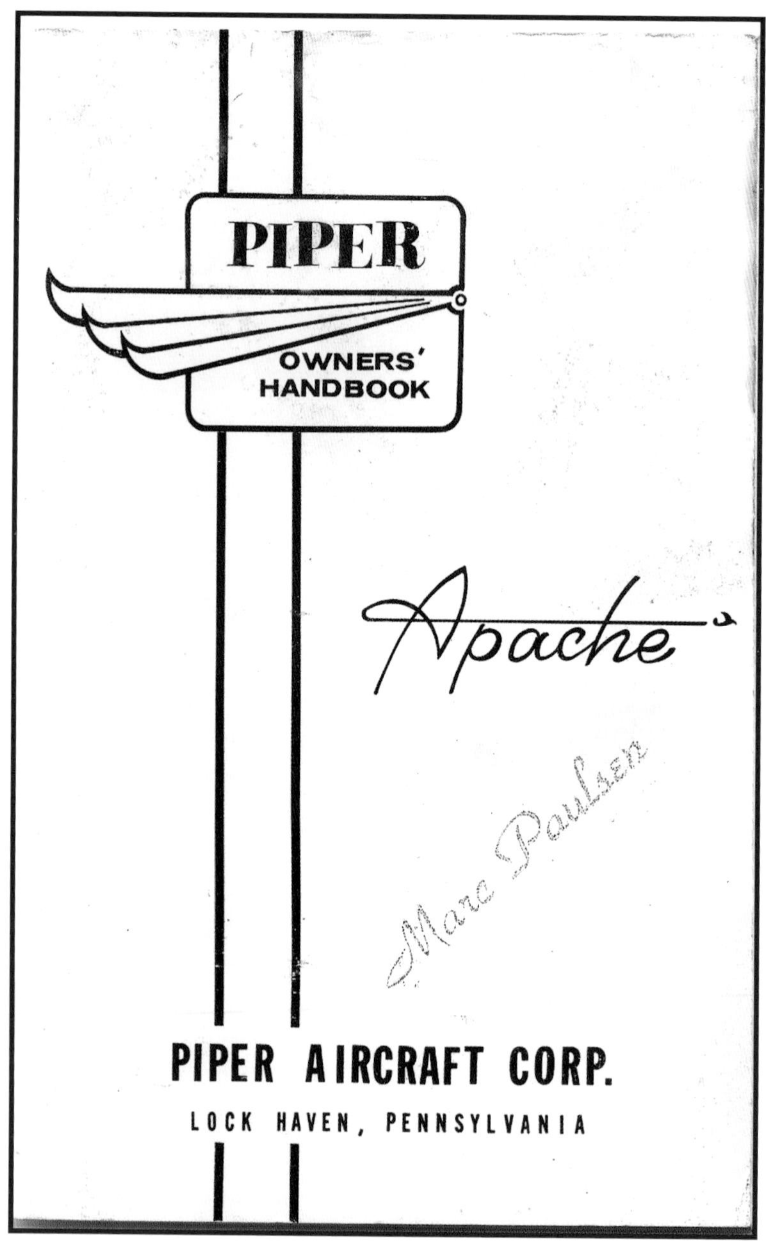
PIPER
OWNERS' HANDBOOK
Apache
Marc Paulsen
PIPER AIRCRAFT CORP.
LOCK HAVEN, PENNSYLVANIA

Ed

He was gazing at our wall of photos quietly checking out all the airplanes in the photographs that showed happy people involved with their passion, *the world of flight.* Then, he moved over to the wall which was entirely covered with aeronautical charts...pasted on like wallpaper. The wall presented a fascinating sight for anyone not completely familiar with aviation. Little blue and red and black lines going here and there and odd-looking codified symbols indicating various elements of the earth...that pilots darn well better be familiar with (if they want to find their way home). Even the very newest flight student knew this was an important wall for flight planning. The fellow studied it for quite a time...and then sauntered over to the front window…and looked out to check the source of the latest roaring engine.

As an airplane salesman, I had learned a very interesting basic fact. If those who showed up at the airport seemed delightfully happy when viewing the action and loved to talk about planes and aviation, there was one heck of a good possibility they might have an interest in learning to fly. It didn't really take a lot of deep thinking to figure that out. And learning to fly...frequently leads to *airplane ownership.*

I walked over to where he was standing and opened with... "Hi, I'm Marc," and held out my hand. Somewhat surprised, he turned to face me directly and, a shade hesitantly, eased his hand toward mine. "Oh, ah, ah… I'm Ed," he returned sounding almost apologetic.

I'd learned another interesting fact in the short time I'd been working as the plane salesman at Rogue Valley Skyways in Medford, Oregon. Even though being very welcoming and friendly obviously should be in the best interest of all who work at an airport flight operation, many of the employees go about their work and pay only cursory attention to people wandering in the area. Never did figure that one out. And another thing, some people who are interested in flight but brand new to the activity frequently feel highly insecure and intimidated by those "old hands" around an airport, to whom flying is commonplace.

"Well, Ed, it's good to meet you. Are you a pilot?" I was pretty sure he wasn't but that made a great opening line for meeting new aviation prospects. "Oh, no…I…I…just stopped by to sort of see what's going on."

I had learned to analyze this kind of visitor at a glance…and then move to be friendly, helpful and, above all, thoughtful and kind. Because many people are exceedingly uncomfortable in surroundings foreign to them, a flight lounge can be a formidable place indeed to "groundlings." One must keep in mind how difficult it is to become a pilot. If it was easy, then more than one out of every few hundred people would be pilots. I treated newcomers like I'd known them forever, immediately invited them to be part of our scene and did everything within reason to make them feel at home.

I offered Ed a cup of coffee.

"Thanks, that'd be nice." Ed's voice was very soft and pleasant.

Working here, I'd learned a lot about an airplane flight operation that I should have observed earlier when I was a customer of such places. When you fly in with *your own airplane*, the employees pay a fair amount of attention to you but, if you are just wandering around, few will take the time to stop and be friendly. Many times, they walk right past you as if you weren't there…just like other businesses. But the aviation business isn't just *any old business*. Oh, nooooo…absolutely not! Flying is *extremely unique!* Pilots and airplanes make up a very exclusive club in this world. No getting around the fact. You need a brain and money (or be very careful with the money you have) and tremendous inner drive to be a pilot...and own and fly your own airplane. You'll never find a dull poverty-stricken airplane owner. Won't happen! So, I treated everyone who came through the door as if they had the potential to be a pilot and, frequently, my approach paid off!

"Here you are, Ed," I handed him a cup of coffee.

"Are you taking lessons?"

"No, but I've been thinking about learning to fly."

Just what I wanted to hear!

His features and actions ran quickly through my mental "qualifying" process. He had a "ruddy" face, medium build and was just a bit heavy. He was wearing work clothes that suggested the logging industry.

"Tell ya what, Ed (checking his interest level), I was just getting ready to take my own plane up for a short flight. How would you like to go along?" To get a fix on his reaction, I looked him over with an awareness developed for this business...and checked his countenance. He instantly *glowed!*

"Really?"

"Yes, I want to go up and do a little more 'getting-used-to' my plane which I just bought recently. I'm working on becoming as proficient as possible with the ship and you're welcome to ride along. I'm the salesman here." (I threw that in to get things off to the right start.)

"That's great, I'd sure like that."

"Well, we'll finish our coffees and head out to the plane."

That was how I met *Ed.* One thing I knew as absolute fact. There weren't many airplane salespeople who offered passersby or even fairly serious prospects...rides in *their own airplanes*. There weren't many airplane salespeople who even had their own plane. I'd found airplane ownership a great way to start conversations when meeting new people at the airport and, although the current market had been downright terrible, I still managed to gain some business with this approach. Obviously, to discover "prospects" this way, one needed one's own airplane, and I had an outstanding plane for the purpose…a *twin-engine* ship!

Like other salespeople in my line of work, I used company planes most of the time but, when someone looked a bit more promising than usual, I wanted to get them into a more exotic ship. The company planes to which I had access were all "single-engine" and fairly simple. A twin-engine plane with all the levers, gauges, dials, switches, flashing lights and buttons...*was far more impressive.*

Well…glory be! Although one never would have guessed from his placid demeanor, Ed was a very successful logging contractor. He was in the process of taking over a business his father-in-law had built into a "going concern." At first glance, Ed definitely did not look the part. He appeared more like one of his employees than the head man. Looks *can be deceiving!*

"This is a really nice plane," Ed commented as we walked up to my ship at the nearby tie-down area.

"Yep, got it in San Jose just a month ago. It's a 1957 Piper "Apache." The man who owned it was a former Air Force ground-crewman. He kept it in immaculate condition. It's like brand new throughout!"

Ed followed me as I performed my "walk-around" inspection. I explained the various elements involved as I checked them off. It was very obvious Ed was very enthused about the idea of flight.

Out on the runway and cleared for takeoff, I pushed the throttles forward and felt the exciting rush one always gets from the solid acceleration of two engines. Out of the corner of my eye, I could see Ed's face exhibiting a satisfied smile, which would remain there for the rest of the flight. I directed the plane out of the local area to do some "air-work." We flew around and about for the next half hour as I explained the various elements of flight and operation of the assorted devices inside the plane.

Next, for the sport of it, I lowered the landing gear and touched the plane down on the top of a nearby table rock mountain which had a dirt landing strip. We rolled for a short distance at landing speed and then I quickly pushed the throttles forward to full power, cleared the ground and moved the gear-retract handle up. We went airborne like a rocket! (Well...as much as an Apache can be a rocket.)

The table rock was about a thousand feet high with almost vertical ends...and when we pilots did this little maneuver...as we got to the very edge of the cliff, we would pull the control wheel all the way back and put the plane up into a very steep climb. With the additional thousand feet of instant space suddenly beneath...the plane seemed to "shoot" skyward as it passed the cliff edge. For a few moments, it was as if one had suddenly left earth and were headed for space. ***Ed was thrilled!***

Back at the airport, we parked the plane and I showed Ed how we tied the plane to the steel loops set in the tarmac.

A week later, *Ed was back.* He signed up for a complete course of flight training. He appeared as excited as a little kid with the only talking toy in the nursery. He thanked me again for the great ride given him. I told him I did that for people because, when I was a kid and crazy to go flying, every time I went to an airport nobody paid any attention to me and no one ever had volunteered to take *me* for a ride. It seemed almost criminal to me, I added, for a plane owner to go out for a simple pleasure flight with empty seats and not take along a nearby eager aspiring pilot.

Ed replied, "That's what helped me make a decision to come back. After the flight with you, I knew I wanted to get started...*so here I am!"*

Ed didn't *only* learn to fly, he ***bought an airplane even before*** getting his pilot's license. In the process, I got a sales commission...and there was happiness all around!

Then, Ed traded up the next airplane step to a more powerful ship. He was having the time of his life. So was I. I *got another sales commission!*

Then Ed traded up one more step...to a *much more powerful* ship. He was simply thrilled with the concept of flying his own airplane. Unfortunately, I didn't get that sales commission. He became so excited over a beautiful plane with retractable landing gear (the next logical step up for him) located at a distant airport he visited, that he bought the ship on the spot. And, the plane was indeed a beauty. Almost new...and *very fast*. Ed had moved up from a mere earthling to become a moderately-sophisticated pilot in just a couple of years and he had owned three airplanes in the process. Just goes to show what can be accomplished by treating someone in a down-to-earth humane fashion. I always enjoyed seeing Ed arrive at the airport because he was an all-around nice guy with a great outlook on life, and always had a good word to say to everybody.

Another year passed and I was reading the newspaper one morning. An airplane had crashed. And...*it was Ed who crashed!*

Ed and his wife and another couple were on their way back from an excursion to Reno, Nevada, and got trapped in a snowstorm. He was flying the very fast retractable-gear ship and hadn't yet learned how to fly "blind" on "instruments." *They were all killed!*

The first thought that rushed back to me was of that fine summer day when we first met and hit it off so well. And...I was partly responsible for his involvement with aviation.

It took me a couple of months to get over the shock. What a heck of a nice guy and fine gentleman Ed had been! Why did it have to be Ed? I've always wondered how fate makes selections. Does fate really have to pick such nice people to suffer such tragic endings?

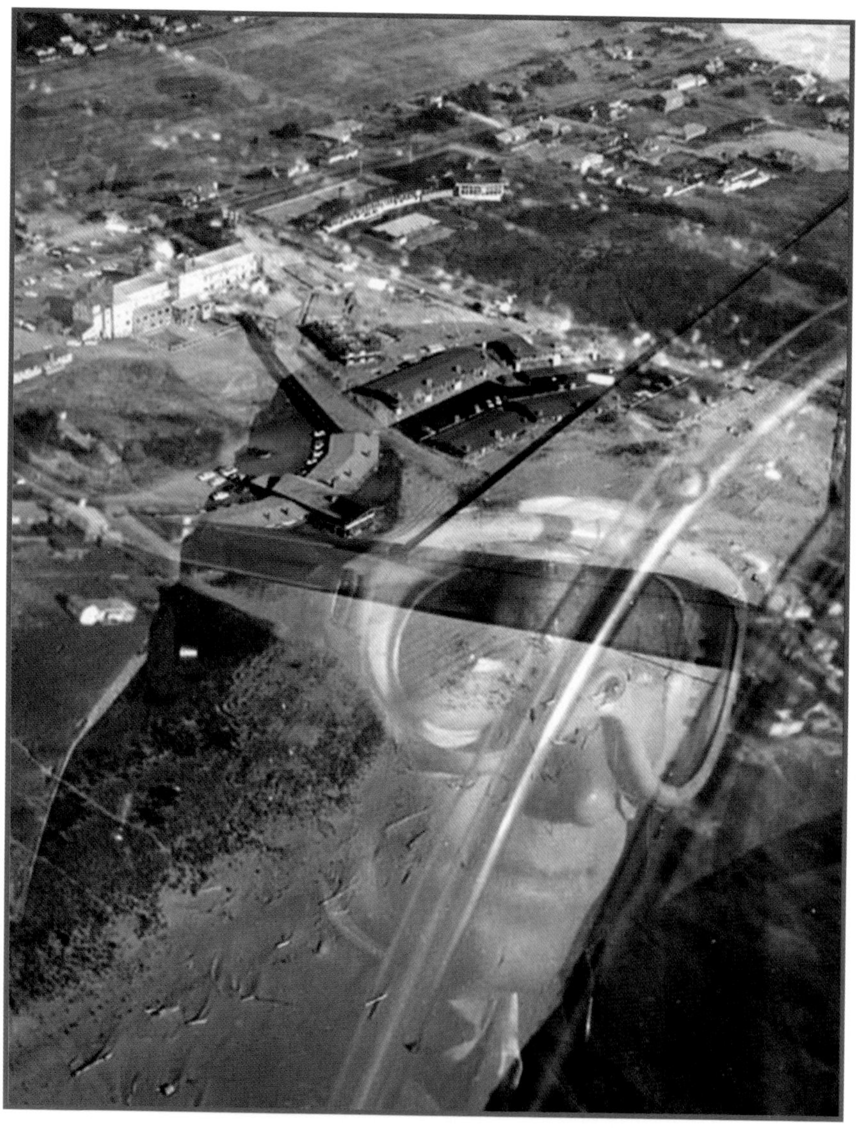

A double-exposure photo taken in the Meyers OTW biplane while performing aerobatics over the Pacific Ocean. Seaside, Oregon, 1967.

Crow Canyon Hangover

Some things you don't forget right away…and some things you don't forget…***ever!*** Those, they put right in the box with you along with that favorite suit…when you check out. And this was one of those!

The metal salvage business was treating me well in 1977. That is, if one would say that driving a paid-for late-model Rolls Royce is doing well. Yep...that was true! I'd made enough money in twenty working days on just one project to pay for the car (and the income taxes, too). "On a roll," I'd done four projects in a row that all worked out exceptionally well! We all deserve a little of that at least once in our lives...and this was my once! (Wouldn't it be great if all projects worked out like that?)

My operation was in the East Bay area of San Francisco, the area the locals call "Ebay," south by Fremont and Newark. I'd been working hard at the business for a couple of weeks four hundred miles from home. Wanting to go home to Medford, Oregon, for a few days, I'd been putting in very long hours and was in no mood to drive if that could be avoided. So, to make the trip easier, with my valid private pilot's license I'd drive to the Oakland airport, rent an airplane and fly home. Simple.

Always, I've been an avid newspaper reader and, when working out of town, I read even more to fill up hours before and after work. The day before I planned to rent the plane, a local newspaper carried a report describing a midair collision between two small planes over nearby "Crow Canyon." Nobody walked away from that one! To myself I thought, "Well…the former open-cockpit WWII Army Air Corps cadet-instructor-pilot Hank Troh, who gave me early flight lessons, gave me solid instruction regarding air traffic!" Hank always yelled at me over the din of the engine, "Pretend your head is on a swivel…and always be looking in every direction for traffic in the air." Then, he would watch me working the "control-stick" in the seat in front of him and, if he got the idea that I wasn't scanning the skies for traffic on a regular basis, he would rap the back of my head with the edge of a fifty-cent piece...***hard!*** You can believe that got my attention. Having become very conscientious about watching for other airplane traffic, collisions wouldn't be one of ***my*** problems.

Not exactly a neophyte regarding small airplanes, at this period of my life I'd owned ten different planes…from a biplane to a twin-engine. I was checked out to fly thirty-four different types, had crashed five times, two fairly serious (walked away without a scratch every time…don't ask…I don't want to talk about them) and had worked as an airplane salesman. Good at giving flight demonstration rides, I'd avoided serious incidents at the hands of amateur pilots any number of times. So, the idea of renting an airplane was not new to me. I'd done that successfully all over the West.

Finishing work early on Friday evening with quite a bit of daylight left, I headed for the large Oakland airport.

At the airport, I looked around for a general aviation operation which had rental planes. Spotting a likely company, I parked my truck, got out, walked in the front door and to a counter...and could see no one in attendance. Finally, after quite a wait, a man materialized from somewhere in the rear of the building and slowly walked up to the counter where I was standing. He didn't give me a big happy greeting…just nodded to me.

I spoke up, "I'd like to rent a 172 for a couple of days."

"You have a logbook with you?"

"Yup."

"May I see your book?"

"Yup."

I produced my flight "logbook." Good thing. If I hadn't remembered the book, I probably would have had to go through a more extensive check out than usual to rent a plane, if I could have gotten one at all.

I thought I'd make a little conversation. "Noticed an article in the paper about a midair over Crow Canyon. A real shame."

He spoke quietly. "***That was ours!***"

That stopped me cold. That was about the last thing I expected to hear. It simply hadn't occurred to me that the plane might be from this operation. All I could say was, "***Sorry***."

He didn't say any more but spent more time inspecting my logbook than anyone in the history of all my years of flying. Obviously, he was plenty apprehensive about renting a plane to a stranger only one day after they had lost a plane and human lives to a very final crash. And...he was the company's *chief pilot!*

At length, he asked, "Have you flown a *Hawk XP?*"

That was the very latest Cessna iteration of their famed four-place model 172. I had to admit I hadn't. I'd owned a basic early model Cessna 172 and flown many a flight demonstration in late models and new 172s…even had a membership in a flying club that owned a 172 but never had I flown a Cessna 172 "Hawk XP"…which was supposed to have a bit more horsepower than the standard models I'd flown. However, my understanding was that the "Hawk XP" probably didn't have enough additional power to make much difference from the earlier models.

"That's all we have available. You'll have to 'check-out' in the *Hawk.*"

That meant I'd have to demonstrate to him in the airplane that I could fly the plane and handle it properly and well enough to satisfy him. Darn, this was going to eat up some valuable time! In most situations, operators checked my logbook and sent me on my way. But…not today!

He sent me out to do a "walk-around" inspection of the plane and I could see him inside watching me. I'd never seen an aircraft operations pilot as "tightly-strung" as he seemed to be. The fatal crash had apparently shaken the foundations of the entire flight operation…understandably so.

Because I hadn't been a party to their trauma caused by the crash, I had an entirely different attitude. I was still happy from my great success in the metal salvage business making a lot of money. But, here he was, still visibly upset from who-knows-what association he'd had with the deceased pilot and passengers who had just crashed in one of his company's airplanes. Who the heck ever said life is fair…not me. I just wanted to rent an airplane and get home...and this guy was holding me up by being so particular.

I finished my "walk-around" and went back inside the flight office. He was still standing behind the counter doing something...I wasn't sure exactly what. He seemed very distracted. Well…I could understand that.

"The plane's ready to go. So am I."

"O.K. I'll be there in a minute."

"Now, what?" I thought, "Am I ever going to get out of here?"

He went to a rear office for at least another five minutes. I guessed he was on the telephone…but, man alive, this was delaying my time schedule. At any other outfit, I'd have been on my way by now.

Finally, he appeared again and mumbled, "Let's go."

Way more than ready, I wanted to get moving. We'd already used a lot of time with his triple-checking my logbooks and license. Now near twilight, I would end up flying late at night, something I did not like to do with only one engine over mountains and forests, my planned route.

We belted ourselves into what turned out to be a brand new ship. The plane smelled new, looked new and felt new. The controls were tight and smooth. This was going to be a pleasure. I started the engine.

Calling "ground control" on the radio, we were cleared to the taxiway leading to the active runway. Then, moving along at a modest pace, we had covered about two-thirds of the distance to the engine "run-up" area at the end of the runway…when a beautiful shiny 4-place Cessna 182 coming toward us approached the runway directly ahead and to our right a couple of hundred feet.

As we watched in disbelief, the 182 landed too short in rough sod, hit hard, bounced twenty-feet in the air and came down sideways…took the left landing gear out, then spun around twice in an instant and pitched over on one wing...all bent up! Shocking! Dead ahead of us and just short of the active runway…totally unexpected! An immediate radio call from ground-control stopped all ground traffic in its tracks. That included us! We shut off the engine and prepared to wait for an "all-clear."

Although the plane probably was a "total," apparently no one was injured. That didn't stop every emergency vehicle at this huge airport from immediately rushing to the scene! We waited listening to the sirens and watching the flashing lights. Slyly, I peeked over at my chief-pilot passenger…and he seemed to be reliving the events of yesterday in his mind ...after this new disaster that happened right before his eyes. I opted to remain quiet and guessed that this scenario wasn't going to make my check ride any easier.

The emergency folks scurried around for half an hour and then a crew came out to move the plane. Normally, the FAA mandates a plane be left exactly in place (sometimes for a week or more) so they can do a thorough investigation but this airport was so constantly busy that they had to get the plane out of the way immediately.

My check pilot and I waited there for an hour-plus while all this action transpired. Finally, the airport was put back in "active" mode and we were cleared to the runway which the 182 hadn't quite landed on. I pulled up on the run-up apron and went through my takeoff checklist. My check-pilot followed my every movement.

Ready to go, I switched radio frequencies and called "Oakland Tower" for takeoff clearance. That was when I got my next big awakening!

The voice on the other end was that of a woman. Nothing against that, but I had difficulty hearing and understanding her words. The very late afternoon had turned into evening twilight which is always a time of exceedingly heavy traffic at large airports, and the radio chatter was absolutely non-stop. Attempting to sandwich a call in between almost constant transmissions was difficult. By sheer luck, I picked the tower gal's voice out of the din and recognized the call from her that cleared me for takeoff...and responded with an affirmative that I'd heard her transmission.

Then, she called me back!

That was to inform me that a Goodyear Blimp had just arrived and was directly overhead…and "lighter-than-air" has right-of-way…so, stay clear!

Here I was in a strange airplane with a hyper-nervous check-pilot just moments after we'd left a crash scene and now, we had to be concerned about a blimp in the dark while listening to a solid stream of blaring radio calls at a strange airport with planes flying in every direction. Holy cow!

I pushed the throttle full forward! We didn't just roll forward…we shot forward! I wasn't ready for that! This plane had one heck of a lot more power than the 172s I was used to flying.

I began my climb-out. The airspeed moved up rapidly.

"Hold your airspeed at seventy," snarled the check pilot.

I glanced at the airspeed indicator…we were doing ninety. I looked nervously at the blimp.

"I said, ***hold the airspeed at seventy***," he snarled again.

Man…this plane was climbing like crazy! What power! I'd given this forthcoming model "short-shrift" when selling planes and heard the "Hawk" was going to be a much-improved 172. I'll say it was! To reduce the airspeed, I'd have to pull the nose straight up (well...up steeply!) Inadvertently, I had let the airspeed creep back up to ninety and the check-pilot didn't like that one bit.

That was when…***I missed a radio call!***

Thinking back, I later realized that the problem wasn't only that I missed the call, the situation was that…I had lost much of my high-pitch hearing ability at the time and didn't realize the fact. That the tower controller was a woman meant dealing with her high-pitch voice and I did not hear her well. Additionally, there was the tremendous amount of plane traffic plus constant radio calls. Add to that the fact that my most recent flying time had been done at a very low traffic airport without all this frenetic radio activity and…I admittedly was out of practice.

I hadn't even turned downwind when the check-pilot looked over at me with a scowl and growled, "Take er' down, you need some dual!" (Meaning some flight-time with an instructor to sharpen flying skills.)

Alas, that meant the check ride was over. I had failed. The first time in my flying life! I knew I hadn't done well with the radio but hadn't yet figured in the high-pitch hearing loss. Sooo….I called the Tower and requested permission to land.

There were no more occasions for a long time to rent another plane. Four years would pass before I had a hearing test and discovered my high-pitch hearing was almost completely gone which, sadly, precludes flying airplanes. That explained my problem. But, I can tell you this…that was the most intense time I ever spent in an airplane. The air in that Cessna 172 seemed as thick as syrup from the start. Understandable! The check-pilot had visible feelings of deep emotional carryover from the previous day's horrific catastrophe…and then, only hours later…he was forced to watch another airplane crash right before his eyes!

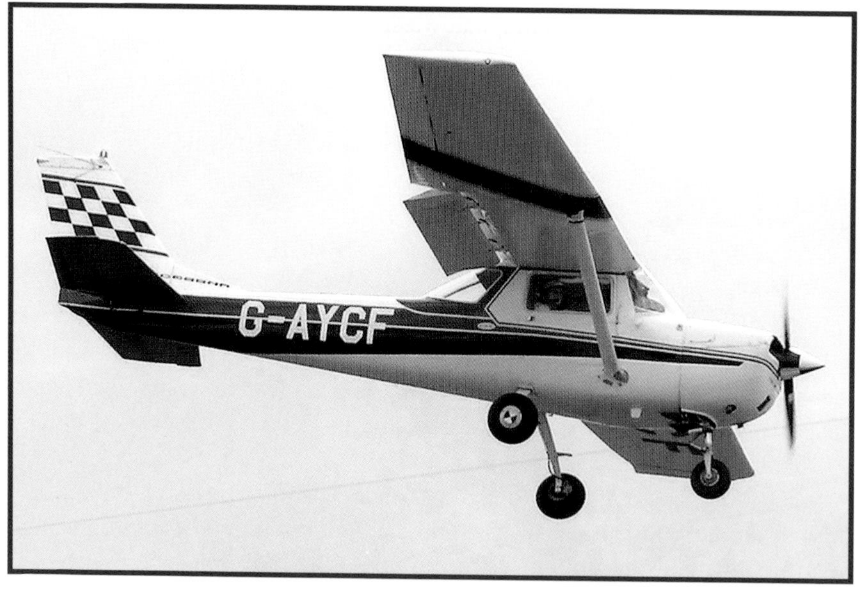

Cessna "Aerobat" - 734 built

Rogue Valley Skyways had a new 1970 Cessna "Aerobat" for a time...and those of us who flew the plane would place a glass of water on top of the instrument panel...and then "***try***" to do barrel rolls without spilling any!

Charmed

"Open…just a bit more."

That was one of the first things Bob ever said to me. Bob…was a dentist. And…not ***just*** a dentist! He was a really nice gentleman and an exceptionally good and dedicated dentist. And, that wasn't all the good news. ***He owned an airplane!***

Why, you might ask…was that such good news? Simply because…I also owned an airplane! That gave us something in common that only a very small percentage of the population has. That's the way it is with pilots. You fly an airplane? Then you and I are very much alike. It's as simple as that!

Interestingly, although we were engaged in very different fields of endeavor, we both had a driving ambition do the finest work we could in our fields. I have found that to be the case with most people who are airplane pilots.

Not only was Bob a fellow pilot, the plane he owned and flew was almost a duplicate of mine. We both flew the legendary "Piper Cub" in a basic "bush-pilot" style. His plane had a bit more horsepower than mine but, essentially, with only that exception, they were almost identical planes. And, we used our planes for the same purposes, "cutting holes in the sky" (flying slang for the pure joy of flying) and transportation to fishing and hunting sites. And so, we became very good friends as well as having the client-patient relationship that had initiated our meeting. An additional trait we had in common was the fact that we were both single and thirty-one years old.

Bob hadn't yet married because he had simply been so busy learning to be a dentist. Intense schooling, getting his practice started and flying his plane on hunting and fishing trips, he just hadn't found the time or had the good fortune to get adequately connected with the opposite sex. But…now he had. At thirty-one! And…***in a big way!***

He had been going with his girlfriend for quite a time and was apparently mightily smitten. Well, noooo, not simply "smitten." He was whatever is waaayyy beyond "head-over-heels" in love. He worshipped her! It didn't look like Bob would be single long.

I was secretly jealous of the gal. Because of "Mary," I figured I wouldn't have my flying friend as a close buddy for long. Shucks!

As Bob "dentisted" along in my mouth, he would alternate his one-way conversation between great flying talk and enlightening me on how neat this fabulous gal was. It was quite a while before I finally met her but before I did…I already knew much of what there was to know about her. Bob had gone on and on about the surprisingly unusual and unique adventures in which they had engaged. They really had a lot in common. They liked the same activities. The things they did ran the gamut all the way from hot-air ballooning to mountain climbing and just about everything in between. This girl was game for it all. And…she loved flying with him in his little ship. It was plain to see their future life together was going to be a thing of beauty and a work of art. At least, to hear Bob, that was exactly where their lives were headed. *Only one thing,* she was just…***nineteen!***

When I did meet Mary, I'd have sworn she was more like thirty. That's how sharp she was; great personality, knowledgeable, articulate, active conversationalist and drop-dead good-looking. She had it all! If you didn't know she was nineteen, you'd have sworn she was much older. I guess that is why she appealed so much to Bob. He thought she was everything he could have dreamed for.

When they were together, they appeared to be a perfect match. As far as I could tell, they were headed for a lifetime of marital bliss. Never did an hour go by when I was alone with Bob that she didn't get at least honorable mention.

Bob had grown up in the "high desert" country of Eastern Oregon and done a lot of "mountain-flying." He had even crashed his plane on the absolute top of a famed ten-thousand-foot high mountain while attempting an amazingly difficult landing. That was just the kind of thing he liked to try. He said one wouldn't believe the difficulty he had in getting the plane back down off the mountain in enough pieces so the plane could be rebuilt. But, he and friends did get it down. Hey, this was a guy on par with my soul. I loved that kind of flying and I had even done a bit of crashing myself (other stories), so we truly spoke the same language.

Bob was an outstanding pilot! On one occasion, as we flew both airplanes along together, I followed him down near the surface of a local river, and I mean…almost *on the surface!* Watching him in awe as he flew lower and lower ahead of me, he then dropped his plane down right *on the river's surface* and bounced his wheels on the water. Bounce…bounce…bounce…bounce! I couldn't believe my eyes. Nobody had told me you do this with an airplane and live to tell about it. He explained later that flying at high speed, there is no way the airplane can get in trouble. The activity looked easy when he did it…but I haven't tried that to this day. Too spooky for me! Obviously, such flying was a "piece of cake" for him but I already said he was good.

He was an exceptionally good dentist, too. I'd had other dental work done and I easily could tell the difference. Another thing at which he was very good was "metallurgy." Turns out a dentist has to learn quite a lot about the specifics of using metal for purposes of making items like tooth "bridges" and "caps;" I'd never given that part of a dentist's work much thought but, when Bob told me a secret and made me promise to keep quiet, I then learned enough to know that working with metal has to be one of the most important "disciplines-within-a-discipline" that makes up a dentist's necessarily large bank of abilities.

Oh yeah…*what was his secret?*

Well…Bob was in the process of making the most fabulous solid sterling silver "charm" bracelet imaginable…for ***Mary***. And, on this amazing project, he was the designer, artist, sculptor, jeweler, metallurgist and foundry-man all rolled up into one. As he first described the piece to me and later showed me the work in progress, I viewed his efforts with absolute thunderstruck awe! This guy could do anything. His work was amazingly beautiful. "Maybe he should have gone into this work instead," I thought. Tiffany or Cartier would have loved this guy.

So…what was the "charm-bracelet" production all about? Why…what else? To celebrate the many exceptional activities he and Mary had engaged in since they met, and…to present it to her as his own unique and very personal…engagement affirmation. Bob reckoned his "effort" to be about the best engagement present any man could possibly give to the woman of his heart. Well, I should think so! I could not imagine any ordinary man working at such a long, drawn-out production to please his love.

When he showed me the work in progress, the bracelet had about ten of the most glorious and perfectly formed solid silver charms I had ever seen anywhere and he still planned to add three more. There had to have been one heck of a lot of outstanding activities they'd done together.

Among the complicated charms he had painstakingly made through the very long and arduous process of "lost-wax" founding, were (naturally) a perfect little airplane like his, a realistic looking hot-air balloon, a mountain, an ocean view, a boat, and representations of other fun things they had done together. A simple ring for Mary? Not from this guy! She was far too special to him for a simple ring. Ordinary fellows do that. ***Not Bob!***

He had been working on this project for months of nights…time he told Mary was spent in the office with evening patients. He wanted the fabulous bracelet to be the perfect secret.

He chortled to himself as he related to me how he had completely fooled her up to this point. His plan was to keep the surprise hidden right up to the end…when he would dramatically present her with his fantastic work of heartfelt sentiment. How a dentist could perform such outstanding works of art was a mystery to me. But…here they were…almost in finished form. He had to be absolutely "head over heels" for this gal. Just a little more time and Mary would be the recipient of what I considered the greatest piece of sentimental work to praise a woman that I had ever seen. It was, in my opinion, only a wee bit short of the famed Taj Mahjal, which also was a tribute to a woman deeply loved.

Our times together in our airplanes made for many fond memories…but, as time went by, Bob had less and less of it to spend with me in the sky. I understood how crazy he was for his lovely little gal friend and I missed him but I knew he was spending more and more time with Mary and also working hard to finish his magnificent charm-bracelet-engagement-offering. I also knew that from the moment he and Mary became man and wife, I would effectively be "cut out of the loop" almost completely. Ah well, that's the way it's been since the beginning.

Then, I didn't see Bob for quite a while. My teeth were O.K. for the time being and he was completely involved with Mary and his important project. More time passed and the next time I saw Bob was purely by accident. I ran into him at the post office. He didn't appear as his usual joyful happy-go-lucky self.

"Hi Bob," I greeted him with the typical great pleasure of accidently running into such a good airplane pilot friend. His response was slow and measured.

"Hi."

That all…Just plain "Hi." No more!

"You all right?" I queried.

"No!...Not really!"

At that point, he looked directly into my eyes...and a big tear began to form in his eye.

"What is it, Bob?"

He tried to speak. Nothing came out.

I waited.

Finally; "***She wouldn't take it!***"

"You mean the...?"

"Yes."

"Why not?"

"Her father!" he faltered...and almost seemed to choke as the words came out.

"And?"

"He said I am...***too old for her***."

"And she?"

"Just couldn't disrespect her father's wishes...***it's over!"***

Now tears were streaming down his face as he stood looking at me wistfully. I was at a complete loss for words. For a bit, I couldn't speak. It was too emotional. We just stared at each other. I could try only to imagine the depth of his feelings. And, I couldn't. I'm sure he knew that.

"Are you all right, Bob?" was about all I could muster.

Finally...using only two words...he quietly (almost unintelligibly) mumbled, "Gotta go!"

"What are you going to do, Bob?"...I gently asked.

"I've already done it," he replied softly.

And that was how, in time that followed, I was able to proudly tell all my other friends and acquaintances that my good friend Bob was performing great services for mankind by helping correct native dental deficiencies in a third-world country in..."The Peace Corps."

Until now, I've never had the heart to tell those same people the rest of the story.

And...don't you ask me what happened to "it." My tear ducts go on autopilot when the very thought of "it" returns!

Peril On The Runway

We couldn't believe what was happening! Our flight planning most certainly had not considered any possibilities this bizarre. This situation had to be resolved…and soon!

An engineer and I had begun the day with a takeoff at 4:00 A.M. and the time was now 2:00 A. M. after 17 hours of hard flying in my Piper Apache twin. An equipment sales trip, we had visited sawmills in Oregon, Idaho, Montana and Wyoming and had decided to spend the night in Rawlins, Wyoming. We had pushed the limits of fatigue and wanted nothing more than to flop down on soft warm beds. Alas, that possibility was not looking good.

The final flight leg had been uneventful and we simply wished to make the last landing a quick one and get to a hotel as quickly as we could. There apparently was no one at the isolated airport due to lack of traffic because our radio calls announcing our arrival went unanswered. So, I set up a long approach, checked the fuel source, set the mixtures to rich, eased back the throttles, moved the prop pitches to flat, turned landing lights on and lowered the flaps and gear. All that remained was touchdown and sleep! This was not to be...yet!

Western Mule Deer

Just at the runway threshold, our landing lights revealed a group of deer directly ahead. Quickly shoving the throttles forward, I eased back on the yoke and we flew over the deer about twenty feet above them. Even more shocking, much of the rest of the runway and the grasses on both sides were teeming with deer! There must have been a couple hundred. There was no way we could land with such a condition.

We decided to try scaring the deer off the runway and made a fast pass over them again with engines screaming. To no avail! They moved very little. We continued to harass them for ten minutes or so when a car appeared and drove down the runway with its horn blaring. That cleared the runway enough for us to land. Later, the man driving the car (a pilot) told us this happened frequently and, when he would hear a plane buzzing around and around, he immediately knew what the situation was and, as a Good Samaritan, he'd quickly drive to the airport to help resolve the problem.

Planes...For A Song!

In the late 1950s, I knew a fellow who was quite mechanical and dabbled in buying and selling miscellaneous construction equipment. Visiting him at a warehouse he had for equipment being prepared for sale, I was shocked to see a massive (to me) olive-drab Howard DGA airplane, minus its wings, parked right in the middle of his clutter. The wings were resting against one wall.

Surprised to see an airplane in the ownership of one who was not a pilot, I quizzed him. "I got this plane for four hundred bucks at an equipment auction. It's war surplus!" was his reply. "I just couldn't pass up the deal!" "What are you going to do about flying the ship?" I inquired. "Oh, that shouldn't be a problem...I'll just learn to fly," was his response. Then he excitedly informed me he was going to go through the ship and put it in first-class mechanical condition.

Howard "DGA" 15-P - 520 built

When I asked him what he knew about airplanes, he said he didn't think there could be much difference from the other equipment he was used to working on. I shook my head in awe at the idea of a rank-amateur taking on the task of reworking such a large airplane...and then attempting to learn to fly beginning in this ship. He practically glowed all over when he exclaimed, "The guys who sold this to me said the "DGA" designation stands for "Damned Good Airplane!" He thought that was one of the funniest things he had ever heard. So did I!

I visited him a few more times in the next couple of years but never saw much progress with his airplane project. I believe his excitement at the thought of flying this big hulk of a plane simply overcame his good judgment at the auction. His purchase price did, however, illustrate the tremendous values that could be found for quite a few years after World War II.

1970 Cessna 310Q - 5,737 built (all variants)
Price F.A.F.(Fly Away Factory) $67,950.

That price was the basic airplane devoid of any and all accessories and options. Going through an original price sheet that lists all the necessary or desired extras such as radios, autopilot, de-icing systems and oxygen setup...plus many additional options such as different paint schemes and a host of other possibilities, it quickly is obvious that a 310 equipped as many buyers wanted most likely increased the price to about double the base figure. Still, the figure was reasonably low when compared to the astounding escalation of prices of similar planes in later years.

Cessna 310 Follies

In December, 1969, two of us from the Rogue Valley Skyways flight operation in Medford, Oregon, where I worked as a salesman, attended Cessna Aircraft's annual international sales meeting in Wichita, Kansas. After the meeting most attendees ferried new aircraft home to their bases. My associate and I and two other Oregon Cessna aircraft dealers were given a shiny new 1970 Cessna 310Q twin (like the one pictured above) to fly back to "Western Skyways" located at Troutdale, Oregon...a Cessna distributor for a large area. It was my good fortune to gain the command-pilot's seat. I wanted to get as much multi-engine time as possible for experience and my logbook entries. On the trip home we faced mostly very low, cold, cloudy weather. In our group, I was the only pilot lacking an instrument "rating" but in our weather situation, that was not important…we planned to fly the distance VFR (visual flight rules) only. The distributor-owner wanted us to avoid damp cold weather at all costs (well…almost all) to preclude the possibility of getting into cloud-icing conditions which might result in damaged fuselage paint caused by broken ice flung from propellers.

During the trip we experienced clouds so low (and some snow) that, to avoid getting into the solid icy clouds above, in southeastern Oregon we flew just under them ***as low as 100 feet of altitude*** over the chilly high desert sagebrush. The weather was so bad that it brought to mind an old aviation gag-line: "Even the birds were walking!" It was a bit nerve-wracking for *me* to fly at the 310's lowest reasonable speed (about 120 mph) while dodging hills, mountains, trees and miscellaneous objects, *all with exceedingly low forward visibility*. All cockpit chatter ceased as eight eyeballs strained to their limits attempting to pierce the dim view ahead.

Fortunately, we made it without damaging the all-important beautiful paint job from chunks of flying ice, and I got to log the flight time...but, in the process, the tense flight made me one very uneasy low-time multi-engine pilot.

Another interesting 310 anecdote: During my tenure as a plane salesman, a logging operator bought an older "straight-tail" 310 (1959 and earlier) and took his multi-engine dual instruction at our operation. On one flight, he and the instructor went out at night to practice. At another airfield, the instructor asked him to execute a landing. The relative novice twin-pilot reduced all power and, after crossing the runway threshold, pulled back gently on the controls into a landing stall (about fifteen feet above ground). The plane hit the hard surface with a big thud and a tremendous bounce. It hit hard enough to make the instructor nervous and curious so he had the student taxi over to the parking ramp where they got out and checked the plane over. Sure enough, much to their mutual chagrin, the heavy hit (with about ¾ full wingtip tanks exerting additional leverage) had wrinkled the bottom of the wings severely. They parked the plane, called for someone to pick them up…and that plane was "totaled" by the insurance company…***never to fly again!***

Cessna 206 Turbo Skywagon

The 21st Century: Pilots never tire of flying...it is always a new thrill! I've flown a lot of trips in this beautiful ship. My friend pilot/owner added many flight-improving upgrades.

Grumman Widgeon - 317 built

Marc (left) talks flying with Tom Young in front of Tom's beautifully restored amphibian, one of the most revered planes of its type.

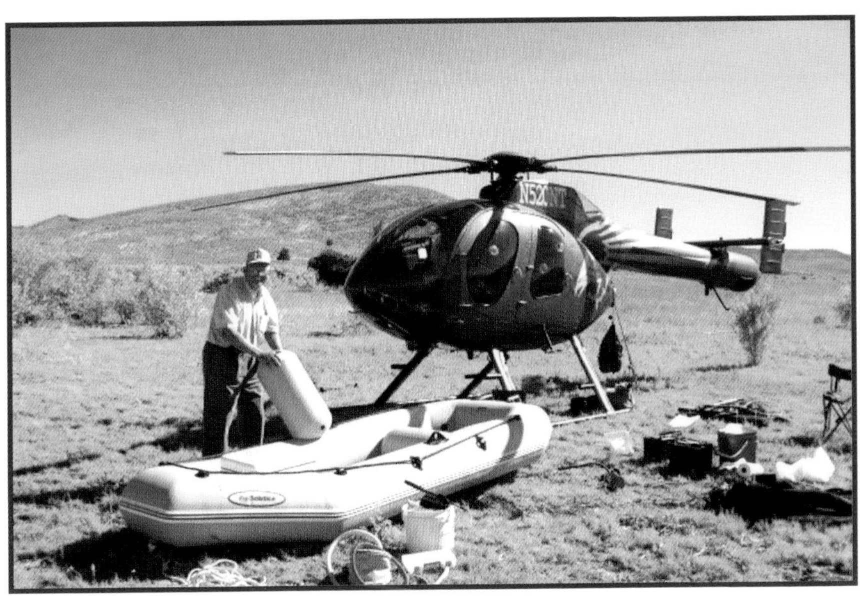

McDonnell Douglas (Hughes) 520N (no tail rotor)
Flying in friend Vahan Dinihanian's helicopter...*fishing the easy way!*

It's hard to beat a state-of-the-art helicopter!

Airplanes are great and helicopters are fantastic. Experiencing the multiple utilities of a "chopper" can make a "fixed-wing" flyer seriously jealous! Marc on the left...pilot/owner Vahan Dinihanian at controls.

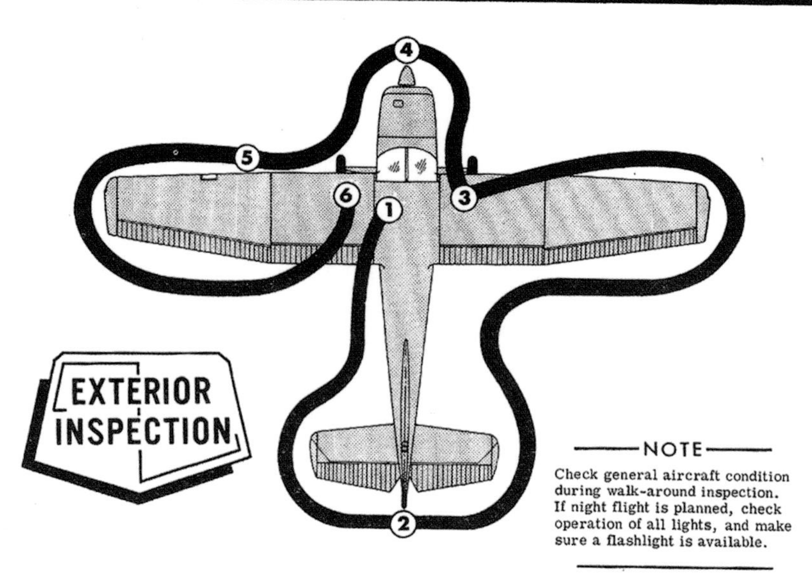
4
5
6
1
3
EXTERIOR
INSPECTION
2
NOTE
Check general aircraft condition during walk-around inspection. If night flight is planned, check operation of all lights, and make sure a flashlight is available.

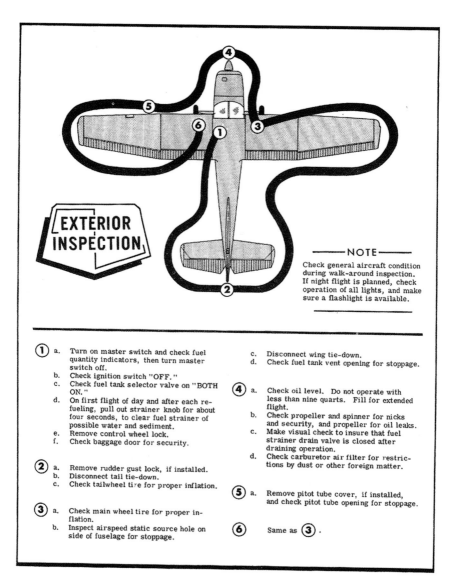

(1)
a. Turn on master switch and check fuel quantity indicators, then turn master switch off.
b. Check ignition switch "OFF."
c. Check fuel tank selector valve on "BOTH ON."
d. On first flight of day and after each refueling, pull out strainer knob for about four seconds, to clear fuel strainer of possible water and sediment.
e. Remove control wheel lock.
f. Check baggage door for security.

(2)
a. Remove rudder gust lock, if installed.
b. Disconnect tail tie-down.
c. Check tailwheel tire for proper inflation.

(3)
a. Check main wheel tire for proper inflation.
b. Inspect airspeed static source hole on side of fuselage for stoppage.
c. Disconnect wing tie-down.
d. Check fuel tank vent opening for stoppage.

(4)
a. Check oil level. Do not operate with less than nine quarts. Fill for extended flight.
b. Check propeller and spinner for nicks and security, and propeller for oil leaks.
c. Make visual check to insure that fuel strainer drain valve is closed after draining operation.
d. Check carburetor air filter for restrictions by dust or other foreign matter.

(5)
a. Remove pitot tube cover, if installed, and check pitot tube opening for stoppage.

(6)
Same as (3).

Cessna 180 pre-flight "Walk-around inspection" Check-List

Many aviation "incidents" have been the result of *inadequate* pre-flight "walk-around-inspections."

In Memoriam: Flyers I Have Known

It is fascinating to consider that, of the many auto accidents taken place during my lifetime, I can remember only four people I've known personally who were killed by automobile accident.

It is a completely different story with people I've known or known of who were involved in aviation. The number to meet their end by airplane flight (including two in foregoing stories) is twenty...all I had dealings with and knew personally to one degree or another. Most surprising, many of these flyers had significant amounts of flight time in a broad range of airplanes. A number had ratings well beyond the basic "Private Pilot, Single-Engine Land" designation. Some had "Flight Instructor" ratings. Others were serious "Commercial" pilots and some highly experienced aerobatic performers. Benefits of maturity, experience and wisdom to make careful choices can elude us at critical times (especially in aviation in which poor decisions or what might seem minor mistakes can escalate into unfortunate results). These were all good people going about their daily lives doing what they loved…they were simply less fortunate than others. Some names have been changed for lack of complete data for all events.

May the mysterious hidden Pilot's Lounge in the Universe be a place of comfort and happiness and may they experience the very best in their flights through eternity.

Here are the stories of their encounters with destiny:

Bill

I met Bill in the flight lounge while taking a break from studying ground school to complete training for my private pilot's license. Bill gave the appearance of a pilot who had broad experience with airplanes and knew a lot about flying. The fact is, he did. A certified flight instructor, he was rated to teach single and multi-engine students. Where I took my "ground school" training, he also served as occasional pilot-in-command of a large twin-engine twenty passenger Douglas DC-3 for Pacific Power & Light Corporation. I'll always remember the last time I saw him...as a dashing visage leaning out of the DC-3 window and calling out to a friend as he taxied out to the active runway…to then roar away into the blue in one of the most legendary of planes.

Another day I picked up the morning newspaper to see a photo of a small mound of crumpled metal in the middle of a plowed field about a hundred yards off a local highway. The caption: "Twin-engine business plane crashes in field…*two dead*." Bill was one of the two. I estimated his age to be about 35. It seems that he was giving a twin-engine aircraft owner some flight training in the owner's airplane. I don't remember what the FAA concluded as the cause but the day of flight had been crystal clear and beautiful, certainly not a day one would think a young flying career was to end so rudely. Bill was a pleasant fellow with an extensive flying background, but fate intervened. Second-guessing fate is an exercise in futility. One day he was here…and the next day he was gone! One would think he would escape such a fate.

Dick

Dick was one of the youngest of flight operation owners and managers at about twenty-eight when I went to work as his in-house airplane salesman. He had a couple of investor-owners as partners but he was the general manager of the business. He had a flight instructor's rating, an instrument rating, a multi-engine rating and a commercial charter license. He had accumulated a very large number of flying hours in a fairly short period of time and was checked out to fly many different planes. He was a safe and intelligent well-trained pilot. Why was it that he died on a weekend while demonstrating an airplane to a prospective buyer with whom I typically would have been flying?

I'd taken the weekend off to go fishing. Returning by auto and approaching town from about twenty miles out, I heard the news on the car radio. Dick had taken two very heavy men up in a single-engine plane to give them a sales demonstration. Shortly after takeoff, when the plane had reached a couple hundred feet of altitude and was still flying at relatively low climb-out airspeed, the engine quit (later determined to be a fuel supply problem). For reasons known only to fate…Dick attempted to execute a 180 degree turn back to the runway to (hopefully) land the plane safely. Most people really don't understand that airplanes do not fly well at low airspeeds and especially in sharp low-airspeed turns. The ship stalled (stopped flying) about a hundred feet above ground, went into an uncontrollable bank and ended up going almost straight down.

Gordy

Only a large-truck driver or mechanic could know the depths of my embarrassment when Gordy came into the flight lounge, spotted me and asked in front of others if I knew I had left the "Jake-brake" on when I had parked the truck in front of our building. Gordy, our main charter pilot, had been a diesel truck mechanic and therefore, recognized the high-pitched sound coming from the borrowed "idling" Freightliner flatbed I had parked minutes before. It would be a few years later that I would learn that I had a severe high-pitch hearing loss. Gordy had worked very hard to learn to fly and then gain enough flight ratings to become a professional pilot. Because he had been a successful truck mechanic and was knowledgeable about many things mechanical, he would be asked to take company planes up for check-rides after the shop had worked on them.

A few years later, I was saddened to read in the local daily paper that Gordy and another pilot met their end in a strange and unusual way. He and the owner of an older Cessna four-place plane took to the air to check the success of the shop in isolating and repairing an engine problem. While still in the traffic pattern on a downwind leg, the engine cowling ripped completely loose and went right through the windshield, incapacitating both Gordy and the owner. The abrupt catastrophic event caused them to lose control of the plane and it went down in a sharp angle at high speed, ending the great professional-pilot-future Gordy had worked so hard to achieve. He was twenty-nine.

Bob

Bob was a cropduster. Not just ***any*** cropduster. How many cropdusters…or for that matter…how many pilots can land a small airplane on top of a 12,281 foot snow-covered mountain peak, get out, take photos of the accomplishment and take off to fly another day? He showed me the photos the day I met him to talk about buying a Piper Cub wreck he had for sale. I had gone to visit him because I had a Piper Cub with a small engine and the wreck he was selling had a larger one I wanted. It seemed he had given his wife basic flight instruction and, while still a student pilot, she landed his Cub just short of the runway in some deciduous trees. The leafy obstructions let the plane down relatively safely and she walked away…but, the Cub's fuselage and wings were bent up to a major degree. Later, I would see Bob at assorted "fly-ins" when he would arrive in a very large antique single engine Stinson "Reliant" airplane…and usually do a magnificent aerobatic "snap-roll" just as he entered the traffic pattern. Man, oh man…this guy could fly!

So…it was with great surprise I was to learn one day that he had met his demise in a crop-dusting plane. The particulars of the incident were a little sketchy but it seemed he "spun in" (headed steeply nose-down and spinning around rapidly) after somehow losing control of the plane. I was told that Bob had been having family problems…and my informant speculated that Bob might have crashed intentionally. That sounded a little "iffy" to me after knowing how handy Bob was with a plane…but then, who knows?

Harold

I met Harold at an air show where he was the star attraction. He flew a former WWII biplane trainer ("Great Lakes") and did aerobatics that left viewers breathless. I had a great talk with him and he gave me a lot of pointers about how to fly my own biplane in aerobatic maneuvers. Harold gave me a list of the future dates he was to fly so I could visit the shows and watch him perform again…and maybe get some more pointers on aerobatic flying. The next time I saw him perform, he seemed to be doing even more and more striking "air-work." A year or so later I found a book he had written on aerobatics which I purchased. The book is still here…but the author isn't.

Over the years, I learned a truism about many professional aerobatic pilots. In a surprising number of cases, they fly very successfully for a few years and then…you don't hear of them anymore. It just happened that one day they made a tiny mistake. That is, a "tiny" mistake if measured in feet, inches or configuration of flight. The challenge with aerobatic flying is that a "tiny" mistake or miscalculation, which in most businesses can be easily remedied, can be catastrophic. In the aerobatic flying business, a significant aberration is usually fatal. And, that is precisely what removed my acquaintance Harold…from this life.

Jack

He was one of the best-looking kids to appear in the flight lounge. He was well educated and came from a highly respected family which owned a successful local business. And, he was learning to fly when I met him. I'd just begun selling planes at the operation and he was taking regular flying lessons. I guessed him to be about twenty-two. We had great conversations about the world of flight and he couldn't wait to get his pilot's license. In a few months, he was successful in receiving his license and, on frequent occasions, rented expensive single-engine planes from the operation. He continued flying lessons, eventually getting a multi-engine rating (but, not an instrument rating).

Only a year or so later, I was stunned to learn he had crashed and died in a relatively complex late model Cessna 310 twin-engine plane. The rest of the story was even more stunning. It developed that the plane he was flying was loaded (according to reports, overloaded) with marijuana. He allegedly had loaded the plane in Mexico, crossed the border just east of San Diego and headed into the mountains to try to elude the narcotics police. It was a fairly dark night and, in his haste to get away, he made a sharp turn right into the side of a mountain. Later, I would learn that his family had earlier cut him off from his easy money supply and forced him out onto his own. Apparently, he was paying for his twin-engine flight lessons with money from "pot" dealing. This was one of the more unique flight-deaths that touched me because he seemed to be a really nice ordinary kid. I hadn't realized that a "drug dealer" could be so inconspicuous.

Myrna

We all wondered why this nice old gal was learning to fly. It seemed she spent a lot more than the usual amount of time flying "dual" with her instructor, a consideration which sometimes indicates the person may not have the aptitude to be a pilot. However, she persisted. We thought it possible she felt a bit "pressured" by family, some of whom were already reasonably accomplished pilots. She definitely did not exhibit the sharpness and calculated decision-making that is native to most aspiring pilots.

So, it was a surprise when she showed up one day in a sporty-looking brand new Cessna "Cardinal," a moderately-performing single engine fixed-gear ship which more than a few pilots considered significantly underpowered. Myrna then continued flight lessons in her own ship and appeared finally to be getting the hang of piloting…or, so it seemed.

I'd gone on to endeavors beyond airplane sales when I heard the story. According to my informant, Myrna flew away from our small city to visit the largest city in the state. To return, the usual path was directly over the Cascade Mountain Range. The day she began her flight home, cloudy weather obscured most of the mountain passes on her planned route. Told of a pass which could frequently be "open" when all others were closed, she aimed for that hoping for an open notch (cloud-free) in the high hills.

The remnants of the plane and of poor Myrna were found after a week-long search. The "hot tip" she had been given regarding a possibly "clear mountain pass" turned out to be unreliable.

Eldon

Eldon was Myrna's husband. He was friendly enough but seemed a little quirky. Like Myrna, he was in his fifties and did not appear to pilots to be typical flyer material. Few people learn to fly after fifty years of age for whatever reason. It isn't that such folks can't learn... it is a fact that many of that age and beyond don't make the best pilots. The reason for that? Possibly the same reason few people over fifty begin music lessons and then achieve virtuoso status. The fact is, flying is a pursuit that most begin at a much younger age. However, I found Eldon very interesting to talk with because his work was in the manufacture of mechanical equipment and I'm mechanical so we had something in common. He managed to acquire his pilot's license after substantially more than the usual number of flying hours for a typical student.

A couple of years after his wife died in the family plane, Eldon began flying his brother's small single-engine low-wing semi-sport plane. His demise and his much-mangled plane were discovered near a highway just short of the top of a low coastal mountain pass through which he had attempted to fly…another victim of low clouds and low fog. It is absolutely amazing how many private pilots die as a result of attempting to fly under clouds and fog which meet the ground in front of them…and obscure all vision.

Al

I met Al when I was thirteen. Al and his friend Kenny taught me how to shoot pool. They also contributed to my delinquency by buying beer for me. Al had a "laid-back" personality which made him a pleasure to be around. He was about five years older than I but we got along well, maybe because I was very big for my age and seemed much older. A couple of years later, Al met a big burly fellow named Ben from the South Sea Islands and they worked together in the construction business for a few years. Al took flying lessons and got his pilot's license. Later, when I ran into the two of them one night at a pool hall, Al said he had saved money diligently and was about to buy into a flight operation in Alaska. Sounded pretty neat to me. At the time, I could only dream about flying so anyone who could actually be in the business had my full attention.

Al left the area and became a success in Alaska. I'd hear about him from time to time usually when he would visit the "lower 48" to buy another airplane for the flight operation. I envied his apparent grand

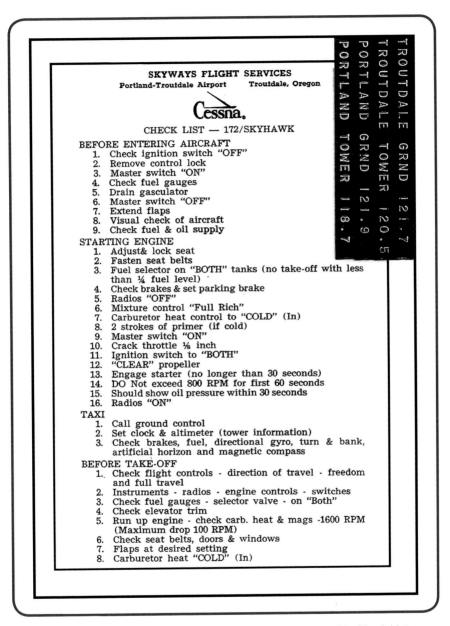

SKYWAYS FLIGHT SERVICES

Portland-Troutdale Airport **Troutdale, Oregon**

Cessna.

TROUTDALE GRND 121.7
TROUTDALE TOWER 120.5
PORTLAND GRND 121.9
PORTLAND TOWER 118.7

CHECK LIST — 172/SKYHAWK

BEFORE ENTERING AIRCRAFT

1. Check ignition switch "OFF"
2. Remove control lock
3. Master switch "ON"
4. Check fuel gauges
5. Drain gasculator
6. Master switch "OFF"
7. Extend flaps
8. Visual check of aircraft
9. Check fuel & oil supply

STARTING ENGINE

1. Adjust& lock seat
2. Fasten seat belts
3. Fuel selector on "BOTH" tanks (no take-off with less than ¼ fuel level)
4. Check brakes & set parking brake
5. Radios "OFF"
6. Mixture control "Full Rich"
7. Carburetor heat control to "COLD" (In)
8. 2 strokes of primer (if cold)
9. Master switch "ON"
10. Crack throttle ⅛ inch
11. Ignition switch to "BOTH"
12. "CLEAR" propeller
13. Engage starter (no longer than 30 seconds)
14. DO Not exceed 800 RPM for first 60 seconds
15. Should show oil pressure within 30 seconds
16. Radios "ON"

TAXI

1. Call ground control
2. Set clock & altimeter (tower information)
3. Check brakes, fuel, directional gyro, turn & bank, artificial horizon and magnetic compass

BEFORE TAKE-OFF

1. Check flight controls - direction of travel - freedom and full travel
2. Instruments - radios - engine controls - switches
3. Check fuel gauges - selector valve - on "Both"
4. Check elevator trim
5. Run up engine - check carb. heat & mags -1600 RPM (Maximum drop 100 RPM)
6. Check seat belts, doors & windows
7. Flaps at desired setting
8. Carburetor heat "COLD" (In)

Pilots who wish to fly another day...pay serious attention to this Check List.

success in the flying business. I don't remember where or exactly when I later ran into Al's friend, Ben, but I definitely remember the first thing Ben said to me: "Al is gone!" "Gone?" I mumbled. "Yep, gone!" "What happened?" "Well…from the statements of the FAA accident investigators, the best they could determine was that Al came down from Alaska, bought a plane, headed back north…and flew so many continuous hours that he went to sleep at the controls and flew right down into a forest of large trees. The plane had enough fuel that it caught fire and burned. There wasn't much left." I was stunned! Al was a nice guy who had worked hard and long to achieve much…and to end up a little pile of burnt rubble in the middle of nowhere! That must be about the time I decided that destiny has no heart!

Matt

The plane made a sweeping low turn toward us, reduced power and glided neatly onto the water directly behind our anchored yacht... making hardly a splash. I hadn't seen many seaplanes up close and didn't know much about them but I could tell this guy really knew water aviation. It was impressive to see when he then turned the engine off, deftly climbed out onto the left float while the plane was still moving slowly and stood there until the tip of the float eased right up to the swim-step of the boat. We're talking inches here… "coasting in" from maybe forty or fifty feet out after engine-cutoff. Then, with a rope in hand, he nonchalantly stepped gently off the plane's float onto the swim-step and tied the plane to the yacht. I was mesmerized! He did this in the middle of a large river with the current running at eight to ten miles an hour. How anyone could manage such an accurate approach under those conditions with a floatplane seemed almost unbelievable. He was a good friend of my host, the boat's owner, and was introduced all around. He and I were the only pilots there so we talked flying for quite a while. He said that he had purchased the Cessna 172 on floats just after he began taking flying lessons and, of his more than a thousand hours of total flight time, almost all of it was in this plane on and over water. He said he felt much more comfortable flying over water than over land.

The headline read, "Four Die In River Plane Crash!" I read on. Yep, it was Matt! It seems he had sold the 172 and bought a de Havilland Beaver on floats. The "Beaver" is one of the most famous planes ever put on floats. It is considered a "pilots' airplane" if ever there was one. That is what made this headline so strange. Anybody who has more than a thousand hours of floatplane flying time and flies the famous Beaver theoretically should be well beyond danger on water.

The circumstances of the deaths were surprising. Matt had taken off in almost the exact spot where I had met him. His family owned a large summer property at that location and he had stopped by to pick up three of his four children to go for a plane ride. Upon takeoff, he apparently made a tight circle, stalled in the turn…and went down into the water (with no survivors). No reasonable explanation. He crashed right in front of the waterfront home as the grandparents watched in shock and horror. So much for substantial "in type" flying experience!

Owen

Owen was an engaging fellow. He was a barber. And, if there was one thing in this life he wanted, it was a Meyers OTW biplane. He had a partner who was a pilot and felt the same way. They answered an ad I'd put in the newspaper to sell my OTW. I'll bet they spent a month trying every effort they could think of to get me to lower my price. They just didn't have enough money between them. They finally gave up but, in the process of meeting with them several times, I got to know them quite well. They were very decent guys but I needed the money for other projects and knew I could get it from someone, so I didn't lower the price. A year or so later, they somehow did get enough money and found an OTW they could afford. They were overjoyed. Now, they, too, could relish the wind blowing in their faces at altitude in an antique biplane. It must have been a longtime dream for them. I ran into them occasionally at small airports while flying about the area and they always seemed to be in "seventh-heaven" with their newly-acquired delight.

Maybe I should have been a bit surprised when reading it in the newspaper that day. It was about Owen and his partner. Seems they had visited an antique airplane air show for the day and left for home. They never arrived! What happened was never exactly determined. They were found in a tangled mass of wood, wire and aluminum in a thinly wooded grove of trees…dead! From the first day I met them, I'd always harbored a hidden feeling that they weren't really airplane "types." They hadn't seemed all that mechanical. Mechanical types usually can tell whether another person is a soul of similar trait. Although these fellows had the desire right from the first, they didn't strike me as the types for flying a biplane. Could that have been premonition?

Ann

She always seemed to be a bit grumpy when I pulled my plane into her family operation for fuel. The reality was that Ann simply was born that way. According to her student pilots, she was as good as they get at flying a plane. Like many fixed base operators, she was a commercial pilot with a certified flight instructor rating, multi-engine rating and an instrument "ticket." She also had a helicopter rating and was checked out for float-plane operation. She could "do it all." And…I couldn't count the many compliments to her I'd heard voiced by former student pilots regarding her ability to teach well. They all thought she was the greatest! Why was it, then, that all her hard-won flying abilities failed her at a time when they were most needed?

She accepted a charter job to fly a customer up to a high mountain lake in her small Piper single-engine plane. She always liked to fly it because it had an extra wide rear seat that gave her plenty of room. She flew the plane into a short narrow Forest Service airstrip not far from the lake and her passenger was picked up by family. The passenger's family then drove away to the lake without the faintest idea of what was to happen next. Ann got back in the plane, revved it up and aimed for the sky. She didn't make it! The only details I remember from reading about what happened (and from hearing bits and pieces of various ideas posed by other pilots), was that the day was unusually hot in the mountains, the strip was very short, the altitude was high and the air thin. It didn't seem that she could be overloaded because she had discharged her passenger and had also used a large share of her fuel getting to the destination. Nonetheless, her flying career (and her life) ended in a jumble at the bottom of the tall Douglas Fir tree she had collided with in a dense forest just a tiny distance from the main highway.

Sam

There aren't a lot of 60-year-old-plus "private-pilot" flyers doing aerobatics who will make a true full-professional aerobatic pilot sit up and take notice. But…Sam was one of them! I met him at an air show and was so amazed at his obvious mastery of his little "Pitts" aerobatic biplane that I visited a number of additional shows and managed to talk to him about flying each time. I always looked forward to watching him perform with both great pleasure and great apprehension. It was a delight to see him execute almost unbelievable maneuvers but I always wondered if the day would come when something would go wrong and I'd be forced to witness the unthinkable. He could do just about everything the "pros" could do with his little ship. One of his most spectacular stunts was a triple "snap roll" only a few feet over the runway. On one occasion, I watched him very intensely as he performed this very dangerous maneuver...and I counted four rotations! Not three...but four! The odds of doing it successfully are not good and the penalty for failing is...death! And...he walked away! When he got out of his plane, I asked him about the maneuver. "Sam, I counted four rotations and it looked like you almost caught a wing on the runway." His answer: "Well, I guess I lost count."

About six years later newspapers described Sam's last flight. Fortunately for me, I hadn't attended that air show...one I hadn't missed in eight or ten years.

Antique airplanes and their pilots gathered every year at a small suburban airport to show off their planes and socialize with other "antiquers." Sam had been a main attraction there for a number of years because he did dramatic aerobatics, lived relatively close and charged only a minimal amount to cover his basic costs. The show he put on was always about as good as most of the stunt pilots on the national circuit so everybody was quite happy with this arrangement. He did this simply because of his great love for flying. It was good that he loved flying so much because it was at this show that he joined those pilots who now make their permanent homes in the sky. How did it happen? And why? One fact is clear. He spiraled straight into the ground at very high speed doing a very simple "spin." The "spin" is one of the simplest of all aerobatic routines and appears to onlookers to be the most dangerous...therefore very dramatic and crowd-pleasing. Sam didn't recover from that one. *It was his last!*

Rex

Moments after I landed on his private strip, Rex rode up on a motorcycle and waved hello. I'd been told this man was very friendly and enjoyed talking with anyone landing on his property. Yep...just like I'd heard, Rex loved everything about flying and welcomed me. Many owners of private airstrips are a bit hesitant about allowing strangers to land...and, unless they know a pilot well and give permission, they would just as soon you stay away. Potential liability may be a big part of that. Or...maybe they get tired of listening to newly-minted pilots (which I was at the time) who get a thrill from landing here and there and everywhere. Rex operated a very large farm and was exceedingly prosperous. His personal choice of airplane was the famed Piper "Super Cub" and he flew his frequently between his scattered farm operations. I visited him on quite a few occasions and we always got along well. I flew a "Cub" and he flew a "Cub" so that made us "birds of a feather!"

During the ownership of my Cub, I had four minor crashes (I like to call them "incidents") and a major "one" that finally ended the plane's useful life. I "walked-away" unscathed in all events, with my guardian angel relieved every step of the way. Unlike my narrow escapes, Rex was not treated as well by destiny.

Another pilot told me what he heard of Rex's "final" event. Rex had flown his Cub to Alaska along with a couple of other planes filled with friends…for some great fishing and hunting. They all landed on the shores of a river, fished very successfully for a few hours and then took off to fly back to their lodgings and an evening dinner. Rex never showed up!

Later, a large contingent of anxious area pilots searching for him discovered what was left of Rex and his Super Cub…in trees at the head of a deep canyon. Earlier, when Rex and his friends left the river, the weather had begun to deteriorate rapidly. Need more be said? Rex joined that significant number of airborne adventurers who in unforgiving Alaskan terrain underestimated the danger of it...when combined with Mother Nature's foibles.

Sarah

I knew Sarah for well over thirty years. We were introduced at a political function. She and her sister were very involved in politics and worked exceptionally hard for their party. Sarah worked as a flight attendant for a major U.S. airline for many years. I lost track of the sisters but came in contact with them again when I sold real estate. They owned a house together and decided to sell it. They were selling because the eldest sister was soon to retire from her long-time airline job and the two of them were going to move to another locality and start a business. The house sold, the sisters moved and I thought no more about them…until I read a newspaper report. The headlines read, "Airliner Goes Down In Atlantic!" Yep…Sarah was on it! I was dumbstruck! And…she had only days to go until her retirement. This was to be her last flight. Well…it was! It made a very strong impression on me because she is the only person I have known to die in a commercial airliner crash.

Kevin

I'd heard nothing but good things about an aircraft operator in Washington State when…darned if I didn't sell him an airplane. As an airplane salesman, I'd had the good fortune to buy a four-year-old single engine Cessna 206 at an unbelievably low price. Although it had a "run-out" engine, it had four very good aircraft radios and I got it for a price so low that, if I quoted it here, I would be called a liar. A week hadn't gone by when the operator from Washington state called me. He had heard about the "206" through the "grape-vine" and needed such a plane. We made a tentative deal on the phone (subject to his approval upon my delivering the ship). I ferried the plane to his operation and was delighted to meet one of the gentlest men in aviation. While there, he proudly introduced me to Kevin, his eleven-year old son, a boy he said had a great future in aviation. He told of Kevin flying at least seven or eight different types of small planes. Dad was always in the right seat to be a "safety pilot" but, according to him, his son could control the planes very well. The boy was unusually well-mannered, entered into conversations easily and it was obvious why his dad was so pleased with him.

One more statistic is what Kevin's future turned out to be. Almost everyone has family troubles and problems of one kind or another. Kevin (at the age of fifteen) and his father apparently had some that disturbed the boy to the point that he and another boy essentially "stole" one of his dad's planes and went for a long "joy-ride." The ride ended in a fiery crash on a short little private airstrip with high trees at both ends…and both boys lost their lives. As in so many plane crashes, the cause was attributed to "failure to maintain flying speed," which is to say, the plane

simply "stalled" on takeoff for lack of sufficient flying airspeed. The underlying reason? The boy lacked the training and experience necessary to successfully fly in and out of such an unusual and demanding airstrip.

George

The airport management asked me to serve on an airport "committee." I was the only full-time airplane salesman working at the airport and considered the invitation quite an honor...and was even more pleased when I found myself seated next to the chief controller of our airport's control "tower." A man of much more than local renown, he had been the moving force behind the initiation of an air ambulance operation which became a model for many throughout the world. Early on, the non-profit "mercy" flight service he helped initiate flew a Cessna 180, a couple of donated planes and a WWII Beechcraft model 18 twin-engine ship. He had many flight ratings and was the "check-pilot" for the operation.

I was especially taken with idea of flying in a Beech 18. The plane was more or less legendary as a radial-engine-equipped workhorse of the air. The "18" makes a fabulous sound when those big round engines crank up. So…after a few committee meetings, I came to know George well enough to make a deal with him. I owned a "Hallicrafters Model TRV 128A" portable VHF aircraft transceiver which I'd used when flying my Piper Cub. The radio name is well remembered because it was one of the very first VHF portables and the battery pack alone weighed an unbelievable twelve pounds. The radio had become surplus to me so I asked George if the operation (Mercy Flights) might have a use for it. He asked, "Sure, how much?" Knowing it was becoming a bit obsolete and not worth much, I responded, "How about trading it for some "right-seat" (co-pilot) time in the Beech 18?" He accepted and I gave him the radio. He said I could fly eight hours in the "right-seat," flight time most young pilots would give their right arm for. For one reason or another, I never did get around to collecting that highly desirable flight time.

Drifting away from flying after a few years, I still lived in the area and ran into George occasionally. We would talk flying and he would bring me up to date on some of the things the air-ambulance operation was doing. At one sitting, he proudly told me they had just purchased a beautiful modern twin-engine Aero Commander to replace the Beech 18. He said he was checking out operation pilots in the "Commander" one by one. He described how much faster and more efficient the new plane was than the Beech 18, and said that now, because the new ship had great instrumentation, pilots could fly safely in just about any weather, a fact which would help save even more lives.

Some time later, I went out to the mailbox for my newspaper…and stared at a shocking headline. "Mercy Flights Founder Dies In Airplane Crash!" And which airplane took him out? Yes, his latest acquisition, the Aero Commander! It seemed he and his co-pilot misunderstood which radio signal came from which source when they were on a solid cloud-cover "instrument" approach to our local airport and the plane crashed in a shower of fractured metal, a typical result when meeting the earth with a very fast, heavy airplane. It was a severe final exit for this grand man and a blow for aviation…he was one of the very last guys you'd expect would meet his end in an airplane.

Alex

After doing well financially in a sector of the energy industry, Alex then invested successfully in real estate. In solid condition financially and retiring at a relatively early age, Alex applied his private-pilot background and mechanical knowledge to the restoration of classic WWII airplanes. He got caught up in the exciting sport of professional air racing and rebuilt an advanced trainer to compete in the biggest annual race in the country. Although he didn't feel quite up to the task of flying the race plane himself, he did fly all of the many planes he restored. I had the pleasure of working on his "pit crew" at one of the big races.

Alex continued to buy even more planes to restore because his growing airplane knowledge made it possible for him to know good deals when he saw them. During one of my visits to his large private operation in the later years of his life, he said he owned fourteen assorted planes, a number of which were loaned to and stored in aviation museums for lack of storage space in his home hangars. Of everyone I ever knew in aviation, he was the most deeply immersed in private airplane ownership. I didn't know what flight "ratings" he had but he certainly had flown a lot of different types of planes. One might think that a person who had flown for more than half of his life could, at the age of eighty-five and in apparent good health, still be able to handle an airplane with no problem.

It was a surprise that, when reading the newspaper one morning, Alex's name caught my attention. It was not a happy story. For whatever reason (none was determined at press time), Alex, alone in a retractable-gear single-engine ship he frequently flew for transportation, crashed a few hundred yards from his home airport. According to the report, there was little left of his ship. Apparently it met the earth at a very steep angle at considerable speed. Such an event usually indicates the plane lost all forward flying speed, "stalled," and then fell out of control to the ground. It was all over…in a moment.

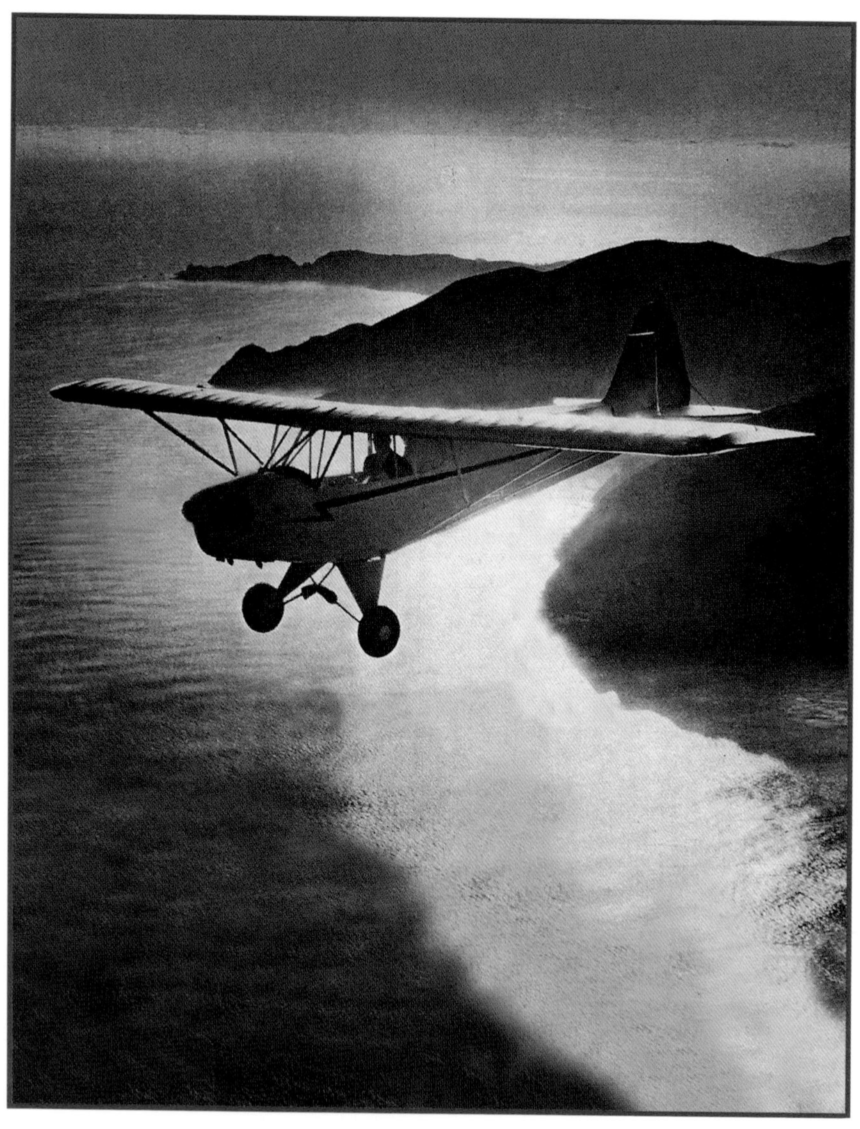

Piper Cub Model J-3, 1939.

Epilogue

Back From Oblivion...

J-3 Cub N7074H...*Flies Again!*

If Orville and Wilbur were alive today, I believe their main interests would be *not* in viewing exotic constructions like the astoundingly high-priced and complicated space shuttle...or even in the very latest iterations of commercial passenger airplanes. Rather, their interests might lie in the amazing total restorations of simple early aircraft like the ubiquitous 75-year-old Piper Cub and other earlier forms of heavier-than-air craft…all proven throughout many decades of operation to be safe, reliable and long-lasting. Would they be surprised to see these enduring planes still in the air? I don't think so!

These uncomplicated "utility" flight machines introduced fundamental flight dynamics to countless thousands of adventurous souls, allowing them to soar with eagles and break free of the "forever before" bonds of gravity.

The Wright brothers' might be surprised at the number of airplanes reclaimed from time-imposed degradation. Even more would be their admiration for the extremely high quality of workmanship exhibited on the finest restored examples. The following is a surprising story about one of those restorations.

The story begins back on page 253 detailing the crashing end of my beloved Piper Cub J-3 N7074H. With the plane upside-down in tall trees almost at the bottom of a fairly deep canyon, my thought as I climbed out unscathed and struggled up the steep grade…was that my cherished ship obviously was a total wreck.

How could I have made such an imbecilic maneuver? The loss of my most-prized possession proved to be a haunting memory for years to come. My subconscious thought processes often brought back the many pleasant memories of freedom in the skies while cruising along with nothing more to interfere than an infrequent bump from shifting air masses. The excitement, thrills, chills, exhilaration and pure ecstasy enjoyed during my time flying the little plane ultimately transitioned into warm distant personal history.

As this book neared publication, an interesting thought overcame me. What happened to my little Cub after I essentially "walked away" from the crash? Allow me to elaborate….

After climbing up from the crash, I approached the "Aircraft & Engine" mechanic (Cliff Krum) who had done considerable work on the plane, lived adjacent to the airport and was on the scene. Knowing the airplane was unflyable, I offered to him: "You can have the airframe if you can figure how to get the parts out of the canyon. If you do, I'd like to have the engine."

Unharmed in the crash, the engine had only 300 hours of flight time and was close to brand new, so some money could be recovered from a sale. As far as the airframe was concerned, I calculated that Cliff and his talented son Dale possibly could rebuild the ship (if they could get the remains up out of the abyss). He agreed on the spot! I had a biplane in the process of restoration by Cliff and Dale so I was still involved with aviation (that is, as long as the FAA did not stifle my activities because of my foolish crash).

My young friend William "Butch" Richards (a witness to the crash... and a pilot and plane owner in later years) did get the engine up out of the gorge. How? The hard way...on an overgrown logging road in a construction wheelbarrow with a friend of his tugging away on a long rope attached! And what exactly happened to the airframe? I didn't have a clue what Cliff and Dale did with it and wanted only to begin again…and put the crash as far behind me as possible. The engine was sold for $400 cash and that was the last of the saga except for good-time memories.

Now, with this book nearing completion, what might have happened to Cub J-3 N7074H weighed on my mind. At their end, many airplanes are simply scrapped, while others are reclaimed from the dust bin of history with total restorations. Airplane mechanics and airplane enthusiasts can be totally dedicated and persistent when their goal is putting a ship back in the sky!

One of the most (if not ***the*** most) *extreme* examples of bringing an airplane back from extinction happened with a WWII Lockheed P-38 fighter plane. On July 15, 1942, a flight of six P-38s and two B-17 bombers with a total of 25 crew members became lost and low on fuel over remotest Greenland...landed...left the planes behind and were rescued.

Fifty years later, in 1992, a group assembled to recover one of the P-38s. A *half century* of snow had become a ***264 foot thick ice cover*** over the planes. In likely the most difficult airplane recovery in history, one of the planes was recovered. The airplane was restored and ***flew again*** on October 26, 2002! The intensive effort clearly illustrates the lengths "airplane-people" will go to bring back a significant piece of history from an almost impossible situation.

My search for N7074H began on the amazing "personal" computer. Entering the plane's number into the "Internet" was unproductive. Then, entering the name of the "A&E" mechanic given the remnants of the ship forty-eight years ago illustrated that aircraft mechanics' acronyms have changed. Today, "A&E" (Aircraft and Engine) refers to mechanics who work on airframes and "reciprocating" engines. "A&P" (Airframe and Powerplant) is a new designation referring to mechanics also rated to work on "turbine" engines. But…no results there, either!

Days later, in a "last gasp" effort, there appeared a website which charged $4.95 to search out details of airplane registration numbers so I paid the price ...and was overjoyed to learn that the plane still existed. I was dismayed that, according to the report, the plane had been exported to Mexico in 2003. There were two names connected to the information…and one name's Oregon address was in Gresham, ***the town in which I grew up*** and near the very areas where I'd flown N7074H! ***(Amazing!)***

Excitedly, I wrote to the Gresham resident!

If the airplane had been rebuilt and one of the two people mentioned had owned plane, were there some relatively recent photos which I might include in this book? I explained that I'd owned (and crashed) Piper Cub N7074H many years ago. Then, I waited…..

To my shocked and happy surprise, about a week later I received a telephone call from Norman DesJardins, an aircraft mechanic. The first thing he told me dashed my hopes. He said, "You've been given erroneous information. In fact, in 2003 the plane was still in pieces much as they were when you crashed it. The plane couldn't possibly have been exported to Mexico as a flyable ship. But…it still *existed!*" Then…he *amazed me!*

He said, "My partner Jack and I have the plane in our possession and… we have just finished completely restoring it to original condition! Only now…the plane is painted "original" Piper Cub "yellow" and has many necessary modern extras! The plane is currently located in our hangar at Troutdale Airport. (Which, astonishingly, is only about ten miles from where I crashed the ship.)

"Excited and overjoyed" are major understated words describing my state of mind upon hearing this news. Norman cordially invited me to drive out and see the finished product of his and partner Jack Barne's efforts. He said, "Yes, the registration number on the plane indicates the plane to be the very one you flew those many years ago. Come by when you can. We'll look forward to meeting you."

I couldn't wait. Only one day passed and I decided to forego making an appointment. The anticipation was too great...I just ***had*** to see that airplane!

"Norm" informed me that he had spent the last number of years operating a company named "Premier Aircraft Engines, Inc.," an airplane engine overhaul and repair facility which produces high-quality work. The plane was located at Troutdale Airport not much over a ***hundred yards*** from where I'd occasionally parked the Cub many years before. What a coincidental miracle!

Upon entering Norm's offices at his airport shop building, I was pleasantly surprised to view a beautifully-presented aircraft engine mounted on a stand in the vestibule. The engine was meticulously prepared as a teaching tool to help neophyte aviation devotees learn the basics of engine operation. Norm machined "cut-a-ways" of various critical parts to visually explain in the simplest way how the engine functions. He had then motorized the engine with an auxiliary electric motor so internal moving parts could be seen doing their jobs in motion and completed the assembly by making it exquisitely clean and sharply finished. Truly impressive! The only similar production I'd ever seen as neatly done as this was a giant airplane engine cut-a-way done during WWII to educate civilian and military mechanics. Norm proudly led me over to the most perfect Piper J-3 Cub I have ever seen, and I've seen quite a few. This was not simply another Piper Cub restoration and rebuild…this was, and is, one of the finest examples of highly-refined mechanical airplane craftsmanship I have ever viewed.

Norm explained how he and Jack had discovered the remnants of the plane for sale only a few miles north in Vancouver, Washington, in 2008… and had purchased them with a complete rebuild in mind. It appeared that

Norm's display engine (*Premier Aircraft Engines, Inc.*)

the carcass of the plane had been in the general area for the prior forty-five years still in the "as-crashed" condition. When found, the "airframe" was still sound enough to restore…but only with extraordinary amounts of effort. Norm is mostly retired, which made it possible for him to devote the many hours required to play his part in changing a pile of mechanical rubble into a master-craftsman's work of art.

Time and effort are only two of the components which make such a restoration possible. In this age, such efforts also take a lot of money and, to get the project to the extreme level of flawless quality that Norm and Jack have achieved, people are required who have dedicated their lives to learning how to do exceedingly meticulous work.

From every quarter, all I could see was perfection. Seeing this fabulous work made me secretly wish I had learned to be an aircraft mechanic…learning only from experts like Norm and Jack. The interior of the ship is every bit as exact, precise, smooth and exquisite as all parts of the exterior. The airplane is just so perfect that it is hard to imagine allowing anyone to climb in and scuff the floor. They've built the plane to fly and that is what they've said...but to visualize even a bug splattered on the windshield is to think of violating perfection. And, wonder of wonders...this was my plane and I was the last to fly it before Norm and Jack got their hands on it. Although it was considered a beautiful plane when I was the owner, it was nothing like the astoundingly pristine treasure it is today. If inspecting the plane with jeweler's loop exactitude...I'd give the ship a "15"...on a scale of ten!

When I crashed Piper Cub N7074H in 1963, the value was about $3,000. The engine had only 300 hours of engine time, the upholstery was new, the fabric cover only a couple of years old and I'd had a baggage compartment and a long tinted window installed in the top of the fuselage, plus extra instruments in an enlarged panel.

Values are, of course, subject to many different interpretations and conditions but Norm and Jack, owners of the now beautifully-restored N7074H, have stated they would turn down...***$100,000*** for the ship!

Baggage compartment I had installed in N7074H in 1962..*still there!*

N7074H...after 45 years in storage

Cub N7074H's remains went through a few owners over those many years but, when Norm and Jack discovered the plane remnants for sale on "Barnstormers.Com," the Aircraft Registration Certificate was still in my name, "Marc Paulsen."

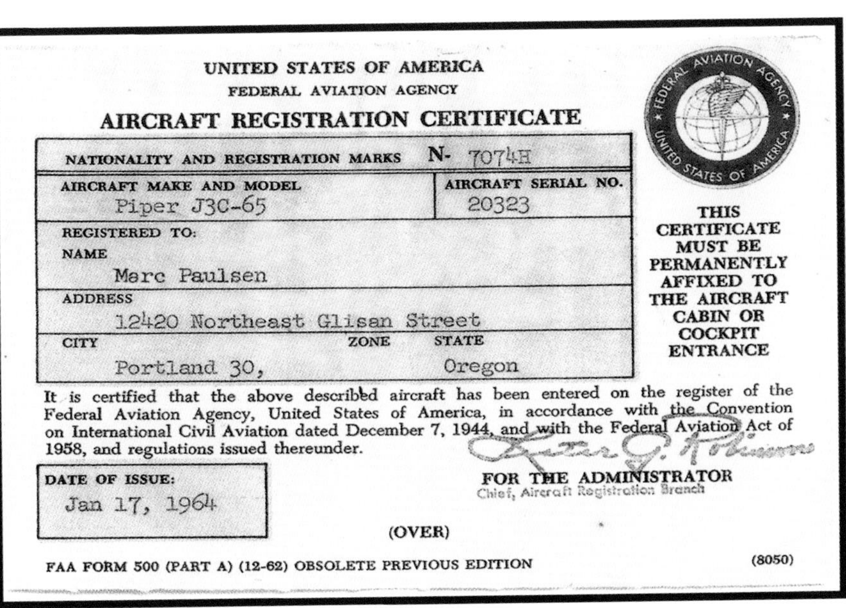

UNITED STATES OF AMERICA
FEDERAL AVIATION AGENCY

AIRCRAFT REGISTRATION CERTIFICATE

NATIONALITY AND REGISTRATION MARKS	N- 7074H
AIRCRAFT MAKE AND MODEL: Piper J3C-65	AIRCRAFT SERIAL NO.: 20323
REGISTERED TO: NAME: Marc Paulsen	
ADDRESS: 12420 Northeast Glisan Street	
CITY: Portland 30, ZONE	STATE: Oregon

FEDERAL AVIATION AGENCY • UNITED STATES OF AMERICA •

THIS CERTIFICATE MUST BE PERMANENTLY AFFIXED TO THE AIRCRAFT CABIN OR COCKPIT ENTRANCE

It is certified that the above described aircraft has been entered on the register of the Federal Aviation Agency, United States of America, in accordance with the Convention on International Civil Aviation dated December 7, 1944, and with the Federal Aviation Act of 1958, and regulations issued thereunder.

DATE OF ISSUE: Jan 17, 1964

FOR THE ADMINISTRATOR
Chief, Aircraft Registration Branch

(OVER)

FAA FORM 500 (PART A) (12-62) OBSOLETE PREVIOUS EDITION (8050)

N7074H Registration still in my name, "Marc Paulsen."

Piper J-3 Cub N7074H fusilage - ***The restoration begins...***

Wing construction in process

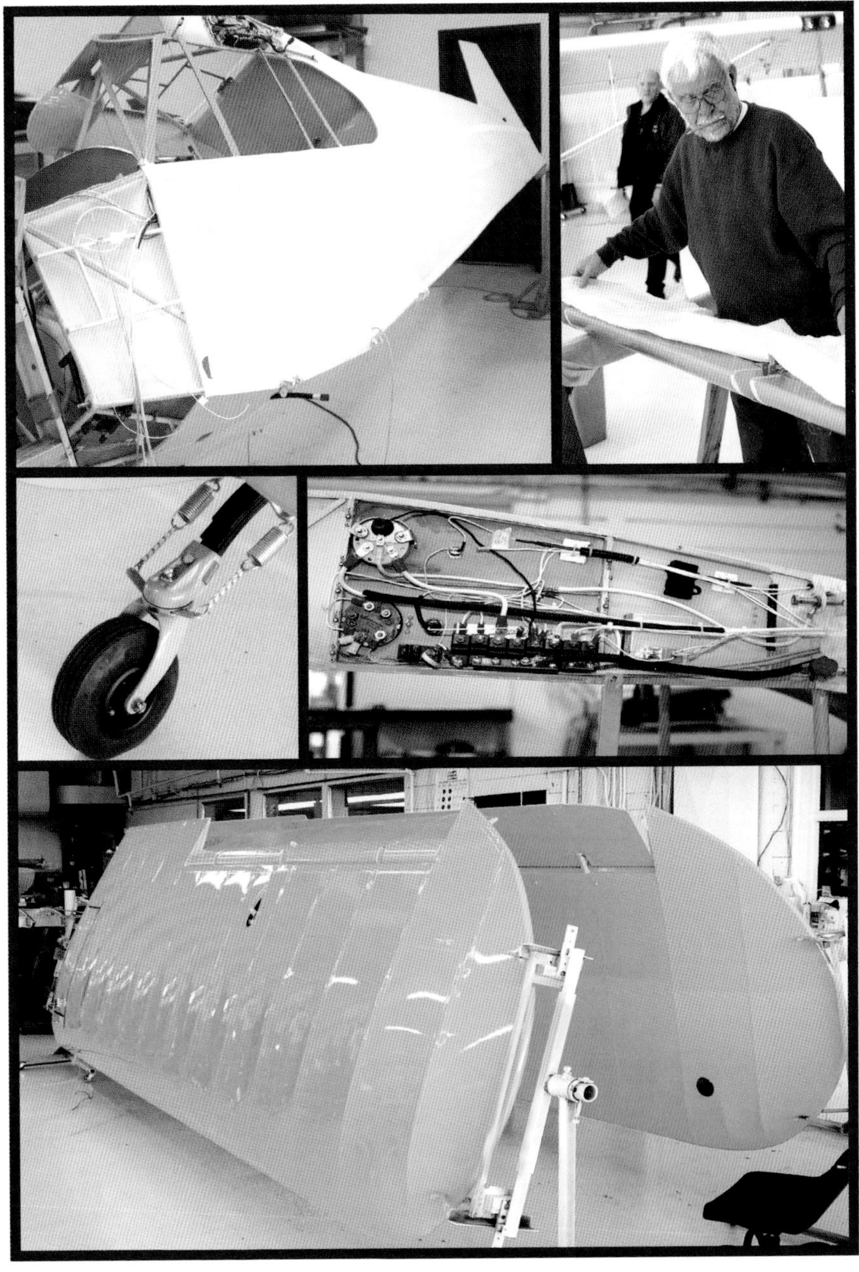

Jack Barnes hard at work on N7074H

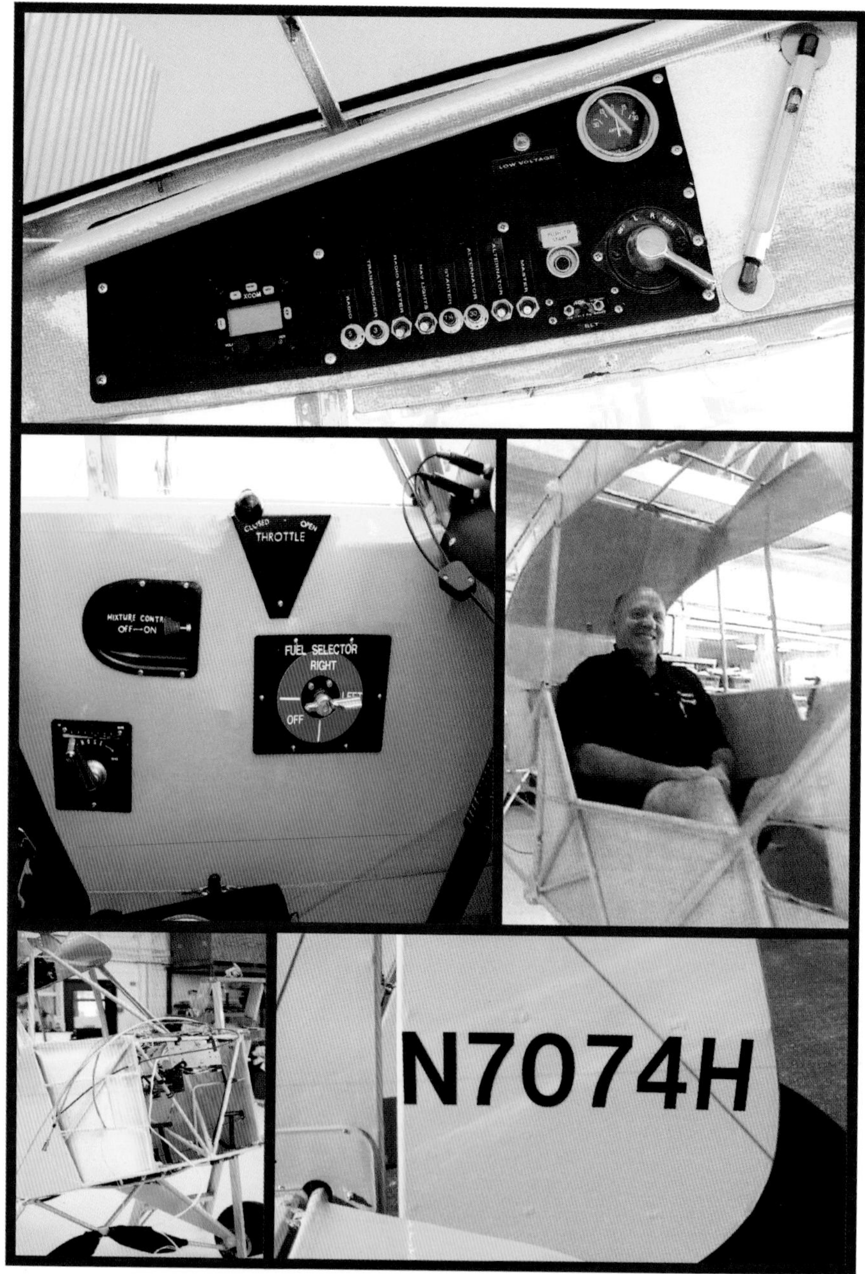

Norm DesJardins enjoying the process

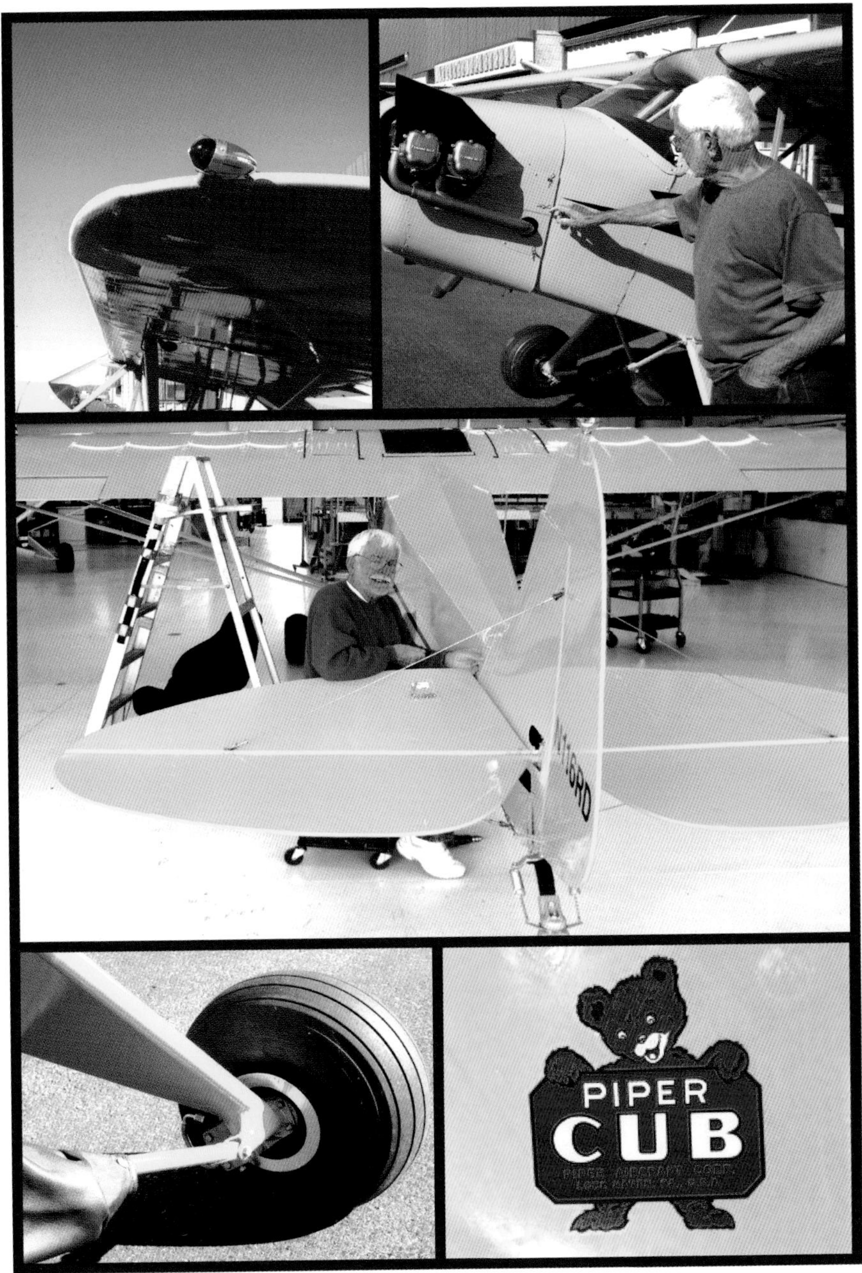

Jack Barnes applies finishing touches

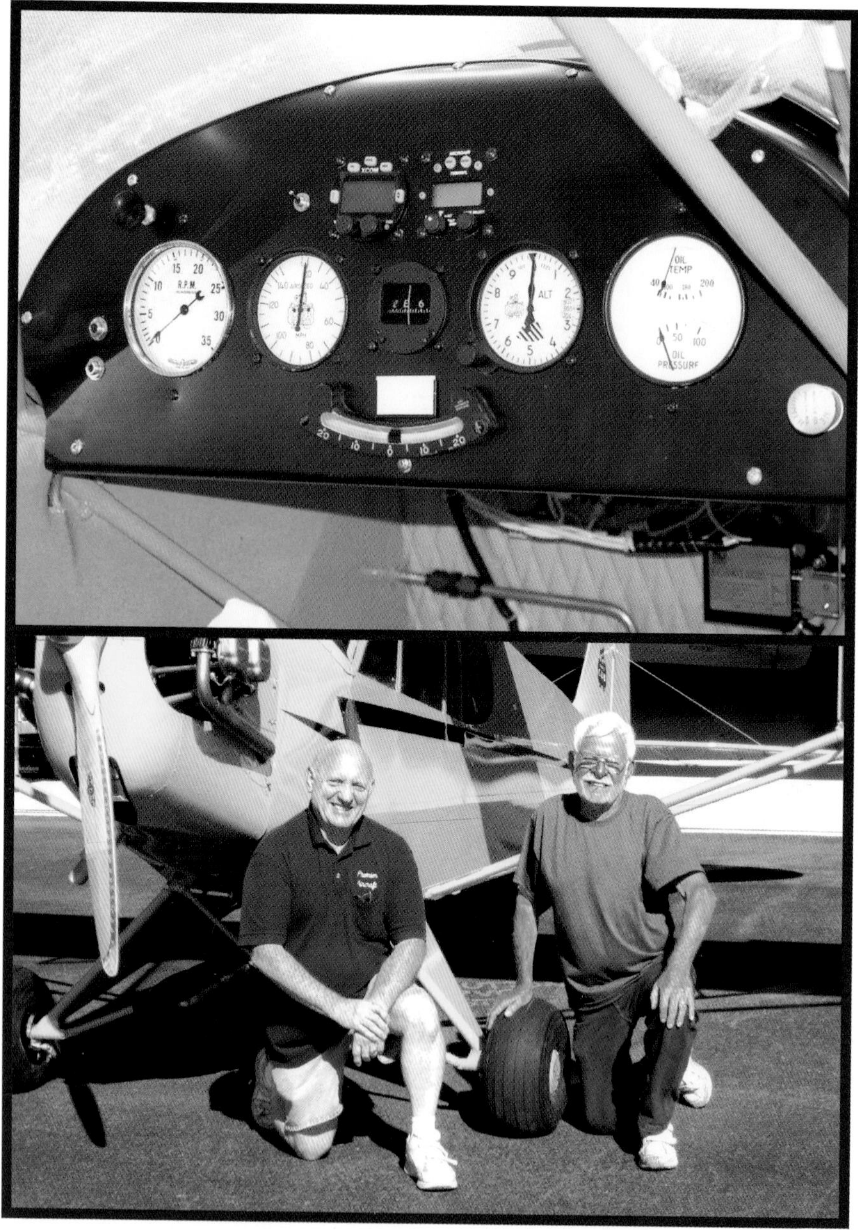

Norm DesJardins and Jack Barnes
with their outstanding Piper J-3 Cub N7074H restoration

The finished J-3 N7074H...*Exceptional!*